# Essays In Our Changing Order

## Transaction Books by Thorstein Veblen

*Absentee Ownership*

*The Engineers and the Price System*

*Essays in Our Changing Order*

*The Higher Learning in America*

*Imperial Germany and the Industrial Revolution*

*The Instinct of Workmanship and
the State of Industrial Arts*

*The Place of Science in Modern Civilization*

*The Theory of Business Enterprise*

*The Theory of the Leisure Class*

# Essays In Our Changing Order

## Thorstein Veblen

with a new introduction by
Scott R. Bowman

edited by
Leon Ardzrooni

Transaction Publishers
New Brunswick (U.S.A.) and London (U.K.)

Library of Congress Catalog Number: 97-24839
ISBN: 1-56000-964-0
Printed in the United States of America

Library of Congress Cataloging-in-Publication Data

Veblen, Thorstein, 1857–1929.
    Essays in our changing order / Thorstein Veblen ; edited by Leon Ardzrooni ; with a new introduction by Scott R. Bowman.
        p. cm.
    Originally published: New York : Viking Press, 1934.
    Includes bibliographical references.
    ISBN 1-56000-964-0 (pbk.)
    1. Economics.  2. World War, 1914–1918.  3. World politics—1900–1945.  I. Ardzrooni, Leon, 1884–    .  II. Title.
HB34.V38   1997
330—dc21                                                        97-24839
                                                                        CIP

# CONTENTS

### III. War Essays

# INTRODUCTION TO THE
# TRANSACTION EDITION

## I

THORSTEIN BUNDE VEBLEN was born on a frontier farm in Wisconsin on July 30, 1857, and died in Palo Alto, California, on August 3, 1929. His lifetime coincided with the rise of modern industrial capitalism and concomitant growth of integrated national markets, the resurgence of monopolies through various forms of corporate combination, and the subsequent transformation of economic, social, and political life under the regime of corporate capitalism. Like many of his contemporaries, Veblen sought to decipher the driving forces behind these developments. In that endeavor, he succeeded brilliantly and entirely on his own terms. What he documented more lucidly and with greater depth than any other scholar of his generation was the manner in which the rise of the large corporation had fomented a reorganization of the structure of power in American society. It is a testimony to the ideological propensities of social scientists, about which Veblen had much to say, that this monumental contribution is not widely appreciated today.

Veblen occupies a unique position in the pantheon of American political and social thinkers. Standing astride two centuries with a foot firmly planted in each, he was both a social theorist in the grand tradition of the nineteenth century and a contemporary critical thinker whose

vii

radical vision reshaped the contours of intellectual debate in the twentieth century. His writings invite comparisons with such luminaries as Karl Marx, Auguste Comte, Herbert Spencer, Max Weber, Emile Durkheim, Sigmund Freud, Vilfredo Pareto, John Dewey, and Charles Beard. Evolutionary theorist, economist, philosopher, anthropologist, ethnologist, sociologist, and political theorist of the corporation, Veblen refused to cabin his expansive intellect within the specialized precincts of the academic disciplines. Our intellectual lives are incalculably richer for that decision.

This collection of essays was published posthumously in 1934, at the direction of Leon Ardzrooni, a close friend and former student of Veblen. It spans the entirety of Veblen's intellectual life and offers a panoramic view of the breadth and variety of his scholarship. The book intersects in some fashion with virtually all of the author's seminal ideas. In many cases, essays in this anthology articulated or anticipated the themes of Veblen's major works. It is helpful to know these connections, and I will point them out as I proceed. However, *Essays in Our Changing Order* does stand on its own as an introduction to an extraordinary intellectual legacy. Indeed, it is the most diverse and representative group of writings under one cover by this prolific author.

By all accounts, Veblen was quite eccentric and undisciplined in his personal affairs, remarkably disciplined and focused in his intellectual life, erudite but uninspiring as a teacher, and iconoclastic to the point of infuriating and regularly offending the powers that be in higher education.[1] He is something of a folk hero to anti-establishment intellectuals and academic free spirits. His professional life, however, was more often than not a source of frustration and frequent disappointment. He did not ascend above the lowest rungs of the academic ladder of success, even after having attained considerable fame as an author. His unconventional views did sometimes frighten publishers. On more than one occasion he paid for the costs of publishing a book. But, clearly, his own errors in judgment greatly contributed to his misfortunes making his academic sojourn more difficult than it might have been. His philandering was well known and widely discussed. Scandals drove him from one institution to another, and still he refused to behave. In this regard, it is accurate to say that his reputation always preceded him.

A moral deviant by Victorian standards, Veblen was also an intellectual misfit in the genteel environment of higher education. His parents were Norwegian immigrant farmers. For the first seventeen years of his life, Veblen lived in culturally insular and often embattled Norwegian-American communities in which the native tongue was the primary language spoken both at home and in school. This formative experience greatly contributed to his defiant ways and especially his intellectual self-image as an outsider. Although a miscreant in some respects, Veblen possessed tremendous integrity as a scholar and craftsman of ideas. Deeply committed to the pursuit of truth in higher education, he believed that academic professionalization and its ethic of "salesmanship" signaled the eclipse of a venerable institution by the businesslike leaders of the modern university system.

Veblen is perhaps best known as a founder of institutional economics, champion of technocracy, bitter foe of finance capitalism, and savvy social critic who exposed the hypocrisies and absurdities of upper-class mores and institutions. No doubt his first book, *The Theory of the*

*Leisure Class* (1899), which has sustained its popularity for nearly a century, is largely responsible for this widely held, yet incomplete, assessment of his work. Veblen's analysis in that early work of the evolutionary origins of modern pecuniary culture shaped the entirety of his thought, but the whole fabric of his social theory was not woven together until his later works completed the tapestry, especially *The Theory of Business Enterprise* (1904), *The Instinct of Workmanship* (1914), and *Absentee Ownership* (1923). His theory did not undergo dramatic shifts or evolutionary leaps so much as it matured with age. One will not find in his voluminous writings an "early Veblen" comparable to an "early Marx," for example. Veblen's analysis of history, culture, politics, economics, and social change remained remarkably consistent from beginning to end, from his cultural critique of the leisure class in the late 1890s, to his analysis of war and peace two decades later.

It is difficult to do justice to Veblen's social theory from the standpoints of current disciplinary perspectives. To appreciate the profundity of his work we must seek a vantage point that allows us to survey all of its intellectual terrain. I propose to reconstruct Veblen's social theory with reference to its central unifying themes: (1) the dynamic interrelationships between instinct, habits of thought, environment, and social change in human evolution; (2) the essential contradiction between business and industry rooted in the evolutionary past and sustained by the instinctual dominance of "pecuniary exploit" over "workmanlike efficiency"; and (3) the self-delusion of the species through ideological and animistic thinking and its implications for the state of our knowledge and social engineering.

I hope to show that these elements embrace the whole of Veblen's social and political thought and related writings. In the course of this reconstruction, I will highlight numerous essays in this anthology to demonstrate their relevance to the texture of his thinking. Moreover, my reconstructive efforts will require frequent departures from the editor's organization of the text. The sequence of discussion, however, does follow a certain logic and endeavors to impose its own order on the material consistent with the themes outlined above.

## II

Veblen maintained that from its earliest beginnings, the social existence of human beings, like that of other species, was a struggle for survival. In the course of this struggle, a process of natural selection had compelled the gradual adaptation of human nature and behavior to changing social conditions. Human institutions and their corresponding modes or habits of thought, however, were not only a result of a "selective and adaptive process," but they were in themselves "efficient factors of selection."[2] Social change or evolution, according to Veblen, was therefore a product of a complex process in which human thought and behavior, by adapting to a changing social environment, transformed the institutional basis for later selection. The fact that selective adaptation would take different forms in societies, depending upon the character of the people, further complicated this process. In other words, the dominance of certain innate characteristics in a nation or a people would either facilitate or hamper the process of adaptation. To fully grasp Veblen's theory of social change, therefore, we must examine the theory of instincts and conception of human nature that informed it.

Human behavior, Veblen observed, was rooted in and conditioned by a complex of "instinctive proclivities and tropismatic attitudes." Instinctive action was purposeful or teleological; that is, it involved "consciousness and adaptation to an end aimed at." Unlike tropismatic behavior, which was purely psychological and could not be consciously altered or controlled, instinctive behavior was shaped by social norms, customs, and habits. Consequently, even though human instincts were innate, the way in which the instinctive ends of life were worked out would depend upon a host of cultural factors.[3]

Veblen's analysis of instinctive behavior focused primarily on three major instincts—workmanship, the parental bent, and idle curiosity. Essential to the material well-being of a people, workmanship referred to the human propensity for effective work including the efficient use of resources and technological mastery: "[man] is in an eminent sense an intelligent agent...possessed of a discriminatory sense of purpose, by force of which all futility of life or of action is distasteful to him." The parental bent induced a concern not only for the welfare of one's off-spring, but for the community as a whole. Like the instinct of workmanship, the parental bent was also necessary to the survival of the species. Idle curiosity motivated the quest for knowledge for its own sake. Human curiosity was "idle," Veblen argued, because it had no utilitarian aim. This did not imply, however, that knowledge produced by this instinctive disposition could have no practical application. Indeed, the development of science and technology provided ample evidence to the contrary.[4]

Instinctive action, according to Veblen, was always a product of an interplay and overlapping of the various instinctive dispositions. Because of the interdependence of human instincts, the modification or accentuation of one instinct due to environmental factors would result in a "mutual contamination" of other instincts and thereby bias the process of selective adaptation.[5] At any given point in the evolution of a society, human nature therefore consisted of a set of instinctive proclivities which had been selected for specific economic and social conditions. But once modified, instinctive dispositions would affect future selection by either facilitating or hampering adaptation. In the author's view, this fact clearly revealed the fallacy of the simplistic idea of progress often associated with human social evolution. In fact, Veblen characterized the notion that "the institutional outcome of men's native dispositions will be sound and salutary" as "an article of uncritical faith [taken] from the historic belief in a beneficent Order of Nature." This is not to say that he rejected the idea of survival of the fittest, only that what was fit and unfit carried no normative connotation.[6]

While Veblen believed human beings to be purposeful creatures—agents "seeking in every act the accomplishment of some concrete, objective, impersonal end"—his analysis of the evolutionary process suggested that human behavior was largely constrained and determined by external forces. Societies evolved, he argued, when individuals were compelled to adapt their habits of thought and hence their institutions to an "altered environment." Social change therefore occurred "in response to pressure from without," which was "of the nature of a response to a stimulus." Whereas a variety of factors contributed to the evolution of societies, "the forces which made for readjustment of institutions, especially in the case of a modern industrial community," Veblen related, were, "in the last analysis, almost exclusively of an economic nature."[7] Forces generated by existing economic institutions eventually outgrew their institutional mode: "as population increases, and as mens' knowledge and skill in directing the forces of nature widen, the habitual methods of relations between the members of the group, and the habitual method of carrying on the life process of the group as a whole, no longer give the same result as before."[8]

Social evolution therefore was largely induced by changing economic forces which, in turn, were driven by advances in the industrial arts, that is, by technological improvements. Veblen's theory of social change clearly embodies a type of technological determinism, albeit qualified by his premise that the development and application of technology will be affected by the institutions and instinctive proclivities of a people. Furthermore, he argued that the impact of technological change on human behavior and thought might vary within a society depending upon the degree to which different groups or classes had been exposed to the forces of change. Prospects for change must also be weighed in light of the fact that power was usually exercised to conserve and not to transform social arrangements. Veblen also contended that, as creatures of habit, human beings generally resisted innovation. Thus, when adaptation finally did occur, however haltingly, the adjusted institutions and habits of thought once again were on the verge of being outmoded by newly arisen economic forces.[9]

Because this process of selective adaptation could "never catch up with the progressively changing situation in which the community finds itself at a given time," the dominant beliefs and institutions of a society would be conservative, though some more so than others. This evolutionary process of adaptation resulted in a more or less persistent condition of cultural lag in which the knowledge, beliefs, and customs of a society (with the exception of scientific knowledge) did not accord with the material advances made possible by technological change. This state of affairs, moreover, legitimated prevailing power relationships since the dominant ideas of a society were those of its rulers. Veblen's theory of social evolution therefore would seem to imply that individuals can never completely control their own destinies precisely because human thought and behavior always lag behind economic change.[10]

In four classic essays first published in the 1890s— "The Beginnings of Ownership," "The Barbarian Status of Women," "The Economic Theory of Women's Dress," and "The Instinct of Workmanship and the Irksomeness of Labor"—Veblen outlined the basic themes of his evolutionary theory. Although he had not fully developed his theory of instincts, he already had worked out his critical anthropological analysis of ownership and its relationship to patriarchy, as well as the relevance of these institutions to American economic and cultural life. These seminal essays, which were published shortly before *The Theory of the Leisure Class*, introduce us to the Veblenian concepts or interpretations of pecuniary emulation, animism, the instinct of workmanship, conspicuous consumption, conspicuous waste, the leisure class, and the institution of ownership-marriage. One will also encounter the penetrating intelligence, iconoclastic style, and sharp wit that would become his hallmark for the remainder of his intellectual life.

While rejecting the notion that human social evolution proceeded according to immutable laws of development, Veblen maintained, on the basis of evidence, that certain broad generalizations were possible. Throughout his writings, he identified four major eras or periods of social evolution in human history, each of which corresponded to a different stage in the advance of technology and social organization—the era of primitive or peaceable savagery, the barbaric or predatory era, the era of the handicraft economy, and the modern era of machine technology. It was during the transition from the period of peaceable savagery, which was characterized by a crude technology and a subsistence economy, to the stage of barbarism, that the institution of ownership emerged.[11]

Veblen observed that despite the fact they occupied "the two extremes of economic speculation," classical economists and socialists both agreed that "productive labor" was the foundation of the institution of property ownership. This "conjectural history of the origin of property," which was based on "the preconceptions of Natural Rights and a coercive Order of Nature," assumed that the institution of ownership, and with it production and wealth, derived from a "self-sufficing individual."[12] Besides being illogical (production is necessarily a social, as opposed to individual, activity that requires cooperation and sharing of technical knowledge and tools), this natural rights preconception prevented economists from understanding the actual origins of ownership. Indeed, to grasp the very beginnings of this institution in the early barbarian culture, the scholar must adopt the point of view of that culture.

As a habit of thought that presupposed a way of viewing people and things, ownership could not exist until individuals distinguished between their organic persons and things that were not a part of their organic persons. The primitive savage, who viewed material and immaterial things as extensions of personality, made no such distinction. Ownership, therefore, did not derive from instinctual capacities; rather, it was a "cultural fact which [had] grown into an institution in the past through a long course of habituation." Ownership was established when societies recognized an individual's "customary right of use and abuse over an object which was obviously not an organic part of his person." Veblen argued that this practice first appeared in cultures in which nonconsumable goods and people, especially women, were seized and hence claimed as property, and that the ownership of property presupposed certain technological advances which made possible the accumulation of wealth which, in turn, often encouraged aggression.[13] Captive humans were obviously not part of the organic person of the captor and could be readily apprehended as possessions or trophies of war. As trophies, women brought distinction to their male owners who eventually created the institution of marriage as a means of laying exclusive claim to their captive property. Veblen thus concluded that the institution of "ownership-marriage" seemed to be "the original both of private property and of the patriarchal household."[14]

Veblen's analysis of the original marriage ceremony provides insight into the pervasiveness in both predatory and modern societies of "animism," the practice of attributing a teleology or purpose to inanimate things or events. The barbarian, he observed, "looks upon external objects and sequences naively, as organic and individual things, and as expressions of a propensity working toward an end." Ritual is accepted as reality by the animis-

tic mind: "if once the motions leading to a desired consummation have been rehearsed in the accredited form
and sequence, the same substantial result will be attained
as that produced by the process imitated." Understood in
this way, religious ceremonies, anthropomorphic beliefs,
superstitions, and ritualized social practices all have their
basis in animistic thinking. The very concept of ownership is animistic in that it attributes to the individual certain intangible powers (e.g., prowess or force) associated
with capture or possession, whereas, in reality, ownership is a social institution. Emulative behavior—for example, competition designed to produce invidious
distinctions—is also animistic because it involves the
same mental process whereby humans project onto things
or events a teleology.[15]

As the institution of ownership-marriage acquired legitimacy and came to represent "the good and beautiful
attitude of the man toward the woman," it became necessary to arrange the marriage of free women, especially
the daughters of men of high standing. By the same token, status and reputability among males, which was
achieved by a more or less constant demonstration of
prowess, could not be sustained without marrying (own-
ing) a woman or women. For these reasons, Veblen surmised, the marriage ritual or ceremony of "feigned
capture" originated and, in time, came "to be appreciated
unreflectingly as a deliverance of common-sense and enlightened reason." The price of social acceptance for
women was servitude. Free women—that is, "masterless,
unattached" women—were shunned or relegated to a
lower social status than "captured" women. Exceptions
to this social convention could be found in societies that
had enjoyed a long period of "peaceable industrial life"

in which the maternal household had thrived. In these (nonpredatory) maternal cultures, "the household of the unattached woman" developed in place of ownership-marriage, although the two institutions usually blended to create a hybrid form at a much later date.[16]

Veblen's account of the historical development of ownership significantly influenced his general theory of social evolution. The institution of ownership-marriage in predatory societies, he argued, gave rise to a class division—a leisure class and a working class—based on a discrimination between employments: the "honorific employments which involve a large measure of prowess" and "the humiliating employments, which call for diligence and into which the sturdier virtues do not enter."[17] Veblen explained that the "invidious distinction" between exploit (prowess) and industry flowed from the institution of ownership and its underlying motive of pecuniary emulation. The possession of wealth became a symbol of prowess and thereby conferred honor just as the lack of wealth relegated one to an ordinary or ignoble social position. One will find, the author observed, that the material and psychological foundations of the leisure class—the institution of ownership and pecuniary emulation—had been substantially developed in predatory societies and, from that point on, remained basically unchanged, even though the class itself did not fully mature until a later stage of social evolution.

Both patriarchy and class domination, therefore, had their origin in the institution of ownership-marriage which nourished, and was nourished by, predatory and animistic habits of thought. Besides ownership-marriage, no other convention better illustrated the barbarian status of women in modern society than did the social rules that applied to women's dress. Dress (which must be distinguished from mere clothing) originated with "adornment" in primitive peoples and evolved to represent the wealth of the "social unit" in more advanced predatory societies. As trophies and later (captive) wives, women, "in a peculiar degree," served the purpose of exhibiting "the pecuniary strength" of the male owner-husband "by means of a conspicuously unproductive consumption of goods." Conspicuous consumption demonstrated prowess by virtue of the capacity of the male head of household to display "conspicuous waste." The practice of conspicuous waste, Veblen observed, adhered to three "cardinal principles": expensiveness ("with respect to its effectiveness as clothing, apparel must be uneconomical"), novelty ("apparel must afford prima facie evidence of having been worn but for a relatively short time"), and ineptitude (the apparel "must afford prima facie evidence of incapacitating the wearer for any gainful occupation"). The "highest manifestation" of this form of dress was "unquestionably seen in the apparel of the women of the most advanced modern communities." Thus, the "most advanced" cultures of the modern world were also the most sophisticated of the predatory societies.[18]

Not only dress, but virtually all of upper-class culture, as well as popular culture (which aped the upper class), especially sporting contests, were outgrowths of a long habituation to predatory life and its corresponding modes of thought. During the evolutionary process, pecuniary exploit had thoroughly "contaminated" the instinct of workmanship and, in modern times, had become the dominant propensity of the two. However, this instinctual blend is a more complex matter in Veblen's theory than this descriptive account suggests. Veblen argued that, in primitive societies, the instinct of workmanship created its own nemesis in the form of a competition or emulation that began when individuals aspired to an "ideal of efficiency." With the growth of technology, especially weapons, predatory culture slowly emerged and supplanted the peaceable industrial community in which the predominance of the instinct of workmanship had become manifest in the values of efficiency, serviceability, and group solidarity. Certain conditions had to be present for predatory culture to develop (e.g., increase in populations, confrontations between groups), but to a large extent, exploit actually grew out of the early industrial culture in which the instinct of workmanship predominated. In short, the psychological propensity necessary for predatory societies to develop was present from the beginning.

Emulation and competitive behavior, therefore, would seem to be part of the human condition. Indeed, Veblen observed that these propensities were also present in the peaceable savage communities in the form of competition for food and sex.[19] He underscored this point in *The Instinct of Workmanship* where he argued that "the most destructive derangement that besets workmanship" was its "self-contamination." This phenomenon was endemic to the activity of work because human beings naturally endowed their actions with significance, thereby imputing a teleology to objects and events. Out of this mental process grew myth and religion which supplanted naive animism with a more sophisticated anthropomorphism.[20] This same innate teleological process, moreover, produced emulative behavior. The putative superiority (or prowess) that invidious distinctions aimed to establish was the ability to control or influence environmental forces. In other words, prowess was not only, or even primarily, a function of demonstrating physical domination. It was a matter of an individual apparently exercising power or, as Veblen would say, "force" over the course of events.

Another way of stating the problem is that Veblen did not believe that human history should be viewed either as a tragic loss of innocence or an idyllic past betrayed. Rather, he argued that both emulation (rooted in animism) and workmanship had co-existed from the beginning and that the development of technology and the advent of predatory culture were inextricable insofar as technical knowledge led to more sophisticated methods of production. Thereafter, workmanship and exploit were blended, with one or the other having greater influence on social institutions, which is to say, habits of thought. The irony of human history, so to speak, was that the prime mover in the evolutionary process was technology (technical knowledge), which initially served the salutary ends of workmanship but, in so doing, also contributed to emulative behavior and the beginnings of predatory society. Technology largely determined the economic structure of a society and hence the conditions under which instinctual proclivities would be expressed. Measured solely by the growth of technology, each era in human history represented an advance over its predecessor. At the same time, the habits of thought that directed the application of technical knowledge continued to be shaped by a mixture of workmanlike efficiency and exploit. The essential contradiction of this developmental process, as Veblen explained it, was that insofar as human beings remained captive to predatory habits of thought, they could not realize the full productive potential of their own creations; but these habits of thought also encouraged the growth of technology and industry.

In Veblen's evolutionary scheme, the handicraft era marked the transition from the predatory to the peaceable commercial phase of pecuniary culture. This stage roughly corresponds to what scholars generally label the transitional period from feudalism to capitalism. For Veblen, the era of handicraft constituted the pre-industrial phase of capitalism, the stage in which the small-scale competitive economy developed around the activities of craftsmen and petty traders.[21] By combining technological mastery with the quest for profit, the craftsman joined the skills of industry and business. Both of these skills "counted equally," for the handicraft system remained "a practicable plan of economic life only so long as the craftsman [could] combine both of these capacities in good force and only so long as the technological exigencies [would] admit the exercise of both in conjunction."[22]

As it became increasingly productive, the handicraft system planted the seeds of its own destruction. Technological advances in various crafts eventually made the cost of equipment prohibitive for most craftsmen. Soon crafts became organized within industrial plants that were owned by individuals with sufficient wealth to purchase the means of production. Improvements in methods of communication, transportation, and trade facilitated, directly and indirectly, the process of industrial advance. Eventually, the handicraft system broke down, or perhaps outgrew itself, and the rudiments of an industrial system began to take shape. In the process, however, a division of labor separated the two skills once embodied in the craftsman. Under the new system, pecuniary control was vested in a class of owners while the tasks of production were consigned to a propertyless class of workers.[23]

Although the Industrial Revolution in England definitively ushered in the era of machine technology, its formative principle—the dominance of business over industry—
grew out of the handicraft economy. The progressive
separation of these two realms of economic activity constituted the dominant trend of modern technological development. With the ascendancy of the business class,
moreover, new relationships of power were established:

The transition from the original predatory phase of the
pecuniary culture to the succeeding commercial phase signifies the emergence of a middle class in such forces as presently to recast the working arrangements of the cultural
scheme and make peaceable business (gainful traffic) the
ruling interest of the community.... It is the conscious interest of this class to further the gainfulness of industry, and as
this end is correlated with the productiveness of industry it
is also, though less directly, correlated with improvements
in technology.[24]

Society thus became organized in the interests of business or profit making; and pecuniary principles or habits
of thought soon acquired "supreme dominance...both as
standards of efficiency and as canons of conduct." This
"pecuniary system of social organization" further instituted
"class divergence of material interests, class prerogative
and differential hardship, and an accentuated class disparity in the consumption of goods."[25] The rise of the bourgeoisie in the era of modern industry had initiated the final
stage of the conquest of exploit over industry.

### III

Veblen reminds us throughout his writings that the split

between business and industry did not occur suddenly but developed very gradually with the growth of modern industry. This division initially became apparent with the phasing out of the independent craftsman and the ascendancy of the first great class of business leaders, the so-called "captains of industry." The captains of industry were in actuality entrepreneurs who possessed, in varying degrees, considerable industrial expertise.[26] It was during the "era of free competition"—roughly the period which "lies between the Industrial Revolution of the eighteenth century and the rise of corporation finance in the nineteenth"—that the captain of industry emerged as a major economic, political, and social force. For nearly a century, the captain of industry was "the dominant figure in civilized life, about whose deeds and interests law and custom have turned, the central and paramount personal agency in Occidental civilization." Yet, as technology became more complex and scientific in character, as the efficiency and output of industrial production increased, and as business transactions expanded, "the function of the entrepreneur, the captain of industry, gradually fell apart in a two-fold division of labor, between the business manager and the office work on the one side and the technician and the industrial work on the other side."[27] With this most recent split between business and industry, which amounted to a division between financial and industrial management with the former retaining ultimate control, the era of corporate dominance began.

The rise of the corporation in the late nineteenth century, Veblen argued, coincided with the failure of the competitive system to prevent excessive (i.e., unprofitable) production. In order to limit production and thereby prevent retrenchment of assets or earnings, the pecuniary captains increasingly resorted to the corporate form of business enterprise. The corporation, he explained, "is a business concern, not an industrial unit"; moreover, it is a "business concern which has been created by a capitalization of funds, and which accordingly rests on credit." While corporations may have indirectly facilitated industrial expansion, their purpose has always been investment for profit. "Business enterprise may be said to have reached its majority," he asserted, "when the corporation came to take first place and became the master institution of civilized life."[28]

The proliferation of corporate enterprise in the last quarter of the nineteenth century marked the beginning of a new order of industry and business.[29] Scientific advances in chemistry and physics revolutionized industrial technology; and the operations of industry increasingly came under the supervision of scientifically trained experts or technicians. The "modern machine process," as Veblen called it, gave rise to greater specialization and division of labor within industry. It created industrial interdependence through standardization of processes, machinery, and labor requirements, and ultimately standardized and routinized all of social existence—work, consumption, leisure—as though it were merely an extension of the mechanical workings of industry. Built upon the precepts of science and "matter-of-fact thinking," the modern machine process held forth the promise of industrial efficiency on a scale hitherto unimagined. This promise, however, was continually thwarted by the overlords of business. Unlike the scientifically oriented technicians and engineers who were concerned with the efficient operation of industry, the business magnates, the czars of finance and the rulers of the great industrial corporations, were driven solely by the quest for profits. Modern business enterprise and the credit economy upon which it rested were designed to stabilize prices, and therefore profits, by regulating competition and limiting production. Because they provided for centralization of control, allowed for routinization of business transactions, and created a greater interdependence within the financial community, corporations constituted the institutional foundation of the new order of business. The rise of the corporation therefore represented the demise of the captain of industry and the triumph of the modern business leader, the "captain of finance."

Veblen's ground-breaking theory of business enterprise focused primarily on three interrelated aspects of the economy—the use of credit, the nature of corporate capital, and the dynamics of business crises and depressions.[30] In "The Overproduction Fallacy," published in 1892, twelve years before the publication of *The Theory of Business Enterprise,* Veblen criticized the inability of conventional economic theorists to explain the phenomenon of overproduction and its relationship to depressions. His enduring contribution to this debate was to shift its footing from the terrain of classical economic theory, which could not account for the economic facts including the decisions of capitalists, to a theory of modern business enterprise that could explain the interrelationships between credit extensions in various forms, their impact on prices and markets, and the cyclical nature of depressions in the era of corporation finance. This same theme runs throughout "Credit and Prices," which was written in response to an issue raised at the American Economic Association annual meeting in 1904: "Does the use of credit raise general prices?" While emphasizing that a rise or fall in prices was correlated with the extension or contraction of credit, Veblen also examined theoretical implications of the causal relationship between credit and prices in this essay.

Veblen maintained that during the era of competitive capitalism and prior to the ascendancy of corporate finance, the extensive use of loan credit gave rise to periods of speculative expansion, rising prices, and business prosperity. Eventually, such periods of prosperity waned and prices dropped, with the result that many businesses had difficulty meeting their financial obligations to creditors. Because loans had been secured on the basis of an inflated earning capacity, a steady drop in prices revealed the extent to which businesses had overextended themselves.[31] The discrepancy between the putative and actual collateral basis of capitalization became apparent to the creditors and a period of liquidation and business depression ensued:

> Such a divergence between the accepted valuation and the actual value of capital may seem an inadequate basis for an economic fact of such magnitude as a period of industrial depression. And yet an industrial depression means, mainly, a readjustment of values. It is primarily, to very great extent, a psychological fact. Secondarily, it is largely a matter of shifting of ownership rather than destruction of wealth or a serious reduction of the aggregate productiveness of industry as measured in goods.[32]

Liquidation resulted in a redistribution of ownership of collateral property among creditors, a period of adjustment and re-capitalization, and eventually another speculative movement. Veblen maintained that prior to the 1870s, the discrepancy between capitalization and actual earning capacity was never too great to prevent a renewed speculative advance. As a consequence, depressions during this period tended to be short-lived and rarely disabled the economy as a whole.[33]

Under modern conditions, however, technological advances reduced costs at such a great rate that there existed a chronic discrepancy between capitalization and earning capacity. As technological improvements persistently out-stripped the readjustment of capitalization, a steady decline in profits resulted, thereby preventing a renewed speculative expansion of the type that had occurred in the earlier decades of the nineteenth century. Furthermore, depressions in the era of modern machine technology took on a systematic character due to the interdependent nature of the industrial system. The technological factor not only complicated the problem of credit inflation, but basically altered the nature of depressions as well. So long as business was conducted on a competitive footing, chronic depression, Veblen observed, was "normal to the industrial situation."[34]

Veblen concluded that competitive business practices were incompatible with the increased efficiency and productivity of modern industry. Accordingly, the dominant business interests in the latter decades of the nineteenth century had sought to eliminate competition by controlling prices and limiting production, mainly through combination and monopoly. In this fashion, the first lords of high finance proceeded to reorganize the economy through mergers and trust building. Thus, high finance—the buying and selling of enterprises, the financing of mergers, and the control of credit—came to dominate business enterprise. The investment banker reigned supreme as the master of high finance, and what the trust builders had initiated in their quest for profits, within a few decades, acquired an institutional basis in the major banks and the Federal Reserve System.[35]

The structure of corporate power, which is to say, the organization of power within the ruling business class, therefore, could be conceived as a hierarchy in which the large financial interests dominated, followed by the business managers of the key industrial corporations, and below them, the managers of the remaining industrial and manufacturing concerns whose livelihood largely depended upon the strategic decisions of the ruling business interests. According to Veblen's theory of modern industrial society, the pecuniary interests of the business class as a whole (which included the leisure class) stood opposed to the community's interest in efficiency and serviceability. Increasingly, this conflict took the form of a confrontation between the interests of the "One Big Union of Financial Interests" and their agents in government, on the one hand, and the vanguard of modern technology, the new class of technicians and engineers, on the other. The contradiction between business and industry, therefore, boiled down to a conflict between an exploitative class interest in profit making and a general social interest in full production and efficient use of technology and resources.[36]

IV

Just as the ascendancy of the captain of finance established the supremacy of pecuniary exploit over workmanlike efficiency, so did the era of corporate dominance represent the highest development of pecuniary culture. In shaping the styles and tastes of the ruling class, and ultimately the underlying population, business principles and ideology also served to justify class rule. Because class governance in advanced capitalist societies depended upon widespread ideological consensus, control over the production and dissemination of ideas was of vital importance to the perpetuation of existing power relationships. Indeed, the institutions of higher learning, according to Veblen, were dominated by individuals thoroughly imbued with pecuniary and nonscientific habits of thought, a fact that was clearly evidenced in the biased curriculum of these schools. While scientific thinking had made some inroads, the system of higher education continued to be administered on the basis of businesslike principles, to propagate the ideas of pecuniary culture, and to serve the needs of the business class.[37] Schools of business and law, and to a lesser extent other vocational schools, "serve the advantage of one class as against another" because they "increase the advantage of such men as already have some advantage over the common run."[38] Thus, even though Veblen did not employ the actual phrase, it is clear that he adhered to a conception of the ideological hegemony of liberalism in the era of corporate rule.

Interpreted within the logic of Veblen's social theory, ideological hegemony was as much a product of cultural lag as of overt control. Ideological justification of the new order of business and industry, he argued, consisted of principles of ownership derived from the era of the handicraft economy.[39] Both the legal and moral foundation of the corporate order rested on the Lockean theory of property rights which posited a unity of ownership and workmanship, that is, of business and industry. This theory, however, like all habits of thought or ideological beliefs, had long since ceased to depict the reality which it justified. In fact, once the split between business and industry had become established in the competitive era, the unity of ownership and workmanship gave way to the institution of absentee ownership. Despite the fact that absentee ownership separated the productive use of property from its ownership, its legal and moral justification stood squarely on Locke's defense of property rights.

Veblen's critique of natural rights preconceptions also included an analysis of animistic habits of thought which, he argued, derived from the earliest primitive societies and remained a factor throughout the evolutionary process. Although its influence was progressively decreasing with the growth of matter-of-fact scientific thinking, Veblen identified animistic preconceptions as a significant influence on the precepts of liberal political thought and classical economic theory. The confluence of animism and liberal ideology was well illustrated by the hedonistic or utilitarian doctrine that informed classical economics and its progeny, such as marginal-utility theory. This latter theory ignored the social reality of production in the era of business enterprise and assumed that a mechanical hedonism was the natural psychological state of humanity from time immemorial. Marginal-utility theory substituted "sufficient reason" (rationalization) for "efficient cause" (cause and effect). It was teleological, Veblen argued, because it assumed an end or purpose rather than demonstrating a causal sequence or process: "this preconception imputes to things a tendency to work out what the instructed common sense of the time accepts as the adequate or worthy end of human effort."[40]

Veblen used the occasion of reviewing two books by economist Irving Fisher, *The Nature of Capital and In-*

*come* (1906) and *The Rate of Interest* (1908), to illustrate how the preconceptions of economic science (marginal-utility theory) limited its ability to explain the reality of economic life. In "Fisher's Capital and Income" and "Fisher's Rate of Interest," published respectively in 1908 and 1909, Veblen took issue with the failure of the author to define the concepts of capital, income, and interest with reference to the actual social context in which they were applied. Veblen deemed Fisher's books to be "taxonomic" works based on a "primordial metaphysical postulate," the "hedonic principle." Although "capital" did not hold the same meaning for businessmen that it did fifty years earlier, practitioners of "modern" economic theory were unable to explain this fact. "Intangible assets," a phenomenon very familiar to real people involved in corporate finance, was not only excluded from Fisher's concept of capital, but was absent altogether from his analysis. This omission, which was to be expected in marginal-utility theory, was a chief cause of its failure "to give an intelligent account of credit and crises." The failure was not Fisher's as such, but that of the theory: the "shortsightedness of the taxonomic economist is a logical consequence of the hedonistic postulates of the school, not a personal peculiarity of the present or any other author."[41]

Fisher's concept of income, "a perfect flower of economic taxonomy," erroneously reduced income to "psychic income" and, for the sake of taxonomic precision, unnecessarily distinguished income from "increase of capital." Income must be assessed in terms of "pecuniary, not of hedonistic magnitudes."[42] Modern business was a pecuniary institution—a credit economy that developed out of a money economy—that had left behind in important ways the simpler economic life that Bentham's utili-

tarian calculus idealized. The same criticism applied to
Fisher's analysis of the rate of interest: the "primordial
metaphysical postulates," those hedonistic preconceptions
of a bygone era, did not (and could not) explain the present
significance of interest, which was "a phenomenon of
credit transactions only." Interest was a quintessential
business (pecuniary) concept of the credit economy: "The
whole matter lies within the range of a definite institutional situation which is to be found only during a relatively brief phase of civilisation that has been preceded
by thousands of years of cultural growth during which
the existence of such a thing as interest was never suspected."[43] Marginal-utility theory failed because it assumed exactly what needed to be explained—namely, the
economic behavior of individuals in society under his-
torically specific conditions.

Veblen argued that both animism and emulation had
contaminated the instinct of workmanship. Animistic
thinking, which was an archaic form of anthropomorphism, was especially important in the development of
religion:

So an animistic conception of things comes presently to
supplement, and in part supplant, the more naive and immediate imputation of workmanship, leading up to farther and
more elaborate myth-making; until in the course of elaboration and refinement there may emerge a monotheistic and
providential Creator seated in an infinitely remote but ubiquitous space of four dimensions.[44]

Monotheistic religions, therefore, developed in conjunction with predatory culture and patriarchy. Like pecuniary
emulation, contemporary religious belief was a throw-
back to the era of barbarism. Both had animistic origins

and both limited or interfered with the instinct of workmanship. This was Veblen's position throughout his writings with one important and curious exception—"Christian Morals and the Competitive System," which he published in 1910. It is not entirely clear why Veblen changed his position in this paper only to abandon it thereafter. Whatever the reason(s) for these decisions, the essay offers an unusual glimpse of another side of the author. There is a hopefulness that pervades the argument, an aberrantly cheerful tone, that is reminiscent of a few other occasions when Veblen perhaps sensed that social change was possible or imminent. Even a theorist of his erudition, it seems, was occasionally prone to wishful thinking.

As he did in all of his research, Veblen sought in "Christian Morals and the Competitive System" to explain habits of thought—in this case, Christian morality and pecuniary emulation—with reference to the material environment and changing social conditions. Noting that both Christian morals and the morality of pecuniary competition were "institutional factors of first-rate importance in this culture" both seemingly occupying a "dominant position," Veblen posed the central issues of the paper in the form of questions: "Taken at their best, do the two further fortify one another? do they work together without mutual help or hindrance? or do they mutually inhibit and defeat each other?"[45]

To answer these queries it was first necessary to identify the basic principles underlying the moral doctrines of Christianity and pecuniary competition, principles that had been present in them from the outset and that still broadly shaped their significance in all of their cultural permutations. The principles of Christianity were "non-resistance (humility) and brotherly love," the latter of which was "in some sort an atavistic trait" inherited from the peaceable communities of savages. Nonresistance, on the other hand, which could not be "traced back as a culturally atavistic trait," belonged "almost wholly to the more highly developed, more coercively organized civilisations, that are possessed of a consistent monotheistic religion and a somewhat arbitrary secular authority." Christianity first took hold under Roman rule "among the lower orders of the populace especially, who had been beaten to a pulp by the hard-handed, systematic, inexorable power of the imperial city." In short, Christianity started out as the religion of the oppressed before it became the official doctrine of the ruling classes during the middle ages. Its enduring appeal, however, had more to do with its compatibility with traits selected during the peaceable savage era of human history ("by far the most protracted and probably the most exacting of any phase of culture in all the life-history of the race") than with any of the institutional forms it had taken on during subsequent centuries.[46] By contrast, the principles of pecuniary competition were derived from the natural rights philosophy of the eighteenth century which had been devised in large part to justify economic changes associated with the growth of handicraft and petty trade. With the transition from feudalism to capitalism, pecuniary exploit had supplanted chivalric exploit. These habits of thought, however, were being outmoded by habits of life instilled in "the current era of machine industry, credit, delegated corporation management, and distant markets."[47]

Veblen concluded that the "two codes of conduct, Christian morals and business principles," were "the institutional by-products of two different cultural situations."

Yet, they also shared common ground: Christian brotherly love had its analogue in the ethic of fair play observed under the regime of pecuniary competition. Indeed, the connection was even stronger in view of the fact that the "very deeprooted and ancient cultural trait" of brotherly love was "forever reasserting itself in economic matters, in the impulsive approval of whatever conduct is serviceable to the common good and in the disapproval of disserviceable conduct even within the limits of legality and natural rights." This principle of Christian morals, Veblen reasoned, seemed to be "nothing else than a specialized manifestation of the instinct of workmanship, and as such it has an indefeasible vitality that belongs to the hereditary traits of human nature." The author's surprising conclusion was that as habits of thought that developed from pecuniary competition during the handicraft era lost their sway in the era of machine industry, the "ancient impulse" of brotherly love (and hence workmanship) would gain ground and eventually eclipse the moral doctrine of pecuniary exploit.[48]

A similarly hopeful view did not characterize Veblen's analysis of the famous protest march on Washington, D.C., by several thousand unemployed men in 1894. Coxey's Army, also known as The Army of the Commonweal, was in reality several separate "armies," only one of which was actually organized and led by Jacob Coxey, a businessman and reformer from Ohio. Members of the Army of the Commonweal demanded that the federal government take action to solve the chronic problem of unemployment. This sentiment was especially widespread in 1894 due to the millions left without jobs as a result of the depression of 1893. In "The Army of the Commonweal," Veblen explained that the conviction among American workers that local economic problems required national solutions was the product of a fundamental and thoroughgoing change in industrial methods and organization: "[T]his attitude is but an expression of the fact latterly emerging into popular consciousness, that the entire community is a single industrial organism, whose integration is advancing day by day, regardless of any traditional or conventional boundary lines or demarcations, whether between classes or between localities." The protest itself was an indication of incipient change in popular perceptions; however, the actual agenda of the protesters reflected an inchoate blend of state-centered and paternalistic ideas of recent years—bimetallism, greenbackism, protectionism, religious (and patriarchal) paternalism, and state socialism. The support for the protest indicated to Veblen that a significant social movement might eventually develop out of this changing sentiment, but to have any effect on the actual course of events, it would have to catch up with the reality of the industrial process.[49]

Veblen came to a similar conclusion in his assessment of the "arts and crafts movement," which sought to restore or rediscover the ethic of an earlier period of handicraft capitalism wherein the artist and craftsman were joined in the same individual. His critique of this romantic quest in his essay, "Arts and Crafts," was incisive and unforgiving. Pointing out that modern industry showed no signs of returning to an earlier stage of technological development, he explained that the machine process "ubiquitously and unremittingly" shaped the workmen's habits of thought rooting out whatever elements were "alien to its own technological requirements and discipline." The implications were fairly obvious to everyone except the aristocratic "Dreamer of dreams, born out of his due time": "'Industrial art,' therefore, which does not work through and in the spirit of the machine technology is, at the best, an exotic. It will not grow into a dandelion-like 'weed of cultivation,' for it has no chance of life beyond the hothouse shelter of decadent aestheticism."[50]

Given his impatience with backward looking reformers and his commitment, in principle, to progressive movements capable of altering the structure of power in American society, one might have expected Veblen to champion the cause of socialist revolution. Despite the many similarities of his social theory with classical Marxism, however, Veblen rejected the Marxist conception of class war between the proletariat and bourgeoisie. Although the business class dominated the whole of society, the potentially decisive class confrontation, in his view, was between the leaders of business and the new class of technicians and trained engineers, the vanguard of modern industrial methods and thinking. Veblen outlined his theory of revolution in a series of hopeful essays written in 1919, subsequently compiled in *The Engineers and the Price System*. While discounting a (Marxist) proletarian revolution as such, he emphasized that the prospect of revolution did indeed depend upon an alliance between the vanguard class and industrial workers. After 1919, Veblen continued to believe that the engineers and technicians could shape the direction of social change, but he never again expressed this view with the same enthusiasm.

## V

Veblen maintained that while the rule of the business class in the United States derived its ideological sustenance, in the main, from the traditional theory of property rights, it also found justification in the sentiment of nationalism. Originally a means for ensuring loyalty to feudal overlords, nationalism or patriotism in its modern form served as a guise to mask the imperialist ambitions of the business class.[51] Through an evolutionary process of adaptation and rationalization in response to changing social circumstances, the institutions of ownership and nationalism continued to justify the predatory aims of society's rulers.

Veblen viewed the state or nation as an institutional outgrowth of the dynastic period of early modern Europe in which "the rival princely or dynastic establishments...each sought its own advantage at the cost of any whom it may concern." In modern times, "the divine right of the prince has passed over into the divine right of the Nation," but the predatory animus of the era of state-making remained in the imperialistic ambitions of the business interests. With the advent of this latest stage of predatory culture, he argued, the ruling class ensured its dominance through control of the state.[52]

In one of his more prescient essays, "Japan's Opportunity," published in 1915, Veblen applied his evolutionary theory of social change and his theory of the state to analyze the unusual blend of monarchical rule and industrial development then at work in Japan. Arguing that an opportunity had presented itself to Japan's rulers to realize their imperialist ambitions, Veblen shrewdly assessed the probable consequences that Japan's rapid industrial development would have on its social and political order. In essence, he argued that Japan had reached a point in its history where it could take advantage of the strengths afforded by a combination of feudalism and capitalism.

Japan's rulers would experience for a short time the best of two worlds, so to speak—a feudal social structure and a modern industrial economy. This transitional phase would last a generation or so after which the deteriorating impact of industrialization on feudal institutions would begin to weaken this powerful combination of dynastic rule and modern technology. The Japanese case resembled in some respects that of the German people who "allowed their new-found technological efficiency to be turned to the service of dynastic politics." Yet Japan had outdistanced all of Europe in the degree to which it had exploited the modern state of industrial arts "by recourse to the servile patriotism of the common man."[53]

In detailing the likely course of change that Japanese social and political institutions would undergo in the coming years, Veblen argued that the business corporation would play an essential role in this transformation both as a means of instilling commercial values and of exploiting the modern state of industrial arts for dynastic ends. However, this bearer of pecuniary culture inculcated the logic of business principles which did not mesh well with the ceremonial trappings of dynastic politics. In the long term, business enterprise would thoroughly transform the face of Japanese society: "Wherever it reaches it carries a 'commercialization' of human relations and social standards, and effects a displacement of such aims and values as cannot be stated in terms of pecuniary gain; and so it throws pecuniary solvency into that position of first consideration that has been occupied by pedigree and putative excellencies of character."[54]

Veblen's writings during World War I covered a wide range of topics that reflected his considerable expertise in international relations, comparative government, economics, philosophy, and what has since been labeled "modernization theory." Many of the essays he wrote during this period reveal the sometimes awkward merger of the realistic social scientist and the social critic still hopeful that progressive change might come out of the most tragic of circumstances. One also suspects that the bitterness Veblen harbored following the many disappointments associated with the War—the failure in his view of the peace agreement to really make the world a safer or better place, the continued oppression of the "common man" at the expense of the vested interests, the mindless backlash against the American left in the wake of the Bolshevik revolution—might have encouraged or fueled the revolutionary zeal he expressed on behalf of the new class of engineers in 1919, while serving as an editor of *The Dial*.

Veblen wrote several papers and one book[55] addressing the philosophical basis and practical implementation of a peace settlement. He contributed two of his papers, "Suggestions Touching the Working Program of an Inquiry into the Prospective Terms of Peace" and "Outline of a Policy for the Control of the 'Economic Penetration' of Backward Countries and of Foreign Investments," to the committee or "Inquiry" formed by Colonel House at the request of President Wilson, in 1917, to explore possible terms of a peace agreement. Four other essays, "The Passing of National Frontiers" (1918), "A Policy of Reconstruction" (1918), "Peace" (1919), and "The Economic Consequences of Peace" (1920) were published in various political and academic journals. A common theme runs throughout all of these papers. When conceived as a permanent condition and not as a temporary or partial solution put in place between wars, peace could be achieved only when the root cause of war—the rivalries between dynastic states fueled by imperialist policies— no longer held sway over the peaceful industrial interests of the great majority of the world's people. In the essays submitted to Colonel House's "Inquiry," Veblen outlined a peace settlement based on a "Pacific League," an idea that might have influenced President Wilson's ill-fated "League of Nations." The vision of the "New Order" that Veblen laid out in these and later papers, however, was not one that Wilson would have fully embraced. Veblen urged that the Pacific League adopt and implement the following policies or objectives: abolition of national frontiers to encourage free trade and the spread of industrial technology, submergence of national distinctions whenever possible through federations or disincentives, protection of natural resources of less developed countries from exploitation by the dominant (imperialist) business interests, and punishment of belligerent nations.[56]

Veblen also argued that the World War had made possible, if not necessitated, a "reconstruction" of the American commonwealth, which entailed "a revision of vested rights, for the common good."[57] Considerations of efficiency in preventing destructive competition among business owners as well as conflict between employers and workers that produced industrial strife and waste justified two "remedial measures":

(1) Disallowance of anything like free discretionary control or management on grounds of ownership alone...whenever the responsible owner of the concern does not at the same time also personally oversee and physically direct the work in which his property is engaged...

(2) To take over and administer as a public utility any going concern that is in control of industrial or commercial work which...[can be] habitually managed from an office by methods of accountancy.[58]

This argument, which seems to anticipate his essays in *The Engineers and the Price System,* illustrated well the blend of realism and hopefulness that characterized so many of his writings during this period. Veblen insisted that his recommendations were "a simple matter of material expediency," and contained neither "socialist iconoclasm" nor the "slightest animus of moral esteem or disesteem."[59]

Veblen supported the war effort but also defended the right of dissenters to oppose it and openly assailed the Red Scare policies that came in its aftermath. In 1918, he had worked five months for the Food Administration in Washington, D.C., writing policy papers. In this capacity, he penned several memoranda, including "Farm Labor for the Period of the War," "Farm Labor and the I.W.W.," "A Memorandum on a Schedule of Prices for the Staple Foodstuffs," and "The War and Higher Learning," and he wrote an article for *The Public,* "Menial Servants During the Period of the War," which was also based on research he had done while working for the Food Administration. Two of these essays are especially noteworthy as examples of Veblen's efforts to influence government policy in conformance with his political ideals. "Farm Labor and the I.W.W.," which ostensibly began as a report on the "conditions surrounding the prospective grain crops of the prairie states," evolved into a very enlightening analysis of the ongoing class warfare between farmers and farm workers, on one side, and the "vested interests" (big business and the commercial clubs) in league with local, state, and federal governments, on the other. In addition to arguing that a labor shortage could be avoided by allowing the 50,000 members of the I.W.W. affiliate, the Agricultural Workers Industrial Union, to work free of harassment and to be paid the minimum wages they demanded, Veblen went out of his way to plead for intervention by the federal government on behalf of many Wobblie members who had been illegally jailed, unfairly punished, or beaten.[60]

Veblen's tack in "The War and Higher Learning" was also ingenious. With many of the academic institutions of Europe in turmoil or in a state of disrepair, which included the lack of financial resources and threats to academic freedom, Veblen sensed an opportunity to propose a two-part plan which, he no doubt believed, might loosen the hold of the vested interests over higher education. First, he proposed that an open door policy for foreign educators would have to be instituted at all American universities. The continued diffusion of knowledge, after all, was in the interest of all nations even if it did run counter in some respects to the American method of businesslike competition among universities. Second, an international forum or center for higher education which involved "an inclusive co-ordination of these American schools" would be established. In addition to preventing duplication and hence wasted funds, a "central office" would "serve as a common point of support and co-ordination, which would at the same time serve as a focus, exchange, and center of diffusion for scholarly pursuits and mutual understanding, as well as an unattached academic house of refuge and entertainment for any guests, strays, and wayfaring men of the republic of learning."[61]

For Veblen, these policies no doubt did not seem idealistic or utopian. They were, in his view, consistent with the direction of social change and with the best interests of the nation as a whole. One might question, however, whether his highly critical assessment of the peace settlement (see "Peace," "Between Bolshevism and War," and "The Economic Consequences of Peace") combined with his strong reaction to the childlike paranoia fomented by the Red Scare (see "Dementia Praecox"), might not also have affected his ability during this period to assess realistically the actual content and direction of Bolshevik policies. In "Bolshevism Is a Menace—to Whom?" published in February of 1919, Veblen observed that "the Bolshevik is the common man who has faced the question: What do I stand to lose? and has come away with the answer: Nothing."[62] Bolshevism was indeed a menace, he surmised, but only to the vested interests. One would expect Veblen to hold this view when the Russian Revolution was fresh and its course had not yet been firmly set. Two years later in 1921, however, he compared the Soviet form of administration to a New England town meeting that had assumed jurisdiction over "all items of absentee ownership" and, in nearly the same breath, he reported matter-of-factly that the Soviet had displaced democracy and representative government because they had "proved to be incompetent and irrelevant for any other purpose than the security and profitable regulation of absentee ownership."[63] This seemingly cavalier attitude toward the squelching of democracy in Russia was more indicative of the hopefulness mixed with desperation and anger Veblen experienced during this period than of a doctrinaire support for communism. Like many other critical thinkers of his generation who had nurtured the hope that the future would bring a more just and humane society, the failure of fundamental social change to occur in the aftermath of the war, combined with the chilling ef-

fect of the anti-Red mob mentality on progressive thinking, eventually left him disillusioned and bitter. Indeed,
in his last and perhaps most comprehensive and mature
work, *Absentee Ownership*, Veblen did not even mention
the prospect of revolutionary change. Rather, he seemed
resigned to the continued dominance of the business class.

## VI

*Essays in Our Changing Order* touches upon every
aspect of Veblen's social theory and political writings. It
is also a volume of firsts and lasts. Veblen's inaugural
academic publication, "Kant's Critique of Judgment,"
marked the first and last time he published a strictly philosophical essay that was not about his own social theory.
This essay appeared in the prestigious *Journal of Speculative Philosophy* in 1884, shortly after Veblen received
his Ph.D. in philosophy from Yale. Unable to secure a
university position in philosophy (most philosophers at
that time were divinity students), he left the academic
world for several years, returning to take graduate courses
at Cornell in 1891, and subsequently embarking on a
career as an economist. Despite the considerable gap in
time (ten years) that separated this first publication from
his later writings on evolutionary theory, the paper is nev-
ertheless useful for understanding Veblen's intellectual
development. It sheds significant light on his methodological assumptions and his insistence on using inductive, as opposed to deductive, reasoning in empirical
research.[64]

Veblen's last published essay (which is first in order of
appearance in this volume), "Economic Theory in the
Calculable Future," might serve equally well as a conclusion to this book. In his inimitable style, Veblen dryly

observed that economists of the coming generation would
be predictably behind the times in their thinking but also
more securely wedded to the creed of businesslike principles. Most economists, he explained, would study only
what is useful to business, just as academic institutions
increasingly would become business schools. "Mr.
Cumming's Strictures on 'The Theory of the Leisure
Class,'" originally published in 1899, was the first and
last time Veblen defended any of his books in print. This
is unfortunate. Veblen's spirited defense is well worth the
read, especially his closing remarks explaining his choice
not to adopt the style of writing that had "long afflicted
economics" and had "given that science its reputed character of sterility."[65] To continue my theme, the last essay
Veblen wrote in his life, "An Experiment in Eugenics,"
which was rejected for publication when he was alive,
was first published in this posthumous collection. A somewhat confusing ethnological analysis that tests eugenics
theory with respect to Scandinavians, this piece is not up
to Veblen's normally high standards. Like many of his
contemporaries influenced by Darwinian theory, Veblen
considered ethnology to be a science. To the contemporary reader, his ethnological or racial generalizations
might give offense or seem comedic depending on the
context. However, many of his writings in this area were
connected with his broader social critique of the predacious habits of thought that sustained modern pecuniary
culture. It should be noted that Veblen rejected as unsci-
entific the notion sometimes associated with eugenics
theory that certain races were superior to others based on
genetic endowment.

In closing, there is one gem left to admire—"The Pre-
eminence of Jews in Modern Europe." This too would
have made a fitting conclusion for this book because it

describes so effectively the intellectual perspective of an outsider. There is no doubt that Veblen identified with those intellectuals and scientists (e.g., Marx, Freud, Einstein) whom he dubbed "renegade Jews," gifted thinkers who became citizens in the "gentile republic of learning."[66] These outsiders were an odd hybrid of cultural influence. Denizens of two worlds, they belonged completely to neither. But their alienated existence was also the wellspring of their intellectual strength and vision. They saw more clearly than those whose eyes were shrouded by convention. They had pierced the veil of accepted wisdom and beheld the naked truth. This paralleled Veblen's own experience. The son of immigrant Norwegian farmers, he had always been a stranger in the land of his birth. Not only did this allow him to study American society with a certain detachment, but he also infused his written observations with an unfamiliar bias, not unlike a social anthropologist whose "objective" assessments of another culture are sifted through the prism of his own life experience. Perhaps this is why Veblen's deadly serious accounts of the ludicrousness of American pecuniary culture often have been mistakenly interpreted as satire. There can be no doubt that Veblen took great pride in his formidable wit and that his playfulness with words often revealed a sardonic sense of humor. He even loved practical jokes. To be sure, some of his writings *were* brilliantly satirical, but one wonders how often he actually intended them to have that effect. The satirist indulges in a form of cultural self-parody, a critique from the inside as it were. It is a literary technique that combines ridicule and irony to delve beneath the layers of conventionality to excavate the truth. Mark Twain, the social conscience of his generation, was a master of satire. Thorstein Veblen, the outsider, was a renegade intellectual. He documented the truth as he saw it, which, we all know, is sometimes much funnier than fiction.

In describing the plight of the Jew in the land of the gentile, Veblen seems to have unwittingly crafted his own eulogy. On second thought, perhaps that is exactly what he wanted us to believe:

> For him as for other men in the like case, the skepticism that goes to make him an effectual factor in the increase and diffusion of knowledge among men involves a loss of that peace of mind that is the birthright of the safe and sane quietist. He becomes a disturber of the intellectual peace, but only at the cost of becoming an intellectual wayfaring man, a wanderer in the intellectual no-man's-land, seeking another place to rest, farther along the road, somewhere over the horizon. They are neither a complaisant nor a contented lot, these aliens of the uneasy feet...[67]

## NOTES

1. The most comprehensive biography of Veblen is Joseph Dorfman's *Thorstein Veblen and His America* (New York: The Viking Press, 1934).

2. Thorstein Veblen, *The Theory of the Leisure Class: An Economic Study of Institutions* (New Brunswick, N.J.: Transaction Publishers, 1991), p. 131; Veblen, *Essays in Our Changing Order*, edited by Leon Ardzrooni (New York: The Viking Press, 1934), p. 80; Veblen, *The Place of Science in Modern Civilization* (New Brunswick, N.J.: Transaction Publishers, 1990), pp. 241–42.

3. *Essays*, pp. 80–81, 85; Veblen, *The Instinct of Workmanship and the State of the Industrial Arts* (New Brunswick, N.J.: Transaction Publishers, 1990), pp. 1, 4, 6–8, 30–31; *Leisure Class*, pp. 29, 146.

4. *Essays*, p. 80; *Leisure Class*, p. 29; *Instinct of Workmanship*, pp. 25–27, 31–37, 84–89; *The Place of Science*, pp. 6–19.

5. *Instinct of Workmanship*, pp. 11, 40–41.

6. Ibid., p. 50, note 1; see also *The Place of Science*, p. 76.

7. *Essays*, pp. 80–81; *Leisure Class*, pp. 29, 133–34; see also *Ab-*

*sentee Ownership and Business Enterprise in Recent Times* (New York: B.W. Huebsch, Inc., 1923), pp. 16–17, 206.

8. *Leisure Class*, p. 134.

9. Ibid.; see also *Instinct of Workmanship*, p. 40; Veblen, *The Theory of Business Enterprise* (New Brunswick, N.J.: Transaction Publishers, 1978, pp. 146–48; *Absentee Ownership*, p. 17.

10. *Leisure Class*, p. 133, 138–42; see also *Absentee Ownership*, pp. 18, 43; Veblen, *The Vested Interests and the Common Man* (New York: The Viking Press, 1933), pp. 4–11.

11. *Essays*, pp. 42–49; *Instinct of Workmanship*, pp. 146–60.

12. *Essays*, p. 33.

13. Ibid., pp. 42–49, 92; *Leisure Class*, pp. 33–34; *Instinct of Workmanship*, pp. 149–61. Veblen's main concern was to locate the beginnings of ownership, not to posit a necessary causal relationship between that institution and a particular social practice. "Whether property provokes to predation or predation initiates ownership," he concluded, "the situation that results in the early phases of the pecuniary culture was much the same" (ibid., p. 160).

14. *Essays*, p. 48.

15. Ibid., p. 58.

16. Ibid., pp. 56–58, 60–61.

17. Ibid., pp. 50, p. 93; *Leisure Class*, pp. 25, 26, 35, 43.

18. *Essays*, pp. 68, 74–75.

19. Ibid., pp. 88–94; *Leisure Class*, pp. 30–32.

20. *Instinct of Workmanship*, pp. 52–61.

21. For Veblen's analysis of the handicraft era, see ibid., pp. 209–98; *Absentee Ownership*, pp. 40–49.

22. *Instinct of Workmanship*, p. 211.

23. Ibid., pp. 210–14, 228–29, 233–34, 277–82.

24. Ibid., pp. 184–85.

25. Ibid., pp. 187, 216. It should be noted that Veblen did not consider pecuniary exploit to be an instinct. Rather, it is a "self-regarding sentiment" or "motive" rooted in pecuniary emulation. Veblen argued that pecuniary exploit, which, of course, is essential to the institution of ownership, had come to thoroughly dominate the behavior and thought of the business (and leisure) class as well as large segments of the rest of society. In short, pecuniary exploit had imposed its own bias on the instinctive proclivities of individuals living in pecuniary culture. Thus, pecuniary exploit and the institution of ownership affected the way in which the instinct of workmanship

was expressed. Veblen argued that with the emergence of pecuniary culture, the system of "free workmanship" (i.e., cooperation, common use of resources and technology, social equality) gave way to pecuniary control of industry (i.e., self-interest, ownership, class distinctions). See ibid., pp. 142–51.

The fact that Veblen did not classify pecuniary exploit (or pecuniary emulation) as an instinct does not seem to be important to his analysis inasmuch as he often referred to pecuniary exploit and/or pecuniary emulation as though it were an instinct. His decision in this matter, however, would appear to serve an ideological purpose since instincts, according to Veblen's theory, were essential to the survival of the species.

26. Veblen's most systematic analyses of the captains of industry will be found in *Absentee Ownership*, pp. 101–18; *The Engineers and the Price System* (New Brunswick, N.J.: Transaction Publishers, 1983), pp. 27–51.

27. *Absentee Ownership*, pp. 101, 102, 106; see also ibid., pp. 70–71. To avoid terminological confusion, it should be noted that the era of machine technology in Veblen's analysis actually comprises two periods or eras—free competition and corporate finance.

28. Ibid., pp. 78–79, 110–11, 331–53; *Business Enterprise*, pp. 115–16, 123–27; *The Engineers*, pp. 36–38; *Absentee Ownership*, pp. 82, 86.

29. Veblen discussed the financial and industrial characteristics of this new order at length in several works. See, generally, ibid., pp. 205–397; *Business Enterprise,* pp. 7–127; *Instinct of Workmanship*, pp. 299–355; *The Engineers,* pp. 38–82; *Vested Interests*, pp. 35–113.

30. For Veblen's theory of business enterprise, see *Business Enterprise,* pp. 49–127; *Absentee Ownership,* pp. 82–100, 326–97.

31. *Essays,* pp. 110–12, 114–20, 126–31. Veblen argued that the extensive use of loan credit, especially in the form of "notes, stock shares, interest-bearing securities, deposits, call loans, etc." had become a normal practice in modern business. In effect, credit of this sort allowed for a greater rate of turnover of capital and served "much the same purpose, as regards the rate of earnings," as did "time-saving improvement in the processes of industry" (*Business Enterprise*, pp. 49–50). Because resort to loan credit provided a competitive advantage, however slight at first, loan credit soon became necessary in order to achieve a "reasonable" return on investment (ibid., pp. 51–52; *Absentee Ownership*, pp. 356–58). The use of credit, however,

also had the effect of enlarging business capital. Recapitalization on the basis of credit extension inflated the money value of an enterprise which at this point diverged from the actual value of the industrial capital upon which the credit was based. This inflated value, plus the intangible asset of "good-will," provided the basis for a further extension of loans, and so on, with the result that the capitalized value of an enterprise came to rest in large part on credit which had no collateral basis (*Business Enterprise*, pp. 52–58; *Absentee Ownership*, pp. 345–48, 218–20). These inflated values therefore created a discrepancy between capitalization or putative earning capacity and actual earning capacity.

32. *Essays*, pp. 112–13.

33. *Business Enterprise*, pp. 94–100, 117–20.

34. Ibid., pp. 109, 120–21.

35. Ibid., pp. 115–16, 123–27. *Absentee Ownership*, pp. 331–53; *The Engineers*, pp. 47–49. On the role of the Federal Reserve system in consolidating the rule of corporate finance, see ibid., pp. 50–51, and *Absentee Ownership*, pp. 223–24 and 352, note 13.

36. Ibid., pp. 229–50. Although Veblen believed that the new class of engineers and technicians constituted the vanguard of social change, he conceived the basic division within society to be between the business (and leisure) class and the "underlying population," i.e., workers, farmers, small business people (ibid., p. 399; *Vested Interests*, p. 175).

37. Veblen, *The Higher Learning in America* (New Brunswick, N.J.: Transaction Publishers, 1993); see also *Leisure Class*, pp. 235–58.

38. *Higher Learning*, p. 212.

39. My reconstruction of Veblen's ideological critique is based upon the following works: *Absentee Ownership*, pp. 12–68, 205–10, 398–445; *Business Enterprise*, pp. 37–48, 128–76; *Leisure Class*, pp. 131–64; *Vested Interests*, pp. 1–34, 114–37, 174–76; *Instinct of Workmanship*, pp. 340–55; *The Place of Science*, pp. 82–251.

40. Ibid., pp. 65, 236–37. Veblen examined this problem in detail in several essays published in *The Place of Science*. Economists regularly indulged in teleological explanations, he argued, precisely because their discipline employed *a priori* or deductive reasoning based on a set of normative principles. Modern economics was, therefore, largely a "taxonomic" or classificatory enterprise.

41. *Essays*, pp. 148–50, 154–57.

42. Ibid., pp. 157–60. "According to the hedonistic postulates the end and incentive is necessarily the pleasurable sensations to be de-

rived from the consumption of goods, what Mr. Fisher calls 'enjoyable income' or psychic income." Hence, "men prefer present to future consumption. This is the beginning of economic (marginal-utility) wisdom; but it is also the end of the wisdom of marginal utility" (ibid., p. 141).

43. Ibid., p. 142.

44. *Instinct of Workmanship,* p. 59.

45. *Essays,* pp. 200–201. John P. Diggins has argued that this essay constituted Veblen's response to Max Weber's *The Protestant Ethic and the Spirit of Capitalism.* See Diggins, *The Bard of Savagery: Thorstein Veblen and Modern Social Theory* (New York: The Seabury Press, 1978), p. 92.

46. *Essays,* pp. 203, 205–207, 209.

47. Ibid., pp. 210–14.

48. Ibid., pp. 214–16.

49. Ibid., pp. 101–103.

50. Ibid., p. 197.

51. *Absentee Ownership*, pp. 35–36, 47.

52. Ibid., pp. 22, 25, 31–39; see also *Vested Interests*, pp. 123–31; and *Business Enterprise*, pp. 135, 139–40.

53. *Essays*, pp. 250–51; see also Veblen, *Imperial Germany and the Industrial Revolution* (New Brunswick, N.J.: Transaction Publishers, 1990).

54. Ibid., p. 262.

55. Veblen, *An Inquiry Into the Nature of Peace and the Terms of its Perpetuation* (New York: B.W. Huebsch, 1917).

56. *Essays,* pp. 355–90.

57. Ibid., p. 391.

58. Ibid., p. 396

59. Ibid., p. 387.

60. Ibid., pp. 319–36.

61. Ibid., p. 345.

62. Ibid., p. 414.

63. Ibid., p. 441.

64. On the relationship between this essay and Veblen's methodological assumptions, see the Murray G. Murphey "Introduction," *The Instinct of Workmanship and the State of the Industrial Arts* (New Brunswick, N.J.: Transaction Publishers, 1990), pp. ix–xiv.

65. Ibid., p. 31.

66. Ibid., p. 226.

67. Ibid., p. 227.

# INTRODUCTION

THORSTEIN VEBLEN died on August 3, 1929. With his passing there was removed from the ranks of social philosophers perhaps the most profound thinker and one of the best informed men of his generation. Among his papers there was found the fragment of a codicil which read:

It is also my wish, in case of death, to be cremated, if it can conveniently be done, as expeditiously and inexpensively as may be, without ritual or ceremony of any kind; that my ashes be thrown loose into the sea, or into some sizable stream running into the sea; that no tombstone, slab, epitaph, effigy, tablet, inscription, or monument of any name or nature be set up in my memory or name in any piece or at any time; that no obituary, memorial, portrait, or biography of me, nor any letters written to or by me, be printed or published or in any way reproduced, copied, or circulated.

It will be seen from this brief testament that he wished to remain as inaccessible to public view after death as he had been during his life. But already a number of obituaries and biographical sketches have appeared and at least one portrait of his is scheduled to adorn the wall of one of the rooms in a university which, having neglected her illustrious son in life, perhaps thinks to make belated amends by thus honoring him in death. As regards the several biographical notices which have so far seen the

light of day, practically all of them have been rather perfunctory and quite inconsequential.[1]

The most important fact about Veblen, however, was
not his private life or his own personal affairs but rather
his contribution particularly to the social sciences and
his influence on the thinking of his time generally. This
fact has become increasingly manifest within the past few
years and is likely to assume still greater significance in
the future. As a result, there have appeared from time to
time some ostensibly serious studies of Veblen calculated
to appraise the scholarly achievements of the man and to
define his proper place in the development of economic
thought in America.

By offering to the public in a compact and easily ac-
cessible form this last collection of early and late papers
written by Veblen it is hoped further to facilitate such
attempts and if possible to assist in a clearer understanding
of Veblen than has been evident in the studies and estimates of Veblen heretofore made. All but one of the papers included in the present volume have appeared in
various publications at one time and another. A few of
them have been published only in recent years since his
death. The present collection, therefore, together with one
published some years ago, contain all the important articles and essays written by Thorstein Veblen in the course
of a mute and unobtrusive but, for all that, memorable
and epoch-making academic career.

Veblen also wrote a number of book reviews and shorter
notes, especially during his tenure at the University of
Chicago and while serving as editor of the *Journal of
Political Economy.* It was planned originally to include
these in the present volume even though they have only a
historical value. But considerations of a practical nature

argued strongly against the feasibility of such a plan, with the result that the book reviews and one or two articles have been left out. For the comfort and convenience of those, however, who may have looked for completeness in a volume of this nature a list of the material omitted is given at the end of the volume.

These papers are reproduced in this volume without emendation or notes, just as they were published originally. Except as it may be necessary to give the proper setting to some of them or to call attention to some of the more flagrant misstatements or misconceptions regarding Veblen and his work, it is not intended in this brief introduction to indicate biographical details or even to dwell on any of the outstanding facts in Veblen's life, nor yet to attempt an appraisal of Veblen's place in American economic thought.

In the process of going over them it turned out that these papers arranged themselves quite conveniently into three main groups. They have been segregated, accordingly, under three headings without particular regard to their chronological order: Essays in Economics, Miscellaneous Papers, and War Essays.

The first essay in this collection, "Economic Theory in the Calculable Future," is the last formal statement of his position with respect to economic theory. In this brief paper Veblen has substantially reaffirmed the position which he assumed when he wrote the series of articles on the "Preconceptions of Economic Science," and "Why Is Not Economics an Evolutionary Science ?"[2]

The rejoinder to "Mr. Cummings's Strictures on *The Theory of the Leisure Class*" reveals Veblen's polemical powers, which were destined to reach their highest expression in "Professor Clark's Economics."[3] Incidentally, it may be remarked that the rejoinder to Mr. Cummings is

the only instance in which Veblen was ever known to have
answered a critic.

Of the other essays in this group, "The Beginnings of
Ownership," "The Barbarian Status of Women," "The
Economic Theory of Woman's Dress," and "The Instinct
of Workmanship and the Irksomeness of Labor," are significant mainly as foreshadowing the course of Veblen's
intellectual development.

In the group of Miscellaneous Essays, "Kant's Critique
of Judgment" is one of the earliest essays written by
Veblen while a student at Yale University. "An Experiment in Eugenics" was written by Veblen shortly before
his death and appears in print now for the first time.

Perhaps the most instructive and interesting are the
War Essays, which reveal Veblen as a keen analyst of
current economic forces and as a man endowed with
something of a prophetic insight into things. The two
papers, for example, dealing with the foreign and domestic policies of Japan are quite as applicable to the
Japanese situation of today as they were at the time of
writing seventeen years ago. The same thing holds true
with regard to affairs in Europe which are discussed in
his review article of Mr. Keynes's The *Economic Consequences of the Peace.* It would not be easy to find a
more accurate and clearer analysis of the forces at work
at the Peace Conference preceding the Versailles Treaty
or a more frank exposure of the motives underlying the
establishment of the League of Nations than is to be
found in this discussion. As Veblen indicated, the only
point upon which the Great Powers were in complete
accord was the suppression of the Soviet Union. In all
other respects the peace treaty was conceived in bitter
hatred and blind vindictiveness and the Covenant of the

League was built on the feeble foundation of insane jealousies and mutual distrust.

It is perhaps needless to point out that Veblen took an intensely partisan interest in the conduct as well as in the final outcome of the Great War. This attitude is quite evident in most of the essays written during this period, especially those in which he deals with domestic industrial problems with a view to furthering the efficient and expeditious conduct of the war.[4] He openly favored the cause of the Allies and more particularly of France as against the Central Powers because in his view France represented all that was best in modern culture and refinement just as Germany symbolized all that was most sinister in modern militant imperialism. Of course, it goes without saying that he was bitterly disappointed in the abrupt conclusion of the war and the uncertain settlement of the peace and the responsibility for all this he laid at the door of the Wilson administration, which was content to play such an indecisive and subordinate role in the whole affair. Not that President Wilson loved peace so much, as Veblen might have expressed it, but that he feared Bolshevism more.

Thus far there have appeared but a few studies of Veblen and they have been quite disappointing, chiefly due to the fact perhaps that for the most part their authors have been concerned more with the hopeless task of vindicating orthodox, "certified," economic theory than with an earnest desire to understand Veblen.[5]

No one, of course, least of all Veblen, would maintain that his work is above criticism, but it may be allowed that base calumny has never been considered a good substitute for honest criticism nor gratuitous abuse for intelligent understanding. At all events those of Veblen's critics who may be endowed with more ambition than good sense would do well to take to heart the counsel of the sage of Concord: "If you criticise a fine genius, the odds are that you are out of your reckoning, and instead of the poet are censuring your own caricature for him. For there is somewhat spheral and infinite in every man, especially in every genius, which, if you can come very near him, sports with all your limitations." To express it in plain language, so dear to the hearts of Veblen's critics, fools should hesitate to rush in where angels fear to tread.

A man's value as a great thinker is to be judged by his insight into the great facts of his own time. In the final analysis this is what distinguishes one whose genius embraces the entire range of the social forces and is able to grasp and analyse actuality from one who is a clearer founder of systems or a shrewd formulator of definitions and principles.

Some of the ill-concealed bitterness of Veblen's critics may also be due not so much to a lack of appreciation and understanding of Veblen's work as to that commonest of human infirmities, envy. It has been observed that we usually envy the man who is our superior and, if in addition it so happens that we feel ourselves under some obligation to him, our bitterness toward such a man is further inflamed by contempt and we finally become indignant. So that this unhappy mixture of envy, contempt, and indignation renders him quite intolerable to us. "For it has been and still is, the fate of superior genius, to be beheld with silent or abusive envy. It makes its way like the sun, which we look upon with pain, unless something passes over him that obscures his glory. We then view with eagerness the shadow, the cloud, or the spot, and are pleased with what eclipses the brightness we otherwise cannot bear."

Perhaps the commonest criticism urged against Veblen has been with regard to his literary style and his peculiar use of words in the English language. Some of his more facetious critics have even felt it to be their duty to offer the prayer that "his style may not spread as an infection among the social philosophers to come." The answer, of course, is that there is not the slightest danger of this. Veblen's style cannot be imitated. In the case of Veblen, perhaps more so than in any other, *le style, c'est l'homme.*

In his analysis of economic factors and institutions Veblen, unlike most of the brethren in the profession, drew freely for his information and illustrative materials upon other sciences, such as anthropology, ethnology, biology, etc., with which the vast majority of American economists were scarcely familiar or references to which in any study of modern business and industrial problems they regarded as irrelevant excursions. The result was that quite frequently Veblen's statements appeared to some of these folks as a meaningless jargon or a jumble of words. For instance, as some one has already pointed out, if the reader was unable to distinguish Veblen's use of the term "sexton beetle" from "sexton beadle," he was likely to charge Veblen with the responsibility for his misfortune.

At all events, whatever may be said of the liberties which Veblen took with the King's English, it cannot be denied that his style always remained readable, attractive, and fascinating—qualities which are notoriously lacking in American economic literature.

But it is to be suspected that the difficulty in understanding Veblen is not to be sought in his intricate and involved style or in his use of new and unusual words and phrases but rather it is to be looked for in the fact of his being concerned with presenting a new point of view

and a new method in economics. He was historical and
empirical, by which it is to be understood that only through
historical interpretation of economic factors and institutions may one be able to have a clear and correct understanding of human activity. In Veblen's view, economics
should be concerned with the problem of how the human
agent views things in the course of his economic activities: what he does with his material equipment and how
and why he does it. The problem in economics is according to this view not the idle classification of the ways and
means which serve the material ends of man. The subject
matter of economic science should be economic activity.
The question is not how things stabilise themselves in a
static state but how they forever grow and change.[6] In a
word, Veblen was essentially interested in the problem of
social change and development. He was not primarily
interested in formulating a plan for a new social order.
Unlike orthodox, "certified" economists of the classical
school, who regard economic categories as fixed and valid
for all time, Veblen emphasised their transitory and evanescent character in the light of changes in the industrial
arts which render the institutional superstructure obsolete and call for a new set of economic categories. Veblen
more than any one else realised the enormous complex-
ity of the factors involved in human behavior, and in spite
of obvious and inherent difficulties he insisted upon taking into consideration these factors in any analysis of
human activity. His method simply offers a guiding principle through the maze of social processes by the aid of
which one is enabled to "explore the past and to understand the present." He was content with merely trying to
place the study of economics on a scientific basis without occupying himself with the task of formulating a new

system of economics. Consequently he left no system in the strict sense of that term and he left no disciples, popular notions to the contrary notwithstanding. His amazing intellect could not be bound by the narrow confines of a petty system nor the sweep of his extraordinary power be restricted to a small circle of disciples. In spite of this, however, Veblen's ideas have permeated all sections of economic thought so that from that "fertile field of suggestions supplied by him there may yet emerge an economics that is science" and a social theory that is something more substantial than "magical incantations" and "logical involutions."

In the case of Veblen as, indeed, in all other cases, theories are only necessary expressions of social conditions. Veblen's claim to everlasting renown as a scholar and philosopher rests on the fact that in him were combined an objective attitude with a high degree of supersensitiveness to changes in the social conditions of his time It is this quality which enables the man of uncommon genius to respond quickly to those changes. He is, therefore, always in advance of his more sluggish contemporaries. To this fact, perhaps more than to any other circumstance, may be traceable the tension and misunderstandings between the man of genius and his public and the consequent lack of appreciation from his fellow men which is the usual fate of men of genius. It requires a very high degree of courage for one to proclaim a new point of view, a new aspect of truth, or to question what hitherto has been accepted as truth by public opinion. As the immortal author of *Penguin Island* has observed, to present men and things in a new light, to give expression to an original idea, is usually to be misunderstood, and that is dangerous. To estimate accurately this quality of Veblen's courage it is only necessary to consider the whole attitude of the lay and academic public of his time toward social questions.

A great scholar really does not want to be misunderstood, for in that case his whole life may be a failure, as was the case with Veblen. Nor did Veblen delight in shocking his audience as is commonly believed. Veblen, like all great men, wanted to be appreciated and loved but he wanted to be loved and appreciated at his own level and that was denied him.

Throughout long years of neglect and discrimination at the hands of university authorities and throughout many years of ostracism and persecution by them[7] Veblen's calm and composure were never ruffled.

Veblen was in reality one of those rare men who may be said to have been ahead of his time—ahead in the sense that what he said and thought was destined to be accepted by succeeding generations though they were rejected by his own generation. "Hence, he was lonely as an alien can be."

LEON ARDZROONI

NOTES

1. Lewis Mumford's "Thorstein Veblen," *New Republic,* August 5, 1931, and more recently, E. S. Bates's "Thorstein Veblen, a Biography," in *Scribner's,* December, 1933, are notable exceptions.

2. *The Place of Science in Modern Civilisation,* New York, 1921.

3. Many years later, in his mellower and more tender moods, Veblen was in the habit of referring to this episode with something of a feeling of filial penitence.

4. There was also a memorandum on a practicable method of fighting submarines written by Veblen and presented by him before a group of military officials at the time, but unfortunately no trace of this

memorandum has been found in spite of painstaking and diligent inquiry.

5. Paul T. Homan, in *Masters of American Social Science*, edited by Howard W. Odum.

T. E. Teggart, *Thorstein Veblen, a Chapter in Economic Thought*, University of California Press. This is an ungracious and unwarranted attack on Veblen, consisting for the most part of gross misrepresentation and wanton abuse of the man. Under the guise of making a study of Veblen, the main purpose of the author seems rather to have been to achieve some momentary notoriety—all of which is, of course, perfectly good and legitimate American business procedure. Incidentally, also, this is one of the most flagrant instances of stultification by an American university appearing in the role of godfather to such an undertaking.

6. Cf. "Economic Theory in the Calculable Future." Also, "Why Is Not Economics an Evolutionary Science?" in *The Place of Science in Modern Civilisation*.

7. During his stay of more than a decade at the University of Chicago, Veblen never attained to a higher rank in the faculty than that of assistant professor. Even after the shameful and shabby treatment accorded him by Stanford University there was at one time a fair chance of his being offered the secretaryship of the Smithsonian Institution which would have reinstated him in the academic world. But the university authorities persisted in hounding him and thus were instrumental in preventing it. For obviously such an appointment would have constituted vindication for Veblen and condemnation of the action of the authorities in dismissing him from Stanford University. Much the same set of circumstances was responsible for the failure, at the last moment, of Cornell University to extend a call to Veblen in 1918, in spite of the fact that some of his friends offered to bear the entire burden of his salary expense at Cornell. Veblen's nearest approach to academic rehabilitation and vindication was his appointment prior to this as lecturer in the University of Missouri, thanks to the efforts of the late H. J. Davenport, the best friend Veblen ever had.

# I

# ESSAYS IN ECONOMICS

# ECONOMIC THEORY IN THE CALCULABLE FUTURE [1]

IT may seem a gratuitous commonplace to say that the calculable future of economic science lies in the hands of the incoming generation of economists and that they are due to create a scheme of economics in their own image. So also, like other men of earlier generations, these incoming economists are due to be the creatures of that heredity and environment out of which they emerge.

On the side of heredity there is not much to be said, nothing much of a distinctive character. There is little if anything in the way of heredity to distinguish this generation of economists from the generations of men that have gone before, say, during the past 10,000 years or so. What is fairly to be presumed is that they will be persons of sound average mentality, of which there is one born every minute, under the broad Malthusian principle of fecundity conditioned by subsistence.

Therefore any distinctive or peculiar traits to be looked for in the science, in the way of scope and method, in the range of its inquiry and the drift and bias of its guiding interest, its logic and its data, will be due to arise out of those characteristic habits of thought that are induced in the incoming generation of economists in the course of that habituation to which

[1] Reprinted by permission from the *American Economic Review*, Vol. XV, No. 1, Supplement, March, 1925.

they will have been exposed during the period of their growth and adolescence and during those marginal years of waning flexibility that make up the initial phase of adult life.

Any critical shift in the course of events during the run of their inquiry will also have its effect in the way of directing their attention and shaping the perspective of their science. Yet these current events with which the economists will be occupied will perforce be apprehended and formulated in terms germane to that scheme of knowledge and belief which has been induced in these economists by their past habituation. As ever, current facts are again due to be made up under those forms and categories that have taken shape in response to past experience, and to be built into a theoretical structure suitable to meet the exigencies of this past experience. It is only that the experience which has given its bias to these latter-day economists is of a later date than that to which their predecessors were exposed; it is of the twentieth century, rather than the nineteenth.

In some substantial, perhaps critical and decisive, respects, therefore, these incoming economists will have that advantage over the passing generation that habitually inures to late-comers. Loosely, the events current during the next quarter-century are due to be made up and handled by them in the terms and with the preconceptions that have been carried over out of the past quarter-century; instead of those more archaic holdovers of knowledge and belief out of the nineteenth century with which the passing generation of economists have gone to their work.

But there is also this further presumptive difference to be anticipated, between this prospective era in the science and any corresponding period that has gone before, that the facts current in this calculable future are presumably due to go on changing, in detail and at large, cumulatively and at an unexampled rate, as time goes on; whereas the mentality of these economists who will have to deal with these elusive current facts of the future, the substance and logic of their knowledge and belief, will have only that rate of flexibility and adaptation that is conditioned by the inveterate tenacity of human preconceptions; and preconceptions are something in the nature of fixed ideas, and they yield and adjust themselves to current changes only tardily and concessively. So that, under these circumstances, it is fairly to be presumed that a sort of effectual discrepancy is again fairly to be looked for between the working categories and formulas employed by the economists, on the one side, and the current exigencies of economic life, on the other side; a discrepancy which should be appreciably more pronounced in this calculable future of the science than at any period in the past, and answering to the more appreciable interval of lag to be looked for, due to the swifter run of events.

The distinctive factors which enter into the case, then, and which are to be counted on to set this prospective phase of economic science off against what has gone before, would accordingly be (*a*) such special habits of thought as have been induced in this generation of economists by the peculiarities of their training and experience, in the way of outlook, intellectual interests, and principles of valuation; and (*b*) that latter-day range of economic events which will provoke their inquiry and on which their science is to spend itself. And under both heads there are novel factors to be taken account of.

The circumstances of life, material and spiritual, have been changing during this quarter-century and more, and they have therefore progressively been inducing something of a change in the effectual outlook, the bias and logic of scientific inquiry, its basis of valuation. The schooling to which this generation of students have been subjected differs also from that which entered into the training of their forbears. At the same time the range of events which will engage their inquiry and determine its direction has been and still is engaged in a process of cumulative change running into the future. What these changes may come to in the calculable future must, of course, be largely a matter of surmise.

By contrast with the nineteenth century, the material conditions of life during the past few decades have been characterised by an accentuated and ever-increasing mechanisation, due to the exigencies of the current industrial arts, which have been going forward on that line unremittingly and have exacted a degree of mechanical standardisation in the workday arts of life, the ways and means of living, such as no earlier generation has been exposed to. This mechanical standardisation has affected urban life most immediately and most profoundly, but no part of the community is or has been immune. Present indications are that this mechanisation of the ways and means of living should go on in the calculable future, presumably at an accelerated rate unless extraneous causes should bring on a collapse or substantial setback in the advance of the industrial arts and the growth of population. Indications are not altogether wanting that something in the nature of such a setback or collapse may conceivably supervene, due to an excessively bellicose patriotism fomented, guided, and driven by business enterprise, leading to bootless adventures in nationalism, with an attendant recrudescence of religious superstitions, after the fashion of what has followed from the Great War. The contingency may seem a remote one, yet it is a contingency not to be wholly overlooked.

From the continued mechanisation in the ways of living it has followed by reason of habituation that in the workday habits of thought of this generation the concrete realities of tangible performance are more insistently and more convincingly present than has been the case in the past. Such is the case of the economists no less than of others; presumably more so, since the schooling of the economists will necessarily bring them more or less intimately in touch with the physical and biological sciences where mechanistic conceptions already rule the road of inquiry with slight abatement. With a wider application than before, the accepted baseline of reality in all knowledge and belief is coming to be tangible performance, objective and impersonal; so much so that even the spiritual realities are by way of being brought within the three dimensions of space, in such a degree as to alarm the spokesmen of the holdovers of the Faith.

Notoriously, scientific inquiry at large is increasingly meticulous in its attention to precise objective measurements and computations, and increasingly negligent of any postulates and values which do not lend themselves to that manner of logic and procedure. The economists are somewhat in arrears in this matter, as might be expected, yet they show a visible drift in this direction, perhaps as much in what they overlook as in what they formally profess. So that those certified articles of theory at large that have meant so much to the passing generation of economists have been falling into decay through obsolescence by disuse during the past quarter-century.

Self-contained systems of economic theory, balanced and compendious, are no longer at the focal center of attention; nor is there a felt need of such. The felt need runs rather along the lines of conjugation between economic science and those fields of knowledge and belief that are cultivated by the material and biological sciences. Meantime, detailed monographic and itemised inquiry, description, analysis, and appraisal of particular processes going forward in industry and business, are engaging the best attention of the economists; instead of that meticulous reconstruction and canvassing of schematic theories that once was of great moment and that then brought comfort and assurance to its adepts and their disciples. There is little prospect that the current generation of economists will work out a compendious system of economic theory at large. They go quite confidently into their work of detailed inquiry with little help from general principles, except it be principles of common-sense, mathematics, and general information.

These principles of common-sense and common information prevalent in this opening quarter of the century are of an evolutionary, or genetic complexion, in that they hold the attention to the changes that are going forward, rather than focus it on that "Natural State of Man," as Nassua Senior called it, to which the movement of history was believed inevitably to tend. The question now before the body of economists is not how things stabilise themselves in a "static state," but how they endlessly grow and change. But in its purview of this genetic proliferation of phases current knowledge and belief see growth and change only in that field in

which the Victorians looked to see an indefeasible stability—the field of human institutions, use and wont,
law and custom, the state of the industrial arts; whereas
this current generation is inhibited from looking for
substantial change where the Victorians found their
comfort in recognising it—in the human factor. There
is for them no "perfectibility of the human race,"
whether through education or through breeding; the
Mendelians forbid it, and in practical effect they are
allowed to have the right of it. *Tempora mutantur sed
nos non mutamur in illis.*

Such is the background and perspective of current
knowledge and belief touching those facts of life with
which the economists will have to make up their account, and it is for the economists to live within the
bounds of the case as well as to live up to their opportunities. As was said above, they are giving their best
attention to monographic work of a detailed and itemised character, dealing with special segments or processes of economic life. And within the run of each detailed process of business or industry so dealt with it
is the run of the process at work and the workday give
and take between this given process and the contiguous
processes in the working sequence, before and after,
that chiefly supply the concepts and categories made use
of in organising the inquiry and formulating its results.
But if these results are to go into the common stock of
knowledge and belief as a substantial contribution they
will have to conform to those canons of knowledge and
belief that rule the road for the time being.

Through all this work of objective and itemised inquiry and analysis there runs, of course, now as ever,
the bias given by the particular economist's personal
equation. This personal bias will commonly run some-

what strong and intemperate; more so perhaps than has been the case in the work of the passing generation. It gives something of a partisan touch to much of this work, and it should presumably continue to do no less in the future. Men should fairly be expected to take sides more obstinately and intolerantly in the absence of any pervasively corrective reference to compendious theoretical formulations.

This drift in the direction of partisan spirit and special pleading is greatly reinforced by the shape in which the data present themselves in the immediate present as contrasted with Victorian times; and the outlook is for an advance on present lines rather than a reversion to anything like Victorian times. Progressively during the past quarter-century the process of economic life at large has suffered a measure of bifurcation, amounting to something very like a dichotomy of the economic community and its work and interests. More and more visibly the economic process has been falling apart into Business and Industry; so that in practical effect any given economist's analysis and canvassing of the data will almost perforce run to a conclusion within the confines of the one segment or the other; the state of the industrial arts or the state of the price-system. Within each field men's initiative and endeavors run their course and round out their purposes in virtual detachment from the aims and exigencies that make up the scheme of things within the other half of this dichotomous economic system. So alien to one another are these complementary halves of the working system, in their logic, their aims, and their data, that they cannot even be said to be consistently at variance. Mr. Taussig has spoken of this bifurcation as a division of the labor of creative leadership between the inventors and the money-makers. On the one side rules the mechanistic logic of technology as it has worked out since the Industrial Revolution; on the other side rules the business logic of the price-system as that has worked out during the same period in response to the exigencies of absentee ownership on a large and ever-increasing scale.

This growth of absentee ownership and business enterprise during their century is one of the things which the economists of the Victorian age overlooked, together with the rise of modern technology. But these things are now the main facts of the economic situation, the dominant institutional factors in the case, and it is the working out of these dominant institutional factors, in common and in conflict, on which the new generation of economists will perforce be engaged. In the economic foreground stands, of course, the organisation of business enterprise, the absentee owners and their agents, in whom vest by law and custom all initiative and discretion in economic affairs. And it is to this work of the business community that the economists are chiefly turning their attention. And such should presumably continue to be the drift and emphasis of economic inquiry and speculations in the calculable future, inasmuch as the promise of things as they run in the immediate present is, unmistakably, that the interests and exigencies of business traffic are and of right must be paramount. These things are visible, understandable, legitimate, and urgent; and like other men the economists are imbued with the preconceptions of the price-system, in terms of which these things are understandable and urgent; but in terms of which the other half, the technological half, of the current economic world is obscure and, at the best, subsidiary.

So that economic science should, for its major incidence and with increasing singleness and clarity, be a science of business traffic, monographic, detailed, exacting, and imbued with a spirit of devotion to things as they are shaping themselves under the paramount exigencies of absentee ownership considered as a working system; and the personnel of the science, the body of economists in ordinary, in the degree in which they run true to form under the training of the schools and the market, should be partisans of this system, and of a reasonably intolerant temper.

Not that there will be no controversy and no dissenters to be looked for, even within the ranks; but the lines of cleavage between these prospective factions and disputants should continue to run within the theoretical domain of the price-system, and the controversies should in an increasing degree run in terms drawn from the current business traffic. Such has been the visible drift of things in the science during the past quarter-century and there is no visible cause why things should take a different turn in the immediate future. Loosely speaking, no argument on economic matters today will get a reasonably wide hearing until it is set out as a "business proposition" in terms drawn from the conduct of business.

This comes to saying that, following the lead given by the workday conduct of business traffic, the attention of the economists and their formulations of theory should converge on the ways and means of differential gain. For business traffic is a quest of differential gains, a pursuit of income over outlay for the particular business concern engaged, and the gains so sought emerge in the form of a price-differential. As in business, so in the scientific inquiry which busies itself with the theory of business enterprise, the emergence or attainment of such a price-differential is the *terminus ad quem,* the final and focal point beyond which neither the business man nor the economist of the business concern can interest himself unless by way of *obiter dictum.*

It is otherwise with the other half, the technological half of the current economic situation. Business traffic seeks a differential gain in terms of price; technological enterprise perforce seeks a gain in productive efficiency at large. Any given business concern may profit by the disabilities of its competitors; its differential gains stand to increase as theirs fall off. Any given technologist is hampered in his work by disabilities on the part of his fellow technicians in the same field. So also the technical efficiency of any given industrial plant and of its personnel is furthered by efficient work on the part of other concerns in the same or related lines of production, and is hampered in its work by whatever hinders them. Technically, in point of workmanlike efficiency, the several industrial concerns are engaged in teamwork; as business units they are competitors engaged in a strategy of mutual defeat. Monopoly is an asset in business, the most valuable of intangible assets. In the technical half of the economic world monopoly is mere waste.

Yet as things have fallen out during this quarter-century of swift advance, and as they promise to fall in the calculable future, any technical advance can get a hearing and reach a practical outcome only if and so far as it can be presented as a "business proposition"; that is to say, so far as it shows a convincing promise of differential gain to some given business concern. So also the economist who ventures to take stock of anything in the technological way and to bring such facts into the framework of his theoretical structures will of necessity handle these matters as a "business proposition," as ways and means of differential gain for one business concern as against others. The realities of the science, those categories that afford the final and conclusive terms of the economist's analysis and on which therefore his analysis converges, are with increasing singleness the realities of business traffic and differential gain. So that the actualities of the industrial arts come to have an economic reality, within the purview of the science, if and in so far as they lend themselves to the pursuit of a differential gain.

And the statesmen, in the policies which they avow and pursue, and in the use which they make of national powers and national frontiers, work together to the same end. To them too economic interests mean advantages in trade, opportunities of differential gain for the business concerns domiciled within the national frontiers as against outsiders. Things have taken such a turn that nations, national interests, national policies, and national armaments no longer have any other use, serve no other purpose, than the differential gain of business concerns doing business in competition with outsiders. The war and that peace of suspicion, bitterness, and bickering in which it has eventuated have made all that plain. National state-craft and patriotic inflation have no other uses. And such economists and commissions of economic inquiry as are drawn into the service of the national establishment are drawn in for no other purpose and on no other qualifications than such as are presumed to serve the bankers and traders of the nation as against outsiders. Economic science, in so far as it enters into the training of the nation's civil servants is perforce of this complexion.

So also the schools are turning their powers to the

same purpose, in so far as they cultivate economic science. Increasingly the faculties of economic science are taken up with instruction in business administration, business finance, national trade, and salesmanship, with particular and growing emphasis on the last-named, the art of salesmanship and the expedients of sales-publicity. Such is the current state of academic economics, and such appears to be its promise as conditioned by the circumstances that promise to surround it in the near future. Of course, there still stand over certain perfunctory antiquities out of the Victorian age, in the way of standard articles of economic theory, and these are given a perfunctory hearing in the schools; but that has little else than a historical interest. It is a matter of survival, not of proliferation.

# MR. CUMMINGS'S STRICTURES ON "THE THEORY OF THE LEISURE CLASS"[1]

In the last issue of this Journal is a paper of some length by Mr. John Cummings, criticising a book lately published for me under the title, *The Theory of the Leisure Class*. The paper is notable for its earnestness no less than for its graceful and cogent discussion. It is needless for me here to express my high appreciation of the attention which the volume has received at Mr. Cummings's hands. But circumstances have made it necessary for me to take this means of calling attention to certain passages in Mr. Cummings's discussion, where the criticism is directed rather against the apparent than against the intended drift of the argument set forth in the volume.

As editor of the Journal it should have been my place, and my privilege, to forestall what I might conceive to be misdirected criticism by making the necessary suggestions to Mr. Cummings before his paper appeared in print; and, but for the untoward chance that the issue in which the paper appears was printed during my absence, this would have been done. As it is, I am constrained to offer my explanations in the ungracious form of a reply to his criticism. There is the more excuse for so doing, since what has proved to be obscure to so acute a critic as Mr. Cummings may be expected to offer at least as great difficulties to others who may

[1] Reprinted from *The Journal of Political Economy*, Vol. VIII, December, 1899.

have the patience to read the book. Had I had the good fortune to say what I intended, and no more, my critic would, I believe, have been saved a good share of the corrections which he is good enough to offer, as well as much of the annoyance which he is at pains to conceal. Indeed, to such an extent does this appear to be true that the greater portion and the weightier of Mr. Cummings's criticisms appears to proceed on misapprehension that might have been obviated by a more facile use of language.

But to speak first of a point on which the difference between the book and its critic is apparently not of this verbal complexion. Mr. Cummings (p. 426) [2] gravely distrusts any "attempt to read modern psychology into primitive conditions," together with attempts at "a psychological reconstruction of primitive society." To the first count I plead guilty, only if "modern" psychology is taken to mean the latest views of psychological science known to me, as contrasted with older theories. Whether this constitutes an offense is, of course, not within my competency to inquire. As to the second count, I plead that any theory of culture, late or early, must have recourse to a psychological analysis, since all culture is substantially a psychological phenomenon. In any modern discussion of culture, and of cultural development, where this recourse is not had openly it is had covertly.

Mr. Cummings's criticism is directed to three main heads: (1) The theory of waste (pp. 427–434); (2) the relation of the leisure class to cultural change (pp. 436–439); (3) the justification of leisure-class incomes (pp. 439–453). On the first of these heads the difference between the book and its critic seems to be

[2] *Journal of Political Economy,* September, 1899.

apparent only, due to a misconception caused by want of explicitness in the argument. As to the second, the difference between Mr. Cummings's views and mine is, I believe, less by half than appears from Mr. Cummings's strictures. Under the third head, running through some fourteen pages, Mr. Cummings develops a point of doctrine with which the book does not concern itself.

Exception is taken (p. 427) to my attempted definition of waste. It should be said that the definition in question aims to promulgate no novel doctrine; the aim being to state discursively what is the content of a judgment concerning waste or futility. The definition may be unfortunate, but its ineptitude does not eliminate the concept of waste from men's habits of thought, nor does it eliminate the word from everyday speech. Men do currently pass opinions on this and that as being wasteful or not wasteful, and there is much evidence that they have long been in the habit of doing so. Sumptuary legislation and the much preaching of the moralists of all ages against lavish habits of life is evidence to this effect. There is also a good deal of a consensus as to what manner of things are wasteful. The brute fact that the word is current shows that. Without something of a passable consensus on that head the word would not be intelligible; that is to say, we should have no such word. As Mr. Cummings earnestly contends (p. 428), it is always the individual that passes an opinion of this kind —as must manifestly be conceded with respect to all opinions. But the consensus that prevails shows that the opinions of individuals on matters touching "the generically human" passably coincide—which, I gather, Mr. Cummings is (p. 428) unwilling to admit. If it were in place to offer instruction here, I should suggest that some reason for this coincidence of views is to be found in a community of descent, traditions, and circumstances, past and present, among men living in any given community, and in a less degree among men in all communities. It is because men's notions of the generically human, of what is the legitimate end of life, does not differ incalculably from man to man that men are able to live in communities and to hold common interests.

It is the use of the word "impersonal," in the sense of non-invidious or non-emulative, that seems particularly to have proved misleading. And this, probably, has provoked Mr. Cummings (p. 429) unguardedly to deny the practical possibility of waste. This result of my escapade, I need not say, I deeply regret. The like is true for the word "invidious," though on this term the critic's quarrel is with the current use of the word, not with any misuse of it at my hands. My critic's discussion at this point also carries the implication that any item of consumption which is in any degree useful, as, e.g., "costly church edifices," cannot at the same time be in any degree wasteful. This seems an unwarranted application of the logical expedient of "exclusion." As bearing on this passage (p. 429), it may be added that even if "the labor expended on the church edifice . . . be considered in any sense wasteful," that need not imply that the edifice or its consumption according to the accepted method is disallowed by economic theory. It is, for all I can see, competent for an economist to inquire how far such an edifice and the employment of time and effort involved in its use may be industrially unproductive, or even industrially disserviceable, if such should be the outcome of the inquiry. Such an endeavor, I believe, need bring no obloquy upon the economist, nor

need he thereby invade the moralist's peculiar domain,
nor need it flutter the keepers of the idols of the tribe.
The economic bearing of any institution is not its only
bearing, nor its weightiest. The ends of human culture
are manifold and multiform and it is but the meaner of
them, if any, that are fairly comprised in that petty side
of life into which it is the economist's lot to inquire. An
electrician might, without blame, speak of the waste of
energy that is inseparable from the use of storage batteries. Indeed, if he is discussing the efficiency of this
means of utilising a source of power, he could not avoid
a detailed inquiry into this feature of their use. But his
endeavor to determine the magnitude of the unavoidable or of the ordinary waste involved would not commit him to a condemnation of the batteries, nor would
it make him an object of suspicion in the eyes of his
fellow-electricians.

The like critical use of exclusion, applied to alternatives which it had not occurred to me to conceive of as
exclusive alternatives, recurs in Mr. Cummings's observations on the conservatism of the leisure class (e.g.,
pp. 437–438), and on the differentiation of employments between the pecuniary and the industrial occupations (pp. 443–453). It is on the strength of such a
needless application of exclusion that Mr. Cummings is
able to say (p. 432): "In Dr. Veblen's philosophy, all
our judgments are based on invidiousness." This should
be so amended as to read: "*Some* of our judgments are
*in part* based on invidiousness." It will be seen that such
an amendment would materially affect Mr. Cummings's
further development of the theme, particularly as regards his strictures on the views advanced in the book.
Similarly the *reductio ad absurdum* on page 434, where
the view that elegance of diction and orthography serve

an invidious purpose is taken logically to contain the further position that speech can serve no purpose but an invidious one, and that the origin and sole use of language lies in the invidious distinction which it lends the user. This resort to excluded middle is in touch with the rhyme of a modern poet, who sings:

> I'd rather have fingers than toes;
> I'd rather have ears than a nose;
>   etc., [3]

overlooking the possibility of combining these several features in a single organism.

These pages (428–435) are a source of comfort and of despair to me. Of comfort in that I find in them a cogent exposition of views which I had attempted to set forth; of despair in showing how my attempted exposition has proved unintelligible even to a reader who had already beforehand reached an articulate recognition of very much of what I attempted to say. For, if I am not mistaken, Mr. Cummings's views on the subject of waste, as set forth fragmentarily in these pages, passably coincide with those intended to be expressed in the volume which he criticises.

Much the same is true for what Mr. Cummings has to say (pp. 436–439) on the conservative effect of the institution of a leisure class. The point at which his development of theory on this head chiefly differs from that of the book—as I had conceived it—is his insistence that this conservative effect is, always and in the nature of things, of a salutary kind. On this I had, perhaps weakly, reserved decision, as I am still compelled to do. Similarly as regards Mr. Cummings's conviction (p.

[3] Gelett Burgess, *The Purple Cow*, San Francisco, 1898.

437) that "Theoretically there is but one right course of social evolution, while the number of wrong courses is infinite." For my part, I have not had the fortune to reach a conclusion, or to attempt one, on this point. I am at a loss to understand what such a thesis may mean to an evolutionist, and I believe it would get the assent of fewer men today than at any previous time. But the main drift of Mr. Cummings's development I gladly assent to. In particular, I am at one with him in his view (p. 437)—which reads like a summary restatement of the argument of the book—that "whatever is, is clearly, at one and the same time, both right and wrong." This proposition Mr. Cummings has, by an unfortunate oversight, placed in contrast with a partial statement of the same view as expressed in the book.

Attention may be called to a further point of detail in this connection. Mr. Cummings (p. 442) takes exception to the view that man's environment changes with the growth of culture. He finds that the environment is "relatively fixed"; that "climate and soil make up pretty much all there is at the basis of that environment, and these change but little." All this is no doubt true if environment be taken to mean climate and topography; but for the purpose of my inquiry—an inquiry as to why and how the habits of life and of thought of the individual come to be modified—for this purpose customs, conventions, and methods of industry are no less effective elements in the environment than climate and topography, and these vary incontinently.

Mr. Cummings also (pp. 440–444, 449–452) offers a theory as to the equity of the existing distribution of property and of the incomes that accrue to the various classes in the community. This discussion is directed to a point not touched upon in my inquiry. But since my critic has been led to read into my argument certain implications on this head which he finds it necessary to refute, it is not improbable that others may read the argument in the same sense and feel the same need of refutation. It may therefore be in place to point out why I have not entered upon a discussion of this topic. The reason is that the whole question of such a justification is beside the point. The argument of the book deals with the causal, not with the moral competence of the phenomena which it takes up. The former is a question for the economist, the latter for the moralist. The manner in which Mr. Cummings has misread the argument—as I conceive it—may be illustrated by citing several specific propositions which are mistakenly conceived to bear upon the argument. He says (p. 440) : "The accumulation at one end is conceived to be at the expense of the other end in the sense that the other end would have more if it had *its just deserts.*" This should read: "is *not* conceived to be at the expense of the other end in the sense," etc. In particular, there is in the volume no reference, express or by implication, to "just deserts." Similarly, unless I am mistaken, it contains no suggestion that a "confiscation" (p. 449) of the products of the "productive laborers" takes place. It does not raise the question as to whether the captain of industry on the one hand or the laborer on the other hand "earn" (pp. 440, 441) their respective incomes. Mr. Cummings (pp. 440–452) assumes the validity of the natural-rights dogma that property rests on production. This relation between production and property rights is a moral, not a causal relation, if it is assumed to subsist at all. As regards Mr. Cummings's advocacy of the claims of the captain of industry to his income, on this ground, it proceeds on the bold though ancient metaphor by force of which bargaining is conceived to produce goods. And as regards the claims of the laborer to a property right in his product, an exhaustive analysis would probably show that they rest on similarly inconclusive grounds. I am therefore unable, in view of well-known facts, to go with Mr. Cummings in his view (p. 453) that a person who does not produce wealth cannot acquire it except by a miracle. One might cite the trite case of the man with the nutshells and the peppercorn, when the miraculous element is, at the best, held to be apparent only.

In a similar connection (p. 448) Mr. Cummings, in a restatement of my argument, says: "it is a game of chance, not of skill, this game of ownership, and the risks assumed are devoid of economic significance." This should read: *"in some part* of chance, *though chiefly* of skill,"* and "the risks assumed are *of the gravest* economic significance." Also (p. 448): "since individual members of the wealthy leisure class resort to chicanery and fraud, therefore nobody else does." This is an instance of Mr. Cummings's use of exclusion. It should read: "individual members of the wealthy leisure class resort to chicanery and fraud, *as do also many other persons."* Again (p. 449): "The unscrupulous man is not, by virtue of his unscrupulousness, a member of any class." To this I beg to give a cordial assent; as also to the proposition (p. 451) that "labor alone [unaided by intelligence] does not produce." So, again, I accept, with a covetous acknowledgment of its aptness, Mr. Cummings's proposition (p. 447) that, instead of its being the sole player in the game, the leisure class "is peculiar in that in playing this game of ownership in which all engage, *its members have succeeded conspicuously."* This statement contains the central position of the argument against which it is directed. The chief difference between the leisure and the industrial classes is conceived to be a larger endowment on the part of the former in respect of those aptitudes and propensities which make for pecuniary success.

In the pages which Mr. Cummings devotes to a defense of the captain of industry and his income the point of serious difference between his exposition and the argument of the book is his rejection of the distinction between "pecuniary" and "industrial" employments. He insists that there is no tenable distinction between the employment of the financier and that of the day laborer, both alike being "productive" and both alike owing their productivity and their income-yielding character to the intelligence exercised. This does not run altogether on the same ground as the argument in the volume, and it seems a less conclusive objection to me than it appears to have been to Mr. Cummings. It seems necessary to explain that the intended point of the argument concerning "pecuniary" and "industrial" employments was to indicate the different economic value of the aptitudes and habits of thought fostered by the one and the other class of employments. The question turns on a difference of kind, not on a difference of degree, in the intelligence and spiritual attitude called for by the different employments, in such a way that the one line of employment calls for more of one range of aptitudes while the other line of employments calls for more of another. It is the ethological bearing of employments that is chiefly in question, my endeavor being to point out how employments differ, for the purpose in hand, in respect of the training and the selective stress to which the character of these employments subjects the persons employed. "The distinction here made between classes of employments is by no means a hard and fast distinction between classes of persons." Few persons escape having some experience of both lines of employment, but the one or the other line of employment commonly is accountable for the greater portion of the serious occupation of any given person. So that while the disciplinary effect of either is seldom unmitigated in any concrete case, still the existing differentiation of occupations commonly confines the attention of any given person chiefly to the one or the other line of employment, and gives his training a bent in the one or the other direction. In the earlier phases of modern industry, where the owner was at the same time the foreman of the shop and the manager of the "business," as well as in those modern industries in which the division of labor is relatively slight, the distinction does not obtrude itself on the attention because the separation of employments is not marked. Probably on this account the distinction is, at least commonly, not made in the received discussions of economic theory, which have for the most part taken their shape under the traditions of a less highly developed differentiation of employments than the existing one. Still, even then the different, or divergent, disciplinary trend of the pecuniary and the industrial activities of any given individual must be held to have had its force, although the unblended effect of the one or the other may not be shown in any concrete case. It is to be added that in the somewhat numerous marginal cases, where these lines of employment cross and blend, as, e.g., in retail shopkeeping, in newspaper work, in popular art, in preaching, in sleight-of-hand, etc., it is perhaps impossible for the nicest discrimination to draw a neat distinction between them.

Since the distinction in question is not an accepted

article of economic theory, it need occasion no surprise that my critic should fail to apprehend it or to admit it; but his failure to apprehend the distinction does not affect its reality. As I conceive it, the distinction at its clearest marks the difference between workmanship and bargaining. Both equally are economic activities, but both are not in the same sense industrial. The "industrial" activities, whose characteristic is workmanship, of course include the work of directing the processes of industry as well as of contriving the aims and ideals of industry—such work as that of the artist, the inventor, the designer, the engineer, and the foreman. This range of employments has to do with adapting the material means of life, and the processes of valuation constantly involved in the work run on the availability of goods and on the material serviceability of the contrivances, materials, persons, or mechanical expedients employed. They have to do with relations of physical cause and effect. In the received scheme of economic theory these employments fall under the head of "Production." The "pecuniary" employments, on the other hand, should, in the received scheme, fall under the head of "Distribution." They have to do with the distribution of wealth —not necessarily with the distribution of goods to consumers. The processes of valuation involved in this work run on the exchange values of goods and on the vendibility of the items with which they are concerned, and on the necessities, solvency, cupidity, or gullibility of the persons whose actions may affect the transaction contemplated. These valuations look to the pecuniary serviceability of the persons and expedients employed. The objective point of the former range of valuations is material use, of the latter pecuniary gain. Indirectly this latter class of employments may have a very considerable effect in shaping industrial life, as witness, e.g., the industrial changes incident to the formation of trusts; and it is this indirect effect that has commonly received the attention of the economists. Similarly, of course, the "industrial" employments rarely if ever are without a pecuniary bearing.

It may be said by way of further characterisation that the pecuniary employments, and the pecuniary institutions to which they give rise, rest on the institution of private property and affect the industrial process by grace of that institution; while the industrial employments, and the industrial differentiation to which they give rise, rest chiefly on the physical conditions of human life; but they have their pecuniary bearing by virtue of the institution of ownership, since all pecuniary phenomena lie within the range of that institution. As J. S. Mill might be conceived to say—as, indeed, he has virtually said—the pecuniary employments are conditioned by human convention, the industrial by the unalterable laws of nature.

Either line of employment may be said to require and to foster a certain intelligence or sagacity in the persons so employed, but the intelligence so fostered is not the same in both cases. The sagacity characteristic of the pecuniary employments is a sagacity in judging what persons will do in the face of given pecuniary circumstances; the sagacity required by the industrial employments is chiefly a sagacity in judging what inanimate things will do under given mechanical conditions. When well developed, sagacity of the former complexion may be expected to make a shrewd salesman, investor, or promoter; intelligence of the latter kind, a competent engineer or mechanician. With the former goes an interest in gain and in contests of shrewdness and personal advantage; with the latter goes an interest in workman-like efficiency and in the play of inanimate forces. It is needless to add that men whose occupations are made up of the latter class of employments also commonly have something of the pecuniary aptitudes and find more or less frequent exercise for them; but it is also bootless to contend that there is no difference between the "pecuniary" and the "industrial" employments in respect of their disciplinary and selective effect upon the character of the persons employed. Neither should it be necessary to point out that the pecuniary employments, with the aptitudes and inclinations that give success in them, are, in their immediate bearing, in no degree serviceable to the community, since their aim is a competitive one. Whereas the latter commonly are serviceable in their immediate effects, except in so far as they are, commonly under the guidance of the pecuniary interest, led into work that is wasteful or disserviceable to the community.

I have permitted myself to speak at length and in this expository way on this point because Mr. Cummings's criticism has shown that the earlier discussion on this topic must have been lacking in clearness, while it has also raised the apprehension in my mind that the distinction between "pecuniary" and "industrial" aptitudes and employments may be more novel and more recondite than I had appreciated.

In conclusion Mr. Cummings speaks in terms of high appreciation of the "clever" use of terminological expedients which he finds in the volume. There is, however, a suggestion that, with all its cleverness, this consummate diction is charged with some malign potency, somewhat after the manner of the evil eye. Sincere, and withal kindly, as may be the intention of these comments on the "consummate cleverness" shown in the choice of terms, I cannot but mistrust that they express the impulses of my critic's heart rather than the deliverances of a serene intelligence. I apprehend they will not commend themselves to thoughtful readers of the volume. For instance, so serious a person as Mr. D. Collin Wells would be able at the most to give but a very materially qualified assent to Mr. Cummings's eulogy. Mr. Wells [4] expresses disappointment on precisely the point that stirs Mr. Cummings's admiration. Indeed, I catch, in Mr. Wells's observations on this matter, something of an inflection of sadness, such as argues a profound solicitude together with a baffled endeavor to find that the diction employed expresses any meaning whatever. In this bewilderment Mr. Wells, I regret to say, is not alone. The difficulty has been noted also by others, and to meet it is a good part of the purpose of what has been said above.

But, while he finds the terminology clever, Mr. Cummings deprecates the resort to terms which, in their current use, convey an attitude of approval or disapproval on the part of those who use them. This, of course, comes to a deprecation of the use of everyday words in their everyday meaning. In their discourse and in their thinking, men constantly and necessarily take an attitude of approval or disapproval toward the institutional facts of which they speak, for it is through such everyday approval or disapproval that any feature of the institutional structure is upheld or altered. It is only to be regretted that a trained scientist should be unable to view these categories of popular thought in a dispassionate light, for these categories, with all the moral

---

[4] *Yale Review*, August 1899, p. 218.

force with which they are charged, designate the motive force of cultural development, and to forgo their use in a genetic handling of this development means avoidance of the substantial facts with which the discussion is concerned. A scientist inquiring into cultural growth, and an evolutionist particularly, must take account of this dynamic content of the categories of popular thought as the most important material with which he has to work. Many persons may find it difficult to divest themselves of the point of view of morality or policy, from which these categories are habitually employed, and to take them up from the point of view of the scientific interest simply. But this difficulty does not set the scientific necessity aside. His inability to keep the cultural value and the moral content of these categories apart may reflect credit upon the state of such a person's sentiments, but it detracts from his scientific competence.

If the free use of unsophisticated vulgar concepts, with whatever content of prejudice and sentiment they may carry, is proscribed, the alternative is a resort to analogies and other figures of speech, such as have long afflicted economics and have given that science its reputed character of sterility. In extenuation of my fault, therefore, if such it must be, it should be said that, if one would avoid paralogistic figures of speech in the analysis of institutions, one must resort to words and concepts that express the thoughts of the men whose habits of thought constitute the institutions in question.

# THE BEGINNINGS OF OWNERSHIP [1]

IN the accepted economic theories the ground of ownership is commonly conceived to be the productive labor
of the owner. This is taken, without reflection or question, to be the legitimate basis of property; he who has
produced a useful thing should possess and enjoy it. On
this head the socialists and the economists of the classical line—the two extremes of economic speculation—
are substantially at one. The point is not in controversy,
or at least it has not been until recently; it has been accepted as an axiomatic premise. With the socialists it
has served as the ground of their demand that the laborer should receive the full product of his labor. To
classical economists the axiom has, perhaps, been as
much trouble as it has been worth. It has given them no
end of bother to explain how the capitalist is the "producer" of the goods that pass into his possession, and
how it is true that the laborer gets what he produces.
Sporadic instances of ownership quite dissociated from
creative industry are recognised and taken account of
as departures from the normal; they are due to disturbing causes. The main position is scarcely questioned,
that in the normal case wealth is distributed in proportion to—and in some cogent sense because of—the recipient's contribution to the product.

Not only is the productive labor of the owner the
definitive ground of his ownership today, but the der-

[1] Reprinted from *The American Journal of Sociology,* Vol. IV,
November, 1898.

ivation of the institution of property is similarly traced to the productive labor of that putative savage hunter who produced two deer or one beaver or twelve fish. The conjectural history of the origin of property, so far as it has been written by the economists, has been constructed out of conjecture proceeding on the preconceptions of Natural Rights and a coercive Order of Nature. To any one who approaches the question of ownership with only an incidental interest in its solution (as is true of the classical, pre-evolutionary economists), and fortified with the preconceptions of natural rights, all this seems plain. It sufficiently accounts for the institution, both in point of logical derivation and in point of historical development. The "natural" owner is the person who has "produced" an article, or who, by a constructively equivalent expenditure of productive force, has found and appropriated an object. It is conceived that such a person becomes the owner of the article by virtue of the immediate logical inclusion of the idea of ownership under the idea of creative industry.

This natural-rights theory of property makes the creative effort of an isolated, self-sufficing individual the basis of the ownership vested in him. In so doing it overlooks the fact that there is no isolated, self-sufficing individual. All production is, in fact, a production in and by the help of the community, and all wealth is such only in society. Within the human period of the race development, it is safe to say, no individual has fallen into industrial isolation, so as to produce any one useful article by his own independent effort alone. Even where there is no mechanical co-operation, men are always guided by the experience of others. The only possible exceptions to this rule are those instances of lost or cast-off children nourished by wild beasts, of which half-authenticated accounts have gained currency from time to time. But the anomalous, half-hypothetical life of these waifs can scarcely have affected social development to the extent of originating the institution of ownership.

Production takes place only in society—only through the co-operation of an industrial community. This industrial community may be large or small; its limits are commonly somewhat vaguely defined; but it always comprises a group large enough to contain and transmit the traditions, tools, technical knowledge, and usages without which there can be no industrial organisation and no economic relation of individuals to one another or to their environment. The isolated individual is not a productive agent. What he can do at best is to live from season to season, as the non-gregarious animals do. There can be no production without technical knowledge; hence no accumulation and no wealth to be owned, in severalty or otherwise. And there is no technical knowledge apart from an industrial community. Since there is no individual production and no individual productivity, the natural-rights preconception that ownership rests on the individually productive labor of the owner reduces itself to absurdity, even under the logic of its own assumptions.

Some writers who have taken up the question from the ethnological side hold that the institution is to be traced to the customary use of weapons and ornaments by individuals. Others have found its origin in the social group's occupation of a given piece of land, which it held forcibly against intruders, and which it came in this way to "own." The latter hypothesis bases the collective ownership of land on a collective act of seizure, or tenure by prowess, so that it differs fundamentally from the view which bases ownership on productive labor.

The view that ownership is an outgrowth of the customary consumption of such things as weapons and ornaments by individuals is well supported by appearances and has also the qualified sanction of the natural-rights preconception. The usages of all known primitive tribes seem at first sight to bear out this view. In all communities the individual members exercise a more or less unrestrained right of use and abuse over their weapons, if they have any, as well as over many articles of ornament, clothing, and the toilet. In the eyes of the modern economist this usage would count as ownership. So that, if the question is construed to be simply a question of material fact, as to the earliest emergence of usages which would in the latter-day classification be brought under the head of ownership, then it would have to be said that ownership must have begun with the conversion of these articles to individual use. But the question will have to be answered in the contrary sense if we shift our ground to the point of view of the primitive men whose institutions are under review. The point in question is the origin of the institution of ownership, as it first takes shape in the habits of thought of the early barbarian. The question concerns the derivation of the idea of ownership or property. What is of interest for the present purpose is not whether we, with our preconceptions, would look upon the relation of the primitive savage or barbarian to his slight personal effects as a relation of ownership, but whether that is his own apprehension of the matter. It is a question as to the light in which the savage himself habitually views these objects that pertain immediately to his person and are set apart for his habitual use. Like all questions of the derivation of institutions, it is essentially a question of folk-psychology, not of mechanical fact; and, when so conceived, it must be answered in the negative.

The unsophisticated man, whether savage or civilised, is prone to conceive phenomena in terms of personality; these being terms with which he has a first-hand acquaintance. This habit is more unbroken in the savage than in civilised men. All obvious manifestations of force are apprehended as expressions of conation—effort put forth for a purpose by some agency similar to the human will. The point of view of the archaic culture is that of forceful, pervading personality, whose unfolding life is the substantial fact held in view in every relation into which men or things enter. This point of view in large measure shapes and colors all the institutions of the early culture—and in a less degree the later phases of culture. Under the guidance of this habit of thought, the relation of any individual to his personal effects is conceived to be of a more intimate kind than that of ownership simply. Ownership is too external and colorless a term to describe the fact.

In the apprehension of the savage and the barbarian the limits of his person do not coincide with the limits which modern biological science would recognise. His individuality is conceived to cover, somewhat vaguely and uncertainly, a pretty wide fringe of facts and objects that pertain to him more or less immediately. To our sense of the matter these items lie outside the limits of his person, and to many of them we would conceive him to stand in an economic rather than in an organic relation. This quasi-personal fringe of facts and objects commonly comprises the man's shadow; the reflection of his image in water or any similar surface; his name;

his peculiar tattoo marks; his totem, if he has one; his glance; his breath, especially when it is visible; the print of his hand and foot; the sound of his voice; any image or representation of his person; any excretions or exhalations from his person; parings of his nails; cuttings of his hair; his ornaments and amulets; clothing that is in daily use, especially what has been shaped to his person, and more particularly if there is wrought into it any totemic or other design peculiar to him; his weapons, especially his favorite weapons and those which he habitually carries. Beyond these there is a great number of other, remoter things which may or may not be included in the quasi-personal fringe.

As regards this entire range of facts and objects, it is to be said that the "zone of influence" of the individual's personality is not conceived to cover them all with the same degree of potency; his individuality shades off by insensible, penumbral gradations into the external world. The objects and facts that fall within the quasi-personal fringe figure in the habits of thought of the savage as personal to him in a vital sense. They are not a congeries of things to which he stands in an economic relation and to which he has an equitable, legal claim. These articles are conceived to be his in much the same sense as his hands and feet are his, or his pulse-beat, or his digestion, or the heat of his body, or the motions of his limbs or brain.

For the satisfaction of any who may be inclined to question this view, appeal may be taken to the usages of almost any people. Some such notion of a pervasive personality, or a penumbra of personality, is implied, for instance, in the giving and keeping of presents and mementos. It is more indubitably present in the working of charms; in all sorcery; in the sacraments and similar devout observances; in such practices as the Tibetan prayer-wheel; in the adoration of relics, images, and symbols; in the almost universal veneration of con-secrated places and structures; in astrology; in divina-tion by means of hair-cuttings, nail-parings, photo-graphs, etc. Perhaps the least debatable evidence of belief in such a quasi-personal fringe is afforded by the practices of sympathetic magic; and the practices are strikingly similar in substance the world over—from the love-charm to the sacrament. Their substantial ground is the belief that a desired effect can be wrought upon a given person through the means of some object lying within his quasi-personal fringe. The person who is approached in this way may be a fellow-mortal, or it may be some potent spiritual agent whose intercession is sought for good or ill. If the sorcerer or any one who works a charm can in any way get at the "penumbra" of a person's individuality, as embodied in his fringe of quasi-personal facts, he will be able to work good or ill to the person to whom the fact or object pertains; and the magic rites performed to this end will work their effect with greater force and precision in proportion as the object which affords the point of attack is more intimately related to the person upon whom the effect is to be wrought. An economic relation, simply, does not afford a handle for sorcery. It may be set down that, whenever the relation of a person to a given object is made use of for the purposes of sympathetic magic, the relation is conceived to be something more vital than simple legal ownership

Such meager belongings of the primitive savage as would under the nomenclature of a later day be classed as personal property are not thought of by him as his property at all; they pertain organically to his person.

Of the things comprised in his quasi-personal fringe all do not pertain to him with the same degree of intimacy or persistency; but those articles which are more remotely or more doubtfully included under his individuality are not therefore conceived to be partly organic to him and partly his property simply. The alternative does not lie between this organic relation and ownership. It may easily happen that a given article lying along the margin of the quasi-personal fringe is eliminated from it and is alienated, either by default through lapse of time or by voluntary severance of the relation. But when this happens, the article is not conceived to escape from the organic relation into a remoter category of things that are owned by and external to the person in question. If an object escapes in this way from the organic sphere of one person, it may pass into the sphere of another; or, if it is an article that lends itself to common use, it may pass into the common stock of the community.

As regards this common stock, no concept of ownership, either communal or individual, applies in the primitive community. The idea of a communal ownership is of relatively late growth, and must by psychological necessity have been preceded by the idea of individual ownership. Ownership is an accredited discretionary power over an object on the ground of a conventional claim; it implies that the owner is a personal agent who takes thought for the disposal of the object owned. A personal agent is an individual, and it is only by an eventual refinement—of the nature of a legal fiction—that any group of men is conceived to exercise a corporate discretion over objects. Ownership implies an individual owner. It is only by reflection, and by extending the scope of a concept which is already familiar, that a quasi-personal corporate discretion and control of this kind comes to be imputed to a group of persons. Corporate ownership is quasi-ownership only; it is therefore necessarily a derivative concept, and cannot have preceded the concept of individual ownership of which it is a counterfeit.

After the idea of ownership has been elaborated and has gained some consistency, it is not unusual to find the notion of pervasion by the user's personality applied to articles owned by him. At the same time a given article may also be recognised as lying within the quasi-personal fringe of one person while it is owned by another—as, for instance, ornaments and other articles of daily use which in a personal sense belong to a slave or to an inferior member of a patriarchal household, but which as property belong to the master or head of the household. The two categories, (*a*) things to which one's personality extends by way of pervasion and (*b*) things owned, by no means coincide; nor does the one supplant the other. The two ideas are so far from identical that the same object may belong to one person under the one concept and to another person under the other; and, on the other hand, the same person may stand in both relations to a given object without the one concept being lost in the other. A given article may change owners without passing out of the quasi-personal fringe of the person under whose "self" it has belonged, as, for instance, a photograph or any other memento. A familiar instance is the mundane ownership of any consecrated place or structure which in the personal sense belongs to the saint or deity to whom it is sacred.

The two concepts are so far distinct, or even disparate, as to make it extremely improbable that the one has been developed out of the other by a process of growth. A transition involving such a substitution of ideas could scarcely take place except on some notable impulse from without. Such a step would amount to the construction of a new category and a reclassification of certain selected facts under the new head. The impulse to reclassify the facts and things that are comprised in the quasi-personal fringe, so as to place some of them, together with certain other things, under the new category of ownership, must come from some constraining exigency of later growth than the concept whose province it invades. The new category is not simply an amplified form of the old. Not every item that was originally conceived to belong to an individual by way of pervasion comes to be counted as an item of his wealth after the idea of wealth has come into vogue. Such items, for instance, as a person's footprint, or his image or effigy, or his name, are very tardily included under the head of articles owned by him, if they are eventually included at all. It is a fortuitous circumstance if they come to be owned by him, but they long continue to hold their place in his quasi-personal fringe. The disparity of the two concepts is well brought out by the case of the domestic animals. These non-human individuals are incapable of ownership, but there is imputed to them the attribute of a pervasive individuality, which extends to such items as their footprints, their stalls, clippings of hair, and the like. These items are made use of for the purposes of sympathetic magic even in modern civilised communities. An illustration that may show this disparity between ownership and pervasion in a still stronger light is afforded by the vulgar belief that the moon's phases may have a propitious or sinister effect on human affairs. The inconstant moon is conceived to work good or ill through a sympathetic influence or spiritual infection which suggests a quasi-personal fringe, but which assuredly does not imply ownership on her part.

Ownership is not a simple and instinctive notion that is naïvely included under the notion of productive effort on the one hand, nor under that of habitual use on the other. It is not something given to begin with, as an item of the isolated individual's mental furniture; something which has to be unlearned in part when men come to co-operate in production and make working arrangements and mutual renunciations under the stress of associated life—after the manner imputed by the social-contract theory. It is a conventional fact and has to be learned; it is a cultural fact which has grown into an institution in the past through a long course of habituation, and which is transmitted from generation to generation as all cultural facts are.

On going back a little way into the cultural history of our own past, we come upon a situation which says that the fact of a person's being engaged in industry was *prima facie* evidence that he could own nothing. Under serfdom and slavery those who work cannot own, and those who own cannot work. Even very recently—culturally speaking—there was no suspicion that a woman's work, in the patriarchal household, should entitle her to own the products of her work. Farther back in the barbarian culture, while the patriarchal household was in better preservation than it is now, this position was accepted with more unquestioning faith. The head of the household alone could hold property; and even the scope of his ownership was greatly qualified if he had a feudal superior. The tenure of property is a tenure by prowess, on the one hand, and a tenure by sufferance at the hands of a superior, on the other hand. The recourse to prowess as the definitive basis of tenure becomes more immediate and more habitual the farther the development is traced back into the early barbarian culture; until, on the lower levels of barbarism or the upper levels of savagery, "the good old plan" prevails with but little mitigation. There are always certain conventions, a certain understanding as to what are the legitimate conditions and circumstances that surround ownership and its transmission, chief among which is the fact of habitual acceptance. What has been currently accepted as the *status quo*—vested interest—is right and good so long as it does not meet a challenge backed by irresistible force. Property rights sanctioned by immemorial usage are inviolable, as all immemorial usage is, except in the face of forcible dispossession. But seizure and forcible retention very shortly gain the legitimation of usage, and the resulting tenure becomes inviolable through habituation. *Beati possidentes.*

Throughout the barbarian culture, where this tenure by prowess prevails, the population falls into two economic classes: those engaged in industrial employments, and those engaged in such non-industrial pursuits as war, government, sports, and religious observances. In the earlier and more naïve stages of barbarism the former, in the normal case, own nothing; the latter own such property as they have seized, or such as has, under the sanction of usage, descended upon them from their forbears who seized and held it. At a still lower level of culture, in the primitive savage horde, the population is not similarly divided into economic classes. There is no leisure class resting its prerogative on coercion, prowess, and immemorial status; and there is also no ownership.

It will hold as a rough generalisation that in communities where there is no invidious distinction between employments, as exploit, on the one hand, and drudgery, on the other, there is also no tenure of property. In the cultural sequence, ownership does not begin before the rise of a canon of exploit; but it is to be added that it also does not seem to begin with the first beginning of exploit as a manly occupation. In these very rude early communities, especially in the unpropertied hordes of peaceable savages, the rule is that the product of any member's effort is consumed by the group to which he belongs; and it is consumed collectively or indiscriminately, without question of individual right or ownership. The question of ownership is not brought up by the fact that an article has been produced or is at hand in finished form for consumption.

The earliest occurrence of ownership seems to fall in the early stages of barbarism, and the emergence of the institution of ownership is apparently a concomitant of the transition from a peaceable to a predatory habit of life. It is a prerogative of that class in the barbarian culture which leads a life of exploit rather than of industry. The pervading characteristic of the barbarian culture, as distinguished from the peaceable phase of life that precedes it, is the element of exploit, coercion, and seizure. In its earlier phases ownership is this habit of coercion and seizure reduced to system and consistency under the surveillance of usage.

The practice of seizing and accumulating goods on individual account could not have come into vogue to the extent of founding a new institution under the peaceable communistic régime of primitive savagery; for the dissensions arising from any such resort to mutual force and fraud among its members would have been fatal to the group. For a similar reason individual ownership of consumable goods could not come in with the first beginnings of predatory life; for the primitive fighting horde still needs to consume its scanty means of subsistence in common, in order to give the collective horde its full fighting efficiency. Otherwise it would succumb before any rival horde that had not yet given up collective consumption.

With the advent of predatory life comes the practice of plundering—seizing goods from the enemy. But in order that the plundering habits should give rise to individual ownership of the things seized, these things must be goods of a somewhat lasting kind, and not immediately consumable means of subsistence. Under the primitive culture the means of subsistence are habitually consumed in common by the group, and the manner in which such goods are consumed is fixed according to an elaborate system of usage. This usage is not readily broken over, for it is a substantial part of the habits of life of every individual member. The practice of collective consumption is at the same time necessary to the survival of the group, and this necessity is present in men's minds and exercises a surveillance over the formation of habits of thought as to what is right and seemly. Any propensity to aggression at this early stage will, therefore, not assert itself in the seizure and retention of consumable goods; nor does the temptation to do so readily present itself, since the idea of individual appropriation of a store of goods is alien to the archaic man's general habits of thought.

The idea of property is not readily attached to anything but tangible and lasting articles. It is only where commercial development is well advanced—where bargain and sale is a large feature in the community's life—

that the more perishable articles of consumption are thought of as items of wealth at all. The still more evanescent results of personal service are still more difficult to bring in under the idea of wealth. So much so that the attempt to classify services as wealth is meaningless to laymen, and even the adept economists hold a divided opinion as to the intelligibility of such a classification. In the common-sense apprehension the idea of property is not currently attached to any but tangible, vendible goods of some durability. This is true even in modern civilised communities, where pecuniary ideas and the pecuniary point of view prevail. In a like manner and for a like reason, in an earlier, non-commercial phase of culture there is less occasion for and greater difficulty in applying the concept of ownership to anything but obviously durable articles.

But durable articles of use and consumption which are seized in the raids of a predatory horde are either articles of general use or they are articles of immediate and continued personal use to the person who has seized them. In the former case the goods are consumed in common by the group, without giving rise to a notion of ownership; in the latter case they fall into the class of things that pertain organically to the person of their user, and they would, therefore, not figure as items of property or make up a store of wealth.

It is difficult to see how an institution of ownership could have arisen in the early days of predatory life through the seizure of goods, but the case is different with the seizure of persons. Captives are items that do not fit into the scheme of communal consumption, and their appropriation by their individual captor works no manifest detriment to the group. At the same time these captives continue to be obviously distinct from their captor in point of individuality, and so are not readily brought in under the quasi-personal fringe. The captives taken under rude conditions are chiefly women. There are good reasons for this. Except where there is a slave class of men, the women are more useful, as well as more easily controlled, in the primitive group. Their labor is worth more to the group than their maintenance, and, as they do not carry weapons, they are less formidable than men captives would be. They serve the purpose of trophies very effectually, and it is therefore worth while for their captor to trace and keep in evidence his relation to them as their captor. To this end he maintains an attitude of dominance and coercion toward women captured by him; and, as being the insignia of his prowess, he does not suffer them to stand at the beck and call of rival warriors. They are fit subjects for command and constraint; it ministers to both his honor and his vanity to domineer over them, and their utility in this respect is very great. But his domineering over them is the evidence of his prowess, and it is incompatible with their utility as trophies that other men should take the liberties with his women which serve as evidence of the coercive relation of captor.

When the practice hardens into custom, the captor comes to exercise a customary right to exclusive use and abuse over the women he has seized; and this customary right of use and abuse over an object which is obviously not an organic part of his person constitutes the relation of ownership, as naïvely apprehended. After this usage of capture has found its way into the habits of the community, the women so held in constraint and in evidence will commonly fall into a conventionally recognised marriage relation with their captor. The result is a new form of marriage, in which the man is master. This ownership-marriage seems to be the original both of private property and of the patriarchal household. Both of these great institutions are, accordingly, of an emulative origin.

The varying details of the development whereby ownership extends to other persons than captured women cannot be taken up here; neither can the further growth of the marriage institution that came into vogue at the same time with ownership. Probably at a point in the economic evolution not far subsequent to the definitive installation of the institution of ownership-marriage comes, as its consequence, the ownership of consumable goods. The women held in servile marriage not only render personal service to their master, but they are also employed in the production of articles of use. All the noncombatant or ignoble members of the community are habitually so employed. And when the habit of looking upon and claiming the persons identified with my invidious interest, or subservient to me, as "mine" has become an accepted and integral part of men's habits of thought, it becomes a relatively easy matter to extend this newly achieved concept of ownership to the products of the labor performed by the persons so held in ownership. And the same propensity for emulation which bears so great a part in shaping the original institution of ownership extends its action to the new category of things owned. Not only are the products of the women's labor claimed and valued for their serviceability in furthering the comfort and fullness of life of the master, but they are valuable also as a conspicuous evidence of his possessing many and efficient servants, and they are therefore useful as an evidence of his superior force. The appropriation and accumulation of consumable goods could scarcely have come into vogue as a direct outgrowth of the primitive horde-communism, but it comes in as an easy and unobtrusive consequence of the ownership of persons.

# THE BARBARIAN STATUS OF WOMEN [1]

IT seems altogether probable that in the primitive groups of mankind, when the race first took to a systematic use of tools, and so emerged upon the properly human plane of life, there was but the very slightest beginning of a system of status, with little of invidious distinction between classes and little of a corresponding division of employments. In an earlier paper, published in this Journal, it has been argued that the early division of labor between classes comes in as the result of an increasing efficiency of labor, due to a growing effectiveness in the use of tools. When, in the early cultural development, the use of tools and the technical command of material forces had reached a certain degree of effectiveness, the employments which occupy the primitive community would fall into two distinct groups—(a) the honorific employments, which involve a large element of prowess, and (b) the humiliating employments, which call for diligence and into which the sturdier virtues do not enter. An appreciable advance in the use of tools must precede this differentiation of employments, because (1) without effective tools (including weapons) men are not sufficiently formidable in conflict with the ferocious beasts to devote themselves so exclusively to the hunting of large game as to develop that occupation into a conventional mode of life reserved for a

[1] Reprinted from *The American Journal of Sociology,* Vol. IV, January, 1899.

distinct class; (2) without tools of some efficiency, industry is not productive enough to support a dense population, and therefore the groups into which the population gathers will not come into such a habitual hostile contact with one another as would give rise to a life of warlike prowess; (3) until industrial methods and knowledge have made some advance, the work of getting a livelihood is too exacting to admit of the consistent exemption of any portion of the community from vulgar labor; (4) the inefficient primitive industry yields no such disposable surplus of accumulated goods as would be worth fighting for, or would tempt an intruder, and therefore there is little provocation to warlike prowess.

With the growth of industry comes the possibility of a predatory life; and if the groups of savages crowd one another in the struggle for subsistence, there is a provocation to hostilities, and a predatory habit of life ensues. There is a consequent growth of a predatory culture, which may for the present purpose be treated as the beginning of the barbarian culture. This predatory culture shows itself in a growth of suitable institutions. The group divides itself conventionally into a fighting and a peace-keeping class, with a corresponding division of labor. Fighting, together with other work that involves a serious element of exploit, becomes the employment of the able-bodied men; the uneventful everyday work of the group falls to the women and the infirm.

In such a community the standards of merit and propriety rest on an invidious distinction between those who are capable fighters and those who are not. Infirmity, that is to say incapacity for exploit, is looked down upon. One of the early consequences of this depreciation of infirmity is a tabu on women and women's employments. In the apprehension of the archaic, animistic barbarian, infirmity is infectious. The infection may work its mischievous effect both by sympathetic influence and by transfusion. Therefore it is well for the able-bodied man who is mindful of his virility to shun all undue contact and conversation with the weaker sex and to avoid all contamination with the employments that are characteristic of the sex. Even the habitual food of women should not be eaten by men, lest their force be thereby impaired. The injunction against womanly employments and foods and against intercourse with women applies with especial rigor during the season of preparation for any work of manly exploit, such as a great hunt or a warlike raid, or induction into some manly dignity or society or mystery. Illustrations of this seasonal tabu abound in the early history of all peoples that have had a warlike or barbarian past. The women, their occupations, their food and clothing, their habitual place in the house or village, and in extreme cases even their speech, become ceremonially unclean to the men. This imputation of ceremonial uncleanness on the ground of their infirmity has lasted on in the later culture as a sense of the unworthiness or Levitical inadequacy of women; so that even now we feel the impropriety of women taking rank with men, or representing the community in any relation that calls for dignity and ritual competency; as, for instance, in priestly or diplomatic offices, or even in representative civil offices, and likewise, and for a like reason, in such offices of domestic and body servants as are of a seriously ceremonial character—footmen, butlers, etc.

The changes that take place in the everyday experiences of a group or horde when it passes from a peaceable to a predatory habit of life have their effect on the habits of thought prevalent in the group. As the hostile contact of one group with another becomes closer and more habitual, the predatory activity and the bellicose animus become more habitual to the members of the group. Fighting comes more and more to occupy men's everyday thoughts, and the other activities of the group fall into the background and become subsidiary to the fighting activity. In the popular apprehension the substantial core of such a group—that on which men's thoughts run when the community and the community's life is thought of—is the body of fighting men. The collective fighting capacity becomes the most serious question that occupies men's minds, and gives the point of view from which persons and conduct are rated. The scheme of life of such a group is substantially a scheme of exploit. There is much of this point of view to be found even in the common-sense views held by modern populations. The inclination to identify the community with its fighting men comes into evidence today whenever warlike interests occupy the popular attention in an appreciable degree.

The work of the predatory barbarian group is gradually specialized and differentiated under the dominance of this ideal of prowess, so as to give rise to a system of status in which the non-fighters fall into a position of subservience to the fighters. The accepted scheme of life or consensus of opinions which guides the conduct of men in such a predatory group and decides what may properly be done of course comprises a great variety of details; but it is, after all, a single scheme—a more or less organic whole—so that the life carried on under its guidance in any case makes up a somewhat consistent and characteristic body of culture. This is necessarily the case, because of the simple fact that the individuals between whom the consensus holds are individuals. The thinking of each one is the thinking of the same individual, on whatever head and in whatever direction his thinking may run. Whatever may be the immediate point or object of his thinking, the frame of mind which governs his aim and manner of reasoning in passing on any given point of conduct is, on the whole, the habitual frame of mind which experience and tradition have enforced upon him. Individuals whose sense of what is right and good departs widely from the accepted views suffer some repression, and in case of an extreme divergence they are eliminated from the effective life of the group through ostracism. Where the fighting class is in the position of dominance and prescriptive legitimacy, the canons of conduct are shaped chiefly by the common-sense of the body of fighting men. Whatever conduct and whatever code of proprieties have the authentication of this common-sense are definitively right and good, for the time being, and the deliverances of this common-sense are, in their turn, shaped by the habits of life of the able-bodied men. Habitual conflict acts, by selection and by habituation, to make these male members tolerant of any infliction of damage and suffering. Habituation to the sight and infliction of suffering, and to the emotions that go with fights and brawls, may even end in making the spectacle of misery a pleasing diversion to them. The result is in any case a more or less consistent attitude of plundering and coercion on the part of the fighting body, and this animus is incorporated into the scheme of life of the community. The discipline of predatory life makes for an attitude of mastery on the part of the able-bodied men in all their relations with the weaker members of the group, and especially in their relations with the women. Men who are trained in predatory ways of life and modes of thinking come by habituation to apprehend this form of the relation between the sexes as good and beautiful.

All the women in the group will share in the class repression and depreciation that belongs to them as women, but the status of women taken from hostile groups has an additional feature. Such a woman not only belongs to a subservient and low class, but she also stands in a special relation to her captor. She is a trophy of the raid, and therefore an evidence of exploit, and on this ground it is to her captor's interest to maintain a peculiarly obvious relation of mastery toward her. And since, in the early culture, it does not detract from her subservience to the life of the group, this peculiar relation of the captive to her captor will meet but slight, if any, objection from the other members of the group. At the same time, since his peculiar coercive relation to the woman serves to mark her as a trophy of his exploit, he will somewhat jealously resent any similar freedom taken by other men, or any attempt on their part to parade a similar coercive authority over her, and so usurp the laurels of his prowess, very much as a warrior would under like circumstances resent a usurpation or an abuse of the scalps or skulls which he had taken from the enemy.

After the habit of appropriating captured women has hardened into custom, and so given rise on the one hand to a form of marriage resting on coercion, and on the other hand to a concept of ownership, a development of certain secondary features of the institution so inaugurated is to be looked for. In time this coercive ownership-marriage receives the sanction of the popular taste and morality. It comes to rest in men's habits of thought as the right form of marriage relation, and it comes at the same time to be gratifying to men's sense of beauty and of honor. The growing predilection for mastery and coercion, as a manly trait, together with the growing moral and æsthetic approbation of marriage on a basis of coercion and ownership, will affect the tastes of the men most immediately and most strongly; but since the men are the superior class whose views determine the current views of the community, their common-sense in the matter will shape the current canons of taste in its own image. The tastes of the women also, in point of morality and of propriety alike, will presently be affected in the same way. Through the precept and example of those who make the vogue, and through selective repression of those who are unable to accept it, the institution of ownership-marriage makes its way into definitive acceptance as the only beautiful and virtuous form of the relation. As the conviction of its legitimacy grows stronger in each succeeding generation, it comes to be appreciated unreflectingly as a deliverance of common-sense and enlightened reason that the good and beautiful attitude of the man toward the woman is an attitude of coercion. "None but the brave deserve the fair."

As the predatory habit of life gains a more unquestioned and undivided sway, other forms of the marriage relation fall under a polite odium. The masterless, unattached woman consequently loses caste. It becomes imperative for all men who would stand well in the eyes of their fellows to attach some woman or women to themselves by the honorable bonds of seizure. In order to a decent standing in the community a man is required to enter into this virtuous and honorific relation of ownership-marriage, and a publicly acknowledged marriage relation which has not the sanction of capture becomes unworthy of able-bodied men. But as the group increases in size, the difficulty of providing wives by capture becomes very great, and it becomes necessary to find a remedy that shall save the requirements of decency and at the same time permit the marriage of women from within the group. To this end the status of women married from within the group is sought to be mended by a mimic or ceremonial capture. The ceremonial capture effects an assimilation of the free woman into the more acceptable class of women who are attached by bonds of coercion to some master, and so gives a ceremonial legitimacy and decency to the resulting marriage relation. The probable motive for adopting the free women into the honorable class of bondwomen in this way is not primarily a wish to improve their standing or their lot, but rather a wish to keep those good men in countenance, who, for dearth of captives, are constrained to seek a substitute from among the home-bred women of the group. The inclinations of men in high standing who are possessed of marriageable daughters would run in the same direction. It would not seem right that a woman of high birth should irretrievably be outclassed by any chance-comer from outside.

According to this view, marriage by feigned capture within the tribe is a case of mimicry—"protective mimicry," to borrow a phrase from the naturalists. It is substantially a case of adoption. As is the case in all human relations where adoption is practiced, this adoption of the free women into the class of the unfree proceeds by as close an imitation as may be of the original fact for which it is a substitute. And as in other cases of adoption, the ceremonial performance is by no means looked upon as a fatuous make-believe. The barbarian has implicit faith in the efficiency of imitation and ceremonial execution as a means of compassing a desired end. The entire range of magic and religious rites is testimony to that effect. He looks upon external objects and sequences naïvely, as organic and individual things, and as expressions of a propensity working toward an end. The unsophisticated common-sense of the primitive barbarian apprehends sequences and events in terms of will-power or inclination. As seen in the light of this animistic preconception, any process is substantially teleological, and the propensity imputed to it will not be thwarted of its legitimate end after the course of events in which it expresses itself has once fallen into shape or got under way. It follows logically, as a matter of course, that, if once the motions leading to a desired consummation have been rehearsed in the accredited form and sequence, the same substantial result will be attained as that produced by the process imitated. This is the ground of whatever efficiency is imputed to ceremonial observances on all planes of culture, and it is especially the chief element in formal adoption and initiation. Hence, probably, the practice of mock-seizure or mock-capture, and hence the formal profession of fealty and submission on the part of the woman in the marriage rites of peoples among whom the household with a male head prevails. This form of the household is almost always associated with some survival or reminiscence of wife-capture. In all such cases, marriage is, by derivation, a ritual of initiation into servitude. In the words of the formula, even after it has been appreciably softened under the latter-day decay of the sense of status, it is the woman's place to love, honor, and obey.

According to this view, the patriarchal household or, in other words, the household with a male head, is an outgrowth of emulation between the members of a war-like community. It is, therefore, in point of derivation, a predatory institution. The ownership and control of women is a gratifying evidence of prowess and high standing. In logical consistency, therefore, the greater the number of women so held, the greater the distinction which their possession confers upon their master. Hence the prevalence of polygamy, which occurs almost universally at one stage of culture among peoples which have the male household. There may, of course, be other reasons for polygamy, but the ideal development of polygamy which is met with in the harems of very powerful patriarchal despots and chieftains can scarcely be explained on other grounds. But whether it works out in a system of polygamy or not, the male household is in any case a detail of a system of status under which the women are included in the class of unfree subjects. The dominant feature in the institutional structure of these communities is that of status, and the groundwork of their economic life is a rigorous system of ownership.

The institution is found at its best, or in its most effectual development, in the communities in which status and ownership prevail with the least mitigation; and with the decline of the sense of status and of the extreme pretensions of ownership, such as has been going on for some time past in the communities of the western culture, the institution of the patriarchal household has also suffered something of a disintegration. There has been some weakening and slackening of the bonds, and this deterioration is most visible in the communities which have departed farthest from the ancient system of status, and have gone farthest in reorganising their economic life on the lines of industrial freedom. And the deference for an indissoluble tie of ownership-marriage, as well as the sense of its definitive virtuousness, has suffered the greatest decline among the classes immediately engaged in the modern industries. So that there seems to be fair ground for saying that the habits of thought fostered by modern industrial life are, on the whole, not favorable to the maintenance of this institution or to that status of women which the institution in its best development implies. The days of its best development are in the past, and the discipline of modern life—if not supplemented by a prudent inculcation of conservative ideals—will scarcely afford the psychological basis for its rehabilitation.

This form of marriage, or of ownership, by which the man becomes the head of the household, the owner of the woman, and the owner and discretionary consumer of the household's output of consumable goods, does not of necessity imply a patriarchal system of consanguinity. The presence or absence of maternal relationship should, therefore, not be given definite weight in this connection. The male household, in some degree of elaboration, may well coexist with a counting of relationship in the female line, as, for instance, among many North American tribes. But where this is the case it seems probable that the ownership of women, together with the invidious distinctions of status from which the practice of such an ownership springs, has come into vogue at so late a stage of the cultural development that the maternal system of relationship had already been thoroughly incorporated into the tribe's scheme of life. The male household in such cases is ordinarily not developed in good form or entirely free from traces of a maternal household. The traces of a maternal household which are found in these cases commonly point to a form of marriage which disregards the man rather than places him under the surveillance of the woman. It may well be named the household of the unattached woman. This condition of things argues that the tribe or race in question has entered upon a predatory life only after a considerable period of peaceable industrial life, and after having achieved a considerable development of social structure under the régime of peace and industry, whereas the unqualified prevalence of the patriarchate, together with the male household, may be taken to indicate that the predatory phase was entered early, culturally speaking.

Where the patriarchal system is in force in fully developed form, including the paternal household, and hampered with no indubitable survivals of a maternal household or a maternal system of relationship, the presumption would be that the people in question has entered upon the predatory culture early, and has adopted the institutions of private property and class prerogative at an early stage of its economic development. On the other hand, where there are well-preserved traces of a maternal household, the presumption is that the predatory phase has been entered by the community in question at a relatively late point in its life history, even if the patriarchal system is, and long has been, the prevalent system of relationship. In the latter case the community, or the group of tribes, may, perhaps for geographical reasons, not have independently attained the predatory culture in accentuated form, but may at a relatively late date have contracted the agnatic system and the paternal household through contact with another, higher, or characteristically different, culture, which has included these institutions among its cultural furniture. The required contact would take place most effectually by way of invasion and conquest by an alien race occupying the higher plane or divergent line of culture. Something of this kind is the probable explanation, for instance, of the equivocal character of the household and relationship system in the early Germanic culture, especially as it is seen in such outlying regions as Scandinavia. The evidence, in this latter case, as in some other communities lying farther south, is somewhat obscure, but it points to a long-continued coexistence of the two forms of the household; of which the maternal seems to have held its place most tenaciously among the subject or lower classes of the population, while the paternal was the honorable form of marriage in vogue among the superior class. In the earliest traceable situation of these tribes there appears to have been a relatively feeble, but growing, preponderance of the male household throughout the community. This mixture of marriage institutions, as well as the correlative mixture or ambiguity of property institutions associated with it in the Germanic culture, seems most easily explicable as being due to the mingling of two distinct racial stocks, whose institutions differed in these respects. The race or tribe which had the maternal household and common property would probably have been the more numerous and the more peaceable at the time the mixing process began, and would fall into some degree of subjection to its more warlike consort race.

No attempt is hereby made to account for the various forms of human marriage, or to show how the institution varies in detail from place to place and from time to time, but only to indicate what seems to have been the range of motives and of exigencies that have given rise to the paternal household, as it has been handed down from the barbarian past of the peoples of the western culture. To this end, nothing but the most general features of the life history of the institution have been touched upon, and even the evidence on which this much of generalisation is based is, perforce, omitted. The purpose of the argument is to point out that there is a close connection, particularly in point of psychological derivation, between individual ownership, the system of status, and the paternal household, as they appear in this culture.

This view of the derivation of private property and of the male household, as already suggested, does not imply the prior existence of a maternal household of the kind in which the woman is the head and master of a household group and exercises a discretionary control over her husband or husbands and over the household effects. Still less does it imply a prior state of promiscuity. What is implied by the hypothesis and by the scant evidence at hand is rather the form of the marriage relation above characterised as the household of the unattached woman. The characteristic feature of this marriage seems to have been an absence of coercion or control in the relation between the sexes. The union (probably monogamic and more or less enduring) seems to have been terminable at will by either party, under the constraint of some slight conventional limitations. The substantial difference introduced into the marriage relation on the adoption of ownership-marriage is the exercise of coercion by the man and the loss on the part of the woman of the power to terminate the relation at will. Evidence running in this direction, and in part hitherto unpublished, is to be found both in the modern and in the earlier culture of Germanic communities.

It is only in cases where circumstances have, in an exceptional degree, favored the development of ownership-marriage that we should expect to find the institution worked out to its logical consequences. Wherever the predatory phase of social life has not come in early and has not prevailed in unqualified form for a long time, or wherever a social group or race with this form of the household has received a strong admixture of another race not possessed of the institution, there the prevalent form of marriage should show something of a departure from this paternal type. And even where neither of these two conditions is present, this type of the marriage relation might be expected in the course of time to break down with the change of circumstances, since it is an institution that has grown up as a detail of a system of status, and, therefore, presumably fits into such a social system, but does not fit into a system of a different kind. It is at present visibly breaking down in modern civilised communities, apparently because it is at variance with the most ancient habits of thought of the race, as well as with the exigencies of a peaceful, industrial mode of life. There may seem some ground for holding that the same reassertion of ancient habits of thought which is now apparently at work to disintegrate the institution of ownership-marriage may be expected also to work a disintegration of the correlative institution of private property; but that is perhaps a question of speculative curiosity rather than of urgent theoretical interest.

# THE ECONOMIC THEORY OF
# WOMAN'S DRESS [1]

In human apparel the element of dress is readily distinguishable from that of clothing. The two functions—of dress and of clothing the person—are to a great extent subserved by the same material goods, although the extent to which the same material serves both purposes will appear very much slighter on second thought than it does at first glance. A differentiation of materials has long been going on, by virtue of which many things that are worn for the one purpose no longer serve, and are no longer expected to serve, the other. The differentiation is by no means complete. Much of human apparel is worn both for physical comfort and for dress; still more of it is worn ostensibly for both purposes. But the differentiation is already very considerable and is visibly progressing.

But, however united in the same object, however the two purposes may be served by the same material goods, the purpose of physical comfort and that of a reputable appearance are not to be confounded by the meanest understanding. The elements of clothing and of dress are distinct; not only that, but they even verge on incompatibility; the purpose of either is frequently best subserved by special means which are adapted to perform only a single line of duty. It is often true, here as elsewhere, that the most efficient tool is the most highly specialised tool.

[1] Reprinted from *Popular Science Monthly*, Vol. XLVI, November, 1894.

Of these two elements of apparel dress came first in order of development, and it continues to hold the primacy to this day. The element of clothing, the quality of affording comfort, was from the beginning, and to a great extent it continues to be, in some sort an afterthought.

The origin of dress is sought in the principle of adornment. This is a well-accepted fact of social evolution. But that principle furnished the point of departure for the evolution of dress rather than the norm of its development. It is true of dress, as of so much else of the apparatus of life, that its initial purpose has not remained its sole or dominant purpose throughout the course of its later growth. It may be stated broadly that adornment, in the *naïve* æsthetic sense, is a factor of relatively slight importance in modern dress.

The line of progress during the initial stage of the evolution of apparel was from the simple concept of adornment of the person by supplementary accessions from without, to the complex concept of an adornment that should render the person pleasing, or of an enviable presence, and at the same time serve to indicate the possession of other virtues than that of a well-favored person only. In this latter direction lies what was to evolve into dress. By the time dress emerged from the primitive efforts of the savage to beautify himself with gaudy additions to his person, it was already an economic factor of some importance. The change from a purely æsthetic character (ornament) to a mixture of the æsthetic and economic took place before the progress had been achieved from pigments and trinkets to what is commonly understood by apparel. Ornament is not properly an economic category, although the trinkets which serve the purpose of ornament may also do duty as an economic factor, and in so far be assimilated to dress. What constitutes dress an economic fact, properly falling within the scope of economic theory, is its function as an index of the wealth of its wearer—or, to be more precise, of its owner, for the wearer and owner are not necessarily the same person. It will hold with respect to more than one half the values currently recognised as "dress," especially that portion with which this paper is immediately concerned—woman's dress—that the wearer and the owner are different persons. But while they need not be united in the same person, they must be organic members of the same economic unit; and the dress is the index of the wealth of the economic unit which the wearer represents.

Under the patriarchal organisation of society, where the social unit was the man (with his dependents), the dress of the women was an exponent of the wealth of the man whose chattels they were. In modern society, where the unit is the household, the woman's dress sets forth the wealth of the household to which she belongs. Still, even today, in spite of the nominal and somewhat celebrated demise of the patriarchal idea, there is that about the dress of women which suggests that the wearer is something in the nature of a chattel; indeed, the theory of woman's dress quite plainly involves the implication that the woman is a chattel. In this respect the dress of women differs from that of men. With this exception, which is not of first-rate importance, the essential principles of woman's dress are not different from those which govern the dress of men; but even apart from this added characteristic the element of dress is to be seen in a more unhampered development in the apparel of women. A discussion of the theory of dress in general will gain in brevity and conciseness by keeping in view the con-

crete facts of the highest manifestation of the principles
with which it has to deal, and this highest manifestation
of dress is unquestionably seen in the apparel of the
women of the most advanced modern communities.

The basis of the award of social rank and popular
respect is the success, or more precisely the efficiency, of
the social unit, as evidenced by its visible success. When
efficiency eventuates in possessions, in pecuniary
strength, as it eminently does in the social system of our
time, the basis of the award of social consideration becomes the visible pecuniary strength of the social unit.
The immediate and obvious index of pecuniary strength
is the visible ability to spend, to consume unproductively;
and men early learned to put in evidence their ability to
spend by displaying costly goods that afford no return to
their owner, either in comfort or in gain. Almost as early
did a differentiation set in, whereby it became the function of woman, in a peculiar degree, to exhibit the pecuniary strength of her social unit by means of a conspicuously unproductive consumption of valuable goods.

Reputability is in the last analysis, and especially in the
long run, pretty fairly coincident with the pecuniary
strength of the social unit in question. Woman, primarily, originally because she was herself a pecuniary
possession, has become in a peculiar way the exponent of
the pecuniary strength of her social group; and with
the progress of specialisation of functions in the social
organism this duty tends to devolve more and more entirely upon the woman. The best, most advanced, most
highly developed societies of our time have reached the
point in their evolution where it has (ideally) become
the great, peculiar, and almost the sole function of woman
in the social system to put in evidence her economic
unit's ability to pay. That is to say, woman's place (ac-

cording to the ideal scheme of our social system) has come to be that of a means of conspicuously unproductive expenditure.

The admissible evidence of the woman's expensiveness has considerable range in respect of form and method, but in substance it is always the same. It may take the form of manners, breeding, and accomplishments that are, *prima facie,* impossible to acquire or maintain without such leisure as bespeaks a considerable and relatively long-continued possession of wealth. It may also express itself in a peculiar manner of life, on the same grounds and with much the same purpose. But the method in vogue always and everywhere, alone or in conjunction with other methods, is that of dress. "Dress," therefore, from the economic point of view, comes pretty near being synonymous with "display of wasteful expenditure."

The extra portion of butter, or other unguent, with which the wives of the magnates of the African interior anoint their persons, beyond what comfort requires, is a form of this kind of expenditure lying on the border between primitive personal embellishment and incipient dress. So also the brass-wire bracelets, anklets, etc., at times aggregating some thirty pounds in weight, worn by the same class of persons, as well as, to a less extent, by the male population of the same countries. So also the pelt of the arctic fur seal, which the women of civilised countries prefer to fabrics that are preferable to it in all respects but that of expense. So also the ostrich plumes and the many curious effigies of plants and animals that are dealt in by the milliners. The list is inexhaustible, for there is scarcely an article of apparel of male or female, civilised or uncivilised, that does not partake largely of this element, and very many may be said, in point of economic principle, to consist of virtually nothing else.

It is not that the wearers or the buyers of these wasteful goods desire the waste. They desire to make manifest their ability to pay. What is sought is not the *de facto* waste, but the appearance of waste. Hence there is a constant effort on the part of the consumers of these goods to obtain them at as good a bargain as may be; and hence also a constant effort on the part of the producers of these goods to lower the cost of their production, and consequently to lower the price. But as fast as the price of the goods declines to such a figure that their consumption is no longer *prima facie* evidence of a considerable ability to pay, the particular goods in question fall out of favor, and consumption is diverted to something which more adequately manifests the wearer's ability to afford wasteful consumption.

This fact, that the object sought is not the waste but the display of waste, develops into a principle of pseudo-economy in the use of material; so that it has come to be recognised as a canon of good form that apparel should not show lavish expenditure simply. The material used must be chosen so as to give evidence of the wearer's (owner's) capacity for making it go as far in the way of display as may be; otherwise it would suggest incapacity on the part of the owner, and so partially defeat the main purpose of the display. But what is more to the point is that such a mere display of crude waste would also suggest that the means of display had been acquired so recently as not to have permitted that long-continued waste of time and effort required for mastering the most effective methods of display. It would argue recent acquisition of means; and we are still near enough to the tradition of pedigree and aristocracy of birth to make long-continued possession of means second in point of desirability only to the possession of large means. The greatness of the means possessed is manifested by the volume of display; the length of possession is, in some degree, evidenced by the manifestation of a thorough habituation to the methods of display. Evidence of a knowledge and habit of good form in dress (as in manners) is chiefly to be valued because it argues that much time has been spent in the acquisition of this accomplishment; and as the accomplishment is in no wise of direct economic value, it argues pecuniary ability to waste time and labor. Such accomplishment, therefore, when possessed in a high degree, is evidence of a life (or of more than one life) spent to no useful purpose; which, for purposes of respectability, goes as far as a very considerable unproductive consumption of goods. The offensiveness of crude taste and vulgar display in matters of dress is, in the last analysis, due to the fact that they argue the absence of ability to afford a reputable amount of waste of time and effort.

Effective use of the means at hand may, further, be taken to argue efficiency in the person making the display; and the display of efficiency, so long as it does not manifestly result in pecuniary gain or increased personal comfort, is a great social desideratum. Hence it happens that, surprising as it may seem at first glance, a principle of pseudo-economy in the use of materials has come to hold a well-secured though pretty narrowly circumscribed place in the theory of dress, as that theory expresses itself in the facts of life. This principle, acting in concert with certain other requirements of dress, produces some curious and otherwise inexplicable results, which will be spoken of in their place.

The first principle of dress, therefore, is conspicuous

expensiveness. As a corollary under this principle, but of such magnificent scope and consequence as to claim rank as a second fundamental principle, there is the evidence of expenditure afforded by a constant supersession of one wasteful garment or trinket by a new one. This principle inculcates the desirability, amounting to a necessity wherever circumstances allow, of wearing nothing that is out of date. In the most advanced communities of our time, and so far as concerns the highest manifestations of dress—e.g., in ball dress and the apparel worn on similar ceremonial occasions, when the canons of dress rule unhampered by extraneous considerations—this principle expresses itself in the maxim that no outer garment may be worn more than once.

This requirement of novelty is the underlying principle of the whole of the difficult and interesting domain of fashion. Fashion does not demand continual flux and change simply because that way of doing is foolish; flux and change and novelty are demanded by the central principle of all dress—conspicuous waste.

This principle of novelty, acting in concert with the motive of pseudo-economy already spoken of, is answerable for that system of shams that figures so largely, openly and aboveboard, in the accepted code of dress. The motive of economy, or effective use of material, furnishes the point of departure, and, this being given, the requirement of novelty acts to develop a complex and extensive system of pretenses, ever varying and transient in point of detail, but each imperative during its allotted time—facings, edgings, and the many (pseudo) deceptive contrivances that will occur to any one that is at all familiar with the technique of dress. This pretense of deception is often developed into a pathetic, childlike make-believe. The realities which it simulates, or rather symbolises, could not be tolerated. They would be in some cases too crudely expensive, in others inexpensive and more nearly adapted to minister to personal comfort than to visible expense; and either alternative is obnoxious to the canons of good form.

But apart from the exhibition of pecuniary strength afforded by an aggressive wasteful expenditure, the same purpose may also be served by conspicuous abstention from useful effort. The woman is, by virtue of the specialisation of social functions, the exponent of the economic unit's pecuniary strength, and it consequently also devolves on her to exhibit the unit's capacity to endure this passive form of pecuniary damage. She can do this by putting in evidence the fact (often a fiction) that she leads a useless life. Dress is her chief means of doing so. The ideal of dress, on this head, is to demonstrate to all observers, and to compel observation of the fact, that the wearer is manifestly incapable of doing anything that is of any use. The modern civilised woman's dress attempts this demonstration of habitual idleness, and succeeds measurably.

Herein lies the secret of the persistence, in modern dress, of the skirt and of all the cumbrous and otherwise meaningless drapery which the skirt typifies. The skirt persists because it is cumbrous. It hampers the movements of the wearer and disables her, in great measure, for any useful occupation. So it serves as an advertisement (often disingenuous) that the wearer is backed by sufficient means to be able to afford the idleness, or impaired efficiency, which the skirt implies. The like is true of the high heel, and in less degree of several other features of modern dress.

Herein is also to be sought the ground of the persistence (probably not the origin) of the one great mutilation practiced by civilised occidental womankind—the constricted waist, as well as of the analogous practice of the abortive foot among their Chinese sisters. This modern mutilation of woman is perhaps not to be classed strictly under the category of dress; but it is scarcely possible to draw the line so as to exclude it from the theory, and it is so closely coincident with that category in point of principle that an outline of the theory would be incomplete without reference to it.

A corollary of some significance follows from this general principle. The fact that voluntarily accepted physical incapacity argues the possession of wealth practically establishes the futility of any attempted reform of woman's dress in the direction of convenience, comfort, or health. It is of the essence of dress that it should (appear to) hamper, incommode, and injure the wearer, for in so doing it proclaims the wearer's pecuniary ability to endure idleness and physical incapacity.

It may be noted, by the way, that this requirement, that women must appear to be idle in order to be respectable, is an unfortunate circumstance for women who are compelled to provide their own livelihood. They have to supply not only the means of living, but also the means of advertising the fiction that they live without any gainful occupation; and they have to do all this while encumbered with garments specially designed to hamper their movements and decrease their industrial efficiency.

The cardinal principles of the theory of woman's dress, then, are these three:

1. Expensiveness: Considered with respect to its effectiveness as clothing, apparel must be uneconomical. It must afford evidence of the ability of the wearer's economic group to pay for things that are in themselves of no use to any one concerned—to pay without getting an

equivalent in comfort or in gain. From this principle there is no exception.

2. Novelty: Woman's apparel must afford *prima facie* evidence of having been worn but for a relatively short time, as well as, with respect to many articles, evidence of inability to withstand any appreciable amount of wear. Exceptions from this rule are such things as are of sufficient permanence to become heirlooms, and of such surpassing expensiveness as normally to be possessed only by persons of superior (pecuniary) rank. The possession of an heirloom is to be commended because it argues the practice of waste through more than one generation.

3. Ineptitude: It must afford *prima facie* evidence of incapacitating the wearer for any gainful occupation; and it should also make it apparent that she is permanently unfit for any useful effort, even after the restraint of the apparel is removed. From this rule there is no exception.

Besides these three, the principle of adornment, in the æsthetic sense, plays some part in dress. It has a certain degree of economic importance, and applies with a good deal of generality; but it is by no means imperatively present, and when it is present its application is closely circumscribed by the three principles already laid down. Indeed, the office of the principle of adornment in dress is that of handmaid to the principle of novelty, rather than that of an independent or co-ordinate factor. There are, further, minor principles that may or may not be present, some of which are derivatives of the great central requisite of conspicuous waste; others are of alien origin, but all are none the less subject to the controlling presence of the three cardinal principles enumerated above. These three are essential and constitute the sub-

stantial norm of woman's dress, and no exigency ca⊔
permanently set them aside so long as the chance of
rivalry between persons in respect of wealth remains.
Given the possibility of a difference in wealth, and the
sway of this norm of dress is inevitable. Some spasm of
sense, or sentiment, or what not, may from time to time
create a temporary and local diversion in woman's apparel; but the great norm of "conspicuous waste" cannot
be set aside or appreciably qualified so long as this its
economic ground remains.

To single out an example of the temporary effect of
a given drift of sentiment, there has, within the past few
years, come, and very nearly gone, a recrudescence of the
element of physical comfort of the wearer, as one of the
usual requirements of good form in dress. The meaning
of this proposition, of course, is not what appears on its
face; that seldom happens in matters of dress. It was the
show of personal comfort that was lately imperative, and
the show was often attained only at the sacrifice of the
substance. This development, by the way, seems to have
been due to a ramification of the sentimental athleticism
(flesh-worship) that has been dominant of late; and
now that the crest of this wave of sentiment has passed,
this alien motive in dress is also receding.

The theory of which an outline has now been given is
claimed to apply in full force only to modern woman's
dress. It is obvious that, if the principles arrived at are
to be applied as all-deciding criteria, "woman's dress"
will include the apparel of a large class of persons who,
in the crude biological sense, are men. This feature does
not act to invalidate the theory. A classification for the
purpose of economic theory must be made on economic
grounds alone, and cannot permit considerations whose
validity does not extend beyond the narrower domain of

the natural sciences to mar its symmetry so far as to exclude this genial volunteer contingent from the ranks of womankind.

There is also a second, very analogous class of persons, whose apparel likewise, though to a less degree, conforms to the canons of woman's dress. This class is made up of the children of civilised society. The children, with some slight reservation of course, are, for the purpose of the theory, to be regarded as ancillary material serving to round out the great function of civilised womankind as the conspicuous consumers of goods. The child in the hands of civilised woman is an accessory organ of conspicuous consumption, much as any tool in the hands of a laborer is an accessory organ of productive efficiency.

# THE INSTINCT OF WORKMANSHIP AND
# THE IRKSOMENESS OF LABOR [1]

IT is one of the commonplaces of the received economic theory that work is irksome. Many a discussion proceeds on this axiom that, so far as regards economic matters, men desire above all things to get the goods produced by labor and to avoid the labor by which the goods are produced. In a general way the common-sense opinion is well in accord with current theory on this head. According to the common-sense ideal, the economic beatitude lies in an unrestrained consumption of goods, without work; whereas the perfect economic affliction is unremunerated labor. Man instinctively revolts at effort that goes to supply the means of life.

No one will accept the proposition when stated in this bald fashion, but even as it stands it is scarcely an over-statement of what is implied in the writings of eminent economists. If such an aversion to useful effort is an integral part of human nature, then the trail of the Edenic serpent should be plain to all men, for this is a unique distinction of the human species. A consistent aversion to whatever activity goes to maintain the life of the species is assuredly found in no other species of animal. Under the selective process through which species are held to have emerged and gained their stability there is no chance for the survival of a species gifted with such an aversion to the furtherance of its

[1] Reprinted from *The American Journal of Sociology*, Vol. IV, September, 1898.

own life process. If man alone is an exception from the selective norm, then the alien propensity in question must have been intruded into his make-up by some malevolent *deus ex machina.*

Yet, for all the apparent absurdity of the thing, there is the fact. With more or less sincerity, people currently avow an aversion to useful effort. The avowal does not cover all effort, but only such as is of some use; it is, more particularly, such effort as is vulgarly recognised to be useful labor. Less repugnance is expressed as regards effort which brings gain without giving a product that is of human use, as, for example, the effort that goes into war, politics, or other employments of a similar nature. And there is commonly no avowed aversion to sports or other similar employments that yield neither a pecuniary gain nor a useful product. Still, the fact that a given line of effort is useless does not of itself save it from being odious, as is shown by the case of menial service; much of this work serves no useful end, but it is none the less repugnant to all people of sensibility.

"The economic man," whose lineaments were traced in outline by the classical economists and filled in by their caricaturists, is an anomaly in the animal world; and yet, to judge by everyday popular expressions of inclination, the portrait is not seriously overdrawn. But if this economic man is to serve as a lay figure upon which to fit the garment of economic doctrines, it is incumbent upon the science to explain what are his limitations and how he has achieved his emancipation from the law of natural selection. His emancipation from the law is, indeed, more apparent than substantial. The difference in this respect between man and his sometime competitors in the struggle for survival lies not in a slighter but in a fuller adjustment of his propensities to the purposes of

the life of the species. He distanced them all in this respect long ago, and by so wide an interval that he is now
able, without jeopardy to the life of the species, to play
fast and loose with the spiritual basis of its survival.

Like other animals, man is an agent that acts in response to stimuli afforded by the environment in which
he lives. Like other species, he is a creature of habit and
propensity. But in a higher degree than other species,
man mentally digests the content of the habits under
whose guidance he acts, and appreciates the trend of
these habits and propensities. He is in an eminent sense
an intelligent agent. By selective necessity he is endowed
with a proclivity for purposeful action. He is possessed
of a discriminating sense of purpose, by force of which
all futility of life or of action is distasteful to him.
There may be a wide divergence between individuals as
regards the form and the direction in which this impulse
expresses itself, but the impulse itself is not a matter of
idiosyncrasy, it is a generic feature of human nature. It
is not a trait that occurs sporadically in a few individuals.
Cases occur in which this proclivity for purposeful action is wanting or is present in obviously scant measure,
but persons endowed in this stepmotherly fashion are
classed as "defective subjects." Lines of descent which
carry this defective human nature dwindle and decay
even under the propitious circumstances of modern life.
The history of hereditarily dependent or defective
families is evidence to this effect.

Man's great advantage over other species in the
struggle for survival has been his superior facility in
turning the forces of the environment to account. It is
to his proclivity for turning the material means of life to
account that he owes his position as lord of creation. It is

not a proclivity to effort, but to achievement—to the compassing of an end. His primacy is in the last resort an industrial or economic primacy. In his economic life man is an agent, not an absorbent; he is an agent seeking in every act the accomplishment of some concrete, objective, impersonal end. As this pervading norm of action guides the life of men in all the use they make of material things, so it must also serve as the point of departure and afford the guiding principle for any science that aims to be a theory of the economic life process. Within the purview of economic theory, the last analysis of any given phenomenon must run back to this ubiquitous human impulse to do the next thing.

All this seems to contradict what has just been said of the conventional aversion to labor. But the contradiction is not so sheer in fact as it appears to be at first sight. Its solution lies in the fact that the aversion to labor is in great part a conventional aversion only. In the intervals of sober reflection, when not harassed with the strain of overwork, men's common-sense speaks unequivocally under the guidance of the instinct of workmanship. They like to see others spend their life to some purpose, and they like to reflect that their own life is of some use. All men have this quasi-æsthetic sense of economic or industrial merit, and to this sense of economic merit futility and inefficiency are distasteful. In its positive expression it is an impulse or instinct of workmanship; negatively it expresses itself in a deprecation of waste. This sense of merit and demerit with respect to the material furtherance or hindrance of life approves the economically effective act and deprecates economic futility. It is needless to point out in detail the close relation between this norm of economic merit and the ethical norm of conduct, on the one hand, and the æsthetic norm of taste, on the other. It is very closely related to both of these, both as regards its biological ground and as regards the scope and method of its award.

This instinct of workmanship apparently stands in sheer conflict with the conventional antipathy to useful effort. The two are found together in full discord in the common run of men; but whenever a deliberate judgment is passed on conduct or on events, the former asserts its primacy in a pervasive way which suggests that it is altogether the more generic, more abiding trait of human nature. There can scarcely be a serious question of precedence between the two. The former is a human trait necessary to the survival of the species; the latter is a habit of thought possible only in a species which has distanced all competitors, and then it prevails only by sufferance and within limits set by the former. The question between them is, Is the aversion to labor a derivative of the instinct of workmanship? and, How has it arisen and gained consistency in spite of its being at variance with that instinct?

Until recently there has been something of a consensus among those who have written on early culture, to the effect that man, as he first emerged upon the properly human plane, was of a contentious disposition, inclined to isolate his own interest and purposes from those of his fellows, and with a penchant for feuds and brawls. Accordingly, even where the view is met with that men are by native proclivity inclined to action, there is still evident a presumption that this native proclivity to action is a proclivity to action of a destructive kind. It is held that men are inclined to fight, not to work—that the end of action in the normal case is damage rather than repair. This view would make the proclivity to purposeful action an impulse to sportsmanship rather than to workmanship. In any attempt to fit this view into an evolutionary scheme of culture it would carry the implication that in the prehuman or proto-anthropoid phase of its life the race was a predacious species, and that the initial phase of human culture, as well as the later cultural development, has been substantially of a predatory kind.

There is much to be said for this view. If mankind is by derivation a race not of workmen but of sportsmen, then there is no need of explaining the conventional aversion to work. Work is unsportsmanlike and therefore distasteful, and perplexity then arises in explaining how men have in any degree become reconciled to any but a predacious life. Apart from the immediate convenience of this view, it is also enforced by much evidence. Most peoples at a lower stage of culture than our own are of a more predatory habit than our people. The history of mankind, as conventionally written, has been a narrative of predatory exploits, and this history is not commonly felt to be one-sided or misinformed. And a sportsmanlike inclination to warfare is also to be found in nearly all modern communities. Similarly, the sense of honor, so-called, whether it is individual or national honor, is also an expression of sportsmanship. The prevalence of notions of honor may, therefore, be taken as evidence going in the same direction. And as if to further fortify the claim of sportsmanship to antiquity and prescriptive standing, the sense of honor is also noticeably more vivid in communities of a somewhat more archaic culture than our own.

Yet there is a considerable body of evidence, both from cultural history and from the present-day phenomena of human life, which traverses this conventionally accepted view that makes man generically a sportsman. Obscurely but persistently, throughout the history of human culture, the great body of the people have almost everywhere, in their everyday life, been at work to turn things to human use. The proximate aim of all industrial improvement has been the better performance of some workmanlike task. Necessarily this work has, on the one hand, proceeded on the basis of an appreciative interest in the work to be done; for there is no other ground on which to obtain anything better than the aimless performance of a task. And necessarily also, on the other hand, the discipline of work has acted to develop a workmanlike attitude. It will not do to say that the work accomplished is entirely due to compulsion under a predatory régime, for the most striking advances in this respect have been wrought where the coercive force of a sportsmanlike exploitation has been least.

The same view is borne out by the expressions of common-sense. As has already been remarked, whenever they dispassionately take thought and pass a judgment on the value of human conduct, the common run of mature men approve workmanship rather than sportsmanship. At the best, they take an apologetic attitude toward the latter. This is well seen in the present (May, 1898) disturbance of the popular temper. While it may well be granted that the warlike raid upon which this community is entering is substantially an access of sportsmanlike exaltation, it is to be noticed that nearly all those who speak for war are at pains to find some colorable motive of another kind. Predatory exploit, simply as such, is not felt to carry its own legitimation, as it should in the apprehension of any species that is primarily of a predacious character. What meets unreserved approval is such conduct as furthers human life on the whole, rather than such as furthers the invidious or predatory interest of one as against another.

efficiency, both as regards men's physical and mental traits and as regards their spiritual attitude.

By selection and by training, the life of man, before a predacious life became possible, would act to develop and to conserve in him an instinct for workmanship. The adaptation to the environment which the situation enforced was of an industrial kind; it required men to acquire facility in shaping things and situations for human use. This does not mean the shaping of things by the individual to his own individual use simply; for archaic man was necessarily a member of a group, and during this early stage, when industrial efficiency was still inconsiderable, no group could have survived except on the basis of a sense of solidarity strong enough to throw self-interest into the background. Self-interest, as an accepted guide of action, is possible only as the concomitant of a predatory life, and a predatory life is possible only after the use of tools has developed so far as to leave a large surplus of product over what is required for the sustenance of the producers. Subsistence by predation implies something substantial to prey upon.

Early man was a member of a group which depended for its survival on the industrial efficiency of its members and on their singleness of purpose in making use of the material means at hand. Some competition between groups for the possession of the fruits of the earth and for advantageous locations there would be even at a relatively early stage, but much hostile contact between groups there could not be; not enough to shape the dominant habits of thought.

What men can do easily is what they do habitually, and this decides what they can think and know easily. They feel at home in the range of ideas which is familiar through their everyday line of action. A habitual line of action constitutes a habitual line of thought, and gives the point of view from which facts and events are apprehended and reduced to a body of knowledge. What is consistent with the habitual course of action is consistent with the habitual line of thought, and gives the definitive ground of knowledge as well as the conventional standard of complacency or approval in any community. Conversely, a process or method of life, once understood, assimilated in thought, works into the scheme of life and becomes a norm of conduct, simply because the thinking, knowing agent is also the acting agent. What is apprehended with facility and is consistent with the process of life and knowledge is thereby apprehended as right and good. All this applies with added force where the habituation is not simply individual and sporadic, but is enforced upon the group or the race by a selective elimination of those individuals and lines of descent that do not conform to the required canon of knowledge and conduct. When this takes place, the acquired proclivity passes from the status of habit to that of aptitude or propensity. It becomes a transmissible trait, and action under its guidance becomes right and good, and the longer and more consistent the selective adaptation through which the aptitude arises, the more firmly is the resulting aptitude settled upon the race, and the more unquestioned becomes the sanction of the resulting canon of conduct.

So far as regards his relation to the material means of life, the canon of thought and of conduct which was in this way enforced upon early man was what is here called the instinct of workmanship. The interest which men took in economic facts on the basis of this propensity, in the days before spoliation came into vogue, was not primarily of a self-regarding character. The necessary dominance of a sense of group solidarity would preclude that. The selective process must eliminate lines of descent unduly gifted with a self-regarding bias. Still, there was some emulation between individuals, even in the most indigent and most peaceable groups. From the readiness with which a scheme of emulation is entered upon where late circumstances favor its development, it seems probable that the proclivity to emulation must have been present also in the earlier days in sufficient force to assert itself to the extent to which the exigencies of the earlier life of the group would permit. But this emulation could not run in the direction of an individual acquisition or accumulation of goods, or of a life consistently given to raids and tumults. It would be emulation such as is found among the peaceable gregarious-animals generally; that is to say, it was primarily and chiefly sexual emulation, recurring with more or less regularity. Beyond this there must also have been some wrangling in the distribution of goods on hand, but neither this nor the rivalry for subsistence could have been the dominant note of life.

Under the canon of conduct imposed by the instinct of workmanship, efficiency, serviceability, commends itself, and inefficiency or futility is odious. Man contemplates his own conduct and that of his neighbors, and passes a judgment of complacency or of dispraise. The degree of effectiveness with which he lives up to the accepted standard of efficiency in great measure determines his contentment with himself and his situation. A wide or persistent discrepancy in this respect is a source of abounding spiritual discomfort.

Judgment may in this way be passed on the intention

of the agent or on the serviceability of the act. In the former case the award of merit or demerit is to be classed as moral; and with award of merit of this kind this paper is not concerned. As regards serviceability or efficiency, men do not only take thought at first hand of the facts of their own conduct; they are also sensitive to rebuke or approval from others. Not only is the immediate consciousness of the achievement of a purpose gratifying and stimulating, but the imputation of efficiency by one's fellows is perhaps no less gratifying or stimulating.

Sensitiveness to rebuke or approval is a matter of selective necessity under the circumstances of associated life. Without it no group of men could carry on a collective life in a material environment that requires shaping to the ends of man. In this respect, again, man shows a spiritual relationship with the gregarious animals rather than with the solitary beasts of prey.

Under the guidance of this taste for good work, men are compared with one another and with the accepted ideals of efficiency, and are rated and graded by the common-sense of their fellows according to a conventional scheme of merit and demerit. The imputation of efficiency necessarily proceeds on evidence of efficiency. The visible achievement of one man is, therefore, compared with that of another, and the award of esteem comes habitually to rest on an invidious comparison of persons instead of on the immediate bearing of the given line of conduct upon the approved end of action. The ground of esteem in this way shifts from a direct appreciation of the expediency of conduct to a comparison of the abilities of different agents. Instead of a valuation of serviceability, there is a gauging of capability on the ground of visible success. And what comes to be compared in an invidious comparison of this kind between agents is the force which the agent is able to put forth, rather than the serviceability of the agent's conduct. So soon, therefore, and in so far, as the esteem awarded to serviceability passes into an invidious esteem of one agent as compared with another, the end sought in action will tend to change from naïve expediency to the manifestation of capacity or force. It becomes the proximate end of effort to put forth evidence of power, rather than to achieve an impersonal end for its own sake, simply as an item of human use. So that, while in its more immediate expression the norm of economic taste stands out as an impulse to workmanship or a taste for serviceability and a distaste for futility, under given circumstances of associated life it comes in some degree to take on the character of an emulative demonstration of force.

Since the imputation of efficiency and of invidious merit goes on the evidence afforded by visible success, the appearance of evil must be avoided in order to escape dispraise. In the early savage culture, while the group is small and while the conditions favorable to a predatory life are still wanting, the resulting emulation between the members of the group runs chiefly to industrial efficiency. It comes to be the appearance of industrial incapacity that is to be avoided. It is in this direction that force or capacity can be put in evidence most consistently and with the best effect for the good name of the individual. It is, therefore, in this direction that a standard of merit and a canon of meritorious conduct will develop. But even for a growth of emulation in the productive use of brain and muscle, the small, rude, peaceable group of savages is not fertile ground. The situation does not favor a vigorous emulative spirit. The conditions favorable to the growth of a habit of emulative demonstration of force are (1) the frequent recurrence of conjunctures that call for a great and sudden strain, and (2) exposure of the individual to a large, and especially to a shifting, human environment whose approval is sought. These conditions are not effectually met on the lower levels of savagery, such as human culture must have been during the early days of the use of tools. Accordingly, relatively little of the emulative spirit is seen in communities that have retained the archaic, peaceable constitution, or that have reverted to it from a higher culture. In such communities a low standard of culture and comfort goes along with an absence of strenuous application to the work in hand, as well as a relative absence of jealousy and gradations of rank. Notions of economic rank and discrimination between persons, whether in point of possessions or in point of comfort, are almost, if not altogether, in abeyance.

With a further development of the use of tools and of human command over the forces of the environment, the habits of life of the savage group change. There is likely to be more of aggression, both in the way of a pursuit of large game and in the way of conflict between groups. As the industrial efficiency of the group increases, and as weapons are brought to greater perfection, the incentives to aggression and the opportunities for achievement along this line increase. The conditions favorable to emulation are more fully met. With the increasing density of population that follows from a heightened industrial efficiency, the group passes, by force of circumstances, from the archaic condition of poverty-stricken peace to a stage of predatory life. This fighting stage—the beginning of barbarism—may involve aggressive predation, or the group may simply be placed on the defensive. One or the other, or both the lines of activity—and commonly both, no doubt—will be forced upon the group, on pain of extermination. This has apparently been the usual course of early social evolution.

When a group emerges into this predatory phase of its development, the employments which most occupy men's attention are employments that involve exploit. The most serious concern of the group, and at the same time the direction in which the most spectacular effect may be achieved by the individual, is conflict with men and beasts. It becomes easy to make a telling comparison between men when their work is a series of exploits carried out against these difficult adversaries or against the formidable movements of the elements. The assertion of the strong hand, successful aggression, usually of a destructive character, becomes the accepted basis of repute. The dominant life interest of the group throws its strong light upon this creditable employment of force and sagacity, and the other, obscurer ways of serving the group's life fall into the background. The guiding animus of the group becomes a militant one, and men's actions are judged from the standpoint of the fighting man. What is recognised, without reflection and without misgiving, as serviceable and effective in such a group is fighting capacity. Exploit becomes the conventional ground of invidious comparison between individuals, and repute comes to rest on prowess.

As the predatory culture reaches a fuller development, there comes a distinction between employments. The tradition of prowess, as the virtue *par excellence,* gains in scope and consistency until prowess comes near being recognised as the sole virtue. Those employments alone are then worthy and reputable which involve the exercise of this virtue. Other employments, in which men are occupied with tamely shaping inert materials to human use, become unworthy and end with becoming debasing. The honorable man must not only show capacity for predatory exploit, but he must also avoid entanglement with the occupations that do not involve exploit. The tame employments, those that involve no obvious destruction of life and no spectacular coercion of refractory antagonists, fall into disrepute and are relegated to those members of the community who are defective in predatory capacity; that is to say, those who are lacking in massiveness, agility, or ferocity. Occupation in these employments argues that the person so occupied falls short of that decent modicum of prowess which would entitle him to be graded as a man in good standing. In order to an unsullied reputation, the appearance of evil must be avoided. Therefore the able-bodied barbarian of the predatory culture, who is at all mindful of his good name, severely leaves all uneventful drudgery to the women and minors of the group. He puts in his time in the manly arts of war and devotes his talents to devising ways and means of disturbing the peace. That way lies honor.

In the barbarian scheme of life the peaceable, industrial employments are women's work. They imply defective force, incapacity for aggression or devastation, and are therefore not of good report. But whatever is accepted as a conventional mark of a shortcoming or a vice comes presently to be accounted intrinsically base. In this way industrial occupations fall under a polite odium and are apprehended to be substantially ignoble. They are unsportsmanlike. Labor carries a taint, and all contamination from vulgar employments must be shunned by self-respecting men.

Where the predatory culture has developed in full consistency, the common-sense apprehension that labor is ignoble has developed into the further refinement that labor is wrong—for those who are not already beneath reproach. Hence certain well-known features of caste and tabu. In the further cultural development, when some wealth has been accumulated and the members of the community fall into a servile class on the one hand and a leisure class on the other, the tradition that labor is ignoble gains an added significance. It is not only a mark of inferior force, but it is also a perquisite of the poor. This is the situation today. Labor is morally impossible by force of the ancient tradition that has come down from early barbarism, and it is shameful by force of its evil association with poverty. It is indecorous.

The irksomeness of labor is a spiritual fact; it lies in the indignity of the thing. The fact of its irksomeness is, of course, none the less real and cogent for its being of a spiritual kind. Indeed, it is all the more substantial and irremediable on that account. Physical irksomeness and distastefulness can be borne, if only the spiritual incentive is present. Witness the attractiveness of warfare, both to the barbarian and to the civilised youth. The most commonplace recital of a campaigner's experience carries a sweeping suggestion of privation, exposure, fatigue, vermin, squalor, sickness, and loathsome death; the incidents and accessories of war are said to be unsavory, unsightly, unwholesome beyond the power of words; yet warfare is an attractive employment if one only is gifted with a suitable habit of mind. Most sports, and many other polite employments that are distressing but creditable, are evidence to the same effect.

Physical irksomeness is an incommodity which men habitually make light of if it is not reinforced by the sanction of decorum; but it is otherwise with the spiritual irksomeness of such labor as is condemned by polite usage. That is a cultural fact. There is no remedy for this kind of irksomeness, short of a subversion of that cultural structure on which our canons of decency rest. Appeal may of course be made to taste and conscience to set aside the conventional aversion to labor; such an appeal is made from time to time by well-meaning and sanguine persons, and some fitful results have been achieved in that way. But the commonplace, common-sense man is bound by the deliverances of common-sense decorum on this head—the heritage of an unbroken cultural line of descent that runs back to the beginning.

# THE ARMY OF THE COMMONWEAL [1]

THE ostensible purpose of the "Army of the Common-weal" has been the creation of a livelihood for a great number of people by means of a creation of employment, to be effected by a creation of capital through the creation of fiat money. That is to say, on the face of it, the heart of the "movement" is an articulate hallucination. In this its elaborate form the hallucination probably holds a secure lodgement only in the minds of a small number of people, including a large part of those who have enrolled themselves in the Army on ground of a serious conviction. By those who have sympathised with and furthered this new-fashioned excursion into the field of economic reform the hallucination probably is rarely harbored in this painstakingly absurd shape. Among the common run of its sympathisers the sentiment with which assent is given to the demonstrations of the Army seems to go no farther, either in its scope or in its elaboration of details, than a general conviction that society owes every honest man a living; but a sentiment going that length certainly has obtained some considerable vogue. How, or under what circumstances, or precisely why "society" is to afford the honest man a livelihood is a thoroughly unprofitable question. The answer, so far, does not go much beyond the general proposition *that* it is to afford it. To the extent to which such a sentiment prevails, even in the vaguest form, it is certainly a

[1] Reprinted from *The Journal of Political Economy,* Vol. II, June, 1894.

sufficiently serious accession to the public sentiment of the community, and a sufficiently striking innovation in the American attitude toward economic questions.

No doubt much of the disturbance is due to demagogism, perhaps more is due to a taste for picturesque adventure and a distaste for serious application to unfamiliar work, and much of the countenance accorded it by outsiders may be less disinterested than would appear at first glance. But the sentiment on which it proceeds must not be conceived to be entirely, or even mainly, spurious. The Army of the Commonweal is a new departure in American methods, whether it is to be considered a departure of grave import or not, and a new departure in any people's manner of life and of looking at things does not come about altogether gratuitously; there must be something more vital than a feigned sentiment behind it. After all deduction is made for the spectacular and the meretricious in this "movement," after allowing for the attraction which it exerts on idlers as a temporary means of subsistence and entertainment, and on the friends of humanity as a means of martyrdom, after allowing for the elements of blackmail and of business shrewdness in the enthusiasm with which these straggling bands have sometimes, especially in the Middle West, been speeded on their way, and for the promptings of discontent that have mingled in the sympathy expressed by outsiders remote from the scene and without personal interest in the demands put forth, there is still left a broad substratum of honest sentiment shared in by an appreciable fraction of the community. What is the economic import of this sentiment?

As near as the bizarre characters in which it is written can yet be deciphered, the message of the Army of the Commonweal says that certain economic concepts are not precisely the same to many people today that they have been to the generation which is passing. "Capital," to this new popular sense, is the "capital" of Karl Marx rather than that of the old-school economists or of the market place. The concept of "property" or of "ownership" is in process of acquiring a flexibility and a limitation that would have puzzled the good American citizen of a generation ago. By what amounts to a subconscious acceptance of Hegelian dialectic it has come about that an increase of a person's wealth, beyond a certain ill-defined point, should not, according to the new canon of equity, be permitted to increase his command over the means of production or the processes which those means serve. Beyond an uncertain point of aggregation, the inviolability of private property, in the new popular conception, declines. In Hegelian phrase, a change in quantity, if it is considerable enough, amounts to a change in kind. A man—still less a corporation—must no longer do what he will with his own, if what is classed as his own appreciably exceeds the average. It is competent for his neighbors to appeal for his guidance to the corporate will of the community, and in default of an expression of the corporate will the neighbors in question may properly act vicariously for the community.

But the content of the new accession to popular sentiment is not exhausted by this question of detail alone. Its scope is more magnificent than petty property relations between one individual and the next. There is a class, shown by the Army of the Commonweal to be larger than was previously apprehended, which is, or has been, drifting away from the old-time holding ground of the constitution. The classic phrase is no longer to read, "life, liberty, and the pursuit of happiness"; what is to be insured to every free-born American citizen under the new dispensation is "life, liberty, and the *means of happiness*." The economic significance of this change of attitude, if the new habit of mind should spread so far as to become the dominant attitude of an effective majority of the American people, is tremendous. It means the difference between the civil republic of the nineteenth century and the industrial republic of the socialists, with the gradual submergence of private initiative under the rising claims of industrial solidarity. But whether any sweeping change of this nature will, or can, come, is extremely doubtful. In order to a continued growth of the sentiment it is necessary that experience should prove the feasibility of paternalism, or socialism, on a scale that is not borne out by the experience of the past.

And the appeal from individual initiative and responsibility is not taken to the local civil body as would have been expected to happen if an analogous disturbance had occurred at any time in the past. The industrial solidarity that is assumed is not a solidarity and autonomy of the local unit. The movement does not contemplate an application of the principle of the town-meeting to solve an economic difficulty. It is not an appeal to local self-help; it is an appeal to Cæsar. These individual unemployed men, whether out of employment by preference or by force of circumstances, are acting on "a wild surmise" that they individually stand in some direct, vital economic relation to the general government, and through the general government to all the rest of the community, without intermediation of any lower or local body. These men disregard the fact of local units and local relations with a facility which bespeaks their complete emancipation from the traditions of local self-government. If the industrial republic is to be floated in

on the wave of sentiment which has carried the Army
of the Commonweal, it will not be the anarchist republic
of autonomous communes held together in a lax and
dubious federation.

It may seem a sweeping generalisation to say that this
attitude is but an expression of the fact latterly emerging into popular consciousness, that the entire community is a single industrial organism, whose integration is
advancing day by day, regardless of any traditional or
conventional boundary lines or demarcations, whether
between classes or between localities. The biologist
might, perhaps, name the process "economic cephalisa-
tion." The aberrations, in which this consciousness—or
half-consciousness—of an increasing industrial coherence is expressing itself, must not be allowed to mask the
significance of the great substantial fact whose distorted
expression they are. That the expression of the fact has
taken a form so nearly farcical is something for which
society may be indebted to the influence of protectionism,
or populism, or to the ethical and the clerical economists
and sociologists, or to any other of the ramifications of
the paternalistic tree of life; but the substance, upon
which these deft artificers may have imposed a vicious
form, has been furnished by the situation. This substratum of sentiment is, as popular sentiment must be, the
product of the environment acting upon the average intelligence available in the community at the time. An intellectually undisciplined populace, especially when under
the guidance of leaders whose prime qualification for
leadership in an intellectual crusade is an intense and
comprehensive sympathy, may not, at the first stroke,
achieve what will prove a tenable theory of the facts
whose presence has stimulated the movement of their
brain; but in no community does an appreciably large

class take a new attitude toward a question of public concern without the provocation of a change in the situation of the community, or of some considerable portion of it.

The result, in the way of public sentiment, wrought out by the action of the environment upon the average intelligence may, within limits, be readily shaped by well-meaning advocates of any doctrine which purports to solve all new questions that arise and remedy all defects that come into view as the economic structure of society grows and changes form. The spell of the bearer of a universal solvent is irresistible, at least until his nostrum has repeatedly failed in the test, or until the generation which has given it credence is dead. Now, we have had at least three lines of professedly infallible hortatory instruction converging upon this point in popular belief. As between these three, the priority in point of the date of its advent into popular teaching, as well as in point of naïveté, belongs to the column which upholds the two-fold principle of fiat money (greenbackism, bimetallism) and of fiat prosperity (protectionism). Second, there is a cloud of witnesses, the gentler-mannered spokesmen of the pulpit, whose discourse runs upon the duties of the rich toward the poor, and of rulers toward their subjects—the duty of a "superior" towards an "inferior" class; these bear testimony to the strength and beauty of the patriarchal relation—the Spencerian relation of *status*. Third, there is the cis-Atlantic line of the Socialists of the Chair, whose point of departure is the divine right of the state; whose catchword is: "Look to the state"; whose maxim of political wisdom is: "The state can do no wrong." A few decades ago these phrases read: "The king," where they now read, "The state." This change of phraseology marks a step in the evolution of language, *et præterea nihil.* The spirit remains the same as ever. It is the spirit of loyalty, petition, and submission to a vicarious providence. This position has been euphemistically termed State Socialism, but it is, in principle, related to Socialism as the absolute monarchy is to the republic. These three variants of paternalism have had the public ear, and have constituted themselves guides and interpreters to the public intelligence during the period in which the increasing coherence and interdependence within the economic organism has been coming into view, and the result is what we see. The ingrained sense and practical tact of the American people (or rather of a fraction of it) have been blurred into reflecting an uncertain image of industrial paternalism. But with it all goes a valuable acquisition in the shape of a crude appreciation of the most striking and characteristic fact in modern industrial evolution.

The changed attitude on an economic question, of which many occurrences connected with the Army of the Commonweal are an evidence, is in substance due to a cumulative organic change in the constitution of the industrial community—a change which may, or may not, be considered to have reached serious proportions; which may, in itself considered, be a change for better or for worse; which may still be in its initial stage or may already have nearly run its course; but in any case it is a change of sufficient magnitude to seek expression, now that the occasion offers. To use a Spencerian phrase, advancing "industrial integration" has gone far enough to obtrude itself as a vital fact upon the consciousness of an appreciable fraction of the common people of the country.

# "THE OVERPRODUCTION FALLACY" [1]

## I

In the April number of this *Journal* Mr. Uriel H. Crocker publishes what purports to be a rehabilitation of the "overproduction" theory of industrial depression. [2] The paper deals specifically with Mill's discussion of the question, and it is particularly Mill's position that is claimed to have been refuted. It may, therefore, not seem ungracious to call to mind that, so long as we employ "demand" and "supply" in the meaning attached to those terms by Mill and commonly accepted by those who are of his way of thinking, the proposition that aggregate demand equals aggregate supply is a truism. General overproduction, as defined by Mill—"a supply of commodities in the aggregate, surpassing the demand" —is a contradiction in terms. Aggregate supply is aggregate demand, neither more nor less.

The above-quoted definition of overproduction occurs in the pages cited from Mill by Mr. Crocker, and can therefore hardly have escaped his notice. But, as it seems not to have furnished any obstacle to the development of Mr. Crocker's argument, the simple calling attention to its significance will hardly be accepted as subverting the position taken by him. Mr. Crocker's position is not a simple, crude denial of Mill's proposition in this general form; but I believe it can be shown that the line of argu-

[1] Reprinted from *The Quarterly Journal of Economics,* Vol. VI, July, 1892.

[2] "The 'Over-Production' Fallacy" by Uriel H. Crocker, Vol. VI, April, 1892.

ment by which that position is supported is no less futile than the naïve overproduction theories that have been laid away by past economic discussion.

To Mr. Crocker's mind, the question as to a possible general overproduction takes form as follows:

Is it possible that there should exist at any time an overproduction of one or more products, unless there is at the same time a corresponding underproduction of some other product or products? In other words, is it possible that one product should be selling for less than the ordinary profit over the cost of its reproduction, unless some other product is at the same time selling at more than the ordinary profit over the cost of its reproduction? (P. 356.)

His answer to this question is the following proposition:

If at any time there is a production of a commodity not based upon and strictly proportioned to the adequate demand for it, but, with the knowledge of the producer, in excess of that demand, then there may at such time be an overproduction of that commodity and no corresponding underproduction of any other commodity. In other words, there may be in such case a general overproduction. (P. 356.)

The final conclusion is stated in this second proposition:

A production of a commodity not based upon and strictly proportioned to the adequate demand for the product, but, with the knowledge of the producer, in excess of that demand, may arise, and has, in some cases, actually arisen, when machinery for the production of the commodity has been created with a capacity of production in excess of the adequate demand for the product. (P. 358.)

The use of the term "adequate demand" is to be noted. "Adequate demand" is "the demand for a commodity at such a value as will afford the ordinary profit over the necessary cost of its reproduction." (P. 355.)

The concept of an "adequate demand" rests on the concept of an "ordinary profit." Now, we can intelligibly speak of adequate demand and ordinary profit without questioning either of those terms, so long as the discussion is concerned with the production of a particular commodity, or with a part, only, of the aggregate of industry. But a closer scrutiny will show that both terms break down when we come to deal with production in the aggregate.

The "ordinary profit," which an adequate demand must cover, is not a satisfactorily definite concept. It may be taken to mean the rate of profit commonly obtainable at the point of time with which the discussion deals, or it may mean the rate of profit that ought to be commonly obtainable at the time, or it may mean the rate of profit commonly obtainable during a more or less indefinite period preceding the time in question. In its colloquial use it has both the latter meanings, mingled in varying proportions. Which of these, or any other possible meaning, Mr. Crocker attaches to the term he does not say. The line of argument pursued by him requires the first of these definitions, or some definition which is like the first above given in being based on the rate of profit actually obtained at the time in question, and, therefore, to a good extent, if not entirely, of the nature of an average of the profits actually obtained.

The ordinary rate of profit, in this sense, notoriously varies from time to time. The variations to which it is subject are due to particular variations in particular occupations. Being of the nature of an average, it varies with the fluctuations of the items that go to make up the average. If, in the manner supposed in Mr. Crocker's first proposition (p. 356), a given commodity comes to be produced at less than the ordinary profit previously obtained, the ordinary profit obtainable thereby suffers a reduction, and, compared with the new ordinary profit therewith established, other commodities are now produced at more than ordinary profit; that is to say, overproduction of one commodity involves, other circumstances remaining unchanged, an underproduction of all other commodities, in the sense attached to "overproduction" by Mr. Crocker. The case supposed by Mr. Crocker resolves itself into a variation in the ordinary rate of profit.

From the general point of view, it is clear that any variation in the rate of profit in any one or more branches of industry, or in the production of any particular commodity, produces a variation, in the same direction, in the ordinary profit obtainable at the time in question, and a consequent divergence of the rate of profit in other occupations, in the opposite direction, from the new "ordinary profit." If the rate of profit in occupation B were to fall, without any change in the absolute rate of profit in occupation A, the ordinary rate of profit obtainable in the aggregate of occupations would fall; and consequently the rate of profit in occupation A would thereby rise, relatively to the altered general rate. The demand which previously was an "adequate demand," and no more, for the product of occupation A, would now have become an over-demand, not, conceivably, because of any change affecting the demand for that product directly, but simply in consequence of a change in the "ordinary profit" with which the rate of profit in occupation A is to be compared.

That is to say, there would be an underproduction in occupation A in consequence of there being an over-production in occupation B. It is accordingly necessary to say that any over-supply of one commodity implies, or rather involves, an under-supply, in the strict economic sense, of some or all other commodities. The first of Mr. Crocker's propositions therefore breaks down.

It is to be remarked that the typical case cited by Mr. Crocker (p. 358) of a production "not based upon . . . the adequate demand" also breaks down when it comes to the concrete application in the second of the two propositions. And the like would probably be true of any conceivable case. It is a case of an excess of production of a particular commodity, due to the creation of more fixed capital of a given kind than the adequate demand for the product would warrant, and resolves itself into a case of misdirected or "ill-sorted" production, such as Mill has specially provided for in his discussion. It is a case of relative overproduction of a special kind of fixed capital, and a consequent depreciation of that fixed capital, either permanent or temporary. The reason for the continued production of goods to be sold at what the producer conceives to be less than a fair return is, professedly, the fact that an undue proportion of the aggregate capital has been fixed for the production of the particular commodity in question.

II

While the doctrine of a general over-supply of goods —in the sense in which it has been criticised in economic theory—is palpably absurd, it must be admitted that the cry of "overproduction" that goes up at every season of industrial depression has a very cogent though perhaps not a very articulate meaning to the men who raise the cry. What is the nature of the fact that is symbolised by the colloquial use of "overproduction," and how it is related to "depression" and "liquidation," has never been satisfactorily made out. But no doubt it stands for an economic fact that merits the attention of any one who is curious to understand the phenomena of hard times and commercial crises.

The passages which Mr. Crocker quotes from D. A. Wells's *Recent Economic Changes*—and, more distinctly, certain other passages of that book—indicate the difficulty rather than solve it. It should be said, by the way, that Mr. Wells claims no originality with respect to the theory, or rather statement, which he puts forth, though he gives it a conciseness which it hardly had before.

General "overproduction," in Mr. Wells's use, means a general production in excess of the "demand at remunerative prices." And a remunerative price may be defined, for the present purpose, as a price that will afford the customary profit on the capital invested. If general prices become "unremunerative," the meaning of that fact, as expressed in terms of this definition, is that the general run of profits has fallen below what is accepted as the customary rate of profits, or below the "ordinary profit," in the sense of what the business community accepts as the proper or adequate rate of profits for the time being.

"Overproduction," in the colloquial use of the word, as appealed to in explanation of depression in trade, is used to describe a situation where goods have been produced in excess of the demand at such prices as will afford the customary profit on the capital employed in their production. The average profit obtainable at the time on the capital invested falls short of the standard accepted as the proper, customary profit. This need not mean that the rate of discount at the time falls short of what is conceived to be the proper, customary rate. The trouble lies not primarily with the rate of profit on new investments, as indicated by the rate of interest on money seeking investment, but with the rate of profit on property already invested and capitalised in the past. The point of complaint is as to the earning capacity of investments already made. There may be much that is unsatisfactory with respect to the making of new investments; but that class of difficulties is evidently an effect, never a cause, of the trouble that exists with respect to the earning capacity of capital already invested and "capitalised" in the past.

The average rate of profit from past investments, indicated by the ratio of their earning capacity to their accepted capitalisation, falls short of the accepted customary profit, indicated by the customary rate of interest on money seeking investment. The precise difficulty is that a divergence has taken place between the accepted nominal value of property, based on its past capitalisation, and its actual present value, indicated by its present earning capacity or the present cost of replacing it. The actual present value of the property, as capitalised on the basis of its present earning capacity or on the cost of replacing it, falls short of its nominal, accepted value; and, as profits continue to be computed on the basis of this accepted nominal value, the rate of profit actually obtainable falls short of what is accepted as the customary and proper rate. The profit, computed on this basis, may even entirely disappear.

The "remunerative price," then, on which Mr. Wells bases his conception of "overproduction," turns out to be such a price as will afford the customary rate of profit to capital, as computed on the basis of its nominal value, or, in other words, on the basis of its accepted capitalisation. Now, whenever the course of industrial development compels a readjustment of the basis of capitalisation (as happens whenever the cost of production has been appreciably lowered), the customary basis on which the remunerative price has been computed becomes obsolete. The price, therefore, also becomes obsolete; and a reluctant acceptance of a new order of things follows, in which the capitalisation and nominal value of property are readjusted on a revised scale of prices, which, in the new epoch, fixes the "remunerative price" that now affords the customary rate of profit on the revised capitalisation.

The immediate economic fact for which "overproduction" stands is, therefore, a divergence between the nominal, accepted valuation and the actual present value of property engaged in production, in consequence of which the nominal earnings of capital (and in some cases the real earnings as measured in means of livelihood) are diminished. The characteristic fact in a case of general "overproduction" is that the basis on which "remunerative prices" and customary profit are computed has become obsolete. This divergence may be due to several different causes, but usually and mainly to two general ones—a speculative movement, and an increased efficiency of industry.[3] The action of the former of these needs no discussion here. A speculative movement may have pushed prices up unwarrantably. A fall

[3] The progressive accumulation of capital, by directly lowering the rate of profits, acts in the same direction as the two causes here mentioned; and some would perhaps rank it abreast with these two as an efficient agency in producing the situation for which an explanation is sought.

of general prices, due to improved processes of production, may have depressed the actual present money value of property engaged in production below its nominal value. For the present purpose the immediate result is in either case much the same: the nominal, accepted valuation of the capital, on which its returns are computed, exceeds its actual value as indicated by its present earning capacity. The property, perhaps the general aggregate property of the community, has come to be rated at a capitalised value above the cost at which it, or its equivalent for purposes of production, could now be replaced.

The hard times of the past decade are an example going to show how this result may be reached by a lowering of the cost of production; or, as some would perhaps prefer to express it, by an increase of the efficiency of industry.

If the analysis were carried a step further, it would appear that the divergence between the accepted valuation and the true present value of property, here ascribed to a lowering of the cost of production, is not due to the lowering of cost of production generally, simply as such, so much as to a lowering of the cost of production of some or all staple commodities as compared with the cost of production of the precious metals. The whole matter is very largely a matter of price—of "values" in the commercial sense.

Such a divergence between the accepted valuation and the actual value of capital may seem an inadequate basis for an economic fact of such magnitude as a period of industrial depression. And yet an industrial depression means, mainly, a readjustment of values. It is primarily, to a very great extent, a psychological fact. Secondarily, it is largely a matter of the shifting of ownership rather than a destruction of wealth or a serious reduction of the aggregate productiveness of industry as measured in goods.

The act of readjusting one's conception of one's own belongings to the scale of a reduced number of dollars, even though the dollar is worth enough more to make up for the nominal depreciation, is in itself a sufficiently painful one, and is submitted to only reluctantly and tardily. But this subjective element, this lesion of the feelings of the property owner, is by no means all that is involved in a decrease of the nominal earning capacity of capital. Whenever the nominal owner of the means of production is not also the real owner, as happens in the case of borrowed capital, he becomes answerable to the real owner—the lender—for any amount by which the actual present value of the property may fall short of the accepted valuation. A decline in the market value of property represented by the debt, therefore, means a real loss to the debtor, although, so far as it is due to increased efficiency of industry, it may be only a nominal loss to the man who has to do with his own capital only, and may be, and generally is, a source of distinct though unrecognised gain to the lender. The borrower assumes the risk of depreciation of the property represented by the debt.

In a case such as has been witnessed in this country during the past ten or twelve years, when there has been a pretty general decline in the cost of production of staple commodities—as compared with the standard of value—and a consequent decline in the nominal earning capacity of property engaged in production, of perhaps 30 percent, this factor is of the very gravest consequence. Especially is this true in the case of a community where so great a proportion of capital is represented by interest-bearing securities.

# CREDIT AND PRICES [1]

AT its last meeting (1904) the American Economic Association gave up one session to a discussion of the relation between credit and prices. The point of the discussion was, in substance, the question: Does the use of credit raise general prices? This was the only strictly theoretical topic taken up at the meeting. It is perhaps needless to say that the question was not finally disposed of, even in the apprehension of those who took part in its discussion. There was apparent a general reluctance to admit that credit is a price-making factor of considerable importance, at the same time that there seemed to prevail an apprehensive hesitancy about saying so in so many words. This is true only with exceptions, however. On the whole, there may be said to have been a rough consensus to the effect that credit does not have much to do with prices in ordinary times and in the general run of business, however opinions may differ as to its effect on prices in exceptional circumstances. It should be added that the discussion at the meeting was directed mainly, or almost wholly, to those forms of credit instruments which serve as currency or as a substitute for currency.

It is, of course, not intended here to offer an off-hand solution of this large question of credit and prices, but certain phases of the use of credit in modern business,

[1] Reprinted from *The Journal of Political Economy*, Vol. XIII, June, 1905.

neglected in the arguments of the association's experts, may well be taken up. What is of immediate interest to modern theory is, of course, the current use of credit in business, and the relation of this business credit to the current price-level, rather than the occasional resort to credit under relatively primitive circumstances. Credit is an expedient of business, and as such it is unquestionably a factor of great importance. The price-level is similarly a fact upon which the business community's hopes and fears center. If one looks to the field of business, simply, and neglects to go behind the immediate facts of business traffic to those of the industrial process and the output of consumable goods, certain commonplace facts bearing on credit stand out in relief—obvious facts which have commonly been overlooked, perhaps because they are too obvious to be seen except with the naked eye. These are such facts as the following: The issuance of a large government loan advances the general rate of discount and depresses the price of investment securities; Business men resort to credit for the sake of gain, the gain being counted in money values; The securities covering the capitalisation of a modern corporation commonly have a larger aggregate market value than the underlying tangible assets have before the incorporation; Banking is profitable, also in terms of money values; Prosperous times are attended with a large extension of credit as well as an advance in general prices; Crises and depression bring a shrinkage of credit and a decline of general prices.

From these and other phenomena of the same commonplace character the rough generalisation may be drawn that an advance of prices commonly accompanies a pronounced expansion of credit. It is not plain from these facts which of the two correlated phenomena is cause and which is effect, but the great generality with which they are found in company indicates that they stand in a causal relation to one another, possibly as being the effects of the same causes. There is nothing in these general facts to preclude the view that they are mutually related as cause and effect. That a pronounced advance in prices results in an increased extension of credit seems plain from what happens during a period of prosperity, or speculative advance. The circumstantial evidence runs to that effect, at the same time that such a result is to be expected from the nature of the case. Notoriously, a period of advancing prosperity is a period of relatively high prices, at least in some of the important branches of industry, and usually it is also a period of advancing prices. Extensions of credit, of course, run in terms of money, and are based on the money value (price) of the property submitted as collateral. If this market value of the collateral advances, then the amount of the credit which it will support will likewise increase. The market value of the collateral may increase immediately, as an incident of the advance of general prices; or it may increase through the increased earning capacity of the business property submitted as collateral, this increased earning capacity being in part due to the increased price at which the output of the business can be disposed of, in part, perhaps, to the increased volume of output which the market will carry off. In the latter case, the increased demand for the output is, at least in part, a consequence of the high course of general prices. In the case of crisis or pronounced depression all this chain of consequences is reversed. Such seems to be the rough and general run of correlation between credit and prices as conditioned by the circumstances of prosperity or depression. A closer analysis would show variations of detail under this general rule, and would afford material for detailed study.

The general statement which these facts seem to warrant is that in this connection an advance or decline of general prices brings an expansion or retrenchment of credit. Further attention to the same range of facts seems to warrant the further generalisation that an expansion of credit in periods of prosperity, at the same time, causes an advance of general prices; while a general retrenchment of credit, such as occurs in time of crises or acute depression, acts to lower general prices. This point has been noted by nearly all writers on crises and inflation, and no argument need be spent in enforcing it. The manner in which it works has also been analysed repeatedly. Movements of general credit and general prices have apparently a mutual accelerating effect upon one another, both in case of advance and in case of decline, giving rise to the well-known cumulative process of expansion or of contraction that marks a period of prosperity or of crisis or depression. In practice this cumulative movement of credit and prices is more or less disguised and disturbed by certain (secondary) phenomena, such as the issuance of large loans, particularly government loans; extensive incorporation of new companies and consolidation of old ones, with the attendant recapitalisation of the various items of wealth involved in these operations; the promotion or—in the case of depression or crisis—the collapse of extra-hazardous, speculative business enterprises, etc. These "disturbing causes" would have to be taken up separately. It will probably be admitted that the cumulative movement of credit and prices spoken of has substantially the character assigned it above.

Among the phenomena that usually accompany a period of marked prosperity, and closely related to the expansion of credit during such a period, is a large volume of new capitalisation in the form of new incorporations or expansions and coalitions of corporations already in existence. The issuance of corporation securities is a credit transaction, in the sense in which economists have been accustomed to use the word. Indeed, the sale of such securities involves the typical form of credit, as contemplated by the older economists, in that its immediate effect is to transfer the use of the property which it covers from the owner to the debtor, who is presumed to be a more competent user than the owner. All this applies perhaps more patently to the sale of preferred stock and bonds than to that of common stock, but for the present purpose there seems to be no very substantial difference between these different descriptions of securities. It is currently believed, probably on sufficient grounds, that the corporations can make more profitable use of the property than the buyers of the securities, particularly a more profitable use than the buyers could make of it without spending additional time and attention in the management of the property. It is this presumed differential advantage in favor of the corporations that makes incorporation practicable on any appreciable scale. Except for the presumed advantage in gainfulness, it is safe to say, the organisation of joint-stock companies would not have become a general practice. This presumed greater earning capacity of the corporations, above the earning capacity of the properties in severalty, may be due to economies of production, superior management, economies of sale, or what not. For the present argument it is only necessary to note that the corporations are presumed to have a greater earning capacity than their underlying properties, and that this presumption shows itself in the market value of the corporations' securities. This market value of the securities is commonly larger in the aggregate than the aggregate value of the underlying properties. That is to say, the credit transaction which results in the organisation of a corporation and an attendant issue of marketable securities commonly increases the aggregate price of the property involved. It is not unusual, latterly, to incorporate a business concern at a nominal capitalisation of about 200 percent of the current market value of the underlying properties; the resulting securities will sell below par; but in the case of an ordinarily sound and sagacious incorporation the total capitalisation will still have a market value of something more than 100 percent of the value of the underlying properties.

In this case, then, a credit transaction raises the price of the property immediately involved. Whether and how it affects the prices of other items of wealth is a question not easily answered. If the advantages of incorporation are in all cases differential advantages only, then the presumption would be that the prices of other property engaged in similar lines of business should be depressed in consequence of the incorporation. It does not seem probable that the depression in the prices of similar property outside of the given corporation, if such a depression results at all, is sufficient to balance the increase in the price of the assets of the corporation. In case the given incorporation results in a monopoly, a more or less extensive enhancement of prices may be expected to follow in its marketable output of goods or services, apparently without any necessary countervailing effect upon the prices of other goods. Price changes of this latter class, however, will probably be regarded as the effects of monopoly rather than of the credit transactions which initiate the monopoly. They need therefore not be discussed here. They could properly be discussed here only in so far as credit relations are to be accounted a necessary basis of any efficient monopoly. Under existing conditions this is probably the case, but the relation between the credit relations which enable monopolies to be organised and to operate and the resulting effect on prices is, after all, so remote that an analysis of its consequences would take the present argument out of its way.

Again, the issuance of a very considerable loan, such as a war loan of the larger sort, is known to lower the general market value (prices) of securities with a fixed interest or dividend charge. At such a juncture, because of the large demand for credit, general interest advances, and the general level of capitalisation correspondingly declines; that is to say, the market value of incorporated business declines, while the "price of money" advances. The prices of such lines of goods as are to be bought with the borrowed funds are likely to advance, and this may induce an advance in such capital as is concerned with the supply of these goods, but all that is an indirect consequence of the credit transaction rather than an immediate effect of it.[2]

2 This phenomenon, of an equilibration between the rate of discount and the market value of securities, is one of the most characteristic and indicative features of the modern business situation. An exhaustive study of it may be expected to result in a revision of the received views of credit, capital, interest, and prices, and of the interdependence of these several phenomena; but it is out of the question to pursue an inquiry of that magnitude here. It seems evident, however, that a fuller inquiry along that line should confirm the view here spoken for, that general credit and prices are intimately bound together in a relation of mutual cause and effect.

The phenomena spoken of so far are of the class which the older economists would call "disturbances," rather than developments in the normal course of business. What happens in the case of such disturbances need not be taken as evidence of the effect of credit upon prices in the regular course of business in ordinary times, where no such perturbations occur, or apart from all perturbations of this kind. In the regular course of business there is, no doubt, a larger aggregate volume of credit, proportionately either to the stock of specie or to the aggregate amount of tangible wealth owned in the community, in use at present and in this country than here formerly or now anywhere else. Will general prices range higher or lower because of such a more extended use of credit? Does the more extended and the increasing use of credit during the past thirty or forty years affect the general course of prices during the same period? This question has been argued by comparing the state of things at present with the corresponding facts of a generation ago, but without conclusive results. No canvass of the statistical material bearing on the case can directly reach a solution of the question, because the variables included in the problem are too many and too unprecise. On the other hand, something in the way of tenable general conclusions may probably be arrived at through an examination of the aims which actuate borrowers and lenders, and of the method by which the work of credit extension is carried on, although such a line of inquiry cannot be expected to yield anything like precise results.

As has just been noted, the credit transaction known as the floating of corporation securities results in an increased market value of the aggregate properties involved. This increased market value is more or less permanent, somewhat in proportion as the capitalisation is more or less "conservative." At the same time, it is one of the reasons for the promoting of new corporations. The promoter's bonus, with other like charges and perquisites, comes out of the margin of increase in price. The incentive to credit extensions of this kind is a prospective gain in terms of price, and in this class of transactions the business man's hope of gain is at least not commonly disappointed, even if the permanent increase of the values which he manipulates may not be as large as his anticipations.

In other credit transactions which differ from the floating of new companies in that they do not materialise in the form of corporation securities, but which are of the same kind in that the borrowed funds are made to serve the conduct of business, the end sought is of the same kind—a gain in terms of price. This gain may appear primarily as an increase in the market value of the property in which the borrowed funds are invested, as in the case of a real-estate speculation and the like; or it may appear only as a secondary effect, as an increase in the aggregate value of the output of an industry in which the funds are invested. The presumption would be that in this case also the hope of gain is not altogether disappointed. But even if the business man's hopes of gain could be shown to be false in the average of cases of this class of loans, it would not follow that credit transactions of this class initiate no enhancement of prices.

Loans of the kind just spoken of, procured with a view to investing the borrowed funds in a somewhat fixed form in business, have the direct effect of enhancing the market value of the general description of property in which they seek investment. The borrowers bid up the kind of property which they seek to buy. Whether there is a countervailing decline in the general prices of other property is doubtful and may be left on one side for the present, particularly as the argument of the next few pages approaches that question from another side.

In the ordinary conduct of business there is an extensive and increasing resort to credit in the way of loans, extended by banks in the form of deposits and by other credit institutions, such as trust companies, insurance companies, and the like, without their taking the form of deposits. In general, but more particularly where such a loan takes the form of a deposit, these extensions of credit would, by economists who hold that normal credit does not affect prices, be considered to be an expedient for facilitating an exchange of goods. The goods which serve as collateral for the loan, it is held, are by a more or less roundabout process of accounting exchanged for the goods paid for out of the deposits. This is in substance the theory which has felicitously been named "the refined system of barter." As bearing on the question of credit and prices, this doctrine declares that such loans do not affect prices, because the borrowed funds are nothing but the fluent form of the value of the underlying collateral. The loan and the collateral are held to offset one another as demand and supply, the loan adding no more to the demand side—the effective purchasing power seeking goods—than the collateral adds to the supply side of the market situation—the effective offering of goods seeking sale. Hence, it is held, no enhancement of price can arise from such loans, the increase of funds offered in purchase being no greater than the underlying increase of goods offered for sale.
A singular query presents itself at this point. Not

only is it true that the funds procured by loans of this kind, in a case of "normal" credit extension, are no larger than the value of the underlying collateral, but in the ordinary run of things the loan is not as large as the value of the collateral. No banker would be held blameless if he should extend his loans to the full ascertained value of the collateral. If the argument of the "refined system" is sound, will it not lead to the conclusion that credit extensions of this class lower general prices, since it should follow that the increase of the market demand due to the borrowed funds is overbalanced by the increase in the supply of goods represented by the collateral? The answer to the question comes into sight, if this argument is pursued a step farther.

The argument for "the refined system of barter" assumes that the collateral is of the nature of a bill of sale. It appears to break down immediately in so far as the collateral is not of this character, if it consists of property not sold or not designed presently to be sold; as, e.g., where the collateral is corporation securities or paper similar to corporation securities in the respect that it represents property which the borrower has not sold and is not trying to sell, but which is held as security during the term of the loan. The doctrine seems tenable only in so far as the collateral is of the nature of a bill of sale. A good share of current deposits and the greater part of other current loans are not of this character. The borrower's resort to credit in these cases is not an incident in the sale of the collateral. The presumption, indeed, is that he does not wish to sell. But it is safe to say that he ordinarily wishes to buy, whether it be goods, securities, or what not. Here the balance which is sought to be established between goods sold and goods bought, in the doctrine of "the refined system of barter," is upset by the fact that property not sold and not designed to be sold is made a basis of credit extension. The (discounted) value of this collateral enters the market as a factor in the demand for goods. If the determination of price is conceived in the customary way to be an outcome of the play of demand and supply, it appears that these considerations force the admission that general prices should advance as a result of these credit extensions. The general demand has been increased by "coining into means of payment" property which is not included in the general supply. It appears that, in so far as it is of this character, as it is to a very large extent, credit should raise prices.

The objection is ready, indeed it has in substance been made by those who speak for the view under discussion, that in the end the borrower must sell something or other in order to meet obligations falling due, and that in this way the balance is maintained and the transaction reduces itself to a virtual barter. All of which may conceivably be true as applies to a given transaction, although it is not unusual for such a transaction to be followed immediately on the maturity of the loan by another like transaction which virtually continues the life of the original loan. But this line of defense overlooks the time element, which is of the essence of any credit transaction. During the credit period the balance between demand and supply is not maintained, supposing the argument of the "refined system" to be otherwise sound. And from this it follows that the balance between general demand and general supply (conceiving supply in terms of goods) fails, constantly and in the nature of things, by the whole amount of outstanding credit obligations, after deducting such loans as have been sunk in the purchase of industrial equipment or have otherwise been withdrawn from the active market as a means of payment—indeed, it may even be an open question whether this deduction should be made, or just what force should be assigned to this qualification. Evidently this argument applies to the whole mass of outstanding credit, whatever the nature of the collateral. During their term the loans secured by ordinary commercial paper constitute an addition to the means of purchase as well as those loans that are secured by property not intended for sale.

Accordingly, such portion of the outstanding mass of credit as is available as a means of purchase must be taken to constitute an effective price-making demand and to have a force, as a price-making factor, equal to that of a like amount of hard cash used as currency. The rest of the credit outstanding at any given time, not available as a means of payment, is, perhaps, larger than this that may be called the mass of active credit, and if this "dormant" credit be deducted it appears that what is left as an active price-making factor is an indeterminate fraction of the whole. The secondary price-making effects of the loans sunk in investment are here disregarded; they seem, on the whole, to go in the direction of an enhancement of general prices, but they are complex and variable, and cannot be taken account of here except as a factor for which an indefinite allowance is to be made. It remains true that the mass of active credit, which serves as a current means of payment and so immediately affects prices, is a function of the whole mass of credit outstanding.

Now, when the mass of outstanding credit shrinks appreciably, as in a period of depression or crisis, the shrinkage ordinarily affects the credit available for current means of payment first or primarily. The consequence is a shrinkage of prices, both of goods in the open market, actively seeking a purchaser, and (secondarily) of the prices of the industrial equipment and similar items of property not intended for direct sale. Herewith the value of the collateral shrinks, forcing a reduction of outstanding loans, leading to a sale of collateral and so to an increased supply of things for sale, at the same time that the effective demand has been reduced by a shrinkage of the credit extensions used as a means of purchase.

In the doctrines of the classical economists, who at this point have not been superseded, the phenomena of credit are formulated in terms of their presumed social expediency. The actual motives and aims which animate those business men who seek credit, as well as those who carry on the traffic in credit—bankers, brokers, etc.—are disregarded, and in the stead of these business motives the presumed beneficial results of the traffic are imputed to these business men as the motives of their traffic. Perhaps for this reason the question of the banker's gain and its relation to credit and prices is commonly not broached in the received doctrines of credit and prices. Without the prospective gain the banker would not do business. So the question suggests itself: Why is banking profitable? And what, if any, relation is there between prices and the profits of banking?

Broadly speaking, banking is profitable chiefly because the banker lends more than he has or borrows. This is his chief, though not his only, source of gain. His gains are derived from payments for two distinct kinds of service which he renders his customers. The two are currently not distinguished, the remuneration for both being indiscriminately spoken of as discount or interest, but for the present purpose a distinction seems desirable. (*a*) Banks discount commercial paper, and (*b*) banks and other concerns doing a credit business make loans on collateral which is not of the nature of a bill of sale.

(*a*) In discounting commercial paper the banker does not create credit or increase the volume of outstanding credit obligations. In substance he guarantees or authenticates the credit extension already created by the writing of the commercial paper which he discounts. A bill of sale for future payment is a credit instrument, and the extension of credit involved in its use is effected in the sale for future payment which it covers. The volume of credit so covered by the bill of sale is by the banker's authentication converted into a form available for circulation. In substance, he insures and authenticates it, and for this service he is paid in the discount of the bill. The form of the transaction gives the appearance of no increased demand for goods, since the volume of credit, and so the volume of money values available for purchase, has not been increased by the banker's intervention. This gives color to the claim that in this transaction there is no addition to the available purchasing power, and therefore no effect on prices; but this color is due to oversight of the fact that the bill itself is an instrument which covers an extension of credit already effected. It is an open question whether the banker's intervention in such a case, as authenticator of an existing volume of credit, is to be conceived as increasing the effective demand for goods. But a negative answer to this question is only an evasion. If the increase of available credit in such a case is not made by the banker, it is made by the makers of the bill. The net result is much the same.

(*b*) In making a loan on collateral which is not of the

nature of a bill of sale, but represents property not intended to be sold, the banker, or any similar concern doing a credit business of this kind, creates a new volume of credit. The remuneration for this service also is called interest or discount. Such a transaction creates credit, and so adds to the borrower's funds available for purchase, and therefore increases the effective demand for goods, and by so doing helps to enhance prices. In such a transaction the banker lends funds which he does not possess. He is enabled to lend more in the aggregate than the whole of the funds which seek emplacement in loans through his agency. Or, to phrase it differently, he coins into means of payment goods which do not change hands in the resulting transactions of purchase and sale. Hence borrowers are enabled to borrow more in the aggregate than all the funds which the ultimate lenders have to dispose of—more than the whole of the funds seeking investment as loans plus that collateral which represents property sold or seeking sale. The purchasing power placed at the disposal of debtors is larger because of the banker's mediation than it would be without it.[3]

From this augmented purchasing power the banker deducts his remuneration as a discount. This discount is not withdrawn from the aggregate loan fund. It serves the same purpose as any other item of banker's assets, and enables him to lend more than the whole of it, or, if the wording be preferred, it enables him to make advances on collateral exceeding its own amount.

[3] It may be that a closer analysis would show that the banker's service to his customers is also in this case, as in case (*a*), that of guarantor or authenticator of their credit and that his remuneration in the discount obtained is of the nature of a payment for responsibility assumed. If this view be taken, the form of the argument changes, but its bearing on the question in hand is not materially changed.

The banker's debtors, of course, negotiate their loans with a view to using the funds as a means of payment. The funds have no other use, except further lending, as in the hands of borrowing bankers. Hence, other things equal, it should follow that bank credit acts to raise prices by as much as it increases the nominal purchasing power in the hands of the business community. When the funds so secured by unmarketed collateral have been spent in the purchase of goods, the goods so purchased may in their turn be hypothecated in the negotiation of a further loan; with the result that there is a further augmentation of the volume of credit, a further increase of the effective demand for goods, and a further effect on prices. The whole movement may therefore take on a cumulative character, as it does in a marked degree in a period of prosperity, or speculative advance. Something of this cumulative character there no doubt is in the credit situation at any given time during ordinary times.

For some time past the mass of outstanding credit has been growing gradually larger, on the whole, and the effect of this movement should logically have been to advance general prices in a corresponding degree. The enhancement of general prices due to this cause has apparently been offset by cheapened production of goods, due to technological improvements. How far this countervailing effect of cheapened production has neutralised, or more than neutralised, the enhancement due to credit cannot be considered here. The volume of goods seeking a market has also greatly increased during the same period, and this should also have a countervailing effect. It should mask or offset the enhancement of prices due to an increased resort to credit, but this is also a matter that does not belong here. So also the relation of credit, as a price-making factor, to the production of the precious metals is no doubt a matter of some consequence in this connection, but that, too, is a question of detail that requires treatment by itself.

# BÖHM-BAWERK'S DEFINITION OF CAPITAL, AND THE SOURCE OF WAGES [1]

In his exposition of the term "capital," Professor Böhm-Bawerk briefly touches on the wages-fund doctrine, so far as to reject summarily the proposition that the means of subsistence of productive laborers is drawn from the capital of the community, although, from the point of view of the employer, these "real wages" are to be regarded as drawn from his private capital. With the distinction which the discussion establishes between social capital and private capital, this position is, of course, in itself perfectly consistent. The position is, indeed, contained in the definition of capital previously arrived at (pp. 42, 43, and 21). The ground of the position taken is the unquestioned or, at all events, unquestionable truth that the laborer is a member of society, and his consumption of products is, in a broad view, a fact of the same kind, and of like theoretical significance with consumption on the part of any other member of society. The satisfaction of wants, whether it be the wants of the laborer or of any other, is the end, not the means, of productive activity.

While the exposition at this point undeniably sheds a strong light on the question, it can hardly be said to have finally disposed of all ground for difference of opinion, still less to have explained away the wages-fund controversy, or that point of the controversy which concerns

[1] Reprinted from *The Quarterly Journal of Economics,* Vol. VI, January, 1892.

the question of the source of wages. And that controversy has been of such extent and earnestness as to raise the presumption that something is to be said for both sides of the dispute, and to leave little hope of its being finally put at rest by any other method than that of explaining away the ground of difference. For reaching this end, I believe Professor Böhm-Bawerk's exposition of capital has given us the means.

It is to be remarked, by the way, however, that there is a lacuna in the exposition at this point which seems, at least, not of first-rate theoretical consequence, and is, perhaps, the result of oversight of a not very important point, but which might afford a foothold for carping criticism. It will be best to speak of it at the outset, and put it out of the way before going on. This difficulty arises from the inclusion, as a subhead under Social Capital, of "stocks of goods for consumption which are still in the hands of producers or dealers" (p. 70) ; that is to say, goods which have not yet passed that final stage of preparation for consumption which consists in their transfer, through the mechanism of exchange, into the ownership of the ultimate consumer.

Now, this classification may afford ground for persons unduly given to nice distinctions to take exception to Professor Böhm-Bawerk's position on the question of the source of wages that, (1) inasmuch as the payment of wages, actually for the most part, and in theory normally, is a transfer to the laborer not of the particular goods he wants, but of an item of value by means of which he may obtain the particular goods through this final productive step of exchange, therefore the payment of wages simply gives the recipient a claim on goods which have not yet passed the final stage of production, and so are as yet a part of the general

capital by the terms of the definition, and which will
pass that stage only in consequence of this claim; (2)
that, without regard to the mechanism by which the
transaction is carried out, the claim on goods, which
accrues to the laborer in the payment of wages, constitutes a drain on the stocks in the hands of producers
or merchants, and tends to diminish such stocks, and
this without regard to the point of time of the payment,
relative to the production of the goods, which ultimately
go to satisfy the laborer's wants. The payment of the
wages, as a matter to be considered in a theory of the
methods of production, precedes the consumption, or the
ownership on the part of the recipient, of the goods
which the claim so transferred to him ultimately puts
into his hands for consumption, and so is a claim that
can be satisfied only by drawing on a class of goods included under the head of social capital. This criticism,
it will be seen, touches a point of classification, and may
perhaps be avoided without deranging the main structure
of the theory.

Now, as to the theory of the source of wages, in the
light of Professor Böhm-Bawerk's definition of capital.
It is not too much to say that the controversy has owed
much of its bitterness and sterility to inadequate definition of the terms employed, especially to a lack of accu-
racy in the concept of capital. The *Positive Theorie des
Kapitales* has given to the concept of capital, and of its
relation to other elements of economic theory, a conciseness and adequacy of which earlier speculators were
sorely in need. If the distinction which this discussion
formulates between social and private capital had been
apprehended earlier, with the same full and clear consciousness, the means would have been at hand by which
the wages-fund controversy might have been put at rest.

But the completed definition of capital does not of itself dispose of the question. A further analysis in the same direction is necessary. It seems to me that economic theory is at this point in the presence of a distinction necessary to be made between "the laborer's share of consumable goods," or "earnings," on the one hand, and "wages," on the other, analogous to the distinction taken by Wagner—and perfected by Professor Böhm-Bawerk—between capital as a "purely economic category" and capital "in a juridico-historical sense." Wages, in this stricter definition, and private capital both are facts of usage, while the laborer's income, or earnings, and social capital both are facts intrinsic and fundamental to any theory of industrial society.

Wages is a fact incident to the relation of employer and employed. It is, in the sense fixed by colloquial use, an economic category whose scope is entirely within the theory of production as carried on by the method based on that relation; and the term is not used in precisely the same sense when the discussion shifts to the standpoint of production simply as such, still less when the point of view is that of distribution or consumption. It is by an unconscious equivocation, in shifting the point of view, that wages is identified with earnings and spoken of as an element in the theory of distribution or consumption. The laborer, from the point of view of consumption of products, is no longer "laborer": he is a member of society simply, and his share of the product of industry is the share of an individual member of society. As consumer, he is not "laborer," and his share of consumable goods is not "wages," in the strict technical sense of the term. Wages may coincide in range of comprehension with the laborer's share of product— with earnings—and may likewise coincide with the aggregate of his consumption; but wages is a category having a different significance for economic theory from that of earnings or of goods consumed. The item of value, which from the point of view of production as carried on by the method of private capital as wages, is, from the point of view of the laborer, as being productively employed in his own interest, earnings. From the point of view of consumption of goods produced, neither of these terms can be employed with entirely the same meaning as they have in the use just specified.

If this distinction be allowed as theoretically legitimate, it appears that Professor Böhm-Bawerk's discussion does not upset the wages-fund doctrine in any of its essential texts. The one proposition, that the sustenance of men while productively employed is drawn from the product of past industry, is of course not impugned; the other, that wages are paid out of capital, is conceded in conceding that it will hold true when capital is understood to mean private capital; for it is only then that the term "wages," in the strict technical sense, can properly be employed. At the same time this discrimination of terms leaves the position of the opponents of the wages-fund doctrine, as to this particular point, perfectly tenable; for whenever "wages" is used in the sense of "earnings," as, I believe, is invariably the case in the usage of these writers, they are undoubtedly drawn from the product of industry, inasmuch as earnings are the product, to the laborer, of his labor.

All this may seem to be a web of excessively fine-spun technicalities, but in apology it is to be said that it is also directed exclusively to a point of pure theory. And the whole controversy about the source of wages has also been in the region of pure theory, having never directly involved questions of physical fact or of expediency.

# FISHER'S RATE OF INTEREST [1]

THERE is less novelty, either in the course of the argument or in the results achieved, in the *Rate of Interest* [2] than in Mr. Fisher's earlier volume on the *Nature of Capital and Income*. Substantially the whole of it lies within the accustomed lines of that marginal-utility school of economics for which its author has so often and so convincingly spoken. It is true to the canons of the school, even to the point of making the usual error of logic in the usual place. But while it makes no material innovation, beyond a new distribution of emphasis among the factors held by the school to determine the rate of interest, it carries out the analysis of these determinants with unexampled thoroughness and circumspection, such, indeed, it may fairly be hoped, as will close the argument, on the main heads of the theory at least, within the school. There is all the breadth and facility of command over materials, which Mr. Fisher's readers have learned to expect, such as to make the book notable even among a group of writers to whom such facility seems native. If fault is to be found with this exposition of the marginal-utility doctrines it is scarcely to be sought in details of fact or unauthorised discrepancies of logic. Exception may be taken to the argument as a whole, but scarcely from the accepted ground of the

[1] Reprinted from *The Political Science Quarterly,* Vol. XXIV, June, 1909.
[2] *The Rate of Interest: Its Nature, Determination and Relation to Economic Phenomena.* By Irving Fisher. New York, 1908.

marginal-utility school. Nor should that remnant of the classical school which has not yet given its adherence to the marginal-utility doctrines readily find fault with an exposition which finds its foundations in so good and authentic a utilitarian theorist as John Rae.

The theory of interest arrived at is the so-called "agio" or discount theory, already familiar to Mr. Fisher's readers and substantially in accord with the like theory spoken for by Böhm-Bawerk. Mr. Fisher takes issue with Böhm-Bawerk on the one grave and far-famed point of doctrine concerning the "Roundabout Process." And on this head, I apprehend, it will be conceded that the later writer occupies the stronger and more consistent position, whatever exceptions may be taken to his line of argument in refutation of the doctrine in dispute. In his critical survey of competing and inadequate interest theories, occupying the first four chapters of the volume, this doctrine of the roundabout process comes in for more serious attention than all the rest; and justly so, since it is an alien in the school—a heresy which has been brought in by oversight. Leaving on one side for the moment all question as to the merits of this doctrine, it may readily be shown not to belong in the same explanation of interest with the agio theory, at least not as a proposition correlative with the theorem about the differential preference for present over future income. Interest and the rate of interest is a matter of value, therefore to be explained in terms of valuation, and so in terms of marginal utility. Within the scheme of value theory for which Mr. Fisher and Böhm-Bawerk are spokesmen no analysis of a value phenomenon can be brought to a conclusion until it is stated in terms of marginal utility. All fundamental propositions, all theorems of the first order in this theoretical scheme must be stated in these terms, since these terms alone are ultimate. Facts of a different order bear on any question of value, in this scheme, only as they bear on the process of valuation, which is a matter to be stated in terms of marginal utility. This scheme of theory is a branch of applied psychology—of that school of psychology which was in vogue in the early nineteenth century; whereas the roundabout process is not a psychological phenomenon—at least not of the same class with the doctrines of marginal utility. It is a technological matter. The roundabout process has a bearing on the rate of interest, therefore, only as it bears on the main theorem concerning the preference for present over future income; that is to say, the doctrine of the greater productivity of the roundabout process is, at the best, a secondary proposition, subsidiary to the main theorem. The valuations out of which the rate of interest emerges take account of various circumstances affecting the desirability of present as contrasted with future goods; among these circumstances may be the greater productivity of the roundabout process; but this is as near to the core of the problem as that phenomenon can be brought. The problem of the rate of interest in the marginal-utility system is a problem of applied psychology, more precisely a problem of the hedonistic calculus; whereas the alleged greater productivity of the roundabout process is a technological phenomenon, an empirical generalisation concerning the mechanical efficiency of given industrial ways and means. As an explanation of interest the doctrine of the roundabout process belongs among the productivity theories, as Mr. Fisher has indicated; and as such it cannot be admitted as a competent, or indeed a relevant, explanation of interest in a system of theory whose purpose is to formulate a scheme of economic conduct in terms of the hedonistic calculus.

It is quite conceivable that in some other system of economic theory, worked out for some other purpose than the hedonistic explanation of value, the roundabout process might be brought into the central place in a doctrine of interest; but such a doctrine would have as its theoretical core, upon which the theorist's attention should be concentrated, the physical production of that increment of wealth that is presumed to go to interest, rather than the pecuniary determination of the rate of interest through which this increment is distributed among its claimants. Such a doctrine would belong in a theory of production, or of industry, not in a theory of distribution, or of business. But the marginal-utility system is primarily a theoretical scheme of distribution, and only secondarily a scheme of production; and, therefore, in so far as it aims to deal with the current economic situation, it is or aims to be primarily a theory of business traffic, not of the processes of industry, particularly not of technological efficiency or of technological changes. This is well shown, e.g., in Mr. Fisher's discussion of invention (ch. x, ch. xi, sec. 4, ch. xvii, sec. 6).

Apart from all question of consistency or conclusiveness within the premises of the marginal-utility school, the test to which Mr. Fisher's theory of interest must finally be brought is the question of its adequacy as an explanation of interest in modern business. Mr. Fisher has recognised this, and the most painstaking and most admirable portions of the volume are those which discuss interest as involved in current business transactions (e.g., ch. xii–xvi). In modern life distribution takes place almost wholly in pecuniary terms and by means of business transactions. In so far as it does not, e.g., in the distribution of consumable goods within the household or in the distributive use of public utilities, it does not bear sensibly on any question of interest, particularly does it not bear immediately as a determinant on the rate of interest. Interest, as demanding the attention of the modern economist, is eminently a pecuniary phenomenon, and its rate is a question of business adjustments. It is in the business community and under the guidance and incitement of business exigencies that the rate is determined. The rate of interest in any other bearing in modern life is wholly subordinate and subsidiary. It is therefore an inversion of the logical sequence when Mr. Fisher, with others of the school, explains pecuniary interest and its rate by appeal to non-pecuniary factors. But such are the traditions of the school, and such a line of analysis is imposed by their premises.

As has been remarked above, Mr. Fisher's development of the doctrine of interest is true to these premises and traditions to a degree of nicety never excelled by any of the adepts. These premises or postulates on which the marginal-utility scheme rests are derived from the English classical economists, and through them from the hedonistic philosophy of the earlier decades of the last century. According to the hedonistic postulates the end and incentive is necessarily the pleasurable sensations to be derived from the consumption of goods, what Mr. Fisher calls "enjoyable income" or "psychic income" (see Glossary, pp. 339–340), and for reasons set forth in his analysis (ch. vi), it is held that, on the whole, men prefer present to future consumption. This is the beginning of economic (marginal-utility) wisdom; but it is also the end of the wisdom of marginal utility. To these elemental terms it has been incumbent on all marginal-utility theorists to reduce their formulations of economic phenomena. And from the acceptance of these limitations follow several characteristic excrescences and incongruities in Mr. Fisher's theory, presently to be spoken of.

To save argument it may be conceded that the hedonistic interpretation of human conduct is fundamentally sound. It is not requisite for the purpose in hand to discard that postulate, however frail it might prove on closer scrutiny. But if it be granted that the elemental motive force of economic life is the hedonistic calculus it does not follow that the same elemental calculus of preference for present over future sensations of consumption is to be directly appealed to in explanation of a phenomenon so far from elementary as the rate of interest. In point of historical fact anything like a consistent rate of interest emerges into the consciousness of mankind only after business traffic has reached some appreciable degree of development; and this development of business enterprise has taken place only on the basis and within the lines of the so-called "money economy," and virtually only on that higher stage of the money economy specifically called a "credit economy." Indeed interest is, strictly, a phenomenon of credit transactions alone. But a money economy and the consequent credit transactions which give rise to the phenomena of interest can emerge only on the basis afforded by the mature development of the institution of property. The whole matter lies within the range of a definite institutional situation which is to be found only during a relatively brief phase of civilisation that has been preceded by thousands of years of cultural growth during which the existence of such a thing as interest was never suspected. In short, interest is a business proposition and is to be explained only in terms of business, not in terms of livelihood, as Mr. Fisher aims to do. Business may be intimately concerned with livelihood, it may even be that in modern life business activity is the sole or chief method of getting a livelihood, but the two are not convertible terms, as Mr. Fisher's argument would require; neither are business gains convertible with the sensations of consumption, as his argument would also require.

The reason why these terms are not convertible, and therefore the reason why an argument proceeding on their convertibility or equivalence must reach a fallacious outcome, is that a growth of institutions intervenes between the two—granting that the hedonistic calculus is the primary incentive and guide of economic activity. In economic life, as in other lines of human conduct, habitual modes of activity and relations have grown up and have by convention settled into a fabric of institutions. These institutions, and the usual concepts involved in them, have a prescriptive, habitual force of their own, although it is not necessary at every move to ravel out and verify the intricate web of precedents, accidents, compromises, indiscretions, and appetites, out of which in the course of centuries the current cultural situation has arisen. If the contrary were true, if men universally acted not on the conventional grounds and values afforded by the fabric of institutions, but solely and directly on the grounds and values afforded by the unconventionalised propensities and aptitudes of hereditary human nature, then there would be no institutions and no culture. But the institutional structure of society subsists and men live within its lines, with more or less questioning, it is true, but with more acquiescence than dissent.

Business proceeds on the ground afforded by the institution of property, more particularly of property as rated in terms of money values. The rate of interest is one of the phenomena involved in this business traffic, and its theoretical explanation must run in terms of business, and so in terms of money. When the question is re-moved from this institutional basis and is pushed back to the grounds on which property and money are conceived to rest, it ceases to be a question of interest and becomes a detail of the analysis of the phenomena of value. But value, as understood by living economists, has no exist-ence apart from the institution of property—since it is concerned with the exchange of property. Interest is a pecuniary concept having no validity (except by force of an ambiguity) outside of the pecuniary relations of the business community, and to construe it in other, pre-sumably more elementary, terms is to explain it away by dissolving it into the elements out of which it is remotely derived, or rather to which it is presumed to be remotely related. The phenomena of modern business, including the rate of interest, can no more be handled in non-pecuniary terms than human physiology can be handled in terms of the amphioxus. The difference is that be-tween explaining current facts and endeavoring to ex-plain them away.

There is (probably) no science except economics in which such an endeavor to explain the phenomena of an institution in terms of one class of the rudiments which have afforded the point of departure for the growth of the institution would be listened to with any degree of civility. The philologists, for example, have various in-firmities of their own, but they would have little patience with a textual critic who should endeavor to reduce the Homeric hymns to terms of those onomatopoetic sounds out of which it is presumed that human speech has grown. What fortune would have overtaken E. B. Tylor's *Re-searches into the Development of Mythology, Philoso-phy, Religion, Language, Art and Custom,* if he had set out to explain away the facts and show that these institutions are of no effect because he knows something about the remote sources from which they have come? Scientific vagaries of that heroic stature are not unknown among ethnologists, but it is to be noted to the credit of the craft that they are known as vagaries.

Mr. Fisher's theory of the rate of interest suffers from the same oversight of this difference between explaining facts and explaining them away, as do the common run of marginal-utility doctrines. So, since interest is to be formulated in terms of consumptive hedonism, instead of in business concepts, and since price is to be formulated in the same terms, there arises an unavoidable confusion between the two, as appears in the discussion of "Appreciation and Interest" (ch. v and elsewhere). In the main, this discussion belongs properly in a theory of prices. Appreciation and depreciation of the standard of payments may of course—so far as they are foreseen —affect the rate of interest; but they are, after all, phenomena of price. Business transactions run in terms of money. Interest is rated in money and paid with a view to a money gain. Many contingencies bear on the chances of such gain, and changes of price are notoriously among these contingencies. Speculative buying and selling look to this contingency chiefly, and may look to such a change in the price of the goods bought or sold as shall offset the interest on the funds tied up in the speculation, but the rate of interest does not thereby come to be conceived or stated in terms of the advance or decline of the price of goods. Appreciation and depreciation, if foreseen, are circumstances to be taken into account by lender and borrower very much as the productivity of the roundabout process (if that doctrine be allowed) will be taken into account in making the rate of interest. But this state of the case does not make either of these phenomena a

rate of interest; nor does it reduce interest to a technological matter on the one hand or to a variation of prices
on the other hand.

Now and again, especially in ch. xiv (pp. 276–285),
Mr. Fisher cites facts showing that neither investment
nor interest are counted in terms of livelihood or in the
sensations of consumption, and showing also that questions of livelihood touch these phenomena only uncertainly and incidentally. He well shows (*a*) that business
men habitually do not (adequately) appreciate variations
in the commodity-value of money, and (*b*) that with rising prices they simply do business at a high money profit
and are content to pay a high rate of interest without
suspecting that all this has any connection with the "commodity interest" of Mr. Fisher. (Cf. the passages cited
from Baxter and from Jevons.) But his hedonistic preconceptions lead him to take note of this state of things
as exceptional and anomalous, whereas, of course, it is
the rule. It is not only the rule, but there is no avoiding
it so long as business is done in terms of money, and in
the absence of a foregone conclusion these facts should
persuade any observer that money value has an institutional force in the counsels of business men.

This chapter (xiv), and in good part the succeeding
one, explain interest without support from or reference
to Mr. Fisher's "agio" theory, although they are offered
as an "inductive verification" of that theory. Except for
the author's recurrent intimations, nothing in this inductive verification bears on, or leans on, the doctrine of
a preference for present over future income. Not only
so, but chapter xiv, incidentally helped out by various
passages elsewhere, goes far to disprove that the rate of
interest is a matter of the preference for present over
future income, taking "income" in Mr. Fisher's sense

of the term. There is a strikingly ingenuous passage in
ch. xv, (p. 315) : "For him [the farmer] the lowest ebb
is in the fall, when gathering and marketing his crops
cause him a sudden expenditure of labor or of money for
the labor of others. To tide him over this period he may
need to borrow. . . . The rate of interest tends up-
ward." The farmer, in other words, bids up the rate of
interest when his crops are in hand or are coming in;
particularly just after he has secured them, when he is
required to meet certain pecuniary obligations. But the
farmer's crops are his "income" in the case assumed, and
when his income has come in, at this springtide of his income stream, his preference for present over future goods
should logically be at its lowest, and, indeed, there need
be little question but such is the case. There is also no
doubt that the farmer is willing to bid high for funds at
this period; and the reason seems to be that then the fresh
access of income enables him to bid high, at the same time
that he needs the funds to meet pecuniary obligations.
His need of borrowing is due to the necessity of marketing his crops and so "realising" on them; that is to say,
it is a business or pecuniary need, not a matter of smooth-
ing out the income stream. Farming is a business venture
in modern times, and the end of business is gain in terms
of money. The cycle of business enterprise closes with
a sale, a conversion of "income" into money values, not
conversely, and the farmer is under more or less pecuniary pressure to bring this pecuniary cycle to a close.

# FISHER'S CAPITAL AND INCOME [1]

THE NATURE OF CAPITAL AND INCOME [2] is of that class of books that have kept the guild of theoretical economists content to do nothing toward "the increase and diffusion of knowledge" during the past quarter of a century. Of this class Mr. Fisher's work is of the best— thoughtful, painstaking, sagacious, exhaustive, lucid, and tenaciously logical. What it lacks is the breath of life; and this lack it shares with the many theoretical productions of the Austrian diversion as well as of the economists of more strictly classical antecedents. Not that Mr. Fisher's work falls short of its promise, and assuredly it does not fall short of the mark set by those many able men who have preceded him in this field. No reader of Mr. Fisher can justly feel disappointed in his performance of the difficult task which he sets himself. The work performs what it promises and does it in compliance with all the rules of the craft. But it does not set out substantially to extend the theory or to contribute to the sum of knowledge, either by bringing hitherto refractory phenomena into the organised structure of the science, or by affording farther or more comprehensive insight into the already familiar processes of modern economic life. Consistently with its aim, it is a work of taxonomy, of definition and classification; and it is car-

[1] Reprinted from *The Political Science Quarterly,* Vol. XXIII, March, 1908.
[2] *The Nature of Capital and Income.* By Irving Fisher. New York, 1906.

ried through wholly within the limits imposed by this its taxonomic aim. There are many shrewd observations on the phenomena of current business, and much evidence of an extensive and intimate acquaintance with such facts of modern culture as are still awaiting scientific treatment at the hands of the economists (e.g., in chapters v and vi, "Capital Accounts" and "Capital Summation," as also in chapters viii, ix, xiii, xiv, "Income Accounts," "Income Summation," "Value of Capital," "Earnings and Income," "The Risk Element"). But the facts of observation so drawn into the discussion are chiefly drawn in to illustrate or fortify an argument, somewhat polemical, not as material calling for theoretical explanation. As affects the development of the theory, these observations and this information run along on the side and are not allowed to disturb the argument in its secure march toward its taxonomic goal.

There is no intention here to decry taxonomy, of course. Definition and classification are as much needed in economics as they are in those other sciences which have already left the exclusively taxonomic standpoint behind. The point of criticism, on this head, is that this class of economic theory differs from the modern sciences in being substantially nothing but definition and classification. Taxonomy for taxonomy's sake, definition and classification for the sake of definition and classification, meets no need of modern science. Work of this class has no value and no claims to consideration except so far as it is of use to the science in its endeavor to know and explain the processes of life. This test of usefulness applies even more broadly in economics and similar sciences of human conduct than in the natural sciences, commonly so-called. It is on this head, as regards the serviceability of his taxonomic results, that Mr. Fisher's work falls short. A modern science has to do with the facts as they come to hand, not with putative phenomena warily led out from a primordial metaphysical postulate, such as the "hedonic principle." To meet the needs of science, therefore, such modern concepts as "capital" and "income" must be defined by observation rather than by ratiocination. Observation will not yield such a hard-and-fast definition of the term as is sought by Mr. Fisher and his co-disputants, a definition which shall mark off a pecuniary concept by physical distinctions, which shall be good for all times and places and all economic situations, ancient and modern, whether there is investment of capital or not.

"Capital" is a concept much employed by modern men of affairs. If it were not for the use of the concept in economic affairs—its growing use for a century past—the science would not be concerned about the meaning of the term today. It is this use of the concept in the conduct of affairs that obtrudes it upon the attention of economists; and it is, primarily at least, for a better knowledge of these pecuniary affairs, in which the concept of capital plays so large a part, that a better knowledge of the concept itself is sought. As it plays its part in these affairs of business, the concept of capital is, substantially, a habit of thought of the men engaged in business, more or less closely defined in practice by the consensus of usage in the business community. A serviceable definition of it, therefore, for the use of modern science, can be got only by observation of the current habits of thought of business men. This painfully longwinded declaration of what must appear to be a patent truism so soon as it is put in words may seem a gratuitous insistence on a stale commonplace. But it is an even more painfully tedious fact that the current polemics about "the capital concept" goes on year after year without recognition of this patent truism.

What may help to cover, rather than to excuse, the failure of many economists to resort to observation for a knowledge of what the term "capital" means is the fact, adverted to by the way in various writers, that business usage of the term is not uniform and stable; it does not remain the same from generation to generation; and it cannot, at least as regards present usage, be identified and defined by physical marks. The specific marks of the concept—the characteristics of the category—in the common usage are not physical marks, and the categories with which it is, in usage, related and contrasted are not categories that admit of definition in material terms; because it is, in usage, a pecuniary concept and stands in pecuniary relations and contrasts with other categories. It is a pecuniary term, primarily a term of investment, and as such, as a habit of thought of the men who have to do with pecuniary affairs, it necessarily changes in response to the changes going forward in the pecuniary situation and in the methods of conducting pecuniary affairs. "Capital," in the usage of current business, undoubtedly has not precisely the same meaning as it had in the corresponding usage of half a century ago; and it is safe to say that it will not retain its present meaning, unimpaired and unimproved, in the usage of ten years hence; nor does it cover just the same details in one connection as in another. Yet business men know what the term means to them. With all its shifting ambiguities, they know it securely enough for their use. The concept has sufficient stability and precision to serve their needs; and, if the economist is to deal with the phenomena of modern life in which this concept serves a use of first-rate importance, he must take the term and the concept as he finds them. It is idle fatigue to endeavor to normalise them into a formula which may suit his prepossessions but which is not true to life. The mountain will not come to Mahomet.

It is not for its idiosyncrasies that Mr. Fisher's analysis and formulation of the "capital concept" merits particular attention, but because it is the most elaborate outcome of classificatory economics to this date. Except for certain minor features—important, no doubt, within the school—his definition of capital is by no means a wide departure. It is only worked out more consistently, painstakingly, and circumspectly than has hitherto been done. Some of these special features peculiar to Mr. Fisher's position have been carefully and very ably discussed by Mr. Fetter.[3] The merits of the discussion of these matters between the critic and his author, with the incidental balancing of accounts, need not detain the present argument. Nor need particular attention here be given to the points in dispute so far as regards their consistency with the general body of theory upheld by Mr. Fisher and other economists who cultivate the classificatory science. But there are some details of the "nature of capital" as set forth by Mr. Fisher—and in large part assented to by Mr. Fetter and others of the like way of thinking— that require particular attention as regards their adequacy for other purposes than that of a science of classification.

(1) In the general definition of "capital" (e.g., pp. 51–53, 66–68, 324), the concept is made to comprise all wealth (in its relation to future income); and "wealth"

[3] *Journal of Political Economy,* March, 1907, "The Nature of Capital and Income." See also Mr. Fisher's reply in the same journal, July, 1907, "Professor Fetter on Capital and Income."

has, in the same as well as in earlier pages, been defined "to signify material objects owned by human beings," which, in turn, includes all persons, as well as other material objects. As an aggregate, therefore, as an outcome of a comprehensive "capital summation," "capital" comprises the material universe in so far as the material universe may be turned to use by man (see p. 328). This general definition includes too much and too little. A serviceable definition of capital, one that shall answer to the concept as it is found in practice in the habits of thought of business men, will not include persons. Hitherto, there is no question, the distinction between the capitalist and his capital is not disregarded by practical men, except possibly by way of an occasional affectation of speech; and it is highly improbable that, at any point in the calculable future, business men can come habitually to confuse these two disparate concepts. Modern business proceeds on the distinction. It is only in pulpit oratory that a man's person is legitimately spoken of as an item of his assets. And as for a business man's capitalising other persons, the law does not allow it, even in the form of peonage. There are also other material objects "under the dominion of man" which are not currently thought of as items of capital.

There are apparently two main perplexities of the mechanical classification which constrain Mr. Fisher to include the person of the owner among the owner's assets as capital: (*a*) Contrary to business usage, he is required by his premises to exclude immaterial wealth because it is not amenable to classification by mechanical tests, and it is therefore necessary to find some roundabout line of approach to such elements as good will, and the like; [4] and (*b*) persons are conceived to yield income (in the

[4] See chapter ii, section 6, pp. 24-31; also section 10.

sense of Mr. Fisher's definition of "income," presently to be noted), and since capital is held to be anything which yields "income"—indeed, "capital" is such by virtue of its yielding "income"—persons are included under "capital" by force of logic, though contrary to fact.

(2) As has already been indicated in passing, "immaterial wealth," or "intangible assets," is excluded from "capital" in Mr. Fisher's analysis. Indeed, the existence of intangible assets is denied. The phrase is held to be an untoward misnomer for certain classes of property rights in material objects which are not wholly owned by the individual to whom these property rights inure. An important part of these incomplete property rights are rights of quasi-ownership in other persons, or claims to services performed by such persons. This denial of immaterial wealth Mr. Fisher intends as a salutary correction of current business usage (see p. 39); and he takes pains to show how, by a cumbersome ratiocination (see chapter ii, sections 6–10), the term "intangible assets" may be avoided without landing the theory in the instant confusion which a simple denial of the concept would bring about. As a correction of current usage the attempted exclusion of intangible assets from "capital" does not seem a wise innovation. It cripples the definition for the purposes which alone would make a definition worth while. The concept of intangible assets is present in current usage on no such doubtful or precarious tenure as could be canceled by a bit of good advice. Its vogue is growing and its use is becoming more secure and more definite. The habit and the necessity of taking account, under one name or another, of the various immaterial items of wealth classed as intangible assets counts for more and more in the conduct of affairs; and any theory that aims to deal with the actualities of modern business

will have to make its peace with the term or terms by which these elements of capital are called, however wrong-headed a habit it may be conceived to be. The men of affairs find the concept serviceable, or rather they find it forced upon them, and the theorist of affairs cannot afford to dispense with a concept which is so large a constituent in the substance of affairs.

But the fault of the definition at this point is more serious than the mere exclusion of a serviceable general term which might be avoided by a circumlocution. "Intangible assets" is not simply a convenient general term covering certain more or less fluctuating property rights in certain material items of wealth. The elements of capital so designated are chiefly of the nature of differential advantages of a given business man, or a given concern, as against another. But they are capitalised in the same way as tangible items of wealth are capitalised, and in large part they are covered by negotiable securities, indistinguishable, and in most cases inseparable from, securities representing tangible assets. So, being blended in the process of capitalisation with the tangible assets, the securities based on the intangible assets create claims of ownership co-ordinate with those based on the material items and enter, in practice, into "capital summation" on the same footing as other items of wealth. Hence they become a basis of credit extensions, serving to increase the aggregate claims of creditors beyond what the hypothecable material wealth of the debtors would satisfy. Hence, in a period of general liquidation, when the differential advantages of the various concerns greatly contract, the legitimate claims of creditors come greatly to exceed the paying capacity of debtors, and the collapse of the credit system follows. The failure of classical theory to give an intelligent account of credit and crises is in great part due to the habitual refusal of economists to recognise intangible assets, and Mr. Fisher's argument is, in effect, an accentuation of this ancient infirmity of the classical theory.

It may be added that differential competitive advantages cannot be added together to make an aggregate, even apart from the tangible items of "capital wealth," since the advantage of one concern is the disadvantage of another. These assets come forth, grow great, and decay, according to the advance or decline of the strategic advantage achieved by given individuals or business concerns. Their "summation" is a spurious summation, in the main, since they represent competitive advantages, in the main; and their capitalisation adds a spurious volume to the aggregate property rights of the community. So that it follows from the capitalisation of these items of differential wealth, particularly when they are covered by vendible securities, that the aggregate property rights of the community come to exceed the aggregate wealth of the community.[5] This is, of course, a sufficiently grave trait of the modern business situation, but the effect of Mr. Fisher's contention is to deny its existence by the turn of a phrase and to put economic theory back where it stood before the modern situation had arisen. There are other turns in modern business affairs traceable to the vogue of this concept of "intangible assets," but this illustration of its grave consequences should be a sufficient caution to any taxonomist who endeavors to simplify his scheme of definition by denying inconvenient facts.

The point is perhaps sufficiently plain from what has been said, but it will bear specific mention that the ap-

[5] Contrary to Mr. Fisher's elaborate doctrine of property rights as defined by mechanical limits.—Chapter ii.

parent success of Mr. Fisher's analysis of intangible assets (pp. 32–40, 96–97) is due to his not going beyond the first move. So soon as the actualities of business complication and the cumulative effects of capitalisation are taken into account, it is evident that, with the best intentions, Mr. Fisher's explanation of intangible assets as a roundabout claim to certain concrete (tangible) items of wealth will not serve. The treatment of credit suffers from a like unwillingness to accept the facts of observation or to look farther than the first move in an analysis. This shortsightedness of the taxonomic economist is a logical consequence of the hedonistic postulates of the school, not a personal peculiarity of the present or any other author.

As to Mr. Fisher's definition and handling of the second concept with which the book is occupied—income— much the same is true as of the discussion of capital. Income is re-defined with a close adherence to the logic of that hedonistic-taxonomic system of theory for which he speaks. The concept of income here offered is more tenaciously consistent with the logical run of current classificatory economics, perhaps, than any that has been offered before. It is the perfect flower of economic taxonomy, and it shows, as no previous exposition of the kind has shown, the inherent futility of this class of work for other than purely taxonomic ends.

The concept of income, like that of capital, is well at home in current business usage; and, professedly, it is the concept of income as it plays its part in the affairs of business that occupies the author's attention. But here, again, as before, the definition—"the nature of income" —is not worked out from observation of current facts, with an endeavor to make the demarcation of the con-

cept square with the habitual apprehension of the phenomena of income in the business community. Taken at
its current import, as the concept is taken in the run of
business and in the economic affair of any community of
men dominated by the animus of business enterprise,
there can be no question but that "income" is a pecuniary
concept; it is money income, or is as an element which is
convertible into terms of money income and amenable
to the pecuniary scheme of accountancy. As a business
proposition, nothing that cannot be rated in terms of
money income is to be accounted income at all; which is
the same as saying that no definition which goes beyond
or behind the pecuniary concept can be a serviceable
definition of income for modern use. There may be
something beyond or behind this pecuniary concept
which it may be desirable to reach and discuss for some
other purpose more or less germane to the affairs of
modern life; but such a something, whatever its nature,
cannot be called "income" in the same sense in which that
term is employed in modern business usage. When the
term is applied to such an extra-pecuniary or præter-
pecuniary concept, such an extension of the term is a
rhetorical license; it is a figure of speech which is bound
to work confusion in any argument or analysis that deals
with the two inconvertible concepts. "Income," in modern usage, is a business concept; "psychic income" is not;
and, as Mr. Fisher is in an eminently good position to
admit, the two are incommensurable, or rather disparate,
magnitudes. The one cannot be reduced to terms of the
other. This state of the case may be deprecated, but it
cannot be denied; and it is no service to the science of
modern economic life to confuse this distinction by running the two in under one technical term.

Chapter xiv ("Earnings and Income"), and more particularly the latter sections of the chapter, illustrate how far from facts one may be led by a consistent adherence to Mr. Fisher's hedonistic working-out of the concept of income. "To regard 'savings' as income is essentially to regard an increase of capital as income" (pp. 254–255). Now, apart from the hedonistic prepossession, there is, of course, no reason for not regarding such an increase of capital as income. The two ideas— "income" and "increase of capital"—are by no means mutually exclusive in the current usage; and ordinarily, so long as the terms are taken in their current (pecuniary) meaning, such an increase of capital would unhesitatingly be rated as income to the owner. The need of making "income" and "increase of capital" mutually exclusive categories is a need incident to a mechanically drawn scheme of classification, and it disappears so soon as classification for classification's sake is given up. It is traceable to a postulated (hedonistic) principle presumed to rule men and things, not to observation of the run of facts in modern life. Indeed, even in Mr. Fisher's analysis the distinction goes into abeyance for a while where, in the doctrine of "capital value" (chapter xiii, especially section 11, and chapter xviii, section 2) the facts will absolutely not tolerate its being kept up. The hedonistic taxonomy breaks down at this juncture. And the fact is significant that this point of doctrine—viz., that capital considered as a magnitude of value "is the discounted value of the expected income"—is the latest and most highly prized advance in economic theory to whose initiation Mr. Fisher's writings give him a defensible claim.[6]

[6] Cf. *Journal of Political Economy,* papers cited above.

The day when Bentham's conception of economic life was serviceable for the purposes of contemporary science lies about one hundred years back, and Mr. Fisher's reduction of "income" to "pyschic income" is late by that much. The absolute merits of the hedonistic conception of economic theory need not be argued here. It was a far-reaching conception, and its length of life has made it a grand conception. But great as may be the due of courtesy to that conception for the long season of placid content which economic theory has spent beneath its spreading chestnut tree, yet the fact is not to be overlooked that its scheme of accountancy is not that of the modern business community. The logic of economic life in a modern community runs in terms of pecuniary, not of hedonistic magnitudes.

Mr. Fisher's farthest advance, his definition and handling of "capital value," involves the breaking down of the classical hedonistic taxonomy; and the breakdown is typical of the best work done by the school. This move of the classifiers is, of course, nothing sudden; nor is it an accident. It means, in substance, only that the modern facts have increasingly shown themselves incompatible with the mechanical scheme of classical definitions, and that this discrepancy between the facts and the received categories has finally forced a breaking away from the old categories. The whole voluminous discussion of the capital concept, for the past twenty years or so, has, indeed, turned about this discrepancy between business practice and the hedonistic classification by means of which economists have tried to deal with this business practice. All expedients of classification, definition, refinement, and interpretation of technical phrases have been tried, except the surrender of the main position—

that economic conduct must be read in terms of the hedonistic calculus.[7]

Under the stress of this controversy of interpretation, the hedonistic concept of capital as a congeries of "productive goods" has gradually and reluctantly, but hitherto not wholly, been replaced by something more serviceable. But this gain in serviceability has been won—in so far as the achievement may be spoken of in the past tense—at some cost to the hedonistic point of view. Such serviceability as the newly achieved interpretation of the capital concept has, it has because, and only so far as, it substitutes a pecuniary for a hedonistic construction of the phenomena of capitalisation. Among those who speak for the new (pecuniary) construction is Mr. Fisher, although he is not by any means the freest of those who are breaking away. His position is, no doubt, deprecated by many taxonomic economists as being an irreverently, brutally iconoclastic innovation, quite indefensible on taxonomic grounds; but, after all, as Mr. Fetter has shown in more courteous words,[8] it is an equivocal, or perhaps rather an irresolute position at the best.

"Capital," in the classical definition, was, as required by the hedonistic point of view, a congeries of what has latterly been named "productive goods." From such a concept of capital, which is hopelessly and increasingly out of touch with business usage, the theorists have been straining away; and Mr. Fisher has borne a large part in the speculations that are leading up to the emancipation of theorists from the chore work required by that white elephant. But he is not content formally to give up the

[7] The argument will return to the hedonistic calculus presently to show how the logic of this calculus has forced the theory at certain points.

[8] *Journal of Political Economy,* as above, pp. 143–144.

heirloom; although, as Mr. Fetter indicates, he now makes little use of it except for parade. He offers two correlate definitions of capital: "capital wealth," i.e., productive goods, and "capital value," i.e., pecuniary capital.[9] The former of these, the authentic hedonistic concept, shortly drops out of the discussion, although it does not drop out so tracelessly as Mr. Fetter's criticism may suggest. The argument then proceeds, almost throughout, on the concept of "capital value." [10] But there is a recurrent, and, one is tempted to say, dutiful, reminder that this "capital value," or capitalisation of values, is to be taken as the value of a congeries of tangible objects (productive goods); whereby a degree of taxonomic consistency with the authentic past and with the hedonistic postulate is formally maintained, and whereby also, dutifully and authentically, intangible assets are excluded from the capital concept, as already indicated above. Capital value is "simply the present worth of the future income from the specified capital" [11] (p. 202); but this capital value, it is held, is always the value of tangible items (including persons?).

It is the uncanny office of the critic to deal impersonally with his author's work as an historical phenomenon. Under cover of this license it may be pardonable to speak baldly and broadly of the logic of this retention of the authentic postulate that physically productive goods

[9] Pp. 66–67, 327, and elsewhere.

[10] Mr. Fetter, in advance of Mr. Fisher in the position taken if not in priority of departure, advocates discarding the older (authentic hedonistic) concept, in form as well as in fact.

[11] In this and similar passages Mr. Fisher appears to be in search of a more competent phrase, which has been used, but which he apparently has not met with—"putative earning-capacity." Certain infirmities of such a definition, whether under one phrase or another, for the taxonomic purpose, will be indicated presently.

(including persons) alone are to be included in the capitalisation out of which capital value emerges. And what is here said in this connection is not to be taken as a presumptuous make-believe of reproducing the sequence of ideas by which Mr. Fisher has arrived at the position set forth in this book. It is only an attempt to trace the logical sequence between the main hedonistic body of theory and the historical outcome of its development at this point.

In the classical-Austrian scheme of theory the center and circumference of economic life is the production of what a writer on ethics has called "pleasant feeling." Pleasant feeling is produced only by tangible, physical objects (including persons), acting somehow upon the sensory. The inflow of pleasant feeling is "income"— "psychic income" net and positive. The purpose of capital is to serve this end—the increase of pleasant feeling— and things are capital, in the authentic hedonistic scheme, by as much as they serve this end. Capital, therefore, must be tangible, material goods, since only tangible goods will stimulate the human sensory pleasantly. Intangible assets, being not physical, do not impinge upon the sensory; therefore they are not capital. Since they unavoidably are thrown prominently on the screen in the show of modern life, they must, consistently with the hedonistic conception, be explained away by construing them in terms of some authentic category of tangible items.

There is a second line of approach to the same conclusion comprised in the logical scheme of hedonistic economics, more cogent on practical grounds than that sketched above and perhaps of equally convincing metaphysical force. The hedonistic (classical-Austrian) economics is a system of taxonomic science—a science of normalities. Its office is the definition and classification of "normal" phenomena, or, perhaps better, phenomena as they occur in the normal case. And in this normal case, when and so far as the laws of nature work out their ends unvitiated, nature does all things well. This is also according to the ancient and authentic canons of taxonomic science. In the hedonistically normal scheme of life wasteful, disserviceable, or futile acts have no place.[12] The current competitive, capitalistic business scheme of life is normal, when rightly seen in the hedonistic light. There is not (normally) present in it anything of a wasteful, disserviceable, or futile character. Whatever phenomena do not fit into the scheme of normal economic life, as tested by the hedonistic postulate, are to be taken account of by way of exception. If there are discrepancies, in the way of waste, disserviceability, or futility, e.g., they are not inherent in the normal scheme and they do not call for incorporation in the theory of the situation in which they occur, except for interpretative elimination and correction. In this course the hedonistic economics, with its undoubting faith that whatever (normally) is is right, simply follows the rule of all authentic taxonomic science.

As indicated above, the normal end of capital, as of all the multifarious phenomena of economic life, is the production of pleasure and the prevention of pain; and in the Benthamite system of theory—which includes the classical-Austrian economics—the normal end of the life of man in society, economic and otherwise, is the greatest happiness of the greatest number. Such may not be the outcome in any given actual situation, but in

[12] Cf., e.g., Clark, *Essentials of Economic Theory*, passim.—"Each man who gets, in a normal way, any income at all performs one or more productive functions" etc.—p. 92.

so far as such is not the outcome the situation departs from the normal; and such departures from the normal do not properly concern the (hedonistic) "science" of economics, but fall authentically to the care of the "art" of economics, whose concern it is to find correctives for these, essentially sporadic, aberrations. Under the rule of normal serviceability nothing can be included in the theoretically right "capital summation" which does not go to swell the aggregate of hedonistic "services" to man—nothing which is not "productive," in the sense of increasing the well-being of mankind at large. Persons may, indeed they "normally" should always, be productive in this sense, and persons, therefore, should properly be included in the capital summation.[13]

In this normalised scheme of economic life all claims

---

[13] What is to be done, theoretically, with persons leading disserviceable or futile lives, "undesirable citizens," does not clearly appear. They are undesirable, but they are of the human breed and so are presumably to be included in the normal human aggregate whose "greatest number" are elected for the "greatest happiness" by the (normally) benevolent laws of nature. The suggestion is, of course, obvious that they should be deducted from the gross aggregate of items—i.e., algebraically added in as negative magnitudes—so as to leave a net algebraic sum of positively serviceable capital goods, including persons. The like might apparently be done with impersonal material items which are wastefully or noxiously employed.

But the converse suggestion is at least equally cogent, that such disserviceable items, personal and impersonal, are simply abnormal, aberrant, exceptional, and that therefore they simply drop tracelessly out of the theoretical scheme, so as to leave the theoretically correct "summation" as large as it would be had these disserviceable negative items not been present. That is to say, the theoretically correct net aggregate serviceability is the same as the gross serviceability, since the negative quantities actually present among the aggregate of items are not normally present, and are, therefore, theoretically non-existent.

There is a third alternative. The abnormal disserviceable items being indubitably present in fact, and some part of them being present with the hedonistically sacred stamp of the human breed, it may represented by negotiable instruments, e.g., must be led back, as is done by Mr. Fisher,[14] to tangible items of serviceable goods; and in its application to the concrete case, the actual situation, it follows from this rule that all such instruments are, normally, evidences of the ownership of such tangible items as serve the material needs of mankind at large. It follows also that there are, normally, no items of differential serviceability included among the property rights covered by negotiable instruments; that in the hedonistic theory of business there are no differential advantages and no differential or competitive gains; that the gain of each business man is, at the most, simply the sum of his own contributions to the aggregate of services that maintain the life and happiness of the community. This optimistic light shed on the business situation by the hedonistic postulate is one of the most valued, and for the wise quietist assuredly the most valuable, of the theoretical results following from the hedonistic taxonomy. And this optimistic light will fall with the surrender of the authentic posi-

---

be that, in the apprehension of the adepts, should this problem of taxonomy present itself to them, at least so much of the disserviceable productive goods as are human beings should be counted in; but, since they are persons, and since it is the normal estate of man to be serviceable to his fellows, they should be theoretically counted as normally serviceable, and therefore included in the net aggregate of serviceability at the magnitude of serviceability normally imputable to them. What rule should guide in fixing the true magnitude of imputed normal serviceability for such disserviceable persons in such a case is a further problem of taxonomy which would take the present argument too far afield. This much seems clear, however, that under this third alternative the net aggregate serviceability to be imputed to the sum of capital goods (including persons) should exceed the actual aggregate serviceability by the addition of an amount approximately equal to the disservice rendered by the disserviceable persons in question.

[14] Chapter ii, especially sections 4–9, and pp. 93–96.

tion that capital is a congeries of physically productive goods. But while this light lasts the hedonistic economist is able to say that, although the scheme of economic life contemplated by him as normal is a competitive system, yet the gains of the competitors are in no degree of a competitive character; no one (normally) gains at the cost of another or at the cost of the community at large; nor does any one (normally) turn any part of his equipment of capital goods to use for a competitive or differential advantage. In this light, the competitive struggle is seen to work out as, in effect, a friendly rivalry in the service of mankind at large, with an eye single to the greatest happiness of the greatest number. If intangible assets are recognised by the theory this comforting outlook on the business situation fails, because intangible assets are, in the main, of a differential effect only. Hence they are excluded by the logic of the hedonistic taxonomy.

Returning to a point left uncovered above (p. 120), it may be in place to look more narrowly into the definition of capital as "capital value" arrived at by Mr. Fisher, ably spoken for by Mr. Fetter, and apparently in train to be accepted by many economists interested in questions of theory.[15] On its face this formulation seems

---

[15] "The value of capital is the discounted value of the expected income" (p. 328). "It is found by discounting (or 'capitalising') the value of the income expected from the wealth of property" (p. 330). "Capital today may be defined as economical wealth expressed in terms of the general unit of value." (Fetter, *Principles of Economics*, p. 115.) . . . "every good becoming capital when it is capitalised, that is, when the totality of its uses is expressed as a present sum of values." (Ibid., p. 116.) It has elsewhere been characterised as "capitalisation of putative earning capacity." The latter is perhaps the more serviceable definition, being nearer to the concept of capital current in the business community.

definite, tangible, and stable enough. Such a concept appears to serve the needs of business traffic. But it is a more delicate question, and more to the present purpose, whether the definition has the requisite stability and mechanical precision for the purposes of a taxonomy such as Mr. Fisher's, which seeks to set up mutually exclusive categories of things distinguished from one another by statistically determined lines of demarcation. The question obtrudes itself, as regards this putative value of expected income: Whose imputation of value is to be accepted? Value, of course, is a fact of imputation; and it may seem a ready solution to say that the decision in this question of appraisement is rendered by a consensus of imputation between or among the parties concerned in the capitalisation. This consensus would be shown concretely by market quotations of securities, and it would be shown in generalised form by the familiar diagrams offered by all taxonomists of the marginal-utility school. But, concretely, there is not always a consensus of imputations as to the expected value of a given flow of income; in the case of unlisted securities, as well as of other capitalisable property in like case, the appeal to a consensus fails. And, in point of taxonomic theory, the marginal-utility curves apply to the case in hand only when and in so far as the property in question is the subject of a bargain; and, further, the diagrams of intersections and the like are of no avail for the cases, frequent enough in practice, where bargains are struck at the same time for different lots of the same line of goods at different heights on the ordinate. It is only by virtue of broad and untenable generalisations concerning the higgling of the market that the diagrams appear to cover a general proposition as to the actual value of property. The upshot of the matter is that a given block of capital need not, in practice it frequently does not, have one particular value at a given time; no more than a given expected flow of income need have one particular value alone imputed to it by all, or by a consensus of, the various parties in interest.

A summary review of an actual case taken from current business traffic may illustrate some of the difficulties of arriving, in detail, at such a definite and stable determination of capital value as will serve the needs of "capital summation" as expounded by Mr. Fisher.

A relatively small and inconspicuous corporation managed by two men, A and B, had for a series of years been doing a successful, conservative business in one of the necessaries of life, and had achieved an enviable reputation for efficiency and reliability; that is to say, it had accumulated a large and valuable body of "good will." The only form of securities outstanding was common stock, unlisted, and held by relatively few stockholders. During the late winter and spring of the present year (1907), the managers of the company gathered from the course of the market that business in their line would probably slacken off appreciably in the immediate future, with small chance of a prompt recovery. They determined to sell out and withdraw to another line of business, not similarly dependant on prices. To this end they set about buying in all the stock of their company, A–B, with a view to selling out the going concern to another corporation, C–D, whose appraisement of the future (imputation of value) was apparently more sanguine than their own. The outstanding shares of stock were bought in, during a period of some six weeks, by A and B bargaining separately with the several stockholders as opportunity offered, at prices ranging from about 105 to about 125. Meantime, negotiations had been going for-

ward with company C–D for the sale of the concern as
a whole on the basis of an inventory of the plant, including the stock of goods on hand. Both the plant and the
stock of goods were somewhat extensive and scattered.
With the inventory as a basis the concern was sold at
an aggregate price which included a fair allowance for
the intangible assets (good will) of the going concern.
The inventory was taken on the basis of the last previous
monthly price-current, and the transfer to C–D took
place on that basis. As counted on by A–B, and as apparently not counted on by C–D, the next succeeding
monthly price-current showed a decline in the market
value of the stock of goods on hand of some nine or
ten percent; and the subsequent course of the market, as
well as of the volume of traffic in this line of business,
has been of the same complexion. The transfer of the
concern, all told, from A–B to C–D took place at figures
which aggregated an advance of some 25 percent over
the cost to A and B, counting the stock of the corporation at an average of the prices paid by them for such
shares of stock as they bought in from other stockholders, which was rather more than one-half of all
the outstanding stock.

The question now is: What, for purposes of "capital
summation," should be taken as the basis of the capital
value of corporation A–B last spring, say, at the date
of the transfer to C–D, or at any date during the
buying-in of the outstanding stock? During all this time
the "capital value" must have been something over
100 percent of the nominal capital, since none of the
stock was bought at less than 105. But the shares of
stocks were bought in, scatteringly, from 105 to 125,
with an average in the neighborhood of 115; while the
aggregate price of the going concern at the same time

seems to have been in the neighborhood of 140 percent of the nominal capitalisation. Should the last transaction in the purchase of stock from day to day, running uncertainly between 105 and 125, be construed to revise the "capital value" of the concern to that date? This would make the "capital value" skip capriciously back and forth within the 20 points of the margin, in attendance upon the last previous "consensus of imputation" between a given seller and one or the other of the two buyers. The final average of, say, 115, had not at that time been established, so that that figure could not be taken as a basis during the interval. Or should the stipulated price of the going concern rule the case, in the face of these transactions taking place at figures incompatible with it? Again, at the date of the transfer to C–D, was the "capital value" immediately before the transfer the (indefinite) rating given by the then owners, A and B; and was it, the next minute, to be counted at the price paid by C–D; or, at the nominal capitalisation; or, at the (indefinite) figure at which C–D might have been willing to sell? What further serves to muddle the whole question is the fact that the transfer price of the going concern had been agreed upon between A–B and C–D before the whole amount of the outstanding stock had been bought in by A–B.

This case, which is after all sufficiently commonplace, offers a chance for further refinements of confusion, but what has been said may serve to illustrate the point in question. The difficulty, it will be noticed, is a difficulty of classification, not of business procedure. There are no difficulties of mutual intelligibility among the various parties engaged in the transactions. The difficulties arise when it is attempted to define the phenomena for some (taxonomic) purpose not germane to the transactions in question, and to draw lines of demarcation that are of no effect in the business affairs in which these phenomena arise. The resulting confusion marks a taxonomic infirmity in the proposed capital concept, due to an endeavor to reach a definition from a metaphysical postulate (of hedonism) not comprised among the postulates on which business traffic proceeds.

This fable teaches that it is a wise hedonist who keeps his capital concept clear of all entanglement with "capital value," and, more particularly, with the live business notion of capitalised earning-capacity.

# II

# MISCELLANEOUS PAPERS

# KANT'S CRITIQUE OF JUDGMENT [1]

THE place of the *Critique of Judgment* in Kant's system of philosophy is that of a mean between the two Critiques of the Pure and of the Practical Reason. A feeling of the lack of coherence between the other two critiques prompted him to the elaboration of this one, and the Doctrine of Method at the close of the work is mainly a sketch of the way in which he conceived that the results of this *Critique* were to be made useful in the system of philosophy to which he regarded all his critical work as preliminary. The outcome of the *Critique of Practical Reason* is the notion of freedom in the person; the outcome of the *Critique of Pure Reason* is the notion of strict determinism, according to natural law, in the world. It will hardly do to say that the two are contradictory, for they are so thoroughly disparate that, taken by themselves only and placed in juxtaposition, they do not even contradict each other. It is well known that it was on account of this disparity of the two notions that Kant was able to hold to the reality of personal freedom at the same time that he held to the doctrine of unavoidable determination according to natural law. But while he found the disparity of the two indispensable in order to the reality of freedom, he also found that, in order to free activity, a mediation between the two was likewise indispensable.

[1] Reprinted from *The Journal of Speculative Philosophy,* Vol. XVIII, July, 1884.

The idea of freedom of moral action contains the requirement that the concepts of morality are to be actualised in the sphere of rational law. Without the possibility of realising the concepts of morality in the realm of nature—without ability to affect events in the course of nature—morality would be only a fiction. The free person must be able to exert a causality on things, or else his freedom would be only an absurdity; but, even if it be granted that the person can and does come into the course of events as an efficient cause, that is not enough. Thus far the conclusions of the *Critique of Practical Reason* reach, but Kant was not satisfied with that. The action of the person must be capable of falling in with the line of activity of the causes among which it comes; otherwise it will act blindly and to no purpose. The agent must know what will be the effect of this or that action, if his activity is not to be nugatory, or worse than nugatory. And, in order to such a knowledge of the results of a contemplated action, the knowledge furnished by simple experience is not sufficient. Simple experience, whether we accept Kant's doctrine concerning the knowledge given by experience, as he has developed it in the *Critique of Pure Reason,* or not, cannot forecast the future. Experience can, at the best, give what is or what has been, but cannot say what is to be. It gives data only, and data never go into the future unaided and of their own accord. Data do not tell what the effect of action will be, except as we are able to judge the future by the help of the data given. Judgment must come in, if experience is to be of any use, and morality anything more than a dream. The power of judgment, or of reasoning, must mediate between theoretical knowledge and moral action; and the kind of judgment that is required is inductive reasoning. All this is simple enough. It is so simple and is so obvious that it is difficult to see it until it has been pointed out, and after it has been pointed out it seems to have been unnecessary to speak of it. Though Kant, in giving his reasons for undertaking the *Critique of Judgment,* speaks mainly of the indispensableness of this power of inductive reasoning for the purposes of morality, it is evident that it is no less indispensable in every other part of practical life. Today any attempt, in any science, which does not furnish us an induction, is counted good for nothing, and it is with this power of inductive reasoning that the most important part of the *Critique of Judgment* has to do.

In Kant's trichotomous scheme of the faculties and capacities of the intellect, the Power of Judgment lies in the middle, between the Understanding and the Reason, just as the faculty of pleasure and pain lies between the faculties of cognition and of desire, and affords a connection and mediation between the two. The Understanding has to do with cognition, and is *a priori* legislative for empirical knowledge; the pure Reason has to do with desire, and is *a priori* legislative for action; by analogy we should be able to say, at least provisionally, that the Power of Judgment has to do with the capacity of pleasure and pain, and legislates *a priori* concerning the adequate or subservient, the commensurate, appropriate, or adapted (*das Zweckmässige*).

The Power of Judgment is, in general, the power of thinking the particular under the universal. "If the universal (the rule, the principle, the law) is given, then the judgment which subsumes the particular under it is *determinative.* [Deductive reasoning.] But if only the particular is given, for which the judgment is to find a universal, then the judgment is only *reflective.* [Inductive reasoning.] (*Kr. d. Urtheilskraft,* ed. K. Kehr-bach, 1878; *Einl.,* IV.) Inasmuch as this Critique is a critique of the *pure* Power of Judgment only—i.e., of the Power of Judgment in so far as none of the principles of its action are borrowed from elsewhere—it has to do only with the reflective judgment; for, in order that the judgment be determinative, the universal which is to serve it as a rule in the work of subsumption must be *given,* and so must be present as a premise, and will condition the action of the judgment working under it. The determinative judgment is simply the activity of the intellect in general in applying the laws given by Understanding and Reason, and, as such, its action has been analysed in the two critiques which treat of those faculties. The determinative judgment, subsuming particular data under general laws which are also data, is nothing but the activity of the Understanding in combining simple experience into a synthetic whole, under those laws of the Understanding which are a necessary condition of experience. Therefore the discussion of the determinative judgment belongs in the critique of the theoretical Reason. The reflective judgment passes beyond the simple data of experience and seeks a universal which is not given in empirical cognition; therefore it must proceed according to a principle not given to it from without. It has a power of self-direction, and therefore calls for a critique of its own.

This is the starting-point of the *Critique of Judgment,* and, if this had been borne in mind, it might have saved many of Kant's critics a good deal of mistaken criticism. As a rule, the criticisms offered on his doctrine of Teleology have gone to work as though his starting-point had been from the developed principle of Final Cause, and as though he had proceeded from that principle to the notion of adaptation, and thence to that of æsthetic appropriateness, which is precisely reversing the truth. They have taken up the Critique wrong end foremost, and it is no wonder that they have found fault with it. Kant's doctrine of Final Cause is arrived at from a consideration of the way in which the reflective judgment works; the nature of the reflective judgment is not deduced from a preconceived notion about finality.

The office of the reflective judgment is to find unity in multiplicity, or to give unity to multiplicity. Its action is not only synthetic, but it is to make a synthesis which shall reach beyond, and include more than what is given in simple experience. The problem of this Critique, as of the other two, is: How are synthetic judgments *a priori* possible? but, while the faculties under consideration in the other two Critiques have to do with laws unavoidably given and unavoidably applied to given data, the reflective judgment has to find the laws to be applied to given data. The reflective judgment is the faculty of search. It is the faculty of adding to our knowledge something which is not and cannot be given in experience. It is to reduce the manifold of nature, the various concepts we have of the things in the world, to a synthetic totality. It has to bring the facts given in experience under laws and principles, and to bring empirical concepts under higher concepts. Whatever is ascertained, and so becomes an item of knowledge, becomes therewith a point of departure for the reflective judgment. The reflective judgment is continually reaching over beyond the known, and grasping at that which cannot come within experience. Its object is a synthesis, a systematisation of whatever is known; and, in order to the attainment of a system, its procedure must be governed by some principle. As the result aimed at lies beyond experience, the principle according to which it is to proceed cannot be given by experience. The principle is not taken from outside the power of judgment, for, if such were the case, the judgment working under that principle would be determinative and not reflective; therefore the principle according to which the reflective judgment proceeds must originate with the reflective judgment itself; or, in other words, it must be an *a priori* principle of the intellect, and must hold its place as a principle only in relation to the reflective judgment. It cannot be the same principle, in the same form, as any of the principles governing the other faculties.

The nature of this principle is to be found from a consideration of the work it is to do. The reflective judgment is to generalise, to reduce our knowledge to a system under more general laws than any given by experience. Its office is to systematise, and to systematise is but another expression for reducing things to intelligent orders; that is, to think things as though they had been made according to the laws of an understanding, to think them as though made by an intelligent cause. But to think things in a system *as though* they were made by an intelligent cause is not the same as to think that they are made by such a cause. So much is not required by the principle. All that is required is that the things be thought as falling under a system of law according to which they adapt themselves to the laws of our understanding—that they are such in the manner of their being as they would be if they were made with a view to the exigencies of our capacity of knowing. The principle of the reflective judgment is, therefore, primarily the requirement of adaptation on the part of the object to the laws of the activity of our faculties of knowledge, or, briefly, adaptation to our faculties.

Now, whenever the intellect finds the objects of its knowledge to be such as to admit of the unhampered activity of the faculties employed about them, there results a gratification such as is always felt on the attainment of an end striven for. The more nearly the concept of the object known approaches to what such a concept might have been if it had been constructed simply under the guidance of the laws of the mind's own activity and without being in any way hindered or modified by external reality—that is, the more nearly the activity of the mind in thinking a given thought coincides with what would be the mind's activity if that activity were guided by its own intrinsic laws alone and were not influenced or hampered by the environment— the more fully will the requirements of the mind's activity be realised, and the more intense will be the gratification felt in contemplating the object of thought which so employs the mind. A feeling of gratification, or the contrary, accordingly, goes along with the activity of the reflective judgment as a sanction and a test of its normality.

What this feeling of gratification testifies to is, that the play of the faculties of the intellect is free, or but little hampered by the empirical element in its knowledge. It therefore indicates that the objects contemplated are, in the form in which they are present in thought, adapted to the faculties. This adaptation of knowledge to our faculties may take place in two different ways, or rather it may take place at two different stages in the elaboration of the material gained by experience. A simple datum may be given to the apprehension such as to

conform to the normal action of our faculty of knowledge, and, by its so conforming, it shows adaptation to
the faculties that are employed about it. In such a case,
the concept which is contemplated and found adapted
is not thereby an item of knowledge which goes to make
up our conception of the world system, or to make a
part of any systematic or organised whole. As a datum
of the apprehension, it is considered singly by itself only
in relation to the apprehending subject, no thought
being given to its making or not making an integral
part of our knowledge of reality. In so far as concerns
the adaptation conceived to belong to the concept, it is
no matter whether any external reality corresponds to
the concept or not; and, therefore, it makes no difference, as to the adaptation, whether the concept is derived from experience or is a pure figment. The adaptation belonging to such a concept, which is only a datum
of the apprehension, is, therefore, subjective only. It
is only a question of the conformation or nonconforma-
tion of a simple concept (*Vorstellung*) to the norms
of the apprehension. The question is, how far the concept given is suited to the normal activity of the faculty
of cognition; whatever may be the objective validity of
the concept, that does not enter into consideration at all.
This being the case, the only way to judge of the adaptation of such a concept is to take cognisance of the way
in which the faculties act on occasion of it, and the
test can only be whether the faculties act unhampered
and satisfactorily; and the only indication of the normal activity of the faculties, again, is the resulting feeling of gratification or dissatisfaction. If the concept,
simply as such, pleases, it is normal or adapted; if it
displeases, it is not. The object corresponding to such
a concept, which pleases in its simple apprehension, is

said to be beautiful, and the reflective judgment, in so far as it proceeds on the simple adaptation of the data of apprehension to the faculties of cognition, is æsthetic judgment. It is of a purely subjective character, and its action is not based on logical, but wholly on pathological grounds. The decision of the æsthetic judgment is made on the ground of the feeling called forth by the apprehension of the concept, and the feeling is, therefore, in this case, the only authority that has a voice in the matter.

From these considerations it follows that there can be no objective principle of æsthetic judgment. The principle which governs taste must accordingly exert its authority, not through the means of logical argument and proof, but by an appeal to the nature of men in respect to reflective judgment in general. "The principle of taste is the subjective principle of the judgment in general" (*Kr. d. U.*, p. 148). The universal validity which a judgment in a matter of taste bespeaks can, therefore, rest only on the assumption of an essential similarity of all men in respect to the feeling involved in such a judgment.

On the other hand, the data of cognition may also be contemplated, with reference to their adaptation, at the stage at which they are no longer simple data of apprehension, but constitute a part of our knowledge of reality. That is, they (the concepts) may be considered as making a part of our knowledge of nature, and, consequently, as entering into a system in which they must stand in relation to other data. Their adaptation will consequently here be found, if at all, in the logical relations of concepts—items of empirical knowledge or laws of nature—to one another, and the conformity of these relations to the normal activity of the faculties;

not in the immediate adaptation of particular items or data of experience to be taken up by the faculties, as was the case in the æsthetic judgment. And since the faculties, in dealing with the relations of concepts as making up our knowledge of reality, have to do with the relations of real objects as known to us, the relations of the concepts, in which the adaptation is supposed to lie, are here conceived to be real relations of objects; the adaptation of these concepts, as standing in logical relations to one another, to the normal activity of the mind, therefore comes to be looked on as a quality of the objects contemplated. The objects are conceived to stand in such relations of dependence and interaction as correspond to the logical relations of the concepts we have of them. Now, as a matter of fact, the connection or relation of our concepts which will be found adapted to our faculties, and which answers the requirements of their normal action, is one according to which they make a systematic, connected whole. The relations of objects which shall correspond in the world of reality to this logical relation of our concepts are such relations of interaction and interdependence as will bind the particular things in the world of reality together into a whole, in which the existence of one thing is dependent on that of another, and in which no one thing can exist without mutually conditioning and being conditioned by every other. That is, the adaptation found, or sought to be found, in concepts when contemplated in their logical aspect, is conceived to be an adaptation of things to one another in such a way that each is at the same time the means and the end of the existence of every other.

Such a conception of the world of reality, in which things are united into an organised whole, can proceed only on the assumption that the particular things which go to make up the organic whole are subject to laws of a character similar to that of the logical laws according to which our mind subsumes the particular under the general, and holds together all the material gained by our cognition in a systematic totality of knowledge; which is the same as saying that in such a conception is contained the idea that the world is made according to laws similar to the laws of our understanding, and therefore that it is made by an intelligent cause, and made with intention and purpose. To put the same thing in another way: To conceive the world in the way required by the reflective judgment is to conceive it as being made so as to harmonise with the laws of our understanding; that is, in being made, it is adapted to our faculties, and therefore made by a cause working according to laws like those of our understanding, and with a view to the exigencies of our understanding in comprehending the world. The cause producing the world must therefore be conceived to have worked it out according to a preconceived notion of what it was to be, and the realization of the form in which the world so created actually exists, accordingly, has its ground in an idea conceived by the cause which created it. The idea of what the world was to be precedes and conditions the world as it actually comes into existence—which is precisely what we mean when we say that the world was created by final cause.

All this argument for a final cause in the world rests on the action of the reflective judgment, and its validity therefore extends only so far as the principle of the reflective judgment reaches. That principle is the requirement of adaptation, on the part of our knowledge, to the normal action of our faculties of knowing; it is therefore of subjective validity only, and can say nothing as to the nature of external reality. The finality which is attributed to external reality, on the ground of the adaptation found by the reflective judgment, is simply and only an imputed finality, and the imputation of it to reality is based on the same ground of feeling as every other act of the reflective judgment. Our imputation of finality to the things of the world, and our teleological arguments for an intelligent cause of the world, proceed on subjective grounds entirely, and give no knowledge of objective fact, and furnish no proof that is available for establishing even a probability in favor of what is claimed.

What is proved by the tenacity with which we cling to our teleological conception of the world is, that the constitution of our intellect demands this conception— that our faculties, in their normal action, must arrive at this before they can find any halting-place. The mind is not satisfied with its knowledge of a thing, or of any event or fact, until it is able to say, not only how the thing is, or how it came about, but also why it is as it is, and what was the purpose of its coming to pass. At least it must be able to assert, before it will rest from its search, that the thing or event has a purpose; the proposition may be put into this general form, and we may be obliged, oftentimes, to leave the matter in this state of generality; but we cannot believe, concerning anything, that there is no reason why it is, or why it is as it is. It is, of course, possible to give our attention to any item of knowledge—to employ ourselves about any object or any process or law in nature—without bringing in the notion of purpose; but our knowledge of it cannot be regarded as complete until we have asked the question why it is.

But though this question of teleology is of extreme importance, yet a knowledge of the teleological end of a given thing, or the purpose of an action or event as considered from the standpoint of the economy of the universe, is not absolutely necessary in order to human life, nor even in order to a high degree of development in moral life. In truth, a knowledge of ultimate particular ends and purposes is of no use whatever in the affairs of everyday life; and, therefore, the principle of teleology, as being the principle of conscious purpose in the world, is not indispensable in order to such knowledge of things as is required by the exigencies of life. The knowledge we need and use can be got, and got in sufficient completeness for all purposes of utility, without any appeal to, or any aid from, the developed principle of finality; and, if the exercise of the reflective judgment, in its logical application, consisted in the decision of teleological questions alone, its value would be small enough. Such, however, is not the case.

The principle of the logical use of the reflective judgment was found to be the general principle of adaptation; and since, in its logical use, the judgment has to do with reality, the principle which shall govern the reflective judgment here will be that of objective adaptation; that is, adaptation which is *conceived* to belong to things objectively. The motive which leads to the application of this principle to our knowledge of things was found to be a feeling of dissatisfaction with our knowledge so long as it consists only in a chaotic manifold of concepts. We are dissatisfied with a conception of reality which makes it only a congeries of things, without connection, system, or order, beyond juxtaposition in space and succession and duration in time. Yet such a congeries is all that unaided experience can give; and the determinative (deductive) judgment can do little to bring further order into this chaos. It is true, we have the general law of cause and effect given, and it looks as though we ought to be able to establish some system by the aid of it, when experience gives us the data to which the law applies; but further thought will show that we should be as helpless with that law as without it if no further principle came in to guide us in the application of it. We should have the law which says: "Every change has a cause and an effect"; and all that the data of experience would enable us to say further would be that this law in general applies to these data. The abstract law and the data, simply under the action of the determinative judgment, could never get so far as to afford us ground for asserting that a given effect has a given cause; still less that a given cause will produce a given effect. The truth of this is shown by the nature of our knowledge of particular causes. We can never designate, with that certainty which belongs to every deliverance of the deductive judgment, what is the cause of any given effect. We may have no doubt as to what is the cause of a given effect; but still, if it should turn out that the effect under consideration has some other cause than the one we counted on, we should not, therefore, conclude that the world is out of joint. It is possible that we may be mistaken in our opinion as to particular cases of cause and effect—even the most certain of them—which would not be the case if we arrived at our knowledge of them by simple deductive reasoning from data of experience and an *a priori* law. There is always an element of probability, however slight, in our knowledge of particular causes; but simple experience—cognition—never has anything to say about probability; it only says what *is,* and leaves no room for doubt or probability.

In order to find what is the cause of a given effect, and, still more, what *will be* the effect of a given cause, we need a guiding principle beyond anything that experience gives. We have to go beyond what is given us, and so we need a principle of search. That is what is afforded by this principle of adaptation. The mind is unsatisfied with things until it can see how they belong together. The principle of adaptation says that the particular things do belong together, and sets the mind hunting to find out how. The principle of adaptation says that, in order to the normal action of the faculties, things must be conceived as adapted to one another so as to form a systematic totality—that things must be conceived to be so co-ordinated in their action as to make up an organized whole—and the mind goes to make its knowledge of reality conform to its own normal activity; or, in other words, to find what particular cases of interaction under the law of cause and effect will stand the test of the principle of adaptation. What the principle of adaptation does for us is, therefore, in the first place, that it makes us guess, and that it guides our guessing. If it were not that we are dissatisfied with our knowledge so long as it remains in the shape of a mere manifold, we should never seek to get beyond a congeries of things in time and space; and, if it were not that the principle of adaptation shows us what we are to seek further, we should never find anything further in our knowledge.

But the principle of adaptation cannot give us any new data, nor can it tell us anything new about the data we have. All it can do is to guide us in guessing about the given data, and then leave it to experience to credit or discredit our guesses. That is, it is a regulative, not a constitutive principle of knowledge, according to the distinction which Kant makes in his classification of *a priori* principles of the mind. Now, as has already been pointed out, the direction in which this principle will lead us is that of generalisation, since no such principle is needed in order to deductive reasoning. In order to analyse the content of our empirical knowledge, there is no guessing necessary; all that is then required is that we take a more complete inventory of what we already know. The guessing, under the principle of adaptation, is in the direction of a higher systematisation of what we know. The principle suggests that, in order to conform to the norms of our faculties, things should fall into a system under laws of such or such a character; that they should stand in such or such relations of interaction and co-ordination; and that the laws which are given *a priori* as applying to things should apply to them in such or such a way; and so it leads to an hypothesis as to the nature of particular things and the laws of their connection. The principle guides us to an hypothesis, but it has nothing to say as to the validity of the hypothesis in the world of reality. It proceeds on the basis of a feeling, and so it can decide whether the hypothesis suits the mind, but not at all whether it applies to reality. Experience alone can say whether the hypothesis fits the things it is intended for; or, rather, it can say whether it appears to fit them, since, inasmuch as an hypothesis never can become an object of experience in the same sense as things are objects of experience, it can also not have that empirical certainty which belongs to our knowledge of individual things. The testimony of experience as to the validity of the hypothesis can only be of a cumulative character, and all it can do is to give it a greater or less degree of probability. It is of the nature of circumstantial evidence.

The principle of adaptation, in its logical use, is accordingly the principle of inductive reasoning. The need felt by the mind of bringing order and systematic coherence into the knowledge it acquires, and therefore of conceiving the things about which it is engaged as adapted to one another, affords, at the same time, the motive and the guiding principle for induction. The unrest felt on account of the inharmonious and forced activity of the faculties, when engaged about a mere manifold or a discordant miscellany, drives the mind to seek a concord for its own activities, and, consequently, a reconciliation of the conflicting elements of its knowledge. The reason for the unrest felt in contemplating external things simply as individual and unconnected things lies in the fact that the mind is adapted to conceive the subject-matter of its knowledge in the form of a connected whole. If the mind had not an inherent capacity for thinking things as connected into a totality, or at least as being connected in a systematic way and under definite laws, it could not feel the lack of totality in contemplating things under the mere form of juxtaposition in time and space. It would not be dissatisfied with things as mere data if it knew of nothing better; and it would not seek for anything different if the conception of things, as a mere congeries, satisfied the requirements of its normal activity. But the requirement of totality, of adaptation of part to part, being present, the mind has no alternative but to reflect and reflect on the material given it, and make the most it can out of it in the way of a systematic whole; and the requirement of adaptation points out the direction which its search must take. One consequence of this is that the search is never ended, as, from the nature of the case, the requirement can never be fulfilled. As soon as a result is obtained by the process of induction, that result becomes, for the purposes of the question in hand, a fact of empirical knowledge, and therefore acquires the character, not of a completed whole, but of an isolated and disconnected datum. As fast as one step of induction is completed it becomes a means to another step, which must inevitably follow it.

According to what has just been said, the motive and guiding principle of inductive reasoning, and, with it, of the teleological judgment, is the requirement of adaptation or totality in our knowledge. When we find this requirement answered, in greater or less degree, the consequence is more or less of a feeling of gratification, just as there is always a feeling of gratification on the successful completion of an undertaking, or the attainment of a desired end. This feeling of gratification may therefore be regarded as a sanction to the principle of the reflective judgment, and, in the last resort, it is this feeling of gratification alone which can decide whether the principle has been applied successfully in any given case.

Therefore, so far as concerns the distinctive characteristics of the reflective judgment—and, therefore, of inductive reasoning—it proceeds on subjective ground entirely. Its motive is subjective, and, though the evidence by which it seeks to establish the results aimed at is of empirical origin, yet the criterion, to which the result must conform in order to answer the purposes for which it is sought to be established, is subjective. The consequence of this subjectivity of the principle of induction is that the results it arrives at are only more or less probable. Yet, singular as it might seem, hardly any part of our knowledge except that got by induction is of any immediate use for practical purposes. For by induction alone can we reduce things to system and connection, and so bring particular things and events under definite laws of interaction; therefore by induction alone can we get such knowledge as will enable us to forecast the future; and knowledge which shall help us to forecast the future—to tell what will take place under given circumstances and as the result of given actions—is the only knowledge which can serve as a guide in practical life, whether moral or otherwise.

# ARTS AND CRAFTS [1]

The primary motive of the arts and crafts movement is, as the name implies, the association of art and labor. Initially an English movement, it has been slowly emerging from the general industrial field for about forty years. . . . On its theoretical side the movement is, of course, much older than forty years, its development as an idea being measured by the lives of Carlyle, Ruskin, and Morris.[2]

THE chapters which make up the greater part of Mr. Triggs's volume give an excellent outline of the work of Carlyle, Ruskin, and Morris in relation to art and industry, followed by a sketch on Ashbee and the Reconstructed Workshop and another on Rookwood. The whole leads up to the practical efforts made in Chicago by the Industrial Art League, of which the author is secretary.

Little need be said here of the facile and engaging manner in which Mr. Triggs presents his plea for the work of regeneration in which the league is engaged, but it may not be out of place to speak of the economic bearing of such a movement as a departure in industrial aims and methods. The purpose is to humanise and beautify industry and to bring art into the everyday work of the industrial classes. This end is sought

[1] Reprinted from *The Journal of Political Economy,* Vol. XI, December, 1902.

[2] *Chapters in the History of the Arts and Crafts Movement.* By Oscar Lovell Triggs. Chicago, 1902.

through a return to handicraft methods of work and an avoidance of competitive commercial methods of management. In the later phases of the propaganda, machine production is not condemned without qualification, except in practice. Particularly is this true of Mr. Triggs's presentation of the case, although the earlier phases represented by Morris, and more especially by Ruskin, renounce the machine and all its works with an animation that is not to be mistaken. But even in the later phases of the movement the recognition of machine production as an unavoidable circumstance, if not indeed an unavoidable evil, is a perfunctory concession to facts rather than an integral element in the principles on which the advocates of the movement go about their work.

The movement, it must be said, runs on sentimental grounds rather than on grounds of reasoned practicability. Industrially it is not a continued growth out of the present, but seeks continuity with a past phase of economic life. This may be a necessity of the case. To find a basis for that "association of art and labor" at which the movement aims, such may perhaps be the only available recourse, and this is scarcely the place to offer criticism on the artistic merits of such a course. But seen from the standpoint of industrial feasibility the whole matter looks somewhat different. Its striking trait in this respect is a certain "lack of contemporaneity. Modern industry, in so far as it is characteristically modern, means the machine process; but according to the arts-and-crafts apprehension, only outside the machine process is there salvation. Since the machine process is indispensable to modern culture, both on business grounds and for reasons of economy, this limits the immediate scope of the arts-and-crafts salva-

tion to those higher levels of consumption where exigencies of business and economy are not decisive. The
greater (90–99 percent of the whole) range of industry
must under present circumstances of business and household management remain untouched by any such proposed alteration of the character of the industrial
process. The "industrial art" methods are too costly for
general business purposes, and the "industrial art"
products are (in point of fact) too expensive for general consumption; indeed it is of the essence of industrial art products, if they are to pass inspection by
the adepts, that they must be sufficiently expensive to
preclude their use by the vulgar.

Culturally the movement is an offshoot of Romanticism, which means archaism, but always a sophisticated archaism. In the arts-and-crafts ritual the
requisite sophistication is had by an insistence on
genuineness, sincerity; which being interpreted in economic terms means a genuine high labor cost. This requirement, of course, boldly traverses the requirements
of modern business enterprise as well as of modern,
that is to say democratic, culture. Business exigencies
demand spurious goods, in the sense that the goods must
cost less than they appear to; while a democratic culture
requires low cost and a large, thoroughly standardised
output of goods.

If the proposed association of art and labor is to go
into effect under modern circumstances, it will have to
mean the association of art with the machine process
and with the technology of that process. Modern industry is machine industry, and the forms of labor for
which there is an outlook under modern circumstances
are those employments which are engaged in the machine industry. Such labor as is not associated with the

machine process and conditioned by its technological requirements is in the position of an inconsequential interloper. Such work as goes on today without being immediately under the guidance of the mechanical technology is, with sporadic exceptions, subsidiary to that main body of work which this technology directly and unquestioningly controls. And the precarious margin of work still left outside the sweep of a rigorously consistent machine technology grows visibly narrower from day to day. Therefore, any movement for the reform of industrial art or for the inculcation of æsthetic ideals must fall into line with the technological exigencies of the machine process, unless it choose to hang as an anæmic fad upon the fringe of modern industry.

Men's, particularly workmen's, habits of thought in industrial matters are machine made, in a progressively more unmitigated degree; and if these habits of thought are to be shaped by any propaganda of ideals, they must be sought out and laid hold on in the field where they grow. The machine process has come, not so much to stay merely, but to go forward and root out of the workmen's scheme of thought whatever elements are alien to its own technological requirements and discipline. It ubiquitously and unremittingly disciplines the workmen into its way of doing, and therefore into its way of apprehending and appreciating things. "Industrial art," therefore, which does not work through and in the spirit of the machine technology is, at the best, an exotic. It will not grow into a dandelion-like "weed of cultivation," for it has no chance of life beyond the hothouse shelter of decadent æstheticism.

But however impracticable, within the frontiers of a democratic culture, may be the (substantially aristocratic) ideals and proposals of the "Dreamer of dreams, born out of his due time," it does not follow from all this that the movement initiated by the Dreamer need be without salutary effect upon the working life of the workmen or the artistic value of their output of goods. Indirectly these ideals, romantic or otherwise, have already had a large effect, and there is every reason to hope that the propaganda of taste carried on by organisations like the Industrial Art League and its congeners will count for much in checking the current ugliness of the apparatus of life.

At its inception the movement was a romanticism, with a smear of lackadaisical æstheticism across its face. But that was not its whole meaning, nor is it the more enduring trait. Archaism and sophistication came of a revulsion against the besetting ugliness of what was present before the eyes of the leaders. The absolute dearth of beauty in the philistine present forced them to hark back to the past. The enduring characteristic is rather an insistence on sensuous beauty of line and color and on visible serviceability in all objects which it touches. And these results can be attained in fuller measure through the technological expedients of which the machine process disposes than by any means within the reach of the industry of a past age.

Now, the particular line of arts and crafts endeavor for which Mr. Triggs speaks, the Industrial Art League, recognises the force of this historical necessity more freely than the arts-and-crafts adepts of the stricter observance. Indeed, this aspiration after contemporaneity on the part of Mr. Triggs and his following is something of a stone of offense to the faithful, this apparently being the substantial reason why the Chicago Society of Arts and Crafts is not on speaking terms with the Industrial Art League. What has been said above, therefore, of the precarious outlook for industrial art under the régime of the machine process applies with less breadth to Mr. Triggs's line of endeavor than to many others.

# CHRISTIAN MORALS AND THE COMPETITIVE SYSTEM [1]

In the light of the current materialistic outlook and the current skepticism touching supernatural matters, some question may fairly be entertained as to the religious cult of Christianity. Its fortunes in the proximate future, as well as its intrinsic value for the current scheme of civilisation, may be subject to doubt. But a similar doubt is not readily entertained as regards the morals of Christianity. In some of its elements this morality is so intimately and organically connected with the scheme of western civilisation that its elimination would signify a cultural revolution whereby occidental culture would lose its occidental characteristics and fall into the ranks of ethnic civilisations at large. Much the same may be said of that pecuniary competition which today rules the economic life of Christendom and in large measure guides western civilisation in much else than the economic respect.

Both are institutional factors of first-rate importance in this culture, and as such it might be difficult or impracticable to assign the primacy to the one or the other, since each appears to be in a dominant position. Western civilisation is both Christian and competitive (pecuniary); and it seems bootless to ask whether its course is more substantially under the guidance of the one than of the other of these two institutional norms. Hence, if it should appear, as is sometimes contended, that there is an irreconcilable discrepancy between the two, the

[1] Reprinted from *The International Journal of Ethics*, Vol. XX, January, 1910.

student of this culture might have to face the question: Will western civilisation dwindle and decay if one or the other, the morals of competition or the morals of Christianity, definitively fall into abeyance?

In a question between the two codes, or systems of conduct, each must be taken at its best and simplest. That is to say, it is a question of agreement or discrepancy in the larger elementary principles of each, not a question of the variegated details, nor of the practice of the common run of Christians, on the one hand, and of competitive business men, on the other. The variety of detailed elaboration and sophistication is fairly endless in both codes; at the same time many Christians are engaged in competitive business, and conversely. Under the diversified exigencies of daily life neither the accepted principles of morality nor those of business competition work out in an untroubled or untempered course of conduct. Circumstances constrain men unremittingly to shrewd adaptations, if not to some degree of compromise, in their endeavors to live up to their accustomed principles of conduct. Yet both of these principles, or codes of conduct, are actively present throughout life in any modern community. For all the shrewd adaptation to which they may be subject in the casuistry of individual practice, they will not have fallen into abeyance so long as the current scheme of life is not radically altered. Both the Christian morality and the morality of pecuniary competition are intimately involved in this occidental scheme of life; for it is out of these and the like habits of thought that the scheme of life is made up. Taken at their best, do the two further and fortify one another? do they work together without mutual help or hindrance? or do they mutually inhibit and defeat each other?

In the light of modern science the principles of Christian morality or of pecuniary competition must, like any other principles of conduct, be taken simply as prevalent habits of thought. And in this light no question can be entertained as to the intrinsic merit, the eternal validity, of either. They are, humanly speaking, institutions which have arisen in the growth of the western civilisation. Their genesis and growth are incidents, or possibly episodes, in the life-history of this culture— habits of thought induced by the discipline of life in the course of this culture's growth, and more or less intrinsic and essential to its character as a phase of civilisation. Therefore, the question of their consistency with one another, or with the cultural scheme in which they are involved, turns into a question as to the conditions to which they owe their rise and continued force as institutions—as to the discipline of experience in the past, out of which each of them has come and to which, therefore, each is (presumably) suited. The exigencies of life and the discipline of experience in a complex cultural situation are many and diverse, and it is always possible that any given phase of culture may give rise to divergent lines of institutional growth, to habits of conduct which are mutually incompatible, and which may at the same time be incompatible with the continued life of that cultural situation which has brought them to pass. The dead civilisations of history, particularly the greater ones, seem commonly to have died of some such malady. If Christian morality and pecuniary competition are the outgrowth of the same or similar lines of habituation, there should presumably be no incompatibility or discrepancy between them; otherwise it is an open question.

Leaving on one side, then, all question of its divine

or supernatural origin, force, and warrant, as well as of its truth and its intrinsic merit or demerit, it may be feasible to trace the human line of derivation of this spirit of Christianity, considered as a spiritual attitude habitual to civilised mankind. The details and mutations of the many variants of the cult and creed might likewise be traced back, by shrewd analysis, to their origins in the habits enforced by past civilised life, and might on this ground be appraised in respect of their fitness to survive under the changing conditions of later culture; but such a work of detailed inquiry is neither practicable nor necessary here. The variants are many and diverse, but for all the diversity and discord among them, they have certain large features in common, by which they are identified as Christian and are contrasted with the ethnic cults and creeds. There is a certain Christian animus which pervades most of them, and marks them off against the non-Christian spiritual world. This is, perhaps, more particularly true of the moral principles of Christianity than of the general fabric of its many creeds and cults. Certain elemental features of this Christian animus stand forth obtrusively in its beginnings, and have, with varying fortunes of dominance and decay, persisted or survived unbroken, on the whole, to the present day. These are non-resistance (humility) and brotherly love. Something further might be added, perhaps, but this much is common, in some degree, to the several variants of Christianity, late or early; and the inclusion of other common principles besides these would be debatable and precarious, except in case of such moral principles as are also common to certain of the ethnic cults as well as to Christianity. Even with respect to the two principles named, there might be some debate as to their belonging peculiarly and characteristically to the Christian spirit, exclusive of all other spiritual habits of mind. But it is at least a tenable position that these principles are intrinsic to the Christian spirit, and that they habitually serve as competent marks of identification. With the exclusion or final obsolescence of either of these, the cult would no longer be Christian, in the current acceptation of the term; though much else, chiefly not of an ethical character, would have to be added to make up a passably complete characterisation of the Christian system, as, e.g., monotheism, sin and atonement, eschatological retribution, and the like. But the two principles named bear immediately on the morals of Christianity; they are, indeed, the spiritual capital with which the Christian movement started out, and they are still the characteristics by force of which it survives.

It is commonly held that these principles are not inherent traits of human nature as such, congenital and hereditary traits of the species which assert themselves instinctively, impulsively, by force of the mere absence of repression. Such, at least, in effect, is the teaching of the Christian creeds, in that they hold these spiritual qualities to be a gift of divine grace, not a heritage of sinful human nature. Such an account of their origin and their acquirement by the successive generations of men does not fit these two main supports of Christian morality in the same degree. It may fairly be questioned as regards the principle of brotherly love, or the impulse to mutual service. While this seems to be a characteristic trait of Christian morals and may serve as a specific mark by which to distinguish this morality from the greater non-Christian cults, it is apparently a trait which Christendom shares with many of the obscurer cultures, and which does not in any higher degree characterise Christendom than it does these other, lower cultures. In the lower, non-Christian cultures, particularly among the more peaceable communities of savages, something of the kind appears to prevail by mere force of hereditary propensity; at least it appears, in some degree, to belong in these lower civilisations without being traceable to special teaching or to a visible interposition of divine grace. And in an obscure and dubious fashion, perhaps sporadically, it recurs throughout the life of human society with such an air of ubiquity as would argue that it is an elemental trait of the species, rather than a cultural product of Christendom. It may not be an overstatement to say that this principle is, in its elements, in some sort an atavistic trait, and that Christendom comes by it through a cultural reversion to the animus of the lower (peaceable) savage culture. But even if such an account be admitted as substantially sound, it does not account for that cultural reversion to which Christendom owes its peculiar partiality for this principle; nor is its association with its fellow principle, non-resistance, thereby accounted for. The two come into play together in the beginnings of Christianity, and are thenceforward associated together, more or less inseparably, throughout the later vicissitudes of the cult and its moral code.

The second-named principle, of non-resistance and renunciation, is placed first in order of importance in the earlier formulations of Christian conduct. This is not similarly to be traced back as a culturally atavistic trait, as the outgrowth of such an archaic cultural situation as if offered by the lower savagery. Non-resistance has no such air of ubiquity and spontaneous recrudescence, and does not show itself, even sporadically, as a matter of course in cultures that are otherwise apparently unrelated; particularly not in the lower cultures, where the hereditary traits of the species should presumably assert themselves, on occasion, in a less sophisticated expression than on the more highly conventionalised levels of civilisation. On the contrary, it belongs almost wholly to the more highly developed, more coercively organised civilisations, that are possessed of a consistent monotheistic religion and a somewhat arbitrary secular authority; and it is not always, indeed not commonly, present in these.

Christianity at its inception did not take over this moral principle, ready-made, from any of the older cults or cultures from which the Christian movement was in a position to draw. It is not found, at least not in appreciable force, in the received Judaism; nor can it be derived from the classical (Græco-Roman) cultures, which had none of it; nor is it to be found among the pagan antiquities of these barbarians whose descendants make up the great body of Christendom today. Yet Christianity sets out with the principle of non-resistance fullblown, in the days of its early diffusion, and finds assent and acceptance for it with such readiness as seems to argue that mankind was prepared beforehand for just such a principle of conduct. Mankind, particularly the populace, within the confines of that Roman dominion within which the early diffusion of Christianity took place, was apparently in a frame of mind to accept such a principle of morality, or such a maxim of conduct; and the same is progressively true for the outlying populations to which Christianity spread in the next four centuries.

To any modern student of human culture, this ready acceptance of such a principle (habit of thought) gives evidence that the section of mankind which had thus shifted its moral footing to a new and revolutionary moral principle must have been trained, by recently past experience, by the discipline of daily life in the immediate past, into such a frame of mind as predisposed them for its acceptance; that is to say, they must have been disciplined into a spiritual attitude to which such a new principle of conduct would commend itself as reasonable, if not as a matter of course. And in due process, as this suitable attitude was enforced upon the other, outlying populations by suitable disciplinary means, Christianity with its gospel of renunciation tended to spread and supplant the outworn cults that no longer fitted the altered cultural situation. But in its later diffusion, among peoples not securely under Roman rule and not reduced to such a frame of mind by a protracted experience of Roman discipline, Christianity makes less capital of the morality of non-resistance.

It was among the peoples subject to the Roman rule that Christianity first arose and spread; among the lower orders of the populace especially, who had been beaten to a pulp by the hard-handed, systematic, inexorable power of the imperial city; who had no rights which the Roman master was bound to respect; who were aliens and practically outlaws under the sway of the Cæsars; and who had acquired, under high pressure, the conviction that non-resistance was the chief of virtues if not the whole duty of man. They had learned to render unto Cæsar that which is Cæsar's, and were in a frame of mind to render unto God that which is God's.

It is a notable fact also that, as a general rule, in its subsequent diffusion to regions and peoples not benefited by the Roman discipline, Christianity spread in proportion to the more or less protracted experience of defeat and helpless submission undergone by these peoples; and that it was the subject populace rather than the master classes that took kindly to the doctrine of non-resistance. In the outlying corners of the western world, such as the Scandinavian and British countries, where subjection to arbitrary rule in temporal matters had been less consistently and less enduringly enforced, the principle of non-resistance took less firm root. And in the days when the peoples of Christendom were sharply differentiated into ruling and subject classes, non-resistance was accepted by the lower rather than by the upper classes.

Much the same, indeed, is true of the companion principle of mutual succor. On the whole, it is not too bold a generalisation to say that these elements of the moral code which distinguish Christianity from the ethnic cults are elements of the morals of low life, of the subject populace. There is, in point of practical morality, not much to choose, e.g., between the upper-class mediæval Christianity and the contemporary Mohammedan morality. It is only in later times, after the western culture had lost its aristocratic-feudalistic character and had become, in its typical form, though not in all its ramifications, a kind of universalised low-life culture—it is only at this later period that these principles of low-life morality also became in some degree universalised principles of Christian duty; and it still remains true that these principles are most at home in the more vulgar divisions of the Christian cult. The higher-class variants of Christianity still differ little in the substance of their morality from Judaism or Islam. The morality of the upper class is in a less degree the morality of non-resistance and brotherly love, and is in a greater degree the morality of coercive control and kindly tutelage, which are in no degree distinctive traits of Christianity, as contrasted with the other great religious systems.

In their experience of Roman devastation and punishment-at-large, which predisposed the populace for this principle of non-resistance, the subject peoples commonly also lost such class distinctions and differential rights and privileges as they had previously enjoyed. They were leveled down to a passably homogeneous state of subjection, in which one class or individual had little to gain at the cost of another, and in which, also, each and all palpably needed the succor of all the rest. The institutional fabric had crumbled, very much as it does in an earthquake. The conventional differentiations, handed down out of the past, had proved vain and meaningless in the face of the current situation. The pride of caste and all the principles of differential dignity and honor fell away, and left mankind naked and unashamed and free to follow the promptings of hereditary savage human nature which make for fellowship and Christian charity.

Barring repressive conventionalities, reversion to the spiritual state of savagery is always easy; for human nature is still substantially savage. The discipline of savage life, selective and adaptive, has been by far the most protracted and probably the most exacting of any phase of culture in all the life-history of the race; so that by heredity human nature still is, and must indefinitely continue to be, savage human nature. This savage spiritual heritage that "springs eternal" when the pressure of conventionality is removed or relieved, seems highly conducive to the two main traits of Christian morality, though more so to the principle of brotherly love than to that of renunciation. And this may well be the chief circumstance that has contributed to the persistence of these principles of conduct even in later times, when the external conditions have not visibly favored or called for their continued exercise.

The principles of conduct underlying pecuniary competition are the principles of Natural Rights, and as such date from the eighteenth century. In respect of their acceptance into the body of commonplace morality and practice and the constraining force which they exercise, they are apparently an outgrowth of modern civilisation—whatever older antiquity may be assigned them in respect of their documentary pedigree. Comparatively speaking, they are absent from the scheme of life and from the common-sense apprehension of rights and duties in mediæval times. They derive their warrant as moral principles from the discipline of life under the cultural situation of early modern times. They are accordingly of relatively recent date as prevalent habits of thought, at least in their fuller and freer development; even though the underlying traits of human nature which have lent themselves to the formation of these habits of thought may be as ancient as any other. The period of their growth coincides somewhat closely with that of the philosophy of egoism, self-interest, or "individualism," as it is less aptly called. This egoistic outlook gradually assumes a dominant place in the occidental scheme of thought during and after the transition from mediæval to modern times; it appears to be a result of the habituation to those new conditions of life which characterise the modern, as contrasted with the mediæval, situation. Assuming, as is now commonly done, that the fundamental and controlling changes which shape and guide the transition from the institutional situation of the mediæval to that of the

modern world are economic changes, one may with
fair confidence trace a connection between these economic changes and the concomitant growth of modern
business principles. The vulgar element, held cheap, kept
under, but massive, in the mediæval order of society,
comes gradually into the foreground and into the controlling position in economic life; so that the aristocratic
or chivalric standards and ideals are gradually supplanted or displaced by the vulgar apprehension of what
is right and best in the conduct of life. The chivalric
canons of destructive exploit and of status give place to
the more sordid canons of workmanlike efficiency and
pecuniary strength. The economic changes which thus
gave a new and hitherto impotent element of society
the primacy in the social order and in the common-sense
apprehensions of what is worth while, are, in the main
and characteristically, the growth of handicraft and
petty trade; giving rise to the industrial towns, to the
growth of markets, to a pecuniary field of individual
enterprise and initiative, and to a valuation of men,
things, and events in pecuniary terms.

It is impossible here to go narrowly into the traits of
culture and of human nature which were evolved in the
rise and progress of handicraft and the petty trade, and
brought about the decay of mediævalism and the rise of
the modern cultural scheme. But so much seems plain
on the face of things : there is at work in all this growth
of the new, pecuniary culture, a large element of emulation, both in the acquisition of goods and in their
conspicuous consumption. Pecuniary exploit in a degree
supplies the place of chivalric exploit. But emulation is
not the whole of the motive force of the new order, nor
does it supply all the canons of conduct and standards
of merit under the new order. In its earlier stages, while

dominated by the exigencies of handicraft and the petty trade, the modern culture is fully as much shaped and guided by considerations of livelihood, as by the ideals of differential gain.

The material conditions of the new economic situation would not tolerate the institutional conditions of the old situation. There was being enforced upon the community, primarily upon that workday element into whose hands the new industrial exigencies were shifting the directive force, a new range of habitual notions as to what was needful and what was right. In both of the characteristically modern lines of occupation—handicraft and the petty trade—the individual, the workman or trader, is the central and efficient factor, on whose initiative, force, diligence, and discretion his own economic fortunes and those of the community visibly turn. It is an economic situation in which, necessarily, individual deals with individual on a footing of pecuniary efficiency; where the ties of group solidarity, which control the individual's economic (and social) relations, are themselves of a pecuniary character, and are made or broken more or less at the individual's discretion and in pecuniary terms; and it is, moreover, a cultural situation in which the social and civil relations binding the individual are prevailingly and increasingly formed for pecuniary ends, and enforced by pecuniary sanctions. The individualism of the modern era sets out with industrial aims and makes its way by force of industrial efficiency. And since the individual relations under this system take the pecuniary form, the individualism thus worked out and incorporated in the modern institutional fabric is a pecuniary individualism, and is therefore also typically egoistic.

The principles governing right conduct according to

the habits of thought native to this individualistic era are the egoistic principles of natural rights and natural liberty. These rights and this liberty are egoistic rights and liberty of the individual. They are to be summed up as freedom and security of person and of pecuniary transactions. It is a curious fact, significant of the extreme preponderance of the vulgar element in this cultural revolution, that among these natural rights there are included no remnants of those prerogatives and disabilities of birth, office, or station, which seemed matters of course and of common-sense to the earlier generations of men who had grown up under the influence of the mediæval social order. Nor, curiously, are there remnants of the more ancient rights and duties of the bond of kinship, the blood feud, or clan allegiance, such as were once also matters of course and of common-sense in the cultural eras and areas in which the social order of the kinship group or the clan organisation had prevailed. On the other hand, while these institutional elements have (in theory) lost all standing, the analogous institution of property has become an element of the natural order of things. The system of natural rights is natural in the sense of being consonant with the nature of handicraft and petty trade.

Meanwhile, times have changed since the eighteenth century, when this system of pecuniary egoism reached its mature development. That is to say, the material circumstances, the economic exigencies, have changed, and the discipline of habit resulting from the changed situation has, as a consequence, tended to a somewhat different effect—as is evidenced by the fact that the sanctity and sole efficacy of the principles of natural rights are beginning to be called in question. The excellence and sufficiency of an enlightened pecuniary egoism are no longer a matter of course and of common-sense to the mind of this generation, which has experienced the current era of machine industry, credit, delegated corporation management, and distant markets. What fortune may overtake these business principles, these habits of thought native to the handicraft era, in the further sequence of economic changes can, of course, not be foretold; but it is at least certain that they cannot remain standing and effective, in the long run, unless the modern community should return to an economic régime equivalent to the era of handicraft and petty trade. For the business principles in question are of the nature of habits of thought, and habits of thought are made by habits of life; and the habits of life necessary to maintain these principles and to give them their effective sanction in the common-sense convictions of the community are the habits of life enforced by the system of handicraft and petty trade.

It appears, then, that these two codes of conduct, Christian morals and business principles, are the institutional by-products of two different cultural situations. The former, in so far as they are typically Christian, arose out of the abjectly and precariously servile relations in which the populace stood to their masters in late Roman times, as also, in a great, though perhaps less, degree, during the "Dark" and the Middle Ages. The latter, the morals of pecuniary competition, on the other hand, are habits of thought induced by the exigencies of vulgar life under the rule of handicraft and petty trade, out of which has come the peculiar system of rights and duties characteristic of modern Christendom. Yet there is something in common between the two. The Christian principles inculcate brotherly love, mutual succor: Love

thy neighbor as thyself; *Mutuum date, nihil inde sper-
antes.* This principle seems, in its elements at least, to
be a culturally atavistic trait, belonging to the ancient,
not to say primordial, peaceable culture of the lower
savagery. The natural-rights analogue of this principle
of solidarity and mutual succor is the principle of fair
play, which appears to be the nearest approach to the
golden rule that the pecuniary civilisation will admit.
There is no reach of ingenuity or of ingenuousness by
which the one of these may be converted into the other;
nor does the régime of fair play—essentially a régime
of emulation—conduce to the reinforcement of the
golden rule. Yet throughout all the vicissitudes of cultural change, the golden rule of the peaceable savage
has never lost the respect of occidental mankind, and its
hold on men's convictions is, perhaps, stronger now than
at any earlier period of the modern time. It seems incompatible with business principles, but appreciably less
so than with the principles of conduct that ruled the
western world in the days before the Grace of God was
supplanted by the Rights of Man. The distaste for the
spectacle of contemporary life seldom rises to the pitch
of "renunciation of the world" under the new dispensation. While one half of the Christian moral code, that
pious principle which inculcates humility, submission to
irresponsible authority, found easier lodgment in the
mediæval culture, the more humane moral element of
mutual succor seems less alien to the modern culture of
pecuniary self-help.

The presumptive degree of compatibility between the
two codes of morality may be shown by a comparison of
the cultural setting, out of which each has arisen and in
which each should be at home. In the most general outline, and neglecting details as far as may be, we may

describe the upshot of this growth of occidental principles as follows: The ancient Christian principle of humility, renunciation, abnegation, or non-resistance has been virtually eliminated from the moral scheme of Christendom; nothing better than a sophisticated affectation of it has any extensive currency in modern life. The conditions to which it owes its rise—bare-handed despotism and servile helplessness—are, for the immediate present and the recent past, no longer effectual elements in the cultural situation; and it is, of course, in the recent past that the conditions must be sought which have shaped the habits of thought of the immediate present. Its companion principle, brotherly love or mutual service, appears, in its elements at least, to be a very deeprooted and ancient cultural trait, due to an extremely protracted experience of the race in the early stages of human culture, reinforced and defined by the social conditions prevalent in the early days of Christianity. In the naïve and particular formulation given it by the early Christians, this habit of thought has also lost much of its force, or has fallen somewhat into abeyance; being currently represented by a thrifty charity, and, perhaps, by the negative principle of fair play, neither of which can fairly be rated as a competent expression of the Christian spirit. Yet this principle is forever reasserting itself in economic matters, in the impulsive approval of whatever conduct is serviceable to the common good and in the disapproval of disserviceable conduct even within the limits of legality and natural right. It seems, indeed, to be nothing else than a somewhat specialised manifestation of the instinct of workmanship, and as such it has the indefeasible vitality that belongs to the hereditary traits of human nature.

The pecuniary scheme of right conduct is of recent growth, but it is an outcome of a recently past phase of modern culture rather than of the immediate present. This system of natural rights, including the right of ownership and the principles of pecuniary good and evil that go with it, no longer has the consistent support of current events. Under the conditions prevalent in the era of handicraft, the rights of ownership made for equality rather than the reverse, so that their exercise was in effect not notably inconsistent with the ancient bias in favor of mutual aid and human brotherhood. This is more particularly apparent if the particular form of organisation and the spirit of the regulations then ruling in vulgar life be kept in mind. The technology of handicraft, as well as the market relations of the system of petty trade, pushed the individual workman into the foreground and led men to think of economic interests in terms of this workman and his work; the situation emphasised his creative relation to his product, as well as his responsibility for this product and for its serviceability to the common welfare. It was a situation in which the acquisition of property depended, in the main, on the workmanlike serviceability of the man who acquired it, and in which, on the whole, honesty was the best policy. Under such conditions the principles of fair play and the inviolability of ownership would be somewhat closely in touch with the ancient human instinct of workmanship, which approves mutual aid and serviceability to the common good. On the other hand, the current experience of men in the communities of Christendom, now no longer acts to reinforce these habits of thought embodied in the system of natural rights; and it is scarcely conceivable that a conviction of the goodness, sufficiency, and inviolability of the rights of own-ership could arise out of such a condition of things, technological and pecuniary, as now prevails.

Hence there are indications in current events that these principles—habits of thought—are in process of disintegration rather than otherwise. With the revolutionary changes that have supervened in technology and in pecuniary relations, there is no longer such a close and visible touch between the workman and his product as would persuade men that the product belongs to him by force of an extension of his personality; nor is there a visible relation between serviceability and acquisition; nor between the discretionary use of wealth and the common welfare. The principles of fair play and pecuniary discretion have, in great measure, lost the sanction once afforded them by the human propensity for serviceability to the common good, neutral as that sanction has been at its best. Particularly is this true since business has taken on the character of an impersonal, dispassionate, not to say graceless, investment for profit. There is little in the current situation to keep the natural right of pecuniary discretion in touch with the impulsive bias of brotherly love, and there is in the spiritual discipline of this situation much that makes for an effectual discrepancy between the two. Except for a possible reversion to a cultural situation strongly characterised by ideals of emulation and status, the ancient racial bias embodied in the Christian principle of brotherhood should logically continue to gain ground at the expense of the pecuniary morals of competitive business.

# THE INTELLECTUAL PRE-EMINENCE OF JEWS IN MODERN EUROPE [1]

AMONG all the clamorous projects of national self-determination which surround the return of peace, the proposal of the Zionists is notable for sobriety, good will, and a poise of self-assurance. More confidently and perspicuously than all the others, the Zionists propose a rehabilitation of their national integrity under a régime of live and let live, "with charity for all, with malice toward none." Yet it is always a project for withdrawal upon themselves, a scheme of national demarcation between Jew and gentile; indeed, it is a scheme of territorial demarcation and national frontiers of the conventional sort, within which Jews and Jewish traits, traditions, and aspirations are to find scope and breathing space for a home-bred culture and a free unfolding of all that is best and most characteristic in the endowment of the race. There runs through it all a dominant bias of isolation and inbreeding, and a confident persuasion that this isolation and inbreeding will bring great and good results for all concerned. The Zionists aspire to bring to full fruition all that massive endowment of spiritual and intellectual capacities of which their people have given evidence throughout their troubled history, and not least during these concluding centuries of their exile.

The whole project has an idyllic and engaging air.

[1] Reprinted from *The Political Science Quarterly*, Vol. XXXIV, March, 1919.

And any disinterested bystander will be greatly moved to wish them godspeed. Yet there comes in a regret that this experiment in isolation and inbreeding could not have been put to the test at an earlier date, before the new order of large-scale industry and universal intercourse had made any conclusive degree of such national isolation impracticable, before this same new order had so shaped the run of things that any nation or community drawn on this small scale would necessarily be dependent on and subsidiary to the run of things at large. It is now, unhappily, true that any "nation" of the size and geographical emplacement of the projected Zion will, for the present and the calculable future, necessarily be something of a national make-believe. The current state of the industrial arts will necessarily deny it a rounded and self-balanced national integrity in any substantial sense. The days of Solomon and the caravan trade which underlay the glory of Solomon are long past.

Yet much can doubtless be done by taking thought and making the most of that spirit of stubborn clannishness which has never been the least among the traits of this people. But again, to any disinterested bystander there will come the question: What is the use of it all? It is not so much a question of what is aimed at, as of the chances of its working-out. The logic of the Zionist project plainly runs to the effect that, whereas this people have achieved great things while living under conditions of great adversity, scattered piecemeal among the gentiles of Europe, they are due to achieve much greater things and to reach an unexampled prosperity so soon as they shall have a chance to follow their own devices untroubled within the shelter of their own frontiers. But the doubt presents itself that the conditioning circumstances are not the same or of the same kind in the occidental twentieth century A.D. as in the oriental twelfth century B.C.; nor need it follow that those things which scattered Jews have achieved during their dispersion among the gentiles of Europe are a safe index of what things may be expected of a nation of Jews turned in upon themselves within the insulating frontiers of the Holy Land. It is on this latter point that a question is raised here as to the nature and causes of Jewish achievement in gentile Europe; and the contrast of the conditions offered by the projected Zion will present itself without argument.

It is a fact which must strike any dispassionate observer that the Jewish people have contributed much more than an even share to the intellectual life of modern Europe. So also it is plain that the civilisation of Christendom continues today to draw heavily on the Jews for men devoted to science and scholarly pursuits. It is not only that men of Jewish extraction continue to supply more than a proportionate quota to the rank and file engaged in scientific and scholarly work, but a disproportionate number of the men to whom modern science and scholarship look for guidance and leadership are of the same derivation. Particularly is this true of the modern sciences, and it applies perhaps especially in the field of scientific theory, even beyond the extent of its application in the domain of workday detail. So much is notorious.

This notable and indeed highly creditable showing has, of course, not escaped the attention of those men of Jewish race who interest themselves in the fortunes of their own people. Not unusually it is set down as a national trait, as evidence of a peculiarly fortunate intellectual endowment, native and hereditary, in the Jewish people. There is much to be said for such a view, but it should not follow that any inquiry into the place and value of the Jewish people in western civilisation should come to rest with this broad assertion of pre-eminence in point of native endowment.

It is true that the history of the Chosen People, late and early, throws them into a position of distinction among the nations with which they have been associated; and it will commonly be accepted without much argument that they have, both late and early, shown distinctive traits of temperament and aptitude, such as to mark them off more or less sharply from all the gentiles among whom it has been their lot to be thrown. So general is the recognition of special Jewish traits, of character and of capacity, that any refusal to recognise something which may be called a Jewish type of hereditary endowment would come to nothing much better than a borrowing of trouble.

That there should be such a tenacious spiritual and intellectual heritage transmissible within the Jewish community and marking that people off in any perceptible degree from their gentile neighbors is all the more notable in view of the known life-history of the children of Israel. No unbiased ethnologist will question the fact that the Jewish people are a nation of hybrids; that gentile blood of many kinds has been infused into the people in large proportions in the course of time. Indeed, none of the peoples of Christendom has been more unremittingly exposed to hybridisation, in spite of all the stiff conventional precautions that have been taken to keep the breed pure. It is not a question of a surreptitious hybrid strain, such as would show itself in sporadic reversions to an alien type; but rather it is a question whether the Jewish strain itself, racially speaking, can at all reasonably be held to account for one half of the pedigree of the Jewish nation as it stands.

The hybrid antecedents of the Children of Israel are not a mere matter of bookish record. Evidence of their hybrid descent is written all over them, wherever they are to be met with, so that in this respect the Jews of Europe are in the same case as the other Europeans, who are also universally cross-bred. It would perplex any anthropologist to identify a single individual among them all who could safely be set down as embodying the Jewish racial type without abatement. The variations in all the measurable traits that go to identify any individual in the schedules of the anthropologists are wide and ubiquitous as regards both their physical and their spiritual traits, in respect of anthropometric measurements as well as in temperament and capacities. And yet, when all is said in abatement of it, the Jewish type, it must be admitted, asserts itself with amazing persistence through all the disguises with which it has been overlaid in the course of age-long hybridisation. Whatever may be found true elsewhere, in their contact with other racial types than those of Europe, it still appears that within this European racial environment the outcome given by any infusion of Jewish blood in these cross-bred individuals is something which can be identified as Jewish. Cross-breeding commonly results in a gain to the Jewish community rather than conversely; and the hybrid offspring is a child of Israel rather than of the gentiles.

In effect, therefore, it is the contribution of this Jewish-hybrid people to the culture of modern Europe that is in question. The men of this Jewish extraction count for more than their proportionate share in the intellectual life of western civilisation; and they count particularly among the vanguard, the pioneers, the uneasy guild of pathfinders and iconoclasts, in science, scholarship, and institutional change and growth. On its face it appears as if an infusion of Jewish blood, even in some degree of hybrid attenuation, were the one decisive factor in the case; and something of that sort may well be allowed, to avoid argument if for no more substantial reason. But even a casual survey of the available evidence will leave so broad a claim in doubt.

Of course, there is the fact to be allowed for at the outset, so far as need be, that these intellectuals of Jewish extraction are, after all, of hybrid extraction as well; but this feature of the case need be given no undue weight. It is of consequence in its bearing on the case of the Jews only in the same manner and degree as it is of consequence for any other hybrid people. Cross-breeding gives a wider range of variation and a greater diversity of individual endowment than can be had in any passably pure-bred population; from which results a greater effectual flexibility of aptitudes and capacities in such a people when exposed to conditions that make for change. In this respect the Jews are neither more nor less fortunate than their gentile compatriots.

It may be more to the purpose to note that this intellectual pre-eminence of the Jews has come into bearing within the gentile community of peoples, not from the outside; that the men who have been its bearers have been men immersed in this gentile culture in which they have played their part of guidance and incitement, not bearers of a compelling message from afar or proselyters of enlightenment conjuring with a ready formula worked out in the ghetto and carried over into the gentile community for its mental regeneration. In point of fact, neither these nor other Jews have done effectual missionary work, in any ordinary sense of that term, in this or any other connection; nor have they entertained a design to do so. Indeed, the Chosen People have quite characteristically never been addicted to missionary enterprise; nor does the Jewish scheme of right and honest living comprise anything of the kind. This, too, is notorious fact; so much so that this allusion to it may well strike any Jew as foolish insistence on a commonplace matter of course. In their character of a Chosen People, it is not for them to take thought of their unblest neighbors and seek to dispel the darkness that overlies the soul of the gentiles.

The cultural heritage of the Jewish people is large and rich, and it is of ancient and honorable lineage. And from time immemorial this people has shown aptitude for such work as will tax the powers of thought and imagination. Their home-bred achievements of the ancient time, before the Diaspora, are among the secure cultural monuments of mankind; but these achievements of the Jewish ancients neither touch the frontiers of modern science nor do they fall in the lines of modern scholarship. So also the later achievements of the Jewish scholars and savants, in so far as their intellectual enterprise has gone forward on what may be called distinctively Jewish lines, within the confines of their own community and by the leading of their own home-bred interest, untouched by that peculiar drift of inquiry that characterises the speculations of the modern gentile world—this learning of the later generations of home-bred Jewish scholars is also reputed to have run into lucubrations that have no significance for contemporary science or scholarship at large.

It appears to be only when the gifted Jew escapes from the cultural environment created and fed by the particular genius of his own people, only when he falls into the alien lines of gentile inquiry and becomes a naturalised, though hyphenate, citizen in the gentile republic of learning, that he comes into his own as a creative leader in the world's intellectual enterprise. It is by loss of allegiance, or at the best by force of a divided allegiance to the people of his origin, that he finds himself in the vanguard of modern inquiry.

It will not do to say that none but renegade Jews count effectually in the modern sciences. Such a statement would be too broad; but, for all its excessive breadth, it exceeds the fact only by a margin. The margin may seem wide, so wide as to vitiate the general statement, perhaps, or at least wide enough materially to reduce its cogency. But it would be wider of the mark to claim that the renegades are to be counted only as sporadic exceptions among a body of unmitigated Jews who make up the virtual total of that muster of creative men of science which the Jewish people have thrown into the intellectual advance of Christendom.

The first requisite for constructive work in modern science, and indeed for any work of inquiry that shall bring enduring results, is a skeptical frame of mind. The enterprising skeptic alone can be counted on to further the increase of knowledge in any substantial fashion. This will be found true both in the modern sciences and in the field of scholarship at large. Much good and serviceable workmanship of a workday character goes into the grand total of modern scientific achievement; but that pioneering and engineering work of guidance, design, and theoretical correlation, without which the most painstaking collection and canvass of information is irrelevant, incompetent, and impertinent—this intellectual enterprise that goes forward presupposes a degree of exemption from hard-and-fast preconceptions, a skeptical animus, *Unbefangenheit,* release from the dead hand of conventional finality.

The intellectually gifted Jew is in a peculiarly fortunate position in respect of this requisite immunity from the inhibitions of intellectual quietism. But he can come in for such immunity only at the cost of losing his secure place in the scheme of conventions into which he has been born, and at the cost, also, of finding no similarly secure place in that scheme of gentile conventions into which he is thrown. For him as for other men in the like case, the skepticism that goes to make him an effectual factor in the increase and diffusion of knowledge among men involves a loss of that peace of mind that is the birthright of the safe and sane quietist. He becomes a disturber of the intellectual peace, but only at the cost of becoming an intellectual wayfaring man, a wanderer in the intellectual no-man's-land, seeking another place to rest, farther along the road, somewhere over the horizon. They are neither a complaisant nor a contented lot, these aliens of the uneasy feet; but that is, after all, not the point in question.

The young Jew who is at all gifted with a taste for knowledge will unavoidably go afield into that domain of learning where the gentile interests dominate and the gentile orientation gives the outcome. There is nowhere else to go on this quest. He comes forthwith to realise that the scheme of traditions and conventional verities handed down within the pale of his own people are matters of habit handed down by tradition, that they have only such force as belongs to matters of habit and convention, and that they lose their binding force so soon as the habitually accepted outlook is given up or seriously deranged. These nationally binding convictions of what is true, good, and beautiful in the world of the human spirit are forthwith seen to be only contingently good and true; to be binding only so far as the habitual will to believe in them and to seek the truth along their lines remains intact. That is to say, only so long as no scheme of habituation alien to the man's traditional outlook has broken in on him, and has forced him to see that those convictions and verities which hold their place as fundamentally and eternally good and right within the balanced scheme of received traditions prove to be, after all, only an ephemeral web of habits of thought; so soon as his current habits of life no longer continue to fall in those traditional lines that keep these habits of thought in countenance.

Now it happens that the home-bred Jewish scheme of things, human and divine, and the ways and means of knowledge that go with such a scheme, are of an archaic fashion, good and true, perhaps, beyond all praise, for the time and conditions that gave rise to it all, that wove that web of habituation and bound its close-knit tissue of traditional verities and conventions. But it all bears the date-mark, "B.C." It is of a divine complexion, monotheistic even, and perhaps intrinsically thearchic; it is ritualistic, with an exceedingly and beautifully magical efficacy of ritual necessity. It is imperiously self-balanced and self-sufficient, to the point of sanctity; and as is always true of such schemes of sanctity and magical sufficiency, it runs on a logic of personal and spiritual traits, qualities and relations, a class of imponderables which are no longer of the substance of those things that are inquired into by men to whom the ever increasingly mechanistic orientation of the modern time becomes habitual.

When the gifted young Jew, still flexible in respect of

his mental habits, is set loose among the iron pots of this mechanistic orientation, the clay vessel of Jewish archaism suffers that fortune which is due and coming to clay vessels among the iron pots. His beautifully rounded heirloom, trade-marked "B.C.," goes to pieces between his hands, and they are left empty. He is divested of those archaic conventional preconceptions which will not comport with the intellectual environment in which he finds himself. But he is not thereby invested with the gentile's peculiar heritage of conventional preconceptions which have stood over, by inertia of habit, out of the gentile past, which go, on the one hand, to make the safe and sane gentile, conservative and complacent, and which conduce also, on the other hand, to blur the safe and sane gentile's intellectual vision, and to leave him intellectually sessile.

The young Jew finds his own heritage of usage and outlook untenable; but this does not mean that he therefore will take over and inwardly assimilate the traditions of usage and outlook which the gentile world has to offer; or at the most he does not uncritically take over all the intellectual prepossessions that are always standing over among the substantial citizens of the republic of learning. The idols of his own tribe have crumbled in decay and no longer cumber the ground, but that release does not induce him to set up a new line of idols borrowed from an alien tribe to do the same disservice. By consequence he is in a peculiar degree exposed to the unmediated facts of the current situation; and in a peculiar degree, therefore, he takes his orientation from the run of the facts as he finds them, rather than from the traditional interpretation of analogous facts in the past. In short, he is a skeptic by force of circumstances over which he has no control. Which

comes to saying that he is in line to become a guide and
leader of men in that intellectual enterprise out of which
comes the increase and diffusion of knowledge among
men, provided always that he is by native gift endowed
with that net modicum of intelligence which takes effect in the play of the idle curiosity.

Intellectually he is likely to become an alien; spiritually
he is more than likely to remain a Jew; for the heart-
strings of affection and consuetude are tied early, and
they are not readily retied in after life. Nor does the
animus with which the community of safe and sane
gentiles is wont to meet him conduce at all to his personal incorporation in that community, whatever may
befall the intellectual assets which he brings. Their people need not become his people nor their gods his gods,
and indeed the provocation is forever and irritably present all over the place to turn back from following after
them. The most amiable share in the gentile community's
life that is likely to fall to his lot is that of being interned.
One who goes away from home will come to see many
unfamiliar things, and to take note of them; but it
does not follow that he will swear by all the strange gods
whom he meets along the road.

As bearing on the Zionist's enterprise in isolation and
nationality, this fable appears to teach a two-fold moral:
If the adventure is carried to that consummate outcome
which seems to be aimed at, it should apparently be
due to be crowned with a large national complacency
and, possibly, a profound and self-sufficient content on
the part of the Chosen People domiciled once more in
the Chosen Land; and when and in so far as the Jewish
people in this way turn inward on themselves, their
prospective contribution to the world's intellectual output should, in the light of the historical evidence, fairly

be expected to take on the complexion of Talmudic lore, rather than that character of free-swung skeptical initiative which their renegades have habitually infused into the pursuit of the modern sciences abroad among the nations. Doubtless, even so the supply of Jewish renegades would not altogether cease, though it should presumably fall off to a relatively inconsiderable residue. And not all renegades are fit guides and leaders of men on the quest of knowledge, nor is their dominant incentive always or ordinarily the quest of the idle curiosity.

There should be some loss to Christendom at large, and there might be some gain to the repatriated Children of Israel. It is a sufficiently difficult choice between a life of complacent futility at home and a thankless quest of unprofitable knowledge abroad. It is, after all, a matter of the drift of circumstance; and behind that lies a question of taste, about which there is no disputing.

# AN EXPERIMENT IN EUGENICS [1]

LESS attention than their case merits has been given to the life-history of the Scandinavian peoples as it bears on the larger questions of eugenics. Neither those laymen who interest themselves in these things nor the eugenicists by profession have turned the case to full account; indeed, it might rather be said that they have not yet made up their account with it. Their attention has rather converged on experiments and incidents of slighter mass and closer detail.

Yet, in effect, these Scandinavian peoples have all this while been carrying on a large experiment in eugenics, running over a wide interval of time, on a massively comprehensive scale, and with what should seem to be adequate precautions of isolation and control. What they have been doing in this way has of course been quite unintended and incidental to the day's work, being wholly in the nature of historical accident, undesigned and unnoted, driven by the circumstances which have conditioned their life. But, in so far as bears on this question, these controlling circumstances have run singularly uniform and with singularly little mitigation over a period of such duration as should give at least a preponderant weight, if not a conclusive effect, to the outcome of this experiment hitherto.

The case of these Scandinavians is perhaps not unique, even within the circle of European peoples; but it stands out in obvious contrast with the population of the neigh-

[1] Here first published.

boring countries, definite and perspicuous in such a degree as to lend itself to the eugenicist's argument with a minimum of preamble or apparatus. The four Scandinavian peoples, Denmark, Sweden, Norway, and, less obviously, Iceland, are in a striking degree singular among European peoples in the respect that they are now and have through long ages been an area of emigration, with slight, almost negligible, immigration; and this persistent emigration has consistently been, and in a degree continues to be, of a consistently selective character. How far back in the past this selective emigration out of the Scandinavian countries may be conceived to have set in is a moot question; but it is at least clear that the date of its beginning falls somewhere in the remoter ages of prehistory, presumably in the Neolithic rather than at any later period. The interval covered by the experiment, therefore, should be not less than 3000 years, perhaps rather some multiple of that number.

The first intimation which the records or traditions of history afford as to the existence of this Baltic-Scandinavian region mark it down by the one distinctive trait that it was the habitual breeding-ground and home-base from which successive hordes of migrants ran outward and spent themselves by invasion and infiltration among the peoples of Europe and the nearer parts of Asia. When history opens, it is already a settled tradition that no part or corner of the then known world is safe from the incursions of these barbarian invaders out of the hyperborean "Cradle of the Nations."

In the nineteenth century there was a widely held presumption, mainly philological and now defunct, that the barbarian invasions (*Völkerwanderungen*) which habitually troubled the settled parts of Europe were of

an Eastern, Asiatic origin, including among the rest
the barbarians of Germanic speech. Latterly this preconception has given way to reason, and it has become
evident to students of ethnology that the Germanic-
speaking barbarians could be of none but a European
origin; inasmuch as the constituents of these migrant
hordes are not traceable outside of Europe, whether
in point of speech or of their racial affiliations. And
all the known instances of such wandering hordes, in
the degree in which they are known, trace back finally
to the Baltic-Scandinavian home-base and breeding-
ground. Whereas there is no record and no tradition of
anything like a massive immigration into the Baltic-
Scandinavian countries, early or late; until the known
instances of the Lapps and Finns in the north of the
Baltic at some date not far removed from the Christian
era, and the return waves of Germanic invaders, as,
e.g., the Teutonic knighthood, on its southern shores.
None of these reached or seriously troubled the Scandinavian peoples proper, who have accordingly suffered
no substantial admixture of immigrants. Loosely the
case stands, therefore, that, while all other parts and
peoples of Europe have been subject to immigration in
one form and another, early and late, the Scandinavian
peoples are not known to have been seriously touched
by infusion of any new blood from outside since their
life-history began, in the early phases of the Neolithic
period, perhaps some ten or twelve thousand years ago.[2]

[2] As is habitual with broad statements, this may need qualification. There is, e.g., in the legends incorporated in the Eddas, and
notably in the *Rigsthula,* a recurring reference to something like
mass immigration, the last and apparently most authentic being that
which is held to have brought the Asas (*Aesir*) into the Scandinavian lands; or, as seen from the secular side, which brought the
Skjoldungs, as representatives of the race of kings. What these

The one indubitable and substantial factor in the way of immigration into the Scandinavian lands is a sustained infiltration of slaves during the Viking Age, so called, most evident and perhaps most appreciable toward the close of that period. The Viking Age ran for, say, some four or five hundred years, down to the transition from paganism to Christianity in the tenth and eleventh centuries. Virtually all these slaves were of European origin, and therefore not substantially different from the native Scandinavians in point of racial make-up. These slaves made up a very substantial proportion of the population; although it is apparently safe to say that they nowhere accounted for as much as one half of the total, perhaps in no instance as much as one third. It may also be a safe surmise that the ratio of slaves to the total ran rather higher in Norway than in the neighboring countries, at least at the close of the Viking Age. These slaves appear eventually to have been absorbed, bred into the population at large, and so to have disappeared without trace or record of their assimilation. Their infusion into the Scandinavian population appears to have made no sensible difference; unless the slightly more pronounced brunetness of the Norwegian population, especially in the outer seaboard regions, be taken as evidence of an infusion of such alien blood.

That such a continued influx of slaves could be absorbed without sensibly altering the racial complexion of these peoples would go to show that the racial complexion of the Scandinavian peoples had from the outset, in the early phases of the Neolithic, been substantially the same as that of the European population at large. Which brings up the question of what was, in-

legends may signify, in terms of ethnic migration, it seems bootless to guess.

itially, the racial complexion of Europe, including the
Scandinavian peoples, at that early period of the Neolithic which is taken as the point of departure. As is
commonly held, and as there seems no good reason to
question, in respect of its racial, and therefore its hereditary characteristics, the population of Europe was then
what it is now, with negligible exceptions. That is to
say, it was a hybrid population throughout, varying in
such a way as to show more of the brunet blood toward
the south and the Mediterranean seaboard and more of
the dolicho-blond traits toward the northern seaboard.
The contingent of slaves drawn into the Scandinavian
population came out of this hybrid mixture of races
in Europe at large; and the migrant hordes continually
running outward from these Scandinavian countries
flowed into the same wide racial reservoir of hybrids.
The hybrid population of Europe at large therefore
serves the purpose of a "control," or term of comparison, in that it shows what a population composed
of the same racial stocks comes to through the ages
in the absence of that selective breeding to which the
Scandinavians have been subject all this while.

The selection to which they have been subject has not
been strict, but it has been consistent and has been continued over so long a period, so long a series of generations, as should make its showing conclusive. The migrants who were drawn off and sent abroad were drawn
off by a process of self-selection; whereby those individuals who stood out above the common, who were
gifted with initiative and force, were sifted out. Such
persons as were notably big, strong, ambitious, restless,
capable, were sifted out of the home population from
which succeeding generations were to come, and were
sent abroad to die out or to disappear by absorption

into the European common stock of humanity; leaving at home in the Scandinavian countries, as a breeding-stock for succeeding generations, all those who were in any way unfit—the halt, the lame, and the blind, the undersized, the anæmic, and the wry-grown, the timid, the stupid, the superstitious, and the feeble-minded. The slave population which was brought in during the Viking Age, and which in a measure replaced the emigrants drawn off by the Viking traffic, was made up of persons kidnaped or captured from the plundered towns and villages, presumably the more helpless, stupid, and tractable ones among their inhabitants.

Doubtless the selection which took effect in this way was neither strict nor exhaustive; but there is also no doubt of its having been effective and having continued over a sufficient interval of time. Doubtless there would be many persons, particularly among the women, who failed to get away as emigrants even though they might not be unfit, either physically or mentally. But the drain went on through the ages, consistently and unremittingly; and it consistently left the unfit and undesirable ones at home as a breeding-stock, out of whose later generations any efficient individuals would again be drawn off by the like selective process, etc.

From remote antiquity down into the Middle Ages this selective emigration appears to have gone forward with little interruption. Within recorded time there are such as the Gauls, Goths, Visigoths, Ostrogoths, Vandals, Allemanni, Heruli, Burgundians, Franks, Bavarians, Longobards, Jutes, Angles, Saxons, Normans. And back home, in the "Cradle of Nations," all this while the Scandinavian-Baltic peoples go on multiplying on the face of the earth, out of such remnants of humanity as were left in the discard. This process of breeding and persistent extrusion of the fit runs its cyclical course with slight apparent interruption until the high tide of the Middle Ages; when the emigration is virtually discontinued, from the eleventh century to the eighteenth inclusive, to be resumed and continued in the nineteenth.

The date and circumstances of this interruption should be noted, as the incident serves to show the nature of those conditions that have made such a persistent overflow of population possible, as well as the nature of the conditions under which no surplus population will emerge. This interval of virtually no surplus population—loosely, from the eleventh, or perhaps rather the twelfth century, to the eighteenth inclusive—runs from the period when the feudalistic state and the mediæval church were definitely installed in the Scandinavian countries, to the date when both of these institutions began to lose their grip on these peoples. More precisely, its inception coincides with the transition from paganism to Christianity, when the church came in and divided the control of affairs in these countries with the feudalistic state, which had already been coming into control before the date of the transition. The Black Death also came during this interval and ran with exceptional severity over the Scandinavian countries.

Such a sustained selective emigration as is here in question will presume, as its condition precedent, that there is an habitual surplus margin of population; which will presume an habitual margin of livelihood in excess of current needs; which will presume the virtual absence of an idle or non-productive class of ultimate consumers; which will presume that there are no "kept classes" in the community, or nearly none. These conditions appear to have been met in Scandinavian pagan times, at least in such passable fashion as would serve the purpose.

Under the pagan dispensation there was no priesthood in the Scandinavian countries and no other manner of ecclesiastical personnel exempt from industrial employment and drawing its livelihood from the industry of the working population. So also there were (virtually) no "kept classes" of a secular order: no gentry, nobility, or royalty exempt from productive work. Workmanship was then still an honorable distinction to which all classes and conditions of men aspired. Under these circumstances the community's productive work would afford an habitual margin of livelihood over current needs. When this available margin of livelihood is coupled with such a degree of urgent fecundity as is known to prevail throughout the seaboard regions of the Baltic and North Sea, the outcome should be such as has been shown.

With the coming in of the feudalistic state and the mediæval church the situation took a different turn. The courtly, military, official, and ecclesiastical kept classes multiplied on the face of these lands and dominated the community in a teamwork of misrule, extortion, and waste, apparently somewhat beyond what prevailed elsewhere in Europe; with the result that the production of an habitual surplus population ceased, for want of livelihood, and emigration from these countries fell off to the vanishing point.

As touches this question, the substitution of Lutheran ecclesiasticism in the place of Roman Catholicism appears to have made no substantial difference. The Lutheran Church in the Scandinavian countries during these centuries ran on the same old plan of charging all that the traffic would bear. It is true, monasticism presently ceased, but the domestic establishments of the married priesthood served the same purpose of tracelessly consuming any available margin of livelihood, leaving the net result virtually the same as before.

In the early nineteenth century this complexion of things began to change. The grip in which state and church had held the underlying population was shaken loose, in some measure. These organisations of "ultimate consumers" were no longer in a position to absorb all the available margin of livelihood, and a surplus population available for emigration presently emerged. Since then, say, since the second quarter of the nineteenth century, emigration out of these countries has again become habitual.

The case of the Norwegians is perhaps the most instructive. Norway is too poor in agricultural resources, and the like, to support a landed gentry, or a similar proprietary class. Therefore, under the conditions which prevailed in the nineteenth century, and under pressure of that urgent fecundity which still characterises these countries, the available margin of subsistence has habitually been turned to account in the propagation of the species; resulting in an available surplus.

The urgency, among these peoples, of those human propensities which make for fecundity is shown in a felicitous manner, e.g., by the prevalence of illegitimate births among them throughout the nineteenth century; perhaps in an especial degree among the Norwegians. Illegitimate births are, of course, altogether in contravention of the civil law and of the ordinances of Holy Church, whether Lutheran or other; and it should be added that the Norwegians of the past century were sufficiently law-abiding, and devoutly, not to say abjectly, Lutheran. Yet Eilert Sundt (*Om Saedeligheds Tilstanden i Norge*) notes, with due clerical deprecation, about the middle of the century, that illegitimate births in many localities ran as high as twenty percent of the total birthrate; rising in some parishes to thirty or even thirty-five percent. All this in spite of the obstinate endeavors of the clergy to discourage this illicit traffic.[3]

Through the latter half of the nineteenth century and later the propagation of a surplus population has continued as of old and the emigration has been resumed, on the modern plan and with a less pronounced selective effect. During this modern period there has been virtually no immigration of infiltration of alien blood, the slave-trade having ceased with the close of the Viking Age.

What has been the outcome, if any, of this long run of selective emigration of the fit and selective breeding from the unfit, is for the expert spokesmen of eugenics to inquire into and determine. It should imply, as its chief recourse, an objective scrutiny and valuation of the current hereditary traits shown by these Scandinavian peoples, perhaps especially the Norwegian population, in point of physique and mentality, as compared

[3] As Adam Smith might have expressed it, illegitimate births "do not afford a revenue." By reason of this disability they have come in for a negative "prestige value," as not having the countenance of Holy Church. Inasmuch as they are celebrated with no circumstance of publicity, they do not lend themselves to that routine of sacramental excise from which the clerics of Holy Church derive a substantial portion of their livelihood. On these, and perhaps on other grounds, illegitimate births have had the fortune to become sinful, not to say shameful. So that there comes to be about this whole traffic a certain air of reluctant fortuity and irresponsibility, such as will call to mind the "forced movements" of lower animals. In a manner of speaking, such births may be rated as an undesigned triumph of the hormones over the proprieties; or, theologically speaking, as a triumph of the ancient injunction to "be fruitful, and multiply, and replenish the earth," as against those later-devised Divine Ordinances that have been found advisable in view of the Holy Fisc.

with the European population at large; which is made up of the same racial stocks mixed up in the same hybrid fashion, and which has not been subject to such a process of selective breeding.

In this connection it may occur to unwary observers to take the view that the European population at large, outside of the Scandinavian countries, has all this while been subject to selection of a similar, and possibly more drastic, character, in the wars which have continued to devastate Europe at large throughout the period of Christianity, and which have left the Scandinavian countries relatively undisturbed. These wars, the more civilised wars perhaps in an especial degree, have been greatly destructive of life and livelihood; and the casualties of the combat, it is true, have fallen primarily on the fighting men, who are ever a somewhat select body. But it should be noted at the same time that the fatalities brought on by plunder and privation in civilised warfare fall with at least as grave an effect on the infirm and helpless non-combatants, as has appeared, e.g., in the Great War of the past decade; which would appear to leave the selective action of these European wars practically nil, in so far as touches the present argument.

III

WAR ESSAYS

# JAPANESE LOSE HOPE FOR GERMANY [1]

ASSUMING that it is not a ruse designed to be carried out in collusion with the German high command and for the ultimate success of the German cause, the late move by which Japanese forces have been sent into European waters in support of the Entente is the most sinister and convincing episode of the warlike situation in Europe since the failure of the assault on Verdun. Sinister, that is to say, as seen from the German point of view. Assuming always, as has just been said, that it is not a ruse undertaken by oriental statecraft in collusion with the quasi-oriental statecraft of Berlin, it plainly signifies that the statesmen of the Far Eastern empire have cast up the account to date and have concluded that there is no gain to be had for imperial Japan by further playing fast and loose with the European belligerents and keeping open a chance of alliance with imperial Germany at the close of hostilities or at any opportune stage in their further prosecution. The statesmen of imperial Japan have evidently reached the conviction that the chances of ulterior gain for Japan by eventual use of an offensive alliance with Germany are no longer worth serious attention, as against the certainty of a hostile attitude on the part of the nations of the Entente toward any further schemes of Japanese aggrandisement.

Seen in the long and dispassionate perspective af-

[1] Reprinted from *The New Republic,* Vol. XI, June 30, 1917, where it appeared as a communication from Thorstein Veblen.

forded by the Far Eastern point of view, and rated quite unemotionally in terms of prospective profit and loss to the imperial establishment, the European war situation will necessarily present itself as a large question of "alternative uses." It has long been evident that the conservative, that is to say imperialistic and reactionary, statesmen who have controlled the policies of Japan have consistently taken thought to avoid any avoidable offense as against Germany. It is similarly evident that a shrewd imperial policy, whenever a propitious conjuncture may arise, should negotiate a close alliance with Germany and her following for the purpose of making whatever gains might be made during the period of weakness and disorganisation that is expected to take effect among the Entente nations on the close of the present hostilities. But such a policy presumes that the German Empire is to come out of its present difficulties substantially intact; intact, at least, to the extent of still doing business as a German Empire under the rule and policies of the Prussian statesmen. The present move of the Japanese forces would seem to signify that these shrewdest, most callous, and most watchful of all adepts in unashamed statecraft have decided that the chances of so fortunate an eventuality for the German imperial forces are now too slight to be worth serious consideration. It would signify, in other words, that in the apprehension of the Japanese imperial statesmen the German Empire is not to appear on the map of Europe as it is to be redrawn for the day after tomorrow; and it would signify also that in their apprehension there is no help for this sinister eventuality, even if the forces of imperial Japan were to be thrown in unreservedly on the side of the German Empire and its allies. The surmise also suggests itself that it may be America's entrance into the war that so has given the outcome in this Japanese computation of "alternative uses."

# THE OPPORTUNITY OF JAPAN [1]

WHAT is here intended by "the opportunity of Japan" is not so much an outlook of prospective gain for the Japanese people as of aggrandisement for the Japanese state. It will hold true in this instance as in so many others that the advantage of the country's population does not in any sensible degree coincide with that of its directorate, except it be in point of sentiment. For any modern people imbued with a sense of loyalty to their rulers—as is eminently the case with the Japanese people —the dynastic ambitions of their masters are necessarily an object of veneration, and any political success scored by their rulers is of course a source of gratification. And it may fairly be left an open question whether this sentimental value which the people so attach to the political gains achieved by their government is to be rated as a sufficiently substantial matter to admit speaking of these political successes as a substantial gain for the people at large. To speak of any more substantial gain presumed to accrue to the common man from these maneuvers of political aggrandisement—anything like a material advantage, e.g.—would be out of the question, except, of course, in a patriotic harangue. The cost of such dynastic aggrandisement falls, of course, on the people at large ; and equally of course—except in patriotic harangues— such material gains as may accrue from these political successes fall, equally of course, directly to the personnel

[1] Reprinted from *The Journal of Race Development,* Vol. VI, July, 1915.

of the governing class, together with a certain contingent of enterprising business men who are under modern conditions necessary to the conduct of any national enterprise and are in a position to profit by that trade that is said to "follow the flag." This will necessarily hold true with less qualification the more the country's government partakes of that character of absolute and irresponsible mastery that has been exemplified in mediæval and early modern Europe—as, e.g., the Ancien Régime under the Grand Monarch, or, again, the Imperial Regime in Germany under William II; and it holds true in an eminent degree for Japan, where absolute and irresponsible rule is more securely established than it has been in any European power of the first class, barring Turkey perhaps. To the Japanese government, or "state," the country, with its human denizens, is an estate to be husbanded and exploited for the state's ends; which comes near saying, for the prestige of the Mikado's government.

In the material respect, therefore, the division of interest as between the people at large and the governing class is particularly well marked and well maintained; being, indeed, a division after the same fashion as that which holds between servant and master in any community that is organised on a servile footing. So that the people at large, the common man, has no appreciable share and no substantial concern in the measures taken by the governmental agencies, or even in the deliberations of that advisory board of nobility and gentry that has, under the constitution, been installed under the rubric, "Parliament." In effect, the people at large are the government's chattels, to be bred, fed, trained, and consumed as the shrewd economy of dynastic politics may best require. All this is well enough known, though it is not commonly spoken of in such naïve terms. The government established by the revolution, or "restoration," of Meiji is of the nature of an autonomous co-optative bureaucracy, made up out of certain lines and cliques of the nobility (to some extent of a bureaucratic origin), backed by the loyal adhesion of a large body of gentry which differs from the displaced Samurai in its work-day avocations rather than in its spirit of aristocratic fealty or its substantially parasitic livelihood. In point of its substantial powers, as in point of substantial accountability, the current bureaucratic organisation that does business in the name of the Mikado apparently differs in no sensible degree from the Shogunate which it displaced. The Emperor is now paraded instead of being retired behind the screen, and there is much ceremonial dust thrown up about his ostensible share in the measures taken by the bureaucratic directorate; all of which is, doubtless, good management. The powers of the crown —except as they are construed to be identical with the powers of the cabinet—are apparently of much the same *fainéantise* nature as they were under the earlier dispensation, prior to 1868. Of course, none of this characterisation is intended in the least to question or deprecate that peculiar and well-authenticated emanation of virtuous influence whereby this divine ruler magically or preternaturally animates his official servants and, at a farther remove, his subjects more at large; but it is to be noted that apart from such magical control, after the pattern of "absent treatment," it is not evident that the incumbent of the throne exerts any initiative, choice, impulse, guidance, or check in the affairs of state. Power vests in a self-appointed, self-authenticating aristocratic cabinet—under the mask of a piously nourished monarchical fiction—with the advice, but without the consent, of a "parliament" endowed with advisory power.[2]

This bureaucratic organ of control is still animated with the "Spirit of Old Japan," and it still rests on and draws its force from a population animated with the same feudalistic spirit. It is, hitherto, only in respect of its material ways and means, its technological equipment and information, that the "New Japan" differs from the old. That superficial reorganisation and amelioration of its civil and political institutions that went into effect in the Restoration has not yet had time to remove the spiritual landmarks of feudalism or appreciably to weaken the servile-aristocratic bias that still guides the intrigues of the court circle, the policies of state, and the larger maneuvers of diplomacy.

It is in this unique combination of a high-wrought spirit of feudalistic fealty and chivalric honor with the material efficiency given by the modern technology that the strength of the Japanese nation lies. In this respect— in being able anachronistically to combine the use of modern technical ways and means with the mediæval spirit of servile solidarity—the position of the Japanese government is not unique except in the eminent degree of its successful operation. The several governments of Europe are also, and with a varying measure of success, endeavoring similarly to exploit the modern state of the industrial arts by recourse to the servile patriotism of the common man, and for the purposes of a dynastic politics that is substantially of a mediæval character; but in respect of the measure of success which this anachronistic enterprise meets with, these European powers,

[2] See, e.g., the very useful manual on *The Evolution of New Japan,* by Joseph H. Longford, where this complexion of things Japanese is set out in an admirably lucid and succinct manner, although it is apparently done unintentionally and perhaps even unconsciously.

while differing greatly among themselves, each and several fall short of the Japanese pattern by a long interval.

With great, perhaps with exceptional facility, the Japanese have been taking over and assimilating the industrial ways and means offered by the technological knowledge and the material sciences of the western peoples. But, except in the most superficial fashion, their habituation to these technological ways and means and to this matter-of-fact insight in the domain of the material sciences has not yet had its effect on the spiritual outlook and sentimental convictions of the people; nor have these borrowed achievements in the field of matter-of-fact seriously begun to dismantle and reshape those matters of imputation that make up the working specifications of the institutional fabric, the ethical (sentimental) values and conventional principles of conduct by force of which it holds true that "man lives not by bread alone." The Japanese people are learning to gain their "bread" (their fish and rice) by use of the modern, western state of the industrial arts, but they still conduct their life and spend their endeavor in the light of those principles and with an untroubled view to those values that have been handed down from a now obsolescent state of industry and economic organisation in their own recent mediæval past.

In a measure their case is paralleled by that of the German people, e.g., who have recently made an analogous but less immoderate and less precipitate move out of mediævalism into the modern system of industry and science; and in the like analogous way the German people, carrying over much of the servile-aristocratic spirit of mediævalism into their bureaucratic and irresponsible imperial present, have allowed their new-found technological efficiency to be turned to the service of dynastic politics; though herein, again, the rate and ratio of enhanced achievement on the part of the Germans fall short of the spectacular sweep of the Japanese. And by the way, it should be something more than a blind historical accident when the Japanese committee of bureaucrats have found it to their account to draw so largely as they have done from the example of German bureaucratic imperialism, both in their constitutional reorganisation and in the excessively devious and irresponsible ways of their diplomacy.

An analogy farther afield and to a different effect, and yet perhaps even more suggestive in its way, may be found in the case of the English people and their history, both in the industrial and the political respect; but here the analogy is more valuable for its contrasts than for any direct parallelism it may afford. Taking their case over the long run it will be found that, like the Japanese, the English have been a nation of borrowers, particularly borrowers of technological elements. But their borrowings have been extended over an incomparably longer interval of history and have in no case involved so abrupt a break with the people's own cultural past, having commonly been drawn from neighbors occupying a technological plane not conspicuously more advanced than the state of the industrial arts already previously at the command of the English community. And the technological borrowing of the English virtually ceased at a date so far in the past as already to have allowed all borrowed elements not only to be fully assimilated in a virtually home-bred technological system, but also to have so far worked out their secondary, institutional, consequences as to afford an object lesson of what the cultural consequences of any such technological borrowing should necessarily be. Down through the Middle Ages and early modern times the English were, culturally speaking, and particularly in the technological respect, constantly and cumulatively indebted to their Continental neighbors, in a fashion resembling that in which the Japanese throughout their long mediæval experience were, culturally, followers and dependents of China and Korea. But there is in the English case this striking feature of contrast as against the current Japanese situation, that while the English borrowed unremittingly, until such time as the course of events threw them into the lead in Europe's industrial advance, their borrowing took effect at so moderate a pace that the consequently changing state of the industrial arts among them had time and scope concomitantly to work out its effect upon the habits of thought of the community, and so to bring about a state of the institutional conventions answering to the altered state of the industrial arts.

It should, then, confidently be presumed that, as Japan has with great facility and effect taken over the occidental state of the industrial arts, so should its population be due, presently and expeditiously, to fall in with the peculiar habits of thought that make the faults and qualities of the western culture—the spiritual outlook and the principles of conduct and ethical values that have been induced by the exacting discipline of this same state of the industrial arts among the technologically more advanced and mature of the western peoples. For good or ill, life under the conditions imposed by the modern industrial system, and by that economic system of price, business enterprise, and competitive earning and spending that always goes with it, is in the long run incompatible with the prepossessions of mediævalism. So that as soon as her people shall have digested the western state of science and technology and have assimilated its spiritual contents, the "Spirit of Old Japan" will, in effect, have been dissipated. Ravelings of its genial tradition will still trail at the skirts of the new era, but as an asset available for the enterprise in dynastic politics the "Spirit of Old Japan" will have little more than the value of a tale that is told. There will doubtless continue to float through the adolescent brains of Young Japan some yellow vapor of truculence, such as would under other skies be called *el valor español,* and such as may give rise to occasional exploits of abandon, but the joy of living in obscure privation and contumely for the sake of the Emperor's politics and posthumous fame will be lost to the common man.

The opportunity of imperial Japan as a fearsome power in the world's concert of dynastic politics may by consequence confidently be expected to lie within the historical interval that so intervenes between Japan's acquirement of the western state of the industrial arts and its consequent, slower but inevitable, falling into line with those materialistic, commercial, and spendthrift conceptions of right and honest living that make the outcome among the (Christian) peoples that have gone before along the road of industrial dominion and individual self-help.

The "Spirit of Old Japan" is an institutional matter; that is to say it is a matter of acquired habits of thought, of tradition and training, rather than of native endowment peculiar to the race. As such it is necessarily of a transitory, not to say transient, nature, depending for its maintenance on the continued maintenance of those workday habits of life out of which it has arisen and to which it owes its consistency. Barring such retardation as necessarily attached to the growth of new principles and values induced by new circumstances, a radical change in the material ways and means by which the people live must, here as elsewhere, work a consequent change in the people's scheme of life—in the accepted rule of rights and duties. Ideals, ethical values, principles (habits of thought) induced by the conditions of life in the past must presently give place to a different range of ideals, values, and principles, so soon as the range of habituation to which they owe their force has ceased to be operative. The fact that, in the case of the Japanese as in other similar cases, the popular and romantic faith holds the received scheme of habits to be an innate and irreducible specific character peculiar to this people, and therefore holds it to be a national heritage unalterable and indefeasible through the ages—"as it was in the beginning, is now, and ever shall be," etc.; this romantic prejudice need of course not detain us, since it is itself an integral part in that scheme of habits of thought that comes and goes under the compulsion of shifting circumstance.

The Japanese people should be no exception to the common rule in this respect. The elements engaged in their case are of much the same character as those that have been seen at work in the history of the western nations, and they should be amenable to the same discipline of those material circumstances that are now coming to condition the national life. So, in point of their racial make-up, the Japanese are in very much the same case as the occidental nations from whom they are now borrowing ways and means and into the midst of whom they are driving their way by help of these borrowed ways and means.

It is, of course, not intended to claim that there subsists anything like an identity of race, as between the Japanese and the Christian nations, nor even a particularly near or intimate ethnic relationship; but the run of the well-known facts is sufficiently convincing to the effect that the Japanese people readily fall into the same ways of thinking and reasoning, that they readily assimilate the same manner of theoretical constructions in science and technology, that the same scheme of conceptual values and logical sequence carries conviction in Japan as in the Occident. Their intellectual perspective is so nearly the same that the same facts, seen in the same connection, are convincing to the same effect. It need by no means imply an inclusive psychological identity or duplication, but the facility and effect with which the Japanese are taking to western habits of thought in matters of technology and scientific knowledge shows a sufficiently convincing equality or equivalence between them and their western fellow men in respect of their intellectual make-up.

This intellectual similarity or psychological equivalence will stand out in relief when the Japanese case is contrasted with what has befallen certain other peoples, racially alien to the bearers of the western culture, such as the Negro, Polynesian, or East Indian. These others have been exposed to the occidental technological system —the system of the machine industry—but they have been brought to no effectual comprehension of the logic and efficiency of the western technological equipment, have not acquired or assimilated the drift and bias of the material science of the West, and have, even under hard compulsion, been unable to effect anything like a practicable working arrangement with the occidental system of mechanical efficiency and economic control.

And even as the Japanese show this facile apprehension of occidental methods and values in the domain of material knowledge, so also is there apparently a close resemblance in point of emotional complexion, suggested, e.g., by the close similarity between the feudal system as it has prevailed in Japan and, in its time, in western Europe. Similar material circumstances, particularly in respect of the industrial arts, appear to have induced similar institutional results and a parallel range of ideals and ethical values, such as would presume a somewhat closely similar run of human nature in the two cases.

This similarity in point of native traits, if so it can be called, is due not to an identity of race but rather to a parallelism in racial composition. Like the peoples of Christendom, and more particularly like that group of peoples that cluster about the North Sea, and that make up the center of diffusion of the western culture, the Japanese are, racially, a hybrid population. The several racial elements that go to make up the hybrid mixture are, of course, not the same in the two cases under comparison, nor are they, perhaps, at all nearly related in point of racial derivation. But both of these two contrasted populations alike show that wide-ranging variability of individuals that is characteristic of hybrid peoples, both in the absence of uniformity in respect of physical type and in their relatively great variety of intellectual and spiritual endowment, both in degree and in kind. This variability of these hybrid peoples becomes more obvious when they are contrasted with peoples of relatively unmixed stock, or even with the average run of mankind at large. Indeed, it may be set down as an earmark of hybridism. It is a factor of serious consequence for the cultural scheme of any such population, particularly for its stability; since such a wide-fluctuating variability of individuals within any given community will give, in effect, a large available flexibility of type, and so will afford a wide and facile susceptibility to new ideas and new grounds of action.

Such being the character of the human raw material in and by which the Japanese situation is to be worked out, it should presumably follow that, just as the material and matter-of-fact elements of western civilisation are finding ready lodgment and fertile ground among them, so should these intrusive matter-of-fact conceptions presently, and with celerity, induce the working out of a corresponding fabric of matters of imputation—principles of conduct, articles of faith, social conventions, ethical values. The impersonal and materialistic bias of modern science and technology has, among the western peoples, already gone far to dissipate those putative values on which any feudal and autocratic régime must necessarily rest. And since the same impersonal and materialistic frame of mind proves, to all appearance, to be characteristic of the Japanese, they should also expect presently to experience its spiritual, and therefore its institutional consequences.

Hitherto and for the immediate future, therefore, Japan has the usufruct of the modern state of science and the industrial arts, without the faults of its qualities. But in the long run its faults are as inseparable from this system as its structure. How far these faults or infirmities are to be rated as such at large is a question that need not be argued here. They are infirmities for the imperialistic purposes of Great Nippon, and it should be a matter of no great difficulty to see how and why, or even to see that they are already incipiently in process of realisation. This may be better appreciated on calling to mind certain features of the change that is going forward in the economic circumstances of Japan.

Effectually to turn its usufruct of the western science and technology to account, it will be necessary for Japan, in all essential respects, to follow the lead given by the western peoples. Such a course is prescribed by the circumstances of the case; partly in that the modern state of the industrial arts involves a certain kind and degree of popular education and a certain impersonal, mechanistic organisation and co-ordination of the material equipment (mechanical and human) and of the processes employed; partly because nothing like the full advantage of the methods employed can be had except by entering into close relations of give and take, commercially and otherwise, with the other nations that have adopted the scope and method of the mechanical industry. In its full scope this industrial system is necessarily of an international or cosmopolitan character, and any attempt to work it on narrower than international lines must fall short of that highest efficiency which alone can satisfy the imperialistic needs or the national pride of Japan. It is only by way of commerce and a commercialised industry that Japan can get a footing among the commercial nations of the West; and in this necessary commercialisation of its industry and its economic institutions Japan must in all essential respects accept the scheme as it is already in force among the nations of the West. But the unintended consequences of such a course must also follow.

So, a competent system of communication, internal and external, is of the essence of the case, and in this matter the Japanese are already far on their way, with steamships, railway, telegraph, telephone, postal service, and newspapers, as well as an improved and extended system of highways; from which it follows that the isolation, parcelment, and consequent home-bred animus of the people is already beginning to disappear, and the corresponding clannishness and adhesive loyalty to their hereditary local masters is also in process of decay. The feudal organisation, and the spirit of fealty, rests on an industrial system of self-sufficient local units and on discrepancies of usage and convention as between self-sufficient local organisations.

Again, the modern (western) state of the industrial arts requires, in order to its efficient working, a relatively high degree of "intelligence," so-called, among the workmen—it should more accurately be spoken of as a large volume of relatively exact information within the peculiar lines of the material sciences. This involves schooling, of a set and special character, extended far beyond the bounds of what was needed in that way under the earlier industrial system, and specifically it involves, as an imperative requirement, the familiar use of printed matter. (It may be noted by the way that the percentage of illiteracy among the Japanese has fallen off since the Restoration at a rate that is fairly alarming for the stability of the established order.) It is particularly for the sake of matter-of-fact information, serviceable in the mechanically organised system of industry and communication, that this high rate of literacy is indispensable, and the effect of this industrial system and of life organised on these mechanical lines is unavoidably to extend and diffuse information of this kind. At the same time the workday training of the routine of life under this industrial system, and of its ubiquitous and exacting system of communication, goes in a pronouncedly one-sided way to inculcate a matter-of-fact, and especially a materialistic, habit of mind; such as comports ill with those elusive putative verities of occult personal excellence in which the "Spirit of Old Japan" is grounded.

So, e.g., the spread of such matter-of-fact information and such mechanistic conceptions must unavoidably act to dissipate all substantial belief in that *opéra bouffe* mythology that makes up the state religion and supplies the foundation of the Japanese faith in the Emperor's divine pedigree and occult virtues; for these time-worn elements of Shinto are even less viable under the exacting mechanistic discipline of modern industry than are the frayed remnants of the faith that conventionally serve as articles of belief among the Christian peoples.

Under the given conditions, brought on throughout the western world by the machine industry itself and by the antecedent institutional situation out of which it arose, this modern state of the industrial arts can be turned to account for the purposes of any national or dynastic ambitions only by the help or through the mediation of a business organisation of the modern kind. No other method of control or exploitation would serve, because no other system of control will articulate with the industrial organisation of those commercial nations with whom co-ordination and intercourse are requisite to bring the industry of the Japanese people to its best (pecuniary) efficiency. Within the comprehensive community of nations that lies under the dominion of the machine process any degree of isolation counts as a disability. It is a system of interlocking processes; and the mechanism of co-ordination and commutation in the case is the commercial traffic in which all these communities are engaged. Incompetent, or even puerile, as this commercial enterprise may seem when seen in the large and taken as a means of the international co-ordination of industry, it still affords the sole method available for the purpose under the given conditions, because it is one of the chief of the given conditions.

This business enterprise under whose tutelage the industrial system is placed does not directly contemplate or concern itself with serviceability to national, dynastic, or collective ends of any kind. It is a matter of individual enterprise, animated by motives of pecuniary gain and carried on on a competitive basis. Wherever it reaches it carries a "commercialisation" of human relations and social standards, and effects a displacement of such aims and values as cannot be stated in terms of pecuniary gain; and so it throws pecuniary solvency into that position of first consideration that has once been occupied by pedigree and putative excellencies of character.

This pecuniary enterprise that so comes necessarily to take the oversight of the industrial system has certain specific consequences, secondary but essential, which the Japanese community has not yet experienced in full, because the secondary effects of the industrial revolution in Japan have not yet had time to come to a head. The most obvious of these, or at least the one most readily to be stated and appreciated in concrete (material) terms, is what might be called the "sabotage" of capitalism—the competitive working at cross purposes of rival business concerns and the control of industrial processes by considerations of net gain to the managers rather than of material serviceability. By virtue of this pecuniary control it has come about, in all countries in which the modern industrial system has had time to fall into settled lines, that the equipment is rarely, if ever, worked to its capacity—often, over long intervals, at less than one half its capacity—and that the products, whether goods or services, are turned out with a view, in respect of kind, time, place, and sophistication, to their profitable sale rather than to their serviceable consumption. It is presumably well within the mark to say that by force of this unavoidable capitalistic "sabotage" the industries in the maturer commercial countries fall short of their theoretically normal efficiency by something more than fifty percent. The new era in Japan has not yet reached this stage of economic maturity, but there is no reason to presume a different outcome for Japan in this respect, given the necessary time for adjustment.

With competitive gain as the legitimate end of endeavor comes also competitive spending as its legitimate counterfoil, leading to a ubiquitous system of "conspicuous waste." With this canon of right pecuniary living, reinforced by the new ethical principles of self-help and commercial solvency, comes in as a bench-mark in public life the well-worn principle of modern politics that "public office is a means of private gain." Hence the comprehensive system of "graft" that envelopes all civilised affairs of state, and that once, e.g., allowed the great organisation of Russian officials to be defeated by the Japanese. This phase of civilisation must also of right come to the Japanese in due course of maturity.

So, again, through the competitive wage system, as well as by other channels of commerical indoctrination, the same principle of competitive consumption comes to permeate the industrial population and presently induces a higher standard of living, or more accurately of expenditure; which cuts into the disposable margin of production above cost, that might otherwise be drawn to the service of imperial politics.

It would of course be hazardous to guess how long an interval must necessarily elapse between Japan's acquirement of the western state of the industrial arts and the consequent disintegration of that "Spirit of Old Japan" that still is the chief asset of the state as a warlike power; but it may be accepted without hazard that such must be the event, sooner or later. And it is within this interval that Japan's opportunity lies. The spiritual disintegration has already visibly set in, under all the several forms of modernisation spoken of above, but it is presumably still safe to say that hitherto the rate of gross gain in material efficiency due to the new scientific and technological knowledge is more than sufficient to offset this incipient spiritual deterioration; so that, while the climax of the nation's net efficiency as a political or warlike force lies yet in the future, it would seem at least to lie in the calculable future. When this critical point in the country's growing maturity under the new economic dispensation shall be passed, when Japan shall have reached the plane of materialism and commercialisation occupied by the Christian nations, in respect of pecuniary ideals and self-help as well as of technological efficiency; then the advantage that now visibly inures to the government of Japan from the anomalous cultural situation of that country should be at an end, and the efficiency of the Japanese national organisation should then presumably fall to the same level of efficiency per unit of men and of expenditure as is now occupied by the older peoples within the European community of nations. It is the present high efficiency of the Japanese, an efficiency which may be formulated as an exceptionally wide margin between cost of production and output of military force—it is this that makes Japan formidable in the eyes of her western competitors for imperial honors, and in substance it is this on which the Japanese masters of political intrigue rest their sanguine hopes of empire.

As already implied in what has been said above, the Japanese, statesmen and subjects, seeing the rapid rate of gain already made in material efficiency, and failing to see what their own experience has not taught them, that the new industrial era carries the faults of its own qualities; seeing the coefficient of gain, and not discounting the yet incipiently operative coefficient of loss, they count on the present rate of gross gain as a secure basis of prospective net gain. But from the considerations set forth above it follows that if this new-found efficiency is to serve the turn for the dynastic aggrandisement of Japan, it must be turned to account before the cumulatively accelerating rate of institutional deterioration overtakes and neutralises the cumulatively declining rate of gain in material efficiency; which should, humanly speaking, mean that Japan must strike, if at all, within the effective lifetime of the generation that is now coming to maturity. For, facile as the Japanese people have shown themselves to be, there is no reason to doubt that the commercialisation of Japan should be passably complete within that period. It is, therefore, also contained in the premises that, in order to an (imperialistically) successful issue, the imperial government must throw all its available force, without reservation, into one headlong rush; since in the nature of the case no second opportunity of the kind is to be looked for.

# MENIAL SERVANTS
## DURING THE PERIOD OF THE WAR [1]

VISITORS from oversea tell us of a new France and a new
Britain, unsparingly cleared for action, war-weary but
resolute and untiring; where invidious distinctions of
class, sex, wealth, and privilege are giving way before
the exigencies of a war that is to be fought to a finish;
where all resources of material and man power are being
thrown into a common stock of means for the prosecution of a joint enterprise whose demands overbear all
questions of personal gain and immemorial usage.

A year has passed now since America entered on full
partnership in this joint enterprise. During this time, and
the period leading up to it, the Americans have contributed much. They have undertaken a burden of debt, and
they have begun to send their young men into the field.
At the same time they have also begun to redistribute the
industrial forces of the country to meet the material demands of the Great War, and to place these war demands
ahead of many other things. In a measure, it is coming
to be realised that the war is a joint enterprise; but it
is only in words that this realisation has gone so far as to
recognise that the nation's resources are therefore to
be managed as a common stock, devoted to one paramount end. There is much edifying talk on this theme,
and there has been an abundance of moral suasion designed to induce a spirit of sacrifice for the common
good. But of resolute action and a concerted move

[1] Reprinted from *The Public*, Vol. XXI, May 11, 1918.

toward accomplishing something of this kind there has hitherto been surprisingly little. The dominant note still is respect of persons and of those invidious amenities that distinguish peace from a state of war. There still prevails a stubborn reluctance to take such concrete measures as will in any degree derange the settled scheme of things as it runs in time of peace.

Meantime it is becoming increasingly evident that the Great War is to be America's war in the end, if it is to be brought to such a conclusion as the Americans will tolerate. It has already become America's part to supply the food and other means of its carrying on, and before the conclusion comes in sight it will also be America's part to supply the fighting men whose force will bring the decision. Yet it visibly continues to be the chief abiding concern of the Americans to avoid all derangement of the nugatory interests and usages of peace. Popular interest and administrative policy are still bent on the maintenance of the domestic status quo—the status of competitive gain and competitive spending.

The continued production and profitable sale of superfluities must not be materially curtailed; nor must any pressure of a less genial kind than well-bred advice and admonition be brought to bear on that voluminous scheme of competitive waste in which these superfluities are consumed. Only in respect of certain staple articles of food, and less freely in the use of fuel, have the exigencies of the common good been allowed to impose restrictions on the wasteful use of the means in hand; and then only tentatively. Many vested interests, enterprises of private gain, are engaged in the production and sale of these superfluities; and these vested interests still effectually claim the right of way as against an unreserved prosecution of the war. So there are also vested interests in the untrammeled consumption of super-fluities by persons whose craving for social prestige can be gratified only by a conspicuous waste of goods and man power; and this right of untrammeled waste, too, is still upheld as being a good and righteous exercise of personal liberty in the face of the nation's war need.

In the production and competitive sale of superfluities, as well as in their decent consumption, a very large aggregate of labor is employed; at the same time that labor power is urgently needed for productive use in industries necessary to the prosecution of the war. It would be hazardous to offer an estimate of the total volume of labor which is so devoted to deliberate waste, but no man doubts that the total is very large. Not all of this wasted labor force is suitable for use in the war industries. And yet there is little of it that cannot be used to good effect; partly by direct participation in useful industry, partly by substitution to displace other workmen who are fit for useful work.

This wasted labor falls under two heads: (*a*) Employees engaged in the production and sale of super-fluities, and (*b*) those employed in the wasteful consumption of superfluities, including the conspicuous waste of time and effort by caretakers and attendants in many domestic and public establishments.

Typical of the latter class are the many persons to be counted as domestic or "menial servants." Not all of the menials are to be counted in as items of conspicuous waste, without abatement; but it is not to be overlooked that such is ordinarily the nature of their service, with such slight abatement as may be reasonably allowed in any given case.

To appreciate the measure in which menial servants are actually dispensable in the life of the average American household, even in time of peace, it may be called to mind that the ordinary American household gets along without hired domestics; that these domestics themselves ordinarily get along without the use of servants to minister to their own personal wants; and that the number of households which employ domestics is smaller than the number of domestics employed—which leaves the common sort of Americans unprovided with menial servants. "Servant" implies "Master," of course; and the average person, the common man, is not of the master class. Now, in time of stress, when it has become expedient to throw all available resources into a common stock and to forego personal amenities for the common good, it is evident that the lot of the common man must be the lot to which all are called on to submit—for the period of the war.

The chief use of menial servants is to put in evidence their employer's ability to pay. This invidious use of their services commonly masquerades under the profession that they minister to the creature comfort of their masters. But it is plainly the spiritual comfort, the sense of self-complacency and invidious distinction, that is catered to by this class of service, rather than the physical well-being of the employers. It is the "better classes" that employ menial servants—better in point of social prestige. Servants have a "prestige value," as the economists would call it. This prestige value, which represents the "output" of such work, is a matter of invidious distinction. It is altogether of the nature of a spiritual or intangible product; something in the way of a pleasurable state of mind on the part of the employer; an article of "psychic income."

Evidently such psychic income, invidious distinction, prestige value, intangible goods, or whatever term may best cover the output of the menial servant's work, is of very little if any use in the prosecution of the war. In effect, these intangible goods are as sand in the bearings of the great industrial and military mechanism by which the war is to be won. Yet it will be found that many, if not substantially all, of those better classes who profess an unbounded patriotic devotion to the democratic cause for which the war is fought, still continue to draw on the country's labor force for menial service with which to keep themselves in countenance as licensed wasters with ability to pay.

The fortunes of war turn finally on the use of the nation's man power, in productive industry and under arms. Of material resources there is no lack, but of available labor power there is a visible shortage which is bound to grow more serious as time passes and the work to be taken care of increases, at the same time that the drain on the country's man power goes on at a constantly accelerated rate, due to the military and industrial demands of the forces under arms. All the while there is in the background this body of labor force devoted to menial service and the psychic income of the better classes; a body of labor force kept substantially idle, so far as regards any productive work.

So the question presents itself: How can the energies of this large body of idle man-power be turned to account —diverted from this wasteful consumption of superfluities to productive work? It has been suggested, or tentatively hinted, that conscription of this idle labor, simple and direct, might be resorted to with good effect. But such a degree of odium attaches to all manner of coercion, in the mind of the Americans, that conscription could presumably not be put into effect until the case had become inordinately urgent; that is to say, until too late. At the same time conscription in such a case would have to contend with many complications and would be disproportionately costly, in that it would involve an extensive bureaucratic machinery organised for the purpose.

In analogous cases of perplexity the usual expedient has been some ingenious recourse to taxation, which will avoid the formal appearance of coercion at the same time that it is counted on to bring the requisite pressure to bear where it will bring results. This sentimental aversion to coercive measures of all kinds will not apply to a prudently formulated tax, in anything like the same degree; but any tax that is to escape condemnation on this score must be so laid as not to offend the requirement of a formal impartiality. It is in great part a question of the letter of the law rather than of its ulterior purpose.

This idle man-power embodied in the servant class is sorely needed for present use in productive industry, and to that end it should be practicable to lay a steeply progressive tax on those shameless persons who still go on employing a staff of unproductive domestics to uphold their own personal prestige in the face of the nation's sorest need. There will, e.g., be two able-bodied man servants, coachman and footman, in waiting at the curb while their patriotic and spendthrift mistress within the gates sits in self-appointed council on the state of the republic at large with a quorum of ladies as scrupulously ignorant as herself in all those things that have any slightest significance for the work in hand. Indeed, merit is still to be acquired in that way.

As a measure of expediency, for the period of the war, therefore, the suggestion is here offered, tentatively and as a point of departure, that a progressive capitation tax be laid on menial servants, payable by their employers, rising step by step with every additional servant employed in any one household. So it is proposed that any one household of five persons or more be allowed one servant tax-free, provided that such household includes as many as two children under five years of age. It is, of course, to be recognised that the exemption so provided for concedes something to the class of households which habitually employ servants, and that the law would at this point admit a mitigation of the rule which says that in time of stress the common lot must be the lot of all concerned. The suggestion has also been made that the like exemption should apply in the case of households which include one or more invalids requiring personal service; but it is said by those that should know that all such can be more adequately and economically cared for in public hospitals and infirmaries, under the care of properly trained nurses; and for the period of the war some slight home comforts forgone may fairly be overlooked even by well-bred invalids, if their creature comforts are not neglected. It is otherwise as regards households which are made up of bread-winners alone, or whose adult members are to be classed as such. In such cases it would seem reasonable to let the rule of exemption apply. It is true, the common run of households in this country do not, in ordinary times, employ servants to the extent so provided for, under the like circumstances of bread-winning and child-rearing; but it is believed that the common-sense of the community would allow this much of a concession to the established usage, according to which those who are able to pay have habitually employed servants in the past. It is a concession to usage, and it may be a debatable point.

Beginning with the lowest-paid servants in households

not exempt under this concession, or with the second lowest in households entitled to the exemption, it is proposed to impose a tax equal to one hundred percent of the wages paid such servants, or their wages and keep in case the servants' keep is included in the terms of employment. Beyond this, the second taxable domestic would be taxed at the rate of two hundred percent on his cost, the third at three hundred percent, etc.; each successive step in the series going to the next higher-paid employee, and the rate increasing by one hundred percent of the employee's wages at each successive step.

The effect of such a tax should be two-fold: it should set free an appreciable number of persons for use in productive occupations; and it should yield an appreciable revenue. It will be remarked that such a tax will bring no coercive pressure on those who can afford to employ servants, particularly not on those who are accustomed to keep a considerable number of domestics; yet it is fairly to be presumed that such taxation will induce many householders to forgo the use of menial servants, or at least to release a reasonable proportion of the number habitually employed. At the same time it is reasonably to be expected that those persons who still feel constrained by their craving for prestige or for personal comfort to employ a staff of menial servants will be favorably inclined to contribute in due proportion to the funds necessary for the prosecution of the war, and that they will therefore not find the alternative offered them between the payment of the tax and the release of their unproductive servants at all an onerous choice. Indeed, in view of the present and increasing need of workmen in the essential industries, the alternative so offered between the release of unproductive servants and the payment of the proposed tax is to be rated as a concession to the prejudices of those classes who are able to pay.

As has been indicated above, the proposal as it stands is to be regarded only as a point of departure for the contemplated plan to release idle servants by taxation. It is to be taken as a basis on which to deal with other classes of employment and of employees whose services are of the same general nature and supplement or take the place of domestic service in one way and another. So, e.g., it is obvious that the employees of hotels, clubs, theaters, railway stations, sleeping and parlor cars, and an indefinite number of analogous establishments, will have to be drawn in under the same plan, in some degree and in one way and another. It is also an open question how far business concerns engaged in the production and sale of superfluities are to be laid under contribution, in men and money, under the same general plan.

Evidently the production of those superfluities, for the decent consumption of which the menial servants are employed and paid for, is quite as readily dispensable as the decent consumption of the superfluities produced for this purpose; and evidently there is, in point of principle, no defensible ground for the exemption of such business establishments and their employees. They serve the same purpose—conspicuous waste with a view to social prestige—and they are equally disserviceable for the prosecution of the war. There is the difficulty, of course, that many of these establishments produce or deal in goods or services that are of material use, often of necessary use; even when the goods in question have chiefly a prestige value as, e.g., tailors and other producers and sellers of apparel for men, women, and children; department stores of the fashionable sort, or even the unfashionable ones; places of public entertainment, and public vehicles for hire; laundries and bakeshops, etc. But there is also on the other hand the difficulty that in case the proposed measure should lead to an appreciable release of domestics, these establishments so engaged in what may be called personal service would be called on to fill their place in some measure by "out-service"; hence it will become imperative to reach these domestic-service concerns at large, since the domestics whose release is aimed at might otherwise be expected to shift into the employ of these "out-service" concerns, and so continue their work as hired consumers under another style and title, thereby and in so far defeating the intent of the measure. These and the like difficulties will, of course, have to be provided for.

It is also a matter of course that there are many and various objections and exceptions readily to be found by those who may be interested in finding them. E.g., it will be—indeed it has been—said that a large and elaborate house such as commonly requires a retinue of menials for its upkeep and advantageous exhibition, could not advantageously be inhabited, or even kept in running order, without the customary "help." To which is fairly to be replied that such a house is in so far, and for the period of the war, to be classed among the superfluities; that its maintenance and due exhibition in no way conduce to the prosecution of the war; and that the common sort on whom chiefly falls the burden of the war have not the use of houses requiring a retinue of menials even in times of peace. There is also the further consideration that superfluously large houses of this kind, which would in this way be left partly vacant, might so become available for effectual use as habitations by workmen employed in productive work. Some measure should logically be taken to turn such superfluous habitations to account to meet the demands of housing, particularly in the cities and industrial centers. At the same time, country houses that are similarly threatened with decay for want of cheap domestics might reasonably be taken over as recreation grounds for workmen, and more particularly for their women and children, during the period of the war. There is also an ever-increasing need of barracks, billets, hospitals, and infirmaries, which may in part be met by the use of such houses otherwise lying waste. The houses so turned to a baser use, for the period of the war, would presumably not escape some slight defacement in their decorative fittings and some enhanced wear and tear at the hands of underbred tenants; but all that should go in easily and unobtrusively as a willing sacrifice from the side of their owners, for the period of the war.

Again, it is said, with some truth and with more of its counterfeit, that the persons hereby released from domestic service would find themselves homeless, friendless, and useless in an industrial world in which all their previous training would go for naught, resulting in widespread privation and a perplexing problem of unemployment. But it is to be remarked that the community would still save something by the move, even in the wholly improbable case that all these released menials were to fall into the class of the unemployed; since, although the community at large would in that case have to charge itself with their keep, they will at the worst no longer be wasting material resources in the production of superfluities which require their combined efforts to consume. It is also to be noted that, while many of them have been trained into effectual incompetency for useful work, yet it does not follow that even these cannot be made use of

—boys from the farms and villages are trained into serviceable soldiers in the course of weeks and many of them are even made into creditable aviators in a few months. Many will find their place in occupations of much the same kind that they are used to, in the service of the public or of establishments serving the public use; possibly displacing others who are better fit for use in the essential industries; and a large number will fall into place in work for which their training has prepared them. There is no lack of work of the kind demanded of chambermaids and cooks, and footmen and butlers are, typically, an eminently ablebodied sort, who will readily qualify as stevedores and freight handlers so soon as the day's work has somewhat hardened their muscles and reduced their bulk; whereas chauffeurs, mechanicians, plumbers, house-carpenters, electricians, janitors, gardeners, are already urgently in demand for work that is waiting to be done.

This does not by any means exhaust the range of objections to be looked for, but it will be seen that all these and such-like objections are of the nature of underbrush —convenient to hide in for any persons to whom the project is distasteful. They do not touch the substantial merits of the plan, as a measure of present expediency. In effect, they only serve to call attention to minor difficulties in its execution. A more substantial obstacle is likely to be encountered in the known reluctance of any law-giving body to enact a law which might be presumed, incidentally and for the period of the war, to equalise the conditions of life as between the servant-keeping class from which the law-givers are drawn and the common man to whose class the released domestics would bring an increment of numbers and discontent.

# FARM LABOR FOR THE PERIOD
# OF THE WAR [1]

## I

THE Great War has thrown an unexampled strain on
this country's labor force. All industrial undertakings
are suffering from the drain on their labor supply, and
from the disturbance which always comes on with such
a shortage and redistribution of labor. The farm industry of the grain states has its share in this hardship along
with the rest. But there is the difference that grain growing is, just now, a primary requirement, indispensable,
beyond any other branch of industry. The fortunes of
the Great War visibly turn on the American grain-
grower's ability to feed the fighting nations. If the
American grain supply falls below the minimum necessary to keep America's allies in fighting trim, then the
victory will go to the German Empire with all that it
may involve. If a reasonable sufficiency of American
grain continues to be delivered in Europe as required,
then the German Empire will go down to irretrievable
defeat; and it will presumably be taken off the map by
agreement between democratic Europe and the farmers
and workmen of America.

By a combination of circumstances, unexampled and
largely unforeseen, the chances of success or failure
have come to depend immediately on the supply of ship-

[1] Reprinted from *The Public,* Vol. XXI, July 13, 20, 27, August 3,
1919, as an elaboration of an unpublished memorandum which Veblen
prepared for the Food Administration in 1918. See footnote to p. 319.

ping and of foodstuffs; and by force of the same circumstances America's part in the supply of both has
been thrown into the foreground, as indispensable to
the successful prosecution of the war. Of the two the increase of shipping is the more immediately urgent; but
it is also the part which can effectually be pushed to a
working sufficiency by concerted efforts. The need of
shipping can be met in some tolerable measure by drawing on the available materials and consistently pushing
the work in hand; and, indeed, it appears that the measures required to this end have at last been taken and are
bringing the required output.

The production of foodstuffs is a somewhat different
matter. It depends on the seasons, and the rate of production cannot be speeded up beyond the rate at which
the seasons revolve. So that it becomes a question of
how large a volume of output can be turned out within
the run of the season and by use of the resources that
are already employed. In effect, a limit has already been
set to this year's production; a limit which may be approximated, but not passed. There may be some slight
qualification to be made in this broad statement, but it
will have to be allowed to stand as substantially correct.
No appreciable increase of acreage or soil fertility is to
be looked for, and there can be no substantial change in
the methods of cultivating and handling the crops. And
it is to be noted that in American farming the production of other foodstuffs than the grain crops depends,
on the whole and with slight exceptions, on the yield of
the grain crops.

In the last resort American farming is primarily
grain-farming; from which it follows that the American production of foodstuffs rests in the main on the
grain-crops of the Middle West; which in turn centers

in the grain-growing prairie states. So that, by a singular turn of events, the prosecution of the Great War has come to depend on the season's production in the prairie states, more immediately and more critically than on any other one factor. And as the situation now stands, with the crops committed to the soil and the weather, substantially all that can be done by taking thought is to take care that there will be a sufficient labor force of the right kind to take care of the crops and to see that nothing goes to waste out of what the season brings forth.

It has been said that there is no scarcity of foodstuffs to be looked for during the coming crop year; that the prospective harvest, according to the most reliable estimates, promises to be sufficient to meet all the needs of the Americans and their allies throughout the coming year, with reasonable economy. But this appraisal of the situation appears to take account of present rather than prospective needs. It overlooks the fact that the needs both of the Americans and of their allies are bound to be greater during the coming year than ever before; due to a larger consumption by the forces in the field and by those auxiliary forces of man power whose work is indispensable to the support of the forces immediately engaged in military operations—larger by a very considerable amount than the necessary consumption of the same persons would be at home and under the ordinary conditions of the day's work. It also overlooks the added cost of transportation—as counted in terms of consumption—involved in feeding the same number of persons at a distance. It would be a safe underestimate of the case to say that every addition of one man to the nation's fighting forces draws at least two men from the home occupations of the country; and it may also safely be said that the need of foodstuffs for the support of the men under arms will be twice as large, man for man, as the necessary consumption of the same men at home under ordinary conditions.

Meanwhile the supply of farm labor is subject to a steady drain—directly by men enlisting or being drafted into the army or navy, whether from the farms or from the sources from which farm-hands are habitually procured, and indirectly by the like demands of the other industries necessary to the prosecution of the war. This flow of labor from the farms and the farming states is nothing sudden or spectacular, but it is unceasing and it is forever on the increase. Every increase of the American forces in the field, and every extension of the war industries, brings an additional drain on the available labor supply; and the grain states are subject to this drain as much or more than any other section of the country's industry.

It has been said, or rather it has been shrewdly argued in certain quarters, that there is actually no embarrassing shortage of labor in the grain states today. It is argued that what is spoken of as a shortage of labor is in reality only a faulty distribution of the available supply, and that this can easily be remedied by such measures of publicity and management as will place the idle workmen where they are needed for work to be done. There is doubtless a modicum of truth in this contention, but it does not go far to correct the known difficulties which now face the farm situation in the grain states. It would perhaps not do to say that, in effect, it amounts to prevarication so far as concerns the question of farm-hands in the grain states, but it is also difficult to avoid the impression that this contention is put forward by interested parties speaking in behalf of a certain vested interest among the labor organisations.

But whatever may be the state of the case in this respect today, the labor supply is constantly dwindling and the need is growing. The demand for foodstuffs, and particularly for grain, is increasing and is bound to go on increasing. And it is time to look ahead, for the Great War is not yet finished. The reason why the war is not yet finished is, very simply, that the American people have not yet gone to work to finish it. They have not yet been willing effectually to make the war a joint enterprise and to go to work in a joint effort, at the cost of such a disturbance of private interests as will unavoidably be involved in bringing the war to a conclusion of a kind that the Americans will tolerate. The American people have failed to bear their part in the conduct of the war, not because they are unwilling or unable to bear the burden, but because they have been unable to make up their mind to disturb the vested interests that stand in the way of any effectual joint effort. The vested interests are stubbornly unwilling to submit to any measures that will leave them insecure or that will disturb the traffic from which they derive their income; and among these vested interests are to be counted certain corporate organisations of labor, as well as the business concerns with whom the labor organisations habitually deal. And yet it is sufficiently evident to any disinterested observer that if the war is to be won it will have to be at the cost of such derangement of the vested interests, whether of labor or of capital, as may be involved in any unreserved joint use of all available resources, including the nation's man power wherever it is to be found and regardless of private interests that may stand in the way.

As a working force, as a going concern engaged in the prosecution of the war for democracy, the American people is made up of the American farmers and the American workmen. The vested interests are sections and fractions of the community who are vested with something in the way of a customary claim to a preferred share in the community's joint product. Experience teaches that such a vested preference will be surrendered only under pressure of necessity, only when its retention involves palpable risk of its total loss. The work now in hand is work for the American farmers and workmen. The destiny of this nation, and of the other democratic nations as well, rests on the work of these two; and it all resolves itself finally into a question of teamwork between these two free constituents of the American people. What the vested interests will do toward that end is, by and large, a question of what they will be compelled to put up with at the hands of the farmers and workmen.

Meantime, the beginning of wisdom in the prosecution of the war is the growing of grain; and the next grave consideration is the provision of shipping. Both of these call for work and for a labor force to do the work; and, indeed, both of them call for skilled labor, each after its kind. The great and final need in any of the great industries is always skilled labor; and grain-farming is no exception to the rule. Among those persons who know anything about the matter it is well known that any untrained city-bred man who is taken on as a farm-hand is not worth his keep during his first year on the farm; and he will have to be quite exceptional—as, e.g., a trained machinist or teamster—if he is to be worth much more than his keep during his second year. The call of the farm is for skilled labor—skilled and specialised. Any capable farm-hand is a trained workman. He must, in effect, have had several years of special training, such as will amount to an apprenticeship of several years' duration.

This special training is not to be acquired suddenly, by attending a suitable night school; but it is also not lost suddenly or altogether by those farm-hands and farm boys who have shifted into other occupations. One such farm-bred workman who is now employed in some other occupation is worth an indefinite number of equally stout and equally intelligent men who have never had the benefit of farm training. The like rule applies with nearly equal force to newcomers from the agricultural countries of Europe and Asia, where the extensive methods of American prairie farming are not in use. These Europeans and Asiatics—Greeks, Sicilians, Portuguese, Dutch, Lowland Chinese—are capital farmers in their own way; but they are not competent to produce wheat, corn, barley, rye, milk, butter, pork, under the conditions offered by the American prairie states. Here they would be rated as "newcomers," and there would be a doubt as to whether they are worth their keep.

To any one who is familiar with the great grain states and the many country towns scattered over the prairie region, it is evident that these country towns contain a supply of labor suitable for use on the neighboring farms; either immediately or with a short allowance of time to get them back into form. These American country towns consist mainly of retail concerns of many kinds, and retail professional men who help take care of the interests of the retail concerns that make up the town. The retail concerns are very numerous and of many kinds, engaged in buying farm products and forwarding them to the central markets or in selling and distributing all kinds of necessary supplies to the farm population, together with any superfluities which they may be able to induce the farm population to buy.

II

The country town is an organisation of business concerns engaged in buying things from the farmers in order to sell at an advance to the central markets, and in buying things from the central markets in order to sell at an advance to the farmers. The country town is an organisation of "middlemen," and it is out of this difference between the buying price and the selling price that the entire town gets its living, together with whatever its inhabitants are able to lay up. The rest of the town depends on the traffic of its business men who buy and sell and make a profit in buying and selling.

The variety of these retail business concerns is very considerable. Not including professional men, such as lawyers and clergymen, who get a living indirectly out of the general traffic, the list will run something as follows: groceries, drygoods, notions, boots and shoes, clothing, millinery, hardware, laundry, livery, harness, vehicles, jewelry, implements and machinery, grain buyers, stock buyers, express and transfer companies, banks, drugs, lumber, coal, bakeries, meat markets, dairies, hotels and boarding houses, cigar stores, candy kitchens, furniture, seed and feed stores. For any ordinary country town of, say, ten thousand inhabitants, this would not be a complete list; but it includes the greater number of those special business pursuits that are considered indispensable to the traffic of buying and selling, and necessary to the comfort of the town's inhabitants.

There is always more or less duplication among these retail concerns—more or less, but usually a great deal. In such lines as groceries, coal, drygoods, banks, drugs, e.g., the number of concerns actually engaged will sometimes run as high as ten or twenty times the number required to take care of the traffic; and in these lines it seldom amounts to less than four or five times the number needed. A prairie town, county seat, of ten or twelve thousand will be found to support forty groceries, twelve coal yards, seven lumber yards, nine drug stores, ten banks, six hardware stores, an indefinite number of stock buyers, lawyers, real estate and insurance agents, clergymen and detachable politicians, who pick up a livelihood out of the screenings. In some lines the duplication, and the consequent waste of work, may be relatively slight, as, e.g., in express companies, meat markets, or laundries, which are likely to be local agencies of larger concerns located at some larger center.

Indeed, the extent of this duplication of retail establishments varies a good deal, not only from one trade to another, but also from place to place. There appears, on the whole, to be more extensive duplication among retail concerns in the older settled parts of the prairie states, and perhaps more toward the south than toward the north. As near as a general statement can be made to apply to the grain states—the corn belt and the wheat region—it would perhaps do to say that this class of wasteful duplication will foot up to about three fourths of all the equipment and workmen employed. It might appear on closer examination that this estimate is too high; that the wasteful use of men and equipment due to an excessive number of retail concerns in the country towns will not run as high as seventy-five percent of the total; but any deliberate survey of the known facts cannot well avoid placing the estimate of such waste nearer three fourths than one half.

It is also true that the returns on investment in this retail trade will not ordinarily be found to run excessively high, as things commonly go. The rate of profits appears to vary widely, all the way from an extremely high percentage—over one hundred percent in some instances—to a vanishing point among the less fortunate concerns, who will sometimes be found doing business at a loss, and who then presently end in insolvency. On an average the returns on investment may be quite "reasonable"; but the number of concerns among which these "reasonable returns" are divided is much larger than is necessary to take care of the trade in the most economical manner. "Reasonable returns" on something more than twice the investment for which there is any use in the trade will foot up to something over twice the "reasonable" total return that should "reasonably" go to the retailers for doing this work of marketing and distribution in a sane and economical way.

It may also be noted by the way that an appreciable proportion of this retail trade in the country towns is appreciably worse than useless, so far as it has any bearing on the net productive efficiency of the farm community that is served by the trade of the towns. A multiplicity of competing fashion shops, e.g., or of tombstone shops, or furniture stores, serves no better purpose than the encouragement of wasteful expenditure on goods which add to the discomforts of life at the cost of its efficiency. It is true, in ordinary times of peace, when the citizens of any well-conducted democracy are presumed to owe no active duty to the country in which they live—in ordinary times no thoughtful person would be inclined to check up or find fault with habitual waste of this kind that conduces to nothing better than the spread of fashionable discomfort. In time of peace, it is commonly admitted that any citizen who has reached years of discretion should be free to follow his natural bent into all the dips, spurs, and angles of human folly; but in a time of extraordinary stress, when the common good is at stake, when no wasteful use of resources or man power is to be tolerated, this pursuit of "business as usual" in the production of waste and inefficiency takes on another color and becomes a matter of legitimate public concern.

A very considerable proportion of the retail trade in the country towns, as well as in the cities, is taken up with, and gets its profits from, the production and spread of waste, discomfort, and inefficiency, in the name of fashion and respectability. It would not be easy to come to an understanding as to just how much of this retail traffic is occupied chiefly or wholly with supplying the means of fashionable waste and respectable discomfort. In most lines of the trade it is a question of more or less; some trades being devoted almost wholly to useless expenditures, others only in part; but when all due allowance has been made, it will always be found that it foots up to a very considerable amount of the total traffic. Perhaps a fair statistical estimate would run about as follows: Taking one retail concern with another, one third of this retail trade is to be written off as being productive of nothing but waste; which leaves two thirds of the whole to be counted in as being of some use; and of this remaining two thirds, again, an amount running between one half and three fourths— say two thirds—is further to be written off as being mere wasteful duplication of equipment and work among the concerns that are doing partly useful work.

Now, two thirds times two thirds equals four ninths —the amount to be allowed for useless duplication of equipment and working force in that part of the retail trade which serves in part a useful purpose; which is to be added to the one third of the whole that is already accounted for as pure waste; and which so brings the estimated total of useless work and equipment in the retail trade to seven ninths of the whole. Something like seven ninths of all that goes into the retail trade, in the way of stock, equipment, and working force, is accordingly to be set down to the account of useless waste and duplication. It therefore appears, on this showing, that something like two ninths of the number of concerns and of the workmen employed by them are sufficient to take care of all the useful work which the retail merchants of the country towns have to do.

The upshot of this computation is that the country retail trade can afford to set loose something like seven ninths of the working force which it now employs, without interfering with the useful work of marketing farm products and distributing useful goods to the farmers. A closer scrutiny of the whole matter would presumably lead to a more extreme conclusion, since much of the retail trade as now conducted serves the town population; and since this town population is itself for the most part to be regarded as supernumerary, for all material purposes; inasmuch as this town population is either occupied in the retail trade or dependent on the trade for a livelihood.

Something like seven ninths of the town population, perhaps, is to be counted as supernumeraries who contribute nothing to the net productive efficiency of the community from which they derive their livelihood. So

much of the retail traffic, therefore, as serves the needs
of this supernumerary town population is also to be
counted out as being useless. The work of marketing
farm products and distributing goods to the farm population is useful and necessary, of course. Some of the
work that is now done is needed; say one fifth is needed,
according to the estimate and computation. But it is
plainly not useful and necessary that an ordinary county
seat in the prairie states should have thirty to forty
groceries, each with full stock, equipment, and working
force, when three or four groceries would do the necessary work better and with less waste all around. Nor is
it useful and necessary that such a country town should
have ten banks and seven or eight grain buyers, and a
still larger number of regular stock buyers, together
with a small swarm of speculative buyers who dip into
the business when they see a chance. One buyer could
take care of the traffic just as well; and the one local
post office—which is not ordinarily duplicated—could
take care of the necessary banking operations more expeditiously and at a very greatly lower cost.

The objection is ready, of course, that "the benefits
of competition would be lost." But any one who knows
anything about the country towns of the prairie states
knows that the established retailers of the place habitually act in collusion in all matters which seriously interest them, such as prices and competition. The usual
organ of this collusion, or of the conspiracy to restrain
competition, is the local Commercial Club; and back of
the Commercial Club, and serving its purposes, is the
town government, which is much the same thing under
another name; very much after the same fashion as the
municipal government of the larger cities in the prairie
states is commonly a creature of the Chamber of Com-

merce and represents the larger vested interests of the place.

Now, all this arrangement of Commercial Clubs and Chambers of Commerce, and of municipal governments acting as executive committees of these Clubs and Chambers, and taking care of the vested interests back of them—all this may be well enough in ordinary times when there is nothing at stake, beyond the creature comforts of the farming community. That is to say, it is all well enough if the American people—the American farmers and workmen—like to see things done in that way. But just now the life of this American people— the American farmers and workmen—is at stake; their life, their fortunes, and their sacred honor. If America is to make good and win the Great War, all available resources—raw material, equipment, and man power— will have to be placed at the disposal of the American Federal Administration, without reservation and without any foxy intrigue looking to a surreptitious gain for the vested interests. It is time to quit being squeamish about the vested right of the country-town merchants. and speculators to get a "reasonable return" on capital sunk in waste and duplication.

Of course, it is to be admitted without argument or hesitation that these country-town merchants, bankers, and buyers are by law and custom entitled to all the profits which they can get, and as long as they can get them. The law has always said so. These are substantial citizens, pillars of society in a small way, and honorable gentlemen after their kind. And it appears also that according to law and custom the country-town merchants and speculators are within their ancient rights in organising a Commercial Club to take care of their joint interests, to regulate prices and profits, to exclude outside competitors, "and for other purposes." All this maneuvering for private gain and special advantages may be well enough in time of peace. It is the time-honored customary right of the townsman to turn an honest penny at the cost of the countrymen, and no thoughtful person would aim to disturb this vested right of the townsmen in ordinary times of peace. But it is today no longer a question of a sportsmanlike regard for vested rights and legal punctilios. It is a very concrete question of how to set free a force of workmen for use on the farms in the grain states; a labor force which is at present employed by the merchants of the country towns in a wasteful duplication of work, just to enable an excessive number of middlemen to turn an excessive number of honest pennies—more or less honest. Just now, in an extreme emergency, will the grain farmers of the prairie states continue to put up with this endless waste and duplication of work in their country towns? The immediate consequence of letting things drift as they have been doing will be to leave the grain farmers shorthanded on work which has to be done, on pain of national defeat in case of failure.

Most of the men employed in the retail trade of the country towns have in their time been drawn from the farms, after having learned more or less of farm work. The like is true for that great volume of subsidiary employments in the towns, which serve the local trades at the second remove. The greater proportion of these town workmen are fit to do farm work without having to relearn the trade. In fact, they constitute the one great and sufficient reserve of practical farm-hands which the country has to fall back on in the present emergency. So that the practical question is how to turn this force of trained workmen in the country towns to account for the growing of grain and meat, and the prosecution of the war turns visibly on the effectual solution of that problem.

Among those time-tried statesmen who are too wise to attempt anything effectual, the suggestion is very kindly entertained that moral suasion should be brought to play upon the sensibilities of these substantial citizens in the country towns, who are now conducting ten banks and forty grocery stores in a town that has use for only one of each. Circumstantial evidence appears to indicate that this recourse to moral suasion alone has been shrewdly suggested by the Commercial Clubs—the spokesmen of "business as usual." Moral suasion is a potent and valuable factor in human life, no doubt, but experience teaches that its best effects are likely to be slight and transient where it runs counter to a settled legal right. The farmers of this country, and the workmen, too, have in fact quit trusting their interests and ideals to the care of moral suasion in all those matters in which they come in conflict with the vested interests.

When a radical change of policy has become imperative, as in the present juncture, over-ripe statesmen will always endeavor to remedy things without altering them. That is the earmark of over-ripe statecraft, but it is not the way that is taken by the course of events.

### III

To set free this labor supply which is now employed in useless duplication of work in the towns, it will be necessary to derange the business traffic of the country towns to some extent. No considerable number of employees can be set loose without shutting down some of the retail establishments now engaged in the business;

and the larger the number of establishments which are
induced to close down, the larger will be the number of
workmen that will become available for use on the
farms. The obvious line to take is to reduce the margin
of profits in this retail trade to such a figure as to make
it unprofitable for the full number of establishments to
continue in the business. This can be done by administrative regulation and interference, such as will reduce
the total margin of profits derived from the traffic. If
the total profits can be reduced to such a figure as to afford reasonable returns only for a greatly reduced number of retail concerns, then the difficulty will have been
overcome to that extent. All this will bring hardship on
those who are affected by it, by driving them out of a
useless line of enterprise into some useful work, but it
should seem that the emergency will justify such a measure even at the cost of some degree of hardship to one
and another, for the period of the war.

The whole case is simplest on the side of the local
buyers—buyers of grain, hogs, cattle, and produce, who
forward to the central markets, either through commission houses or otherwise. These buyers are comparatively few, as contrasted with the retail sellers, and the
commodities which they handle are of few kinds and can
be standardised and handled under inspector's tests. So
true is this, and so serious and persistent have been the
evasive maneuvers of these buyers, that government
regulation by means of inspection, standard grades, and
tests has already come to be the rule in this field. At the
same time the farmers who have to deal with them are
already thoroughly distrustful of these local buyers, and
are ready to put up with any measures of regulation that
promise to abate the irregularities and evasion of which
the buyers are believed to be guilty. Indeed, a very strict

and comprehensive regulation of this part of the country-town business under Federal authority would be welcomed by the farming community.

It is to be noted by the way that the regulation of local markets and their buyers has hitherto commonly been entrusted to the state authorities, and there has been much dissatisfaction with the way in which the state regulation has worked; there are many complaints that it has been inefficient and unreliable. It is believed that the state authorities are commonly dependent on the goodwill of the Commercial Clubs and Chambers of Commerce for their continued tenure of office; and the Commercial Clubs and the Chambers of Commerce are believed to guard the special business interests of their respective towns, with small regard for the needs and interests of the farm community from which they draw their livelihood. The farmers of the grain states have been learning not to look for an impartial regulation of markets and standards at the hands of any state administration, the roots of whose political tenure run down through the local political organisation to the same persons who make up the Commercial Clubs and the Chambers of Commerce. The established political machinery on which the government of state, county, and town finally rests will commonly be found to be made up of, or owe allegiance to, the same persons who make up these commercial bodies; and these commercial bodies are organised to take care of the vested business interests of the place. Such is the farmers' view of that matter, and so sure are the farmers of the iniquity of this arrangement that they are now organising with all speed to take their case past the established state and local authorities and take over the control under Federal auspices.

From which it follows that if there is to be anything like an unbiased regulation of the marketing of farm produce in the prairie states—or anything which the farmers will believe to be passably unbiased—the whole matter will have to be taken beyond the state authorities and their background of Commercial Clubs, and placed under Federal surveillance. At the same time some care will have to be taken not to let the local interests of congressmen count for much in the case. Congressmen commonly are held in somewhat intimate bonds of goodwill with the Commercial Clubs of their several districts—or rather they are under the necessity of maintaining relations of mutual confidence with the county committees, which are usually made up out of the same class of persons that make up the Commercial Clubs, and are identified with the same local interests. This need not mean that congressmen are consciously partisan in their guidance of public affairs, but only that they are sufficiently human to take on the colors of their best friends. The personal equation counts for something even in the case of the most profound and dispassionate statesmen.

The local marketing of the main staples is a comparatively simple matter, apart from the "tricks of the trade," the businesslike intrigue injected into it by buyers and commission men each seeking his own profit. That is to say, the necessary work of handling these staples, as well as the inspection and grading of them, is simple enough so long as it is not complicated by efforts to evade the rules under which it is carried on; and it should accordingly lend itself readily to administrative regulation, provided always that care is taken to remove all undue opportunity for surreptitious gain. The simple and obvious remedy to apply, as an emergency measure, and for the period of the war, is for the

Administration to take over the marketing, as it is already taking over the surveillance of standards and inspection. Something has already been done in this way under the powers vested in the Grain Corporation. This would involve only a relatively slight increase in official powers, in the necessary number of officials, and in the amount of work to be done. Most if not all private buyers would drop out or would be drawn into the Administration's service; and in so far there would result an economy of personnel and of work. Some, probably few, of these private buyers could be turned to use in other occupations. The many wholly useless ones among them would be no more useless when so retired from business than they now are in carrying on a business that need not be done; while the greater number of their employees are suitable for farm work and would be set free for that use.

The retail trade, in the ordinary sense, is a larger and more complicated proposition. But even as regards this retail trade the magnitude and complications of the task will be found much less in practical fact than they appear from the outside and before the proposed change takes effect. Any reasonable measure of control designed to release farm workmen from their town occupations would necessarily do away with much of the work and management involved in the trade as it runs now. The number of retail concerns would fall off, and the volume of traffic would be greatly reduced, even if the quantity of goods handled remained the same. If, in effect, those who continued in the trade were put on a basis of cost plus a narrow margin on turnover, it is also reasonably to be expected that much of the working at cross purposes that now prevails among them would be discontinued. The number of shipments, deliveries, accountings, payments, etc., would decrease, with or without a decrease in the quantity of goods handled.

This retail trade of the country towns is part of the distributive system of the country. The distributive system comprises also a complete assortment of jobbers, who deal with factories and similar sources of supply on the one side, and with the retailers on the other side. All this involves bargaining at every move, a multiplicity of accounts, cross freights, competitive selling, and compromises of various kinds to safeguard and apportion the gains to be got in the trade. There are several times as many of these jobbing houses as are necessary to take care of the traffic, although the duplication probably does not go so far as in the retail trade; at the same time there appears to be going on a slight relative decrease in the number of jobbers, rather than the contrary.

The nature of the traffic that is to be taken care of, and the recent developments in the management of it, indicate plainly enough what will be the nature of the move which is now due to be made. The traffic is of a two-fold character; or rather it is of a two-sided shape. The staple farm products have to be assembled and forwarded to the central markets, for storage awaiting shipment or to be worked over into finished goods in the mills and packing houses and passed out again into the channels of the retail trade. On the other side, goods suitable for use by the farm community have to be assembled in the same central markets and distributed over the same transportation lines to the same places from which the staple farm products come.

In all this traffic the business men—"middlemen"— are occupied with getting a profit out of it, every time the goods are bought and sold. That is what the business men do business for. The greater the number of times that the goods are bought and sold between the farm and the mill or packing house, or between the mill or factory and the farm, the greater the number of business profits to be deducted from the price which the farmer gets for his produce, or to be added to the price which he has to pay for his necessary supplies; and the greater the uncertainty, miscalculation, and retardation to which the whole traffic is liable, between the farm and the factory, and back again.

Any traffic that is conducted by business men and on business principles—principles of purchase and sale—is necessarily subject to uncertainty, miscalculation, and retardation all along the line; and the greater the number of bargains to be made, the greater the liability to uncertainty and retardation. Conversely, any measures that can be taken to reduce the amount of bargaining—that is to say, of business—necessary to be done in marketing farm produce, or in distributing necessary goods to the farm community, should be very much to the purpose just now, when the urgent requirements of the war situation demand that uncertainty and retardation should be reduced to a minimum. In this connection "Business as usual" means "Uncertainty and retardation as usual."

So far as bargaining—that is to say, business—can be eliminated from the handling of farm produce and farm supplies, the whole country stands to gain in point of expedition and efficiency. Therefore, simply as a matter of expedition and economy, for the period of the war, all this traffic in marketing and distribution in the grain states should best be conducted on a no-profits basis, by disinterested agents of the Administration, and regardless of any vested interests on the part of the business men who would be affected by such a move. The exigencies of the war overbear all questions of private profit, for the period of the war; and wherever disregard of private profits will contribute to the effectual prosecution of the war, it will be simply foolish to let vested interests of this kind stand in the way.

It will not be necessary to take any drastic or forcible measures to displace these superfluous business concerns in the retail trade; such as conscription, confiscation, or penalisation of the supernumerary establishments. All that is needed is to arrange for carrying on the necessary work of marketing and distribution on a no-profits basis, or even on a narrow margin. When this is done, the superfluous retailers will presently withdraw, for the period of the war.

Such a retirement of superfluous business concerns in the country towns is the main fact to be aimed at. Doubtless there is more than one way to accomplish that result. What is needed now, and needed urgently, is the speedy choice of some reliable and expeditious method of doing it. It is a question of releasing the superfluous employees of these superfluous business concerns in time for this year's harvest, if possible; and of leaving them free beyond this season, for the period of the war. It is, therefore, necessary to take such measures at the earliest possible date, and to follow them up consistently until there is no more labor being spent on wasteful duplication of work in the country towns.

The plan which is here spoken for is simple, direct, expeditious, and thorough. And it has the defects which go along with those qualities. It proposes to correct an evil state of things by changing the state of things, in the face of those vested interests that live on this evil state of things. It is, therefore, to be expected that the whole matter will be quite distasteful to those superfluous merchants, bankers, etc., who will be constrained to go into temporary retirement or into some useful occupation for the period of the war. All that sort of thing is to be deplored, of course. At the same time it is to be noted that the proposed measures violate no legal rights and add nothing to the cost of living or the burden of taxation; quite the contrary, in fact.

For the period of the war, the proposed plan contemplates a combination of the methods and working forces employed in three different lines of enterprise that have already proved successful—the Parcel Post, the Chain Stores, and the Mail-Order Houses. It is proposed that the Federal Administration shall, for the period of the war, install a system of farm marketing and of retail distribution of staple merchandise at cost, to be organised as one undivided administrative undertaking under the parcel post division of the U. S. Post Office, and designed to serve all those places and persons whom the parcel post can effectually be made to reach. To this end the Administration will, for the period of the war, take over the traffic of the established mail-order houses, together with so much of their equipment, stocks, and personnel as may be useful for the purpose. And to do this it will also be necessary to discontinue certain restrictions and add something to the discretionary powers of the Post Office.

These mail-order houses already have the ways and means of this traffic in hand, tested, proved, and running smoothly; and the only serious change necessary to be made in their management of the traffic is to combine it with the parcel-post system in such a way as to eliminate all that expensive, vexatious, and unnecessary accounting that is now involved in the shipment and delivery of goods through the Post Office. Many items of work and expense that now have to be counted in among "overhead charges" in the mail-order business will drop out so soon as it is taken over and consolidated with the parcel post; very much as there is a saving of similar items made whenever several independent business concerns are consolidated under one management in the formation of a trust or pool. In the everyday transaction between the parcel post and the mail-order traffic, as it is now conducted, there is always a volume of unnecessary business to be done: fees to be collected and accounted for, risks and margins to be scrutinised and secured, responsibility to be apportioned, evaded, and enforced— all of which results in unnecessary delay, uncertainty, and expense in the transmission of the goods, at the same time that it increases the cost to the customers. It works out in the same way if the mail-order house arranges for the carriage and delivery through an express company or other agency. Delay, vexation, and hindrance come into play at both ends of the line, with no other net result than superfluous fees, invoices, vouchers, correspondence, commissions, and advanced charges.

Among the local business concerns whose traffic and earnings will be likely to suffer by such a measure, therefore, are the express companies and similar common carriers, whose personnel and equipment it is designed to release for useful work. It will accordingly be necessary to remove all restrictions on the size, weight, and character of parcels admitted to carriage by post—in fact to place all facilities of freight handling and transport indiscriminately at the disposal of this distributing system. The express companies and other concerns doing business as common carriers have a vested interest in all these everyday hindrances and expenses connected with the retail distribution of merchandise, and it may well be that they should, in ordinary times, be entitled to something approaching that degree of consideration which has usually been accorded them on this head; but at the present juncture, for the period of the war, it should seem reasonable to ask them to forgo the usual discrimination made in their favor by the laws governing the parcel post. As is well known, though not commonly spoken of, these restrictions have been laid and maintained with a view to the vested interests of the express companies and other common carriers, whom it has seemed wise to protect from the unrestricted competition of the parcel post. But at the present juncture, and for the period of the war, it should seem that expediency for the prosecution of the war must be allowed to take precedence of any vested interest in wasteful practices and special privileges. So it is of the essence of the plan here proposed to release as much as may be of the equipment and workmen now employed by these concerns in work that can more economically be taken care of by the parcel post; thereby setting free considerable number of workmen, teams, vehicles, and motors that will readily be turned to use in the production and handling of grain and other produce. For the period of the war, it should seem expedient to leave their special privileges in abeyance and retire many of these private business concerns from a traffic that can better be taken care of without them.

It may be noted that, even with the handicap imposed by all this superfluous business that is now involved in the transmission of merchandise, the mail-order business has been doing very well; so well, indeed, that it has, on the one hand, earned the undying hatred of the Commercial Clubs, Chambers of Commerce, Town Councils, and such-like bodies who take care of the vested interests in the marketing, carrying, and merchandising trade; at the same time that it has, on the other hand, enabled the leading mail-order houses to capitalise their business at something more than ten times the value of their material assets.

As this business is now conducted, the customer depends on printed descriptions and specifications in making his choice of goods, writes out his order, pays the bill with a postal money-order or its equivalent, commonly with the addition of a fee as well as of postage, transmits the requisite papers through the post office to the office to the mail-order house, where the order is then filled in due course, and the goods started on their transit, with such incidents of delay, expense, and subsequent accounting and adjustment as have already been alluded to above. It is here proposed that the local post office act as agent of the central bureau of distribution, through its office employees and its carriers; to take orders and transmit them with the least possible annoyance or delay; to accept payment, and to make any necessary refunds or adjustments; with no unnecessary writing of instruments or transmission of funds, beyond what is comprised in the ordinary routine of accounting between the local office and the Federal Headquarters.

The money transactions involved, therefore, will best be handled somewhat after the fashion of periodical clearings; and these periodical clearings will be greatly simplified, as compared with what now goes on in the country towns, if the local post office will at the same time take over what would naturally fall to it in the way of a banking business for the convenience of its customers. Particularly will there be a gain in simplicity and expedition if the same general management takes over the marketing of farm produce; so that the local post office also become a station for the purchase or receipt of farm produce as well as for the sale and delivery of staple merchandise. In such a case, the local office will carry a two-sided account with the central office, running roughly even in the long run, as between receipts and disbursements, but with a variable balance to be adjusted from time to time. There is also nothing but the vested interest of the local banks to hinder the local office from carrying on its books the accounts of its customers, subject to draft and settlement after the usual manner of a bank's deposit accounts. All of which will give its money transactions still more of the character of "clearings."

So soon as the post's transactions of purchase and sale in its dealings with its local customers, as well as its receipts and disbursements as a whole, come in this way to be offset against one another, it is evident that the greater part of the remittances which now are involved in the marketing of farm produce, on the one hand, and the sale of merchandise through the retail trade, on the other hand, will best be taken care of by clearings and balancing of accounts. Relatively little remittance of funds, or seasonal provision of funds for "moving the crops," will be needed to keep the balance; particularly if the post office arranges to carry the customers' balances, subject to draft. There will accordingly result a notable decrease in the banking operations necessary to be carried on in the towns.

These and other considerations of a similar bearing indicate unequivocally that, in order to get the full benefit of the proposed system, the post office must also be allowed freely to go into so much of the ordinary work of banking as may seem useful for the purpose. So, e.g., if the local post offices served also as local savings and deposit banks, in correspondence with a similarly empowered central, connected if need be with the Federal Reserve, it is evident that with such an arrangment the whole matter of receipts and disbursements between the parcel post and its customers would be greatly simplified and facilitated; and it is plain that the volume of necessary banking transactions in the local community would be greatly reduced, and that the cost of banking to the customers would also be materially lowered.

There is, in fact, no good reason why the local banks should not come in for the same kind and degree of correction as that which the exigencies of the war and the food supply must presently enforce among the retail merchants. For the prosecution of the war, superfluous banks are no more useful than superfluous buyers and sellers of goods. All the while it is to be kept in mind, of course, that these excessively numerous bankers are very substantial citizens, and that they are an ornament and a comfort to the community in which they live and from which they draw their living. This living that so comes to the bankers is an exceptionally good and respectable living, as a rule; and it is got by an unobtrusive and equitable apportionment of such an honest livelihood as is to be derived from the custody of the municipal and county funds, and from a run of commercial and country credit that could be taken care of at a side-counter in the post office. Their vested interest in so dividing and carrying on an excessively voluminous banking business is not lightly to be set aside; nor is it here proposed to interfere with their gains or to curtail their numbers, except transiently, as a measure of expediency, for the period of the war. As a matter of local pride, in which one will take comfort in time of peace, the spectacle of ten well-fed bankers at the county seat must always appeal to the sensibilities of any community that can afford to pay for it; it is in fact a striking evidence of the community's ability to pay, and as such it is probably worth its cost, in time of peace. But in time of war, when the nation's fortunes are in the balance, it should seem reasonable that the prestige-value of a superfluity of well-fed bankers must not be allowed to cloud the issue of national efficiency.

For the period of the war, the new plan promises to dispense with something more than one half of the banking that is now carried on in the country towns, and to simplify the remainder to such a point as to make it hard to recognise. The banking of the country towns is, after all, mainly commercial banking, and it is accordingly inflated on the same scale as the commercial business which it serves. And so soon as the greater part of the business transactions in the towns is discontinued, that much of the present need of "banking facilities" will also disappear, for the time being.

IV

If one takes note of the experience of the mail-order houses, and so follows out the further logic of the situation, it will necessarily result that this parcel-post system of retail distribution at cost will have to reach back among the jobbers, mills, factories, and packing houses from which the merchandise is drawn. It will be found necessary to enforce standards of quality, purity, cost, and the like, in all the staple lines of merchandise to be dealt in. Even without having taken over or formally standardised any branch of the retail trade as such, the government has already found itself driven to establish and enforce standards and staple specifications in many lines of production; and there are accordingly a considerable body of inspectors and administrative officers already engaged in this work, and these are ready to be drawn on for the same work under the new plan; so that the proposed plan of control and distribution can be put into effect with a relatively slight increase of the staff of administrative officers. The officers would have to be given additional power and discretion, such as would, in effect, put them in the place of those business men who now control the business for their own profit instead of the public service.

It should also be plain in this connection, to any one who is at all acquainted with present conditions in these industries that supply staple goods for the retail trade— e.g., the packing houses and grist mills—that no system of inspection, and no regulation on the basis of inspection, can hope to hold these producers to a *bona fide* observance of the rules made and provided; unless the system of inspection and regulation goes the length of taking all responsibility and control out of the hands of all persons who are in any way interested in the business. In fact, it is now becoming plain beyond debate that it will not do to allow these great industrial enterprises to be managed by their owners for a profit, even under the most stringent standardisation and inspection. The Administration is continually driven to more and more arbitrary measures. The ways to evade specified requirements in detail are too many, too obscure, and too easy, for any system of inspection and legal remedy to keep up with the ingenuity of the interested parties. Legal remedy by litigation after the fact is the merest foolishness in these premises. There is no stopping short of a thorough revision, such as will afford no chance of gain by plausible evasions.

So that the great industries which turn out staple goods for the market will on this plan, and for the period of the war, have to be taken under administrative control; to be operated with a view to produce staple goods in prearranged quantities; to be supplied at the proper times, and at cost, to the distributive system whose nucleus is the parcel post. But again it is evident that the New Order in the retail trade cannot logically stop at that point.

What comes to mind in speaking of the great industries that have to do with the staple supplies is such things as packing houses, flour and other grain mills, pulp and paper mills, lumber mills, coal mining concerns, oil refineries, farm machinery concerns, and the like. Industrially speaking, all these and their like are "halfway houses," where the materials are worked up in their transit from their source to the final consumer of the goods; and their work is conditioned on the supply of materials and the changing circumstances which affect the supply. In some instances, indeed in an appreciable proportion of cases, these "midway" enterprises have already come to control the channels of supply on which they depend, as well as the channels of distribution for their products. Many of these large business concerns engaged in such "midway" industries, as e.g., the packers, already control the channels of supply for their materials and the distribution of their products through "car routes," "branch houses," etc., so that in industries of their class the whole machinery for assembling the materials, working them over into finished products, and distributing them as merchandise to the consumers is already effectually organised under a central management and is ready to be taken over by the Administration at any time, without disturbance of the regular run of the traffic.

All this is referred to here to note that such control of the channels of supply is sufficiently practicable to have taken effect as an ordinary incident in the conduct of business—it is "a sound business proposition"; and to note, further, that in some certain ones of these "midway" industries, as in the packing houses and the grain mills, the supply of materials is drawn from the same farms to which merchandise is supplied by the retail trade; and that the control of the channels of supply by the packers and millers is a source of sore and widespread distrust and irritation among the farmers. The control appears to be wholly effectual, by all accounts, even in these private hands; and since it is exercised for the benefit of the packers and millers it is felt by the farmers that it is exercised at their cost. All of which may or may not be true in fact; but the distrust is unquestionably present in force, and potent for much evil. The logic of the case is plain enough. Under a system of administrative control of such industries as the mills and packing houses it is a simple and obvious further step to extend the system of administrative management to include the marketing and transportation of those farm products which make up the raw materials of the mills and packing houses.

So, in following up the lines along which this postal distributing system will logically carry out its control of the retail trade, it appears that the plan will have to comprise not only the wholesale trade, but also the great industries which supply the great staples on the one side, and which take up and work over the staple products of the farms on the other side. All of which brings the reach of the projected system of handling and distribution at cost back to the country town, for the first as well as for the last link in its chain of operations. It is, in effect, a plan for taking care of the farm products all the way over the circuit from the farm; when the goods leave the farmer's hands at the local market as raw materials; through the process of working them over into staple goods for consumption; and back again through the processes of distribution, until they reach the farmer's hands as wrought goods ready for use.

The Administration already has in hand nearly all the working parts that would go to make up this wide-reaching administrative system, but these working parts will have to be co-ordinated into a balanced system directed from a single center, instead of being left, as now, out of touch and frequently working at cross purposes. And what is lacking to make the system complete can readily be supplied by drawing on the various private concerns that are now engaged in the same kind of work. In fact, all the needed ways and means are ready to hand, both material, equipment, personnel, and corporate organisation; the grand fault of the present working scheme being that it includes more of all these factors, each and several, than there is use for in the work to be done. And the main purpose of the plan here proposed is to release a good part of this supernumerary personnel, at the same time that a saving of equipment and expense is effected by the same move.

Most of the many business transactions now involved in the handling and transmission of products on their way from the farm to the factory would drop out; so would also the like transactions of purchase and sale between the factory and the delivery of the finished goods in the local market; and it is well known that these transactions of purchase and sale are accountable for a very large proportion of the amount by which the retail price of the finished goods exceeds the price of the raw materials—which is sedulously denied by the interested parties.

The market "bureaux," by means of which this plan would take care of the marketing of farm products, would transact very little that could properly be called "business." There would be no bargaining and no salesmanship involved in their work, which would rather be of the nature of traffic management. The prices decided on would be offered quite impersonally, on a basis of standards and tests, as computed in a system of cost accounting.

There need scarcely be any buyers of farm produce, properly speaking, under this arrangement. A "buyer" is of use, as such, only in case there is some unfair advantage to be gained in a bargain. A "buyer's" place and function in the economic system is to "make a good bargain," as it is so called; and in this case there would be no bargain to be made. The Administration, through its local traffic agents connected with the parcel-post distributing system, would make its offer of prices on a cost basis, as adapted by skilled accountants to the special circumstances of each locality; and the producers would "take it or leave it" knowing all the while that the price so made is made without a view to profits and that no man has any motive of gain in determining it. The marketing of such staples as grain and meat under this system would, in fact, not differ greatly from the current practice; and the like is true as regards the marketing of the finished staples through the retail trade; except for the principle underlying the whole traffic. In effect, the present practice is that the large "midway" concerns which gather in, work over, and distribute the produce, as, e.g., the packers, make the price at which the raw materials are bought and at which the finished goods are sold; and the producing farmers, as well as the consumers, are at liberty "to take it or leave it." But the principle on which the price is made by these "midway" business concerns is the principle of "what the traffic will bear"; that is to say, what will bring the largest net profits to those who so make the price. Whereas the principle on which prices are to be made, to both sides, under administrative control, is the principle of net cost. It will be for the producing farmers, on the one hand, and the consumers of the finished goods, on the other hand, "to take it or leave it." And the Administration's part in the management of this system will be so to arrange its schedule of prices as to induce the farming community to turn out the largest practicable output of those staples that are needed for the prosecution of the war.

The details of this price-making cannot be gone into here; neither can the related question of the form of accounts and payments to be adopted under the proposed plan. All that is an extensive matter, into which many other and larger considerations enter. The whole question of finding a practicable base on which to compute the prices of the several staple products, and the ratios or coefficients that should govern the relative prices of these staple farm products, on the one side, and of the staple goods necessary for use by the farm population, on the other side—all that is matter that will have to be worked out as a co-ordinate line of the policy to be pursued in the distribution of the food supply.

It may be in place to say that no administrative pressure is designed to be brought on the local concerns, whether as buyers or sellers, beyond that equitable pressure of competition that is implied in the buying and selling of goods at cost. This pressure would reasonably be expected to induce the greater number of them to quit the trade, whether as buyers or as sellers; but there need be no apprehension that the retail dealers would disappear altogether. Their number would be greatly reduced, perhaps, but some of them would doubtless continue in the trade, to serve the daily minor wants of their customers at least. It is true, the retail buyers would be expected to disappear, or virtually so; and it is not easy to see what place there would be for such concerns as deal in lumber, brick, coal, and similar articles of large bulk and staple grades.

For the convenience of customers, to meet their everyday minor needs and also as a further check on competitive duplication of equipment, this parcel-post distributing system will necessarily comprise a subsidiary system of local branches, of the nature of "general merchandise stores"; which are to be operated on the plan of the "chain stores" now in use, and will carry relatively slight stocks of such commonplace goods as are called for from day to day in small quantity and without notice. The established machinery of the chain stores could advantageously be turned to account; and the existing stocks of the vanishing local retailers would also be expected to go to these branches; which would in the ordinary case most conveniently be housed under the same roof with the post office, and handled in the accustomed way; the substantial difference as contrasted with the present usage being the absence of ordinary profits. These local branches will also be required to handle such local produce as is distributed to local customers without passing through the central markets. At the same time they will take over most of the distribution of the meat supply, and of other perishable articles that are handled in the same general way, as, e.g., fruits and bakery goods. The "car routes" of the packing houses, which already cover the territory in a sufficiently thorough fashion, can be turned to use for this purpose, without delay or disturbance; although it may prove desirable to enlarge the existing "car route" scheme somewhat to take care of a somewhat enlarged traffic in perishable goods, such as would follow from this combination of the meat supply with the general trade in perishables of the same class.

So also, the hotels and inns of the country towns are likely to suffer a marked decline under the new plan. They will presumably run on a greatly reduced volume of traffic, if at all. As is well known, the greater part of their custom is now made up of traveling salesmen and other persons who have to do with the retail trade.

Their local custom is also made up of persons occupied with the same retail trade, in one way or another. Should this retail trade fall off, e.g., by some three fourths or so, the effect on the hotel trade should not be hard to imagine; and as a matter of economy the effect should presumably be altogether salutary. Notoriously, these country-town hotels are extremely wasteful, not only in the use of foodstuffs but in all articles of consumption with which they have to do. So that any reduction of their trade by this means is to be counted on not only to set free a certain labor force now employed in unnecessary work, but it should also result in a very substantial economy in the daily consumption. The hotels are doubtless the most wasteful users of foodstuffs in the country towns.

For the period of the war, such a plan of economy

and expedition in the retail trade will also have a substantial effect on the ordinary country town, as an "urban community." These towns live on the retail trade, directly or indirectly; and in so far as the retail trade suffers a reduction in the amount of work which it now involves or in the number of persons which it now employs, it is fairly to be expected that such of the town's population as are not immediately engaged in the trade will also fall off in the same proportion. Just what this proportion might be would not be easy to say; but it may perhaps be reasonable to expect that the town population at large would decline, for the time being, by something like one half, or two thirds. This reduction of the town population, even if it is only transient, will doubtless bear heavily on the local pride of the town-dwellers; which is to be deplored, but which, it is also fair to expect, will be borne with becoming fortitude in view of the nation's need of diverting all of the available working population to useful work. It is, indeed, not beyond reason to expect that the number of idle inhabitants, rich and poor, may decline by some nine tenths or so. Much of the ground space and buildings may likewise be expected to fall idle, and be turned to more economical use, for the time being; with the result that the local real estate values may be expected, transiently, to decline in a serious fashion; which would be deplored even more loudly.

All this disturbance of the even course of life in the country towns—the retail trade, the real-estate exchange, the hotel traffic, the Commercial Club, and the city council—all this disturbance will seem a grievous burden to those persons whose pleasure or profit is lessened by it; but it is, of course, to be counted as a transient derangement only—as a passing interruption of that régime of wasteful duplication, unearned incomes, and collusive division of profits that now goes to make up the everyday life and habitual interests of the town's population. It is, of course, designed to take effect only for the period of the war, and only as a measure of expedient war-time economy; and it is fairly to be expected that the superfluous townsmen will put up with it all in a cheerful spirit of patriotic sacrifice for the common good; always with a confident view to a speedy return to conditions that will again enable an excessive number of them to turn an excessive number of honest pennies at the cost of their country neighbors—more or less honest.

# FARM LABOR AND THE I.W.W.[1]

THIS memorandum submits impressions gathered in the course of a recent excursion into the grain states of the Northwest, undertaken at the instance of the Food Administration's Statistical Division. The excursion extended to Missouri, Iowa, Illinois, Minnesota, and the

[1] Reprinted from *The Journal of Political Economy,* Vol. XL, December, 1932. It appeared in this Journal under the title "An Unpublished Paper on the I.W.W. by Thorstein Veblen," with the following introductory note by Mr. Joseph Dorfman: "In February, 1918, Thorstein Veblen became a special investigator in the statistical division of the Food Administration. He occupied this position for approximately five months, during which time he prepared several memoranda. The most significant one dealt with the utilisation of the I.W.W. as a source of farm-labor supply.

"General Crowder had just made his first call through the draft for a large quota of men, and complaints were coming into the Food Administration from farmers all over the country, stating that, if their sons were called into service, they would be unable to harvest their crops. Veblen, accompanied by his assistant, Isador Lubin [U. S. Commissioner of Labor Statistics, 1934], then undertook a field investigation through the farm area of the West. On reaching Minneapolis, Veblen was laid up with a severe cold. He went to his home in Columbia, Missouri, to recuperate; and Lubin went on with the work. When Lubin returned to Columbia, he wrote the first draft, and Veblen reworked it.

"The papers of the Food Administration are supposed to be in the government archives, but Veblen's memoranda could not be located. Fortunately one of the carbons of the I.W.W. memorandum was retained by Mr. Lubin, who kindly supplied it to the writer. . . .

"In striking contrast to his published work, but like all his unpublished papers submitted to official or semi-official bodies, this memorandum is written in a simple, straightforward style. Also, unlike his published work, it was accompanied by five exhibits, of which the most significant one ('Exhibit A') is here reproduced. . . ."

Dakotas. It was undertaken with a view to the conditions surrounding the prospective grain crops of the prairie states; more particularly as to the prospects of the spring wheat crop.

In general, it appears certain that the acreage of spring wheat (as well as of winter wheat) will be rather over than under the acreage of 1917. The acreage of corn in the northern prairie states is likely to fall short of the last previous year for want of seed. While the acreage of spring wheat may be expected slightly to exceed that of last year, the spring work of planting and cultivation is apparently not being as carefully and thoroughly done as it should be, for want of a sufficient supply of farm labor.

There appears to be a present shortage of available farm labor in the prairie states, north of Oklahoma and Arkansas, variously estimated at 10–30 percent. The latter figure is almost certainly too high, even for any one of these states. A reasonable estimate would perhaps place this shortage at some 15–18 percent for these prairie states, west of the Mississippi, varying from nearly nothing in the south to a possible 20–25 percent in the north, the severest shortage being found in the Dakotas.

This applies to the present available supply of labor suitable for use in grain farming. At the same time there is a steady and continued drain on this supply, owing to the draft and to the call for workmen in the industries necessary to the prosecution of the war; while the need of skilled workmen for farm use will increase continually through the coming months until the close of the spring-wheat harvest season—September or October. The present situation, therefore, promises a decrease in the available supply, coupled with an increasing demand, so that the effectual shortage may fairly be expected to grow more serious during the season. It is not safe to offer an estimate as to the amount of the resulting shortage at harvest time.

The available farm labor here spoken of is made up of the settled farm-hands, permanently resident in these grain states, and a floating or migratory supply of workmen transiently employed on the farms in increasing numbers, as the season advances. A very large proportion, probably a large majority, of this transient farm labor is enrolled in a special chapter of the I.W.W. known as the Agricultural Workers Industrial Union. So is also an appreciable, and increasing, proportion of the settled farm-hands; although the percentage of the farm-hands affiliated with the I.W.W. is doubtless much lower among the settled workmen than among the transients. This agricultural chapter of the I.W.W. claims a present membership of some 50,000.

These members of the I.W.W., together with many of the workmen who are not formally identified with that organisation, set up the following schedule of terms on which they will do full work through the coming harvest season: (*a*) freedom from illegal restraint; (*b*) proper board and lodgings; (*c*) a 10-hour day; (*d*) a standard wage of $4.00 for the harvest season; and (*e*), tentatively, free transportation in answering any call from a considerable distance.

These are the terms insisted on as a standard requirement; and if these terms are met, the men propose a readiness to give the best work of which they are capable, without reservation. On the other hand, if these terms are not met, in any essential particular, these men will not refuse to work; but, quite unmistakably, they are resolved in that case to fall short of full and efficient work by at least as much as they fall short of getting these terms on which they have agreed among themselves as good and sufficient. It should be added that there is no proposed intention among these men to resort to violence of any kind in case these standard requirements are not complied with. Here, as elsewhere, the proposed and officially sanctioned tactics of the I.W.W. are exclusively the tactics of non-resistance, which does not prevent occasional or sporadic recourse to violence by members of the I.W.W., although the policy of non-resistance appears, on the whole, to be lived up to with a fair degree of consistency. The tactics habitually in use are what may be called a non-resistant *sabotage,* or, in their own phrasing, "deliberate withdrawal of efficiency"—in other words, slacking and malingering.

In this connection it should be noted that the organisation of the I.W.W., whether among agricultural laborers or elsewhere, is of a very loose character. The officials have no coercive powers, so that their control over the members and local chapters is wholly of an advisory kind. Hence, no effectual contracts can be entered into with this body of workmen; the letter of any agreement ceases to bind them so soon as they come to believe that the spirit of the compact is not lived up to. In spite of this loose and irresponsible form of organisation, it is to be noted that these men do surprisingly efficient teamwork in the conduct of their affairs, and that they can consequently be extremely troublesome and disappointing when the occasion offers. All of which has an evident bearing on the ways and means by which it will be expedient to deal with them in the present juncture.

Now, as regards the farmers under whose direction the grain crops of the prairie states are grown, they are to a very large extent enrolled in the National Non-partisan League—indeed, to a greater extent than is commonly believed. The Nonpartisan League is a semi-secret organisation, of a political character, working for industrial ends; and it is made up of farmers, and to a relatively slight extent of farm workmen. The bond of union among them is a felt antagonism between their own material interest, on the one hand, and the interests of the commercial and other business elements of the community, on the other hand. It is a class organisa-tion, seeking a class advantage, and rests on a sentiment of class antagonism. The antagonism lies between those who are engaged in producing grain and meat in the prairie states, on the one side, and the classes that may be spoken of as the "vested interests," on the other side. The sense of antagonism in the case is just now visibly growing, on both sides of this line of cleavage; and it is growing both in the degree of asperity and in the sharpness with which the lines are drawn. The catch-words under which these farmers habitually speak of their antagonists are (*a*) "big business" and (*b*) "the commercial clubs," the latter being the trade organisa-tions of business concerns in the country towns. These are credited at the same time with an irresponsible con-trol of the local authorities, and, in a degree, of the state authorities as well. Hence the political character of the Nonpartisan League, which aims to take the control of state and local administrations out of the hands of these vested interests and turn it to account for the benefit of the farm population.

On the whole, there appears to be no felt antagonism and no working at cross purposes between the Non-partisan League and this agricultural chapter of the I.W.W. At the same time, there is no avowed agreement or official communication between the two organisations; but there is a good deal of unofficial collusion between them, such as to hold them somewhat consistently together on the same side of the line of political cleavage already spoken of, the members of both organisations being largely affected with the same sense of antagonism against the vested interests, and with the same distrust of state and local authorities. (Evidence of a degree of distrust between the farmers and the I.W.W. is by no means wanting. But it remains true that a considerable measure of sympathy and collusion prevails as between the members of the Nonpartisan League and the agricultural chapter of the I.W.W.; and this sense of solidarity is apparently growing.) These public authorities—police, judiciary and administrative, state and municipal—are believed to be strongly biased in favor of the commercial clubs and their aims. The same distrust extends with full vigor to those temporary organisations known as "State Councils of Defense," "Security Leagues," "Committees of Public Safety," etc., which have been instituted for the more effectual prosecution of the war. These Security Leagues are commonly believed to be made up of business men working for the advantage of the commercial interests, as contrasted with the interest of the farmers and workmen. And it is similarly believed or presumed that the charges of disloyalty and violence made by these Committees of Safety and their agents in the prosecution of their aims are in very great measures a cloak to cover other and more sinister purposes than the national defense.

This partisan distrust is mutual, of course, so that the state and municipal authorities, the Security Leagues and Committees of Safety, and the commercial clubs

which underly these administrative organisations all distrust the Nonpartisan League and its affiliated farmers
and workmen as cordially as the latter distrust them.
Each side endeavors to maintain its own rights and con-
tentions; and, as will happen in a partisan contest, both
sides will go to questionable lengths in the prosecution
of their aims. Or at least they will go to lengths that
appear questionable to any outsider who is not moved
by the merits of the controversy. In this contest it happens, unfortunately, that the one party—the party of the
commercial clubs—is in control of the legally constituted administrative apparatus, police and judiciary;
and they are credited by the party of the second part
with a partisan abuse of the power which they so are
in a position to turn to account. Whatever may be the
intrinsic merits of the controversy, and whatever may
be the substantial truth as regards the alleged abuse of
legal authority, this state of the case is unfortunate as
regards the main point here in question—viz., the continued production of a sufficient supply of grain and
meat in the prairie states. It is unfortunate in that the
forces of production involved are thrown into state of
disunion and the cultivation of the farms is by so much
hindered from reaching its best efficiency.

There is the further unfortunate circumstance to be
noted, that inasmuch as the party of the commercial
clubs is the party of the legally constituted authorities
—in the apprehension of the farmers and workmen—
this side of the controversy is in a position to appeal to
the federal authorities, in case of doubt or need. Since
this side speaks in the name of the established law and
order, the federal administration will necessarily appear
initially to come into the controversy on that side of any
given dispute—so long as the legal formalities are com-

plied with in any tolerable degree. To the biased sense of the workmen who find themselves victims of legalized chicanery, as they are inclined to call it, this is coming to mean that the federal administration is lending itself to the purposes of their enemies in the industrial conflict which is going on. And there is, indeed, some circumstantial evidence at hand which will bear that interpretation, particularly when it is viewed from the partisan standpoint of the losing side in the legal proceedings in question. The result is that the federal administration is coming in for a share in the distrust, not to say odium, with which the legal measures alluded to are viewed by the workmen of the prairie states.

Exhibits A and B, appended to this memorandum, submit some of the evidence which so plays into the hands of the malcontents. As being of the same general bearing, and reflecting—in the apprehension of the workmen—the same partisan bias on the part of the constituted authorities, state and federal, the allegation, apparently well founded, may also be cited, that the Post Office has, in connection with the trial now in progress in Chicago, intercepted a very considerable quantity of mail matter designed to procure funds for the conduct of the defense. So also it is alleged, again with the appearance of truth, that in the case of some 150 members of the I.W.W. who have latterly been arrested on formal charges of disloyalty, bail has been fixed at an unnecessarily high figure—some $500—with a view to making it prohibitive. Quite obviously, the ordinary wayfaring man enrolled in the I.W.W. will ordinarily be unable to procure bail in that amount, the consequence being that the men so apprehended face the prospect of incarceration without bail while awaiting a hearing several months hence, on a charge which is com-

monly believed by their fellows to be quite groundless.
Hence more irritation, together with the enforced idleness of such workmen as are immediately concerned in
the case.

So far this memorandum has the appearance of
special pleadings; and, indeed, such is its purpose. It is
intended as special pleadings for the grain crops of the
northern prairie states. Owing to the peculiar circumstances of the case, this purpose gives the argument an
appearance of partiality on the side of the workmen.
The relevant circumstances of the case appear to be
these: The effectual cultivation and harvesting of the
crops demand that all available farm labor be turned
to account forthwith and as economically as may be. A
large proportion of this available farm labor is enrolled
in or affiliated with a special chapter of the I.W.W.
These men cannot be coerced into doing the necessary
work in an efficient manner by any measures of conscription or other authoritative pressure. They will, it
is believed, do good and efficient work on the terms
which they have agreed on among themselves. They are,
it is also believed, deliberately hindered from freely
moving about and finding work on the terms on which
they seek it. The obstruction to their movement and
negotiations for work comes from the commercial clubs
of the country town and the state and municipal
authorities who are politically affiliated with these commercial clubs. On the whole, there appears to be virtually no antagonism between the employing farmers
and these members of the I.W.W. And there is a well-
founded belief that what antagonism comes in evidence
is chiefly of a fictitious character, being in good part due
to mischief-making agitation from outside.

In view of this state of the case, it has been argued

that, quite irrespective of the intrinsic equities involved, it is expedient just now to take measures looking to allay the irritation and distrust that prevails among these workmen; to discountenance and disallow any measures that will bear the appearance of persecution or partisan maneuver; to remove any obstruction that stands in the way of the most efficient use of this or any other available contingent of farm labor. Specifically it is suggested that as a matter of expediency the members of the I.W.W. now under indictment be dealt with as expeditiously and as leniently as the legal formalities will permit; that the mail matter in which their Defense Committee is interested be not detained on any plea of legal expediency; that virtually all charges of disloyalty or sedition in these premises be disallowed; that bail for the men of this class now under indictment be fixed at an amount not to exceed $500; that measures be taken to discontinue the use of force by local authorities seeking to hinder the free movement of workmen in those states; in short, as a matter of present expediency, it is desirable to take a conciliatory stand in relation to this contingent of farm workmen and to go as far as the formalities will allow in cultivating their trust and goodwill. They may not be in the right, but they are one of the factors that will have to be made use of for the production of a sorely needed supply of grain and meat, and they can be used to good effect only by way of generous treatment and fair dealing. It is a case where generosity is the best policy.

It may be in place here to add a word of explanation as regards the present temper of the farm population of these northern prairie states in the matter of loyalty to the Administration and its prosecution of the war.

By way of parenthesis, as bearing on this point, it should be noted that the greater proportion of the membership of these agricultural I.W.W. are apparently of American birth, contrary to what has occasionally been alleged. This generalisation is in part based on a personal inspection of their official files of registered members. The official estimate is that about 80 percent are of American birth. It appears likewise to be true that the greater proportion of members in the Nonpartisan League are of American birth. As to the present temper of this farm population, skilled and transient, there appears a massive and increasing drift in the direction of a more aggressive support of the Administration's war policy. Of the farm population proper, as represented in the Nonpartisan League, it is perhaps safe to say that they are minded to see the war through, at any cost, to the end for which the Administration has spoken. In the region here spoken of, this aggressively warlike temper is distinctly more perceptible now than it was six months ago. The like is fairly to be said for the migratory farm labor affiliated with the I.W.W., but with the reservation that, while this contingent is now prevailingly in a warlike and loyal frame of mind, the cordiality of its continued support of the Administration is in some degree conditioned on the measure of generosity with which the Administration will deal with them during the season.

What has just been said is intended to apply to the present situation, as it bears on the production of this season's crop. But it seems desirable also to look farther ahead and take measures looking to the most efficient use of this farm labor through the coming seasons, for the period of the war. In this connection it is to be kept

in mind that the migratory farm labor of the Northwest is at work on the farms only through the crop
season—some 5-7 months—and that the same workmen are in great part employed in some form of lumber-
ing or sawmill industry through the winter months. In
the seasonal migration which this state of things involves, there is a good deal of scattering and redistribution of the personnel, so that the same workmen will
not be found associated together in the same place from
one season to the next, nor will a given band or gang
be made up of the same workmen year after year. Yet
there is a degree of permanency about any one of these
gangs, so that the gang will have something of a permanent core or nucleus made up of the same men year
by year. There results a certain measure of permanent
regimentation of these migrants, with a degree of continued solidarity and also a degree of continued teamwork. The gang, or chapter, has something of a life-
history of its own and some degree of individuality,
which takes concrete form in its enrolment under its
own official spokesmen in the organisation of the
I.W.W. These spokesmen are officials only in the sense
of standing in an advisory relation to the members of
their particular chapter; and all that can be depended
on to insure concerted action at any juncture is the
teamwork and habitual solidarity of the gang under the
advice of their trusted leaders. Consequently, any agreement entered into is subject to constant revision, with
the result that all employers who deal with these organised workmen are, in effect, placed on their good
behavior. All of which is extremely irksome to the employers, particularly to employers on a large scale, as,
e.g., in the lumber trades, where the contact between

employer and employee is slight and impersonal; but much less so on the farms, where the employer is habitually engaged in the day's work, along with his employees, and where consequently a much closer approach to a personal understanding is commonly had. It may be remarked that suspicion and disagreement between employers and workmen has been much less on the farm than in the lumber camps, although the employees in the two cases are in very great part the same workmen, and in some part organised in the same groups.

As a means of best using this contingent of migratory labor, therefore, both through the open season on the farms and through the winter months in the lumber camps and elsewhere, it is here proposed that the Administration enter into direct and official relations with these workmen through their formal organisations; that a scheme of regimentation be put into effect by which the workmen will be enrolled, under officers of their own choice, as members of a collective labor force to be distributed and employed at the discretion of agents of the Administration with suitable powers—always with the proviso that these agents be vested with advisory rather than coercive powers and be enabled to offer inducements sufficient to give effect to such advice as they may offer; that facilities be constantly afforded for men to enrol in these regiments of workmen, without other necessary qualifications than a willingness to work and to submit to majority rule within their own regiment; and that board, lodging, and needed transportation be provided for the men so enrolled, on the sole condition that they do the work in hand and submit to majority rule. It is believed that under such a scheme of regimentation a permanent body of efficient workmen may be organised and held together in a mobile body which can be shifted readily to any point where they are needed, at the same time that the maintenance of direct and cordial relations between these workmen and the Administration may be expected to call out the highest degree of efficiency of which they are capable. The realisation that they are, in a special and intimate sense, working for their country and its purposes, may fairly be expected to have a happy effect on the temper of these men, as it should have on the temper of any similar body of citizens.

Tentatively, it is further proposed that whatever arrangements may be entered into between the Administration and these workmen should be left in the hands of the Department of War and the Food Administration, preferably in the hands of a joint bureau representing both and consulting with both, but in the last resort answerable to the Secretary of War. There are several considerations leading to this proposal: The work in which this labor force is to be used, summer and winter, is in a paramount sense of the nature of a necessary war industry, in that the production of grain as well as the output of lumber are of prime importance for the prosecution of the war, and no unnecessary apparatus should be allowed to interfere between the War Department's jurisdiction and the factors that enter into these industries. It is, at the same time, a matter which unavoidably falls within the discretion of the Food Administration, which is in this connection to be regarded as an auxiliary branch of the War Administration. In an appreciable degree the Department of Labor is incapacitated for this undertaking by the circumstance that the Department is, in the popular apprehension, somewhat closely identified with the special interests of organised labor, so-called, and more particularly with the interests and special policies which guide the management of the A. F. of L.; and these migratory workmen harbor a lively antagonism and distrust toward the A. F. of L. and its official representatives, and consequently also toward the Department of Labor in so far as that Department is believed to lend its countenance to the particular aims for which the management of the A. F. of L. is believed to be working. In a less degree there appears to be prevalent among these workmen a similar distrust of the Department of Agriculture and its agents in the field, perhaps especially as regards the "county agents," who commonly represent jointly the Department of Agriculture and the state agricultural commissions of the several states. For all that need appear in this argument, this distrust of these two departments and their agents may be quite groundless in fact. The point at issue is the animus of these workmen on this head. If they are effectually to be made use of, the agency by which they are to be made use of should be one to which no antecedent objection of this kind attaches.

In substantiation of the belief expressed above, that generous treatment and a cordial co-operation on the part of the Administration will bring a response in the way of willing and efficient service from these workmen, Exhibits B, C, and D are appended. These exhibits go to show what has been accomplished in detail in other parts of the country and under other circumstances, where the same class of men—indeed, in good part the same men—have been met in a spirit of forbearance, mutual confidence, and partnership, and without recourse to coercive measures.

EXHIBIT A

April 8, 1918

*Mr. Thorstein Veblen,*
*Washington, D.C.*

DEAR SIR:

In compliance with your request of the 6th instant, I am setting forth herein facts pertaining to the Agricultural Workers Organisation No. 400 of the I.W.W. I am going to try and point out to you the reasons why the wheat raised on the farms of the United States last year was not harvested as successfully as it could have been, and also the best possible way for the administration of the United States to guarantee that the wheat crop of 1918 is saved to the last kernel.

Now to begin with, the Agricultural Workers Organisation of the I.W.W. has a membership of some fifty thousand workers. These workers work in the woods during the winter months, and in the harvest fields during the summer months. I can safely say that 80 percent of these workers are American born, and that the one object they have in life is to obtain for themselves and their fellow-workers more wages, shorter hours, and better working conditions, by organising along industrial lines, agreeing to the last man that an injury to one is an injury to all.

We find that the opposition shown toward our members does not come from the farmers who employ these men to sow, cultivate, and harvest their grain, but it comes from the daily press and the commercial clubs, which are composed of bankers, real estate agents, business men, and the local police, the latter arresting the workers and throwing them into jail whenever they attempt at organising workers into the union.

The records of the Agricultural Workers Industrial Union show that there was over ten thousand dollars spent in 1917 for sending attorneys to the different towns throughout the Grain Belt to investigate the cases of our members who had been thrown into jails. All of these investigations show that there were no charges against these men; and when the authorities found that there was some one working in the interests of the workers who were being held by them, they were immediately released.

When the commercial clubs found that they could no longer jail our members and get away with it, they adopted new and more brutal tactics. Whenever a body of organised workers came into towns where these commercial clubs were situated and operating, they were surrounded, taken to jail, where they were held until after dark, loaded into automobiles belonging to the members of the commercial clubs, taken out into the country, their clothes taken off, and with two of these human brutes holding the workers face down to the earth, they were beaten until black and blue, or until they would say that they would have nothing more to do with the organisation or the I.W.W.

To explain to you these outrages in detail would be more than I am capable of doing, but in order that you and the people you represent may understand our side of the question more thoroughly, I am inclosing herewith copies of affidavits made in person by members of the Agricultural Workers Industrial Union No. 400, who were the victims of the commercial clubs of the Grain Belt, because they dared to organise the workers into a union so that they, the workers, may get shorter hours, more wages, and better working conditions.

In conclusion, we wish to plainly state that it has always been and always will be the intention of the members of the Agricultural Workers Industrial Union of the I.W.W. to harvest the grain crops of the world, so that the world may eat. No one understands better th way to harvest the wheat crops than the men who follow up this line of work from year to year, and no one knows better how to save as much grain as possible as the workers who are now members of the Agricultural Workers Industrial Union No. 400 of the I.W.W.

The members of the Agricultural Workers Industrial Union of the I.W.W. will be in the harvest fields this year stronger than ever. They will be there with only one intention, and that intention is that the wheat that feeds the world is harvested successfully under good working conditions, together with reasonable hours and good wages, and that the outrages that are being committed against them shall immediately cease.

Once more assuring you that the Agricultural Workers Organisation of the I.W.W. will do all in its power to harvest the wheat crop of 1918 without wasting a kernel, and doubly insuring you that the members of the Agricultural Workers Industrial Union will under any and all circumstances stand by its motto, "An injury to one is an injury to all," we remain,

Very truly yours,

MAURICE G. BRESNAN

Sec'y-Treas.

AGRICULTURAL WORKERS INDUSTRIAL UNION

No. 400 I.W.W.

CHICAGO, ILLINOIS

# THE WAR AND HIGHER LEARNING [1]

THE modern state of the industrial arts has got its growth and holds its footing by force of an effectual disregard of national demarcations. Not only is it true that this body of industrial knowledge, which makes the material foundation of modern civilisation, is of an international character and that it has been brought into bearing, and continues to be held, as a common stock, common to all the civilised nations; but it is also to be kept in mind that this modern technology always and necessarily draws on the world's resources at large for the means and materials of its work, regardless of national frontiers—in so far as the politicians do not deliberately put obstacles in the way of a free movement of these means and materials. In the realm of industry it is obvious that national frontiers serve no better purpose than a more or less effectual hindrance to the efficient working of the industrial system. Yet in this industrial realm men still argue—that is to say, shortsighted statesmen and interested business men are able to argue—that the nation's industrial interest may best be served by hindering the nation's industry from taking advantage of that freedom of intercourse which the modern industrial system presupposes as an indispensable condition to its best work. So far are men still bound in the ancient web of international jealousy and patriotic animosity.

On the other hand, in the adjacent field of scientific

[1] Reprinted from *The Dial*, Vol. LXV, July 18, 1918.

knowledge it is recognised without reservation that political boundaries have no place and, indeed, no substantial meaning. It is taken as a matter of course that science and its pursuit must be free of all restraints of this character; that it is a matter of "the increase and diffusion of knowledge among men," not merely among the citizens or subjects within the nation. That such is the case, that no politician comes forward to advocate an embargo on knowledge at the national frontier, or a protective customs barrier to serve as a fence against an undue infiltration of enlightenment from abroad—that the national statesmen fail to make mischief at this point is apparently due to the fact that no vested business interest has seen its advantage in taking measures to that end. There is also the difficulty that the international diffusion of knowledge proceeds by such subtle and intangible ways as to make its confinement by statute a perplexing matter.

It is true, something may be done by indirection at least—and the nationally minded statesmen have perhaps done what was possible—to hinder the free passage of knowledge over the national frontiers. They have, for instance, taken thought to impose a restrictive tariff on books and other apparatus made use of in scientific and scholarly pursuits or in the art of teaching; and there are also, now and again, certain restrictive measures taken to hinder aliens from imparting knowledge of any kind to the youth of the land. In all these cases of petty obstruction it will be seen, if one looks into the matter, that there is some vested interest of a businesslike sort which seeks to be benefited by these measures of restraint. But when all is told, these and the like endeavors of retardation are, after all, trifling and nugatory in comparison with that voluminous and many-sided restraint of industrial intercourse that appears to be the chief material use of the national frontiers.

Happily, there is no need of argument among civilised men to gain assent to the proposition that the pursuit and diffusion of knowledge is a matter of joint and undivided interest among all the civilised nations; that it runs on neutral ground, irrespective of national intrigue and ambition; and that no nation has anything to lose in this respect through unguarded co-operation with its neighbors. In respect to this joint interest all are gainers by the gain of any one. Happily, again, this joint interest in the pursuit and diffusion of knowledge is the one end of endeavor which all men and all nations are agreed in rating as the only end of human endeavor that is worth while for its own sake. It may seem a singular state of things, but it will scarcely be questioned on reflection, that this intangible body of knowledge which is in no man's possession and is held as a common stock by the peoples of civilised mankind is not only the most highly valued asset of the civilised world but is at the same time the one indispensable possession which alone can give any community a valid claim to be rated among the civilised peoples. Any substantial loss or defeat on this ground, the ground of what is called the higher learning, would by common consent be accounted the most shameful setback which these nations could suffer; and it is a case where, by common consent, any one's loss is the loss of all.

But at the same time, unhappily, because this pursuit of knowledge is, always and necessarily, of the nature of a collective or joint interest, it results that there is no one class or group of interested persons, no vested interest, which is in a position effectually to parley with the politicians in behalf of this higher learning, in which the civilised world's chief spiritual asset is capitalised. The elements of a political bargain are wanting in the case; and that massive popular sentiment whose pressure can for a time divert the endeavors of the statesmen from the broad and sinuous path of political bargaining is also taken up with other things. And just now, under the strain of desperate work to be done, the material needs involved in the prosecution of the great war take precedence of all else, particularly of all things less tangible. Yet all the while it remains true—and on dispassionate reflection, if such can be had, it will be seen—that this joint pursuit of knowledge which centers and finds expression in the higher learning is the most consequential matter involved in the fortunes of war.

All of which should clear the vision and determine a course of concerted action for those men who still have the interests of science and scholarship at heart, and whose endeavors are not all engrossed with the conduct of the war or with the give and take of political intrigue. The charge which circumstances impose on these keepers of the higher learning is simply the keeping of the ways and means of this pursuit of knowledge well in hand against the time when sober counsels shall again prevail.

Among these keepers of the sacred flame it happens that the hazards of war have thrown the Americans into a position of peculiar responsibility. Through no peculiar merit of their own they have been elected by the singular play of circumstance to take the initiative and largely to shape the prospective fortunes of the republic of learning. Their European copartners have fallen into a state of disorganisation and depletion, both in their personnel and in their equipment, so serious as to leave them, prospectively, very much in arrears. It is perhaps an over-statement to speak of the European world of learning as bankrupt, but it is also to be kept in mind that the misfortunes which make for its undoing are not yet at an end, and will by no means end abruptly with the formal conclusion of the Great War. For one thing, the European community of science and scholarship has been divided into halves between which the war has fixed a great gulf, a gulf so deep and implacable that even for some time after the war it will not be bridged. And within that half in which, by the fortunes of war, the Americans belong—the half which will now have to go into action as a decimated whole—within this half of the pre-war complement the channels of communication have been falling into neglect, the co-ordination of parts has failed, the local units have been depleted, the working capital is exhausted, and the equipment is falling into decay. In short, there is at the best a large depreciation charge to be written off. And all the while there is an indefinite promise of more of the same, and worse.

To put the case in concrete terms, the German men of learning have been and are going through a very trying experience, to choose no harsher expression, and are in such a resulting state of moral dilapidation as should in all likelihood leave them largely incapacitated for sound work in science and scholarship for the term of the passing generation. The visible displacement of judgment and aspirations among them has engendered a profound distrust of their working powers among their colleagues of other nationalities—at least all the distrust which they merit. They are at the same time not being at all fully replaced by a new generation of scholars and scientists, since the war is draining off nearly all the men available for such work as will serve the war, which is also permanently diverting the energies of nearly all the residue to uses that are alien to the higher learning. By force of decimation, diversion, and debauch of scholarly morale—coupled with a stubborn distrust of them by the scholars in other lands—the learned men and the seminaries of the higher learning in the German-speaking world are presumably, in the main, to be counted among the dead, wounded, and missing in so far as concerns the reconstruction now to be entered on in the affairs of the higher learning. Something is plainly to be allowed in abatement of any appraisal of so sweeping a nature; but it is also plain that in the reconstruction now to be undertaken there is no German scholarship to be counted on as a present help, and what is to be counted on in the near future is an indefinite and doubtful quantity. In this respect the German-speaking community is plainly the heaviest loser among all the peoples who are losing by the war, and the loss suffered by the German scholarly community is net loss to the republic of learning at large.

In their degree, though in a less sinister measure than the Germans, the other Europeans are subject to much the same depletion of forces, decay of the spirit, and impoverishment in their material means. The Americans, however, have been less exposed to the disorganising experience of the war, and especially they still command the material means indispensable to the organisation and pursuit of scholarly and scientific inquiry under modern conditions. So that by the play of circumstances the Americans are placed in a position of trust to turn the means at hand to the best use for the conservation and reconstruction of the world's joint enterprise in science and scholarship.

As it is perforce a joint international interest that so calls for initiative and wise conduct at the hands of the American men of learning, so it is only by a disinterested joint action on an impartially international plan that the Americans can hope to take care of the work so entrusted to them. They have the means, or they can find them, and it is for them at this critical tide in the affairs of learning to turn these means to account unreservedly in that spirit of copartnership and self-effacement which alone can hopefully be counted on for anything that shall be worth while in a joint enterprise of such a scope and character.

As an initial move to this end it should reasonably seem obligatory on all those American schools which claim a rating as seminaries of learning to "keep open house"—freely, impartially, and as a matter of routine management to accord unrestricted privileges of sanctuary and entertainment, gratuitously and irrespective of nationality, to all comers who want an opportunity for work as teachers or students and who give evidence of fitness in any respect for this pursuit. It should be a safe rule, particularly under the conditions of bias and inducement now prevailing, to leave full scope for self-selection on this head, and to afford full opportunity for all whose inclination leads them to follow after the idols of the higher learning.

With this as a point of departure there follows a second step, necessitated by the first—an inclusive co-ordination of these American schools, together with a large measure of coalition among them. Such a move of co-ordination and allotment of the work to be done is imperatively called for also on grounds of economy, even apart from the more exacting requirement of economy brought on by such an agreement to keep open house as has been spoken for above. As is well known, though it is more or less ingeniously denied from time to time, the American schools that are of college or university grade have hitherto been competitors for the trade in erudition, somewhat after the fashion of rival merchandising concerns. Indeed, it is just as well to admit frankly that they have been rival concerns, doing a competitive business in student registrations and in the creation of alumni, as also in scholastic real estate and funded endowments. This academic competition has led to an extensive duplication of plant and personnel, and more particularly duplication in the courses of instruction offered by the rival schools, and in the extra-scholastic inducements held out by each to attract a clientele of unscholarly registrants. It is scarcely necessary to insist that this rivalry and duplication have been wasteful, at the same time that it has engendered an undue animus of salesmanship in the place of scholarship. All of which may charitably be held as well enough, or at any rate not to be remedied, in time of peace, prosperity, and universal price-rating. But just now, under pressure of the war demands and the war-time inflation of prices and costs, the wastefulness of this manner of conducting the schools is becoming flagrantly evident, at the same time that the schools are already beginning to fall into distress for want of funds to carry on as usual.

The present should accordingly be a propitious time for a move of co-ordination and a degree of coalescence, such as is spoken for above, particularly as it will be practicable on this plan for the rival schools now to cover their retreat out of the underbrush of rivalry and intrigue with a decent—and unfeigned—avowal of devotion to the greater gain of that learning which they have always professed to cultivate with a single mind, and to which they doubtless have also quite amiably hoped to turn their best endeavors so soon as the more pressing exigencies of intercollegiate rivalry should leave them free to follow their natural bent. If recourse is had to some such measure of co-operation among the schools, they will easily be able to carry any prospective burden of providing for their prospective guests, foreign and domestic, as well as the effective volume of their day's work, which now seems an overload.

Such a pooling of scholastic issues would reasonably give rise to something in the way of a central office to serve as a common point of support and co-ordination, which would at the same time serve as a focus, exchange, and center of diffusion for scholarly pursuits and mutual understanding, as well as an unattached academic house of refuge and entertainment for any guests, strays, and wayfaring men of the republic of learning. This central would then stand as an impersonal, impartial, communal central for the republic of learning, an open house of resort and recuperation through the season of stress and infirmity which the community of scholars is facing. There would be no implied degree of unselfishness on the part of the Americans in so placing their resources and their good offices at the service of the world at large. They would only be serving their own ends as community partners in the pursuit of knowledge; for they can neither increase their own holdings in the domain of learning, nor hold fast that which they conceive themselves to be possessed of, except in copartnership with these others, who now have fallen on evil days.

More specifically, and as affording a concrete point of departure for any enterprise of the kind, provision should be made under the auspices of one or more such centrals for the reorganisation of those channels of communication that have been falling into disuse during the period of the war; for the maintenance and unbroken continuity of the work and the records of the many learned societies that have been falling into abeyance during the same period; and for the keeping of records and the collation and dissemination of materials and bibliographical information, on which the learned men of all countries are in the habit of depending.

The details of this work will be voluminous and diverse, even if it is taken over only as an emergency measure to tide over the period of reconstruction; and the adequate care of it all will call for no small degree of sobriety, insight, and goodwill, and also for no small expenditure of means. But it is hoped that the American scholars are possessed of the requisite large and sober insight (otherwise there is nothing to be done about it) and it is known that, just now, the Americans have the goodwill of all thoughtful men throughout those countries that come into consideration here. It is also known that the Americans command the material means necessary to such an undertaking; and any degree of reflection will show that the American community runs no chance of material impoverishment in the further course of the war, quite the contrary in fact.

# A MEMORANDUM ON A SCHEDULE
# OF PRICES FOR THE STAPLE FOODSTUFFS [1]

PRICE control appears to be the only practical means of regulating the supply of foodstuffs in America. Admonition and advice are likely to be less and less effective for this purpose as time goes on; and no direct coercive control of production would be practicable in this country. At the same time it is desirable to limit the control of prices to as few items as may be, and to adopt a consistent scheme of regulation for the items whose supply it seems necessary to control.

The underlying purpose of any such regulation is the more effectual prosecution of the war; and the first consideration, therefore, is the supply of foodstuffs to the European Allies. Any practical schedule of prices will accordingly have to be drawn with a view primarily to this requirement. The price control will aim to take care of the main staples required by the Allies, and regulate the prices of other articles only so far as may be unavoidable in taking care of these main staples. This will mean that prices are to be regulated with a view to the

[1] Reprinted from *The Southwestern Social Science Quarterly*, Vol. XIII, March, 1933, where it appeared as "An Unpublished Memorandum of Thorstein Veblen on Government Regulation of the Food Supply" with an introductory note by Mr. Joseph Dorfman. According to the note, this Memorandum, along with the preceding one on the I.W.W., was dug out of a barrel in a garret in Washington, D.C., where Mr. Lubin keeps his memories. It was originally written in 1918 for the Statistical Division of the Food Administration. See footnote on p. 319.

supply of grain and meat; and of the grains and meat products, wheat and pork will come in for the chief consideration; wheat because it is the largest and most urgently needed item of the food supply; pork because it can be produced at a lower cost and handled more expeditiously and with less waste than any other available provision of meat and fat.

Hence a price schedule for the control of the American food supply will be based on the requirement of wheat and pork, and will be so drawn as to favor the production and conservation of these two staples. With this primary requirement in mind, it seems expedient to set up a schedule of prices covering three main classes of items: (*a*) the main staple farm products—to include Wheat, Corn, Barley, Rye, Oats, Potatoes, Pork, Beef, Mutton, Eggs, Butter, Cotton, and Tobacco; (*b*) staple articles of import which compete with these domestic products—to include Sugar, Fruits, and Edible Oils and Fats; (*c*) the main staple articles of use on the farms—to include certain standard items of Farm Machinery and Vehicles, Lumber, Fence Wire, Nails, Binder Twine, and perhaps Soft Coal and Gasoline.

Minor staples of import or of domestic production— as, e.g., Rubber, Resins, Hides, Truckfarm Products, Milk, Flax, Peanuts, and the like—may call for regulation on other grounds; but for the Food Administration articles of this general class are of secondary interest and had best be left out of control; partly to afford a free market by observation of which the general level of prices for the main staples can be intelligently readjusted from time to time, and partly to afford a fluctuating margin of employment for such lands and farm work as are not altogether suitable for use in the production of the main staples. There is also the practical reason for leaving such an unregulated margin of minor staples, that it would be extremely difficult to control so scattered and variable a volume of items in any satisfactory way.

Of the three classes of items named above, as being properly subject to regulation for the purposes of the Food Administration, only the first named—the main staple farm products—come directly under the jurisdiction of the Food Administration; the other two are under the surveillance of other branches of the government, and the Food Administration can influence their control only by way of criticism and advice. In effect, the Food Administration will at best be able to set up and carry out a systematic control of the main agricultural staples only, and will have to adjust its control of these staples to the circumstances of the case; prominent among these conditioning circumstances being the dealings of these other organs of government with the other staple items whose competition in the market affects the prices of the agricultural staples. The immediate care of the Food Administration, accordingly, will be the staple farm products, but with a constant regard for the course of prices in those lines that come into relation with the staple foodstuffs, whether on the side of their production or on that of their sale.

It is evident that no rigid and invariable schedule of prices can be adopted, once for all. The seasons vary greatly, and their variation never affects all crops equally. Any schedule will necessarily be subject to revision from time to time to meet the varying conditions of demand and supply. It follows that, in effect, any practicable schedule will take the form of a schedule of price ratios covering the items to be brought under control, drawn with reference to a chosen base and subject to revision as the changing conditions of production may require.

Concretely, to meet these requirements, it is here proposed that the price of wheat during the pre-war years 1911–1914 be taken as a base and reckoned as 100, while the prices of the other staple farm products already named will fall into a series of relative prices taken from the same period and reckoned in percentages of the price of wheat; so giving a series of price ratios or index numbers, to serve as a normal level from which variations will be made to meet special conditions. The general advance of prices that has taken effect during the period of the war will be met by using the ascertained ratio of this general advance as a coefficient to be multiplied into each of the several ratios or index numbers included in the schedule; so raising the general level of prices for farm products by a uniform increase throughout the list. Special disturbances, affecting any given item, such as seasonal variations of supply or demand, will be offset by individually weighting such items in the list as may require it. While special inducements to an increased production of articles that are urgently needed, as, e.g., wheat or beef, may be brought to bear by means of a similar weighting of the corresponding index numbers of the schedule.

It will be seen that this schedule of relative prices is designed to serve as a basis for the continual readjustment of prices to meet varying conditions, rather than a rigid scale to be adhered to in the face of changing conditions. The schedule will also vary from one place to another, by a system of differentials designed to cover differences of nearness to the market, and similar factors that effect the supply; very much after the fashion of the differentials now in use in regulating the price of wheat in different markets under the direction of the Grain Corporation. The result will be a series of price schedules for different markets, but all related to each other through being derived from one base—the schedule of price ratios first spoken of above. Whenever it is desired to change the level of price for any given item— as, e.g., wheat or pork—to encourage or discourage its production or consumption, relatively to the other foodstuffs, these several scales of prices in the local markets can accordingly all be altered at the same time and with a uniform effect by changing the coefficient assigned to the given item in the underlying schedule of price ratios on which the several local schedules are based. The effect of any such change in the underlying schedule of ratios will run uniformly through the entire range of special price schedules, and so maintain an effectual equality of prices throughout the various markets that are to be kept under control.

In so varying the price of any or all of the foodstuffs included in the schedule, there are other circumstances to be taken account of, besides the variations of the seasons and the changes in the export demand; notably changes in the general level of prices, on the one hand, and changes which specially affect the cost of production of the crops, on the other hand. The general price level for the staple foodstuffs will be kept by means of a running reference to (*a*) the current prices of the uncontrolled foodstuffs, as shown in the price bulletins of the Food Administration's Statistical Division, and (*b*) the current price reports of the War Industries Board; while the main variations in cost of production specifically bearing on the production of staple foodstuffs are similarly shown (*a*) in the bulletins of farm-wages published by the Department of Labor, and (*b*) in the pricelists of manufacturers of farm machinery, as well as in the bulletins of the Federal Trade Commission covering farm machinery.

What has been said above bears on the running adjustment of the prices of staple foodstuffs to the current conditions of demand and supply; and the data underlying the argument so far are shown in the subjoined Tables with accompanying Charts.[2] But in addition to such a running adjustment, it will also be incumbent on those who have charge of this price regulation to take care that a sufficient supply of the staples is produced. To this end the farmers should be relieved of the risk of loss due to crop failures or to unforeseen losses of livestock due to drought, hard weather, or disease. As far as practicable the risk of loss should be borne by the nation as a whole—on the well-known principle of mutual insurance. The crop failure in North Dakota in 1917, and the extent to which that misfortune has crippled the farm industry of that state for the current season of 1918, goes to show how serious a mistake it is in the present emergency to let the risk be carried by the individual farmers rather than by the community at large. In the present emergency the production of foodstuffs is quite unmistakably a joint enterprise for the prosecution of the war, and it is imperative that the enterprise should be managed on that basis.

To remedy mischiefs of the class shown by the case of North Dakota, and to offset the discouragement which such a risk of loss always gives rise to, it is necessary to provide beforehand for shifting such risk from the individual producer to the community at large. So far as concerns the main staple foodstuffs this can be done in a passable fashion by guaranteeing the farmers

[2] These have not been included here.

a suitable minimum return per acre of the crops planted, and perhaps a similar insurance per head of livestock in hand at the opening of the season. As is well known the cost of production of the staple crops in American farming is much more nearly proportioned to the acreage than to the total yield; whereas the market value is proportioned to the total yield. The details of any scheme for crop insurance on the basis of acreage will vary somewhat from one place to another, but the general principle will be much the same. As in the case of the market price of the grains, so here it is proposed that a basis on which to compute a practicable minimum per acre may best be found in the value per acre of the various crops in the various localities concerned, during the three years preceding the war. In this connection it may be noted that the three-year average—1911–1914 —coincides closely with the longer, nine-year average, 1909–1917.

For the staple grains, therefore, it should be advisable to set up a schedule of guaranteed minimum returns per acre, to vary from place to place to correspond with the varying conditions of production, but sufficient to relieve the producers of the hazard of loss. Details of method in adjusting such a schedule of guaranteed returns are a matter for advisement between those who will have charge; so also questions of what items are to be counted in as elements of necessary cost, to be covered by the guarantee. So, e.g., the question will come up: How far, if at all, is the rental value of the land to be counted as an item of cost for this purpose?

In like manner the production of the staple meats should be covered with a suitable guarantee against unforeseen loss. This may prove a more delicate matter to arrange. But with the help of the Bureau of Animal

Industry a sufficiently effective method of procedure can doubtless be devised. It is suggested that the control at this point should best proceed on a census of the live-stock population to be taken at the beginning of the crop year.

At this point comes in the close relation which always subsists between the American production of Pork and Beef and the Corn Crop. Much of the pork and beef supply, but more particularly the marginal portion of this supply, comes as a virtual conversion of corn into meat and fat—somewhat at the discretion of the farmer. So much so, that men of experience in this matter—as, e.g., in the Bureau of Animal Industry—have been at pains to work out coefficients, or ratios, governing the proportion between a given increase in the supply of pork or beef and the increased consumption of corn necessary to such increased production. At this point, therefore, the price schedules for the grains and the meats come into necessary correlation; so that the supply of the staple meats comes to be a prime consideration in adjusting the price of corn and fitting it into the price schedule of the staple grains.

# SUGGESTIONS TOUCHING THE WORKING PROGRAM OF AN INQUIRY INTO THE PROSPECTIVE TERMS OF PEACE [1]

I. THE contemplated settlement will take one or another of two contrasted lines of approach: a peace of diplomatic compromise, to include primarily the eight greater Powers, on a footing of parity; or, a league (federation) of the pacific Peoples on a footing of national disclaimer, to include primarily the democratic peoples of the Entente. The part logically to be taken by the United States in such a coalition of peoples will be very materially different according as the one or the other of these two lines of settlement is held in prospect. In the former case—a peace compact of diplomatic com-

[1] This and the succeeding essay are reprinted from *The Political Science Quarterly,* Vol. XLVII, June, 1932, where they appeared together under the title "Two Unpublished Papers of Thorstein Veblen on the Nature of Peace." In his introductory note Mr. Joseph Dorfman has this to say of them: "In the fall of 1917 President Wilson requested Colonel House to institute an Inquiry for the purpose of preparing a memorandum to guide the President in his peace maneuvers. [Veblen submitted] to the Inquiry two highly interesting memoranda which were called 'Suggestions Touching the Working Program of an Inquiry into the Prospective Terms of Peace' and 'An Outline of a Policy for the Control of the "Economic Penetration" of Backward Countries and of Foreign Investments.'

"The latter is still to be found in the papers of the Inquiry, which were placed in the archives of the State Department. A copy of the former, which cannot be found in the archives, was supplied through the courtesy of a friend of Veblen."

promise—America's part logically becomes that of an interested outsider, since the settlement in that case will be primarily an arrangement between the European Powers; whereas in the latter case—a League of the pacific Peoples—America will necessarily come in as an integral factor, perhaps the central and decisive factor in the settlement.

Evidently the range of inquiry with a view to feasible terms of peace will differ notably according to the part which will prospectively be taken by America. In the former case—a diplomatic settlement—America has little interest in what may be called the internal policies of Europe, whether international or intranational; and the range and purpose of this Inquiry would therefore, in that case, be chiefly confined to questions of domestic policy and of maritime trade. In the latter case—a neutral League of Peoples—the range of this Inquiry would necessarily extend to all countries and peoples concerned, but its scope would at the same time be narrowed by neglect of many things which the constitution of such a neutral league would take notice of only to disallow them, e.g., trade discriminations and the commercial engrossing of natural resources. In the former case, America's chief interest should logically be the realignment of its own internal forces, with a view to keeping the peace at home, and to provide against the assured event of its being presently broken abroad. The stipulations of a "diplomatic peace" are of relatively slight interest to America, since they would in any case be observed only so far as the Powers might find it convenient to observe them in the course of preparation for the eventually ensuing war, whereas the measures to be taken in domestic policy in this case, with a view to a solidarity of sentiment and resources under all contingencies, will be of paramount consequence and should claim the chief attention of the Inquiry.

II. To reach a tenable settlement on anything like a democratic footing the support of popular sentiment must be had for all substantial points that are to be agreed on or argued for. Therefore, it is urgently necessary to keep in touch with current opinion and sentiment, to inform all men of what is under advisement as being desirable to be done or possible to be accomplished, and to guide public attention so far as may be in respect of the purposes that are aimed at, and the ways and means and adjustments necessary to their accomplishment. Therefore it becomes incumbent on the Inquiry not only to turn unreservedly to that method of "open diplomacy" that has latterly been made much of, but also deliberately to enter on a campaign of publicity designed to cover all moot questions.

By way of parenthesis it may be suggested that this work of publicity might advantageously take the following forms :—Men associated in the Inquiry should put into the form of written bulletins a detailed presentation of particular questions that are to be taken under advisement, to be published and circulated as bulletins of the Inquiry or of the State Department, but with a specific avowal that the views set out in these bulletins have been submitted to and are taken under advisement by the Inquiry and inviting free discussion and suggestions. Preferably, these bulletins should carry the signatures of their writers, rather than the informal endorsement of the Inquiry, so that their publication should not commit the Inquiry in any official way to the views embodied in the bulletins.

It is hoped that the outcome of such publicity would

be of appreciable use in the way of ascertainment, standardisation, and guidance of popular sentiment touching the ways and means of keeping the peace, as well as the adaptations of policy and administration necessary to be accepted to that end.

III. Any degree of reflection will show that deliberation or debate on these matters must result directly in a two-sided division of opinion and endeavor, in such a way that spokesmen of the vested interests and of the unqualified maintenance of the established order, on the one hand, will be found opposed to the spokesmen of a resolute maintenance of the peace at the cost of any necessary revision or adjustment within this established order, on the other hand; and it should be equally evident that the Inquiry will find itself taking sides and will presently be committed to a position, either favoring the vested interests at some risk to the maintenance of peace at home and abroad, or favoring a workable realignment of the country's available resources designed to keep the peace even at the cost of some appreciable derangements to these vested interests.

What is involved in the logic of the situation is apparently a question of bias, a matter of inclination for or against the vested rights on the one hand, and the domestic and international tranquillity on the other hand; and it would appear that the Inquiry, following the apparent inclination of the Administration, should presently, by force of the logical situation, find itself searching for feasible ways and means of assuring the domestic tranquillity even at the cost of any contingent derangement of the established scheme of vested rights, whether private or national.

IV. Assuming that the settlement will result in a League of the pacific Peoples, drawn on a plan of neutralisation and a pooling of issues, rather than a negotiated compact of diplomatic compromises between rival Powers, then it logically follows that the French and English-speaking Peoples will make up the substantial core of the League, and also that initiative and discretion will continue to vest in these Peoples primarily. But it follows likewise that in such a case, the United States will be thrown into the center, and the initiative and discretion in the formation, structure, and carrying on of the League will in effect come to vest primarily in the American Administration; which so will be put on its honor, and will at the same time be enabled to give effect to its unselfish profession.

At the same time, the sooner the American Administration takes initial measures toward this end the better the chance of its effectually realising its professed ideals, and the better the chance of maturing these ideal aims and progressively embodying them in definitively tenable concrete working arrangements. It is also apparent that a League designed eventually to keep the peace had best be such a League as would now expediently be contrived for achieving an advantageous settlement, from which it follows: (*a*) that an enduring coalition of these chief Entente belligerents (the French and English-speaking Peoples) for the conduct of the war should be arrived at as expeditiously as may be done, and should be an organisation drawn with a view to its continuation as the core of the eventual Pacific League; and (*b*) that this Inquiry, as being an organ of the Administration, should therefore turn its present and continued attention to discovering and presenting the lowest terms and the most neutral claims on which such a working coalition can be made sufficiently compact for this purpose and can be held together as a going concern.

# OUTLINE OF A POLICY FOR THE CONTROL OF THE "ECONOMIC PENETRATION" OF BACKWARD COUNTRIES AND OF FOREIGN INVESTMENTS [1]

IT is assumed as a major premise that the constant and controlling purpose in any arrangements entered into in the prospective settlement will be the keeping of the peace at large; that the need of peace is paramount; that any special interest which may come up for consideration must wait on this paramount exigence of such measures as seem necessary to the state of peace and security at large.

Evidently this paramount consideration will impose a limit and enforce a bias of its own at every point where any measure looking to another purpose is proposed, and wherever the continued expediency of any given item of law or custom is brought under advisement. If the claims of peace and security are to be allowed without reservation, the immediate consequence should be the disallowance and disclaimer of all such special interests and ambitions as may give rise to estrangement or dissension among the peoples associated together for the keeping of the peace.

But the case is not so simple. By tradition and in-

[1] Reprinted by permission from *The Political Science Quarterly,* Vol. XLVII, No. 2, June, 1932. See footnote on p. 355.

grained conceit, all modern nations harbor certain interests and pretensions to which they attach a high value,
whether this value is real or fancied. War is commonly
entered on in defense or furtherance of some such national interest, real or fancied, tangible or intangible.
The current war is an instance in point. And it is even
yet a safe generalisation that no modern nation would
be ready now, out of hand, to disclaim or disavow all
such interests and pretensions tangible and intangible,
commercial and patriotic, even after the national integrity had been duly safeguarded. Therefore it is to be
presumed that the compact, league, or coalition of peoples for the keeping of the peace, which is expected to
be set afoot in the terms of settlement, will take the line
of a mutual concessive disclaimer and disallowance of
such usages, claims, and pretensions as appear to be
patently incompatible with the uninterrupted continuance of peace and security.

The "Pacific League" which is to come out of the
prospective settlement may accordingly be anything,
from a temporary treaty engagement between the pacific
nations, to a close-knit and irrevocable coalition of
peoples who have thrown in their fortunes together and
have subordinated their national ambitions to the common good. And the contemplated "economic penetration," as well as the measures to be taken for its control, will take on a different character according to the
complexion which the Pacific League will take on, and
according to the degree of control which it will be in a
position to exercise. Therefore it appears necessary, by
way of a definition of premises, to indicate at the outset
with what scope and manner of jurisdiction the League
is here conceived to be invested, in so far as bears on
the question in hand. Adequately to control such "eco-

nomic penetration," the Pacific League will have to be vested with a relatively very large discretion; which in turn implies an extensive surrender of powers on the part of the associated peoples of the League.

PROVISIONAL OUTLINE OF A PROJECTED LEAGUE OF THE
PACIFIC PEOPLES; SO FAR AS TOUCHES ITS CONTROL OF
THE "ECONOMIC PENETRATION" OF BACKWARD
COUNTRIES

The abiding purpose of the projected League is to be the keeping of the peace at large; not the furtherance of commercial enterprise, nor the pursuit of national ambitions. Therefore the latter are necessarily and unreservedly to be subordinated to the former. Dissension among nations commonly arises out of conflicting commercial aims and national pretensions; therefore it will be incumbent on the associated pacific peoples, so far as may be, to divest themselves of all commercial discrimination and national ambition. Therefore the projected League can comprise only such of the modern peoples as are content to put away so much of their self-direction and national rivalry as would be incompatible with the maintenance of peace under the League's collective surveillance. And unless a sufficiently large and consequential proportion of civilised mankind can be brought into a sufficiently close coalition, on such terms, the League will prove nugatory. Therefore it is here assumed that the avowedly pacific peoples will be found in such a tolerant frame of mind as will answer the purposes for which the Pacific League is to be formed. Otherwise the argument fails.

In the phrase of President Wilson, the end to be sought in the prospective settlement is to make the world safe for democracy. And within the meaning of the term as employed by the American Administration in its occasional pronouncements, Democracy may be described as that frame of mind by virtue of which a people chooses to be collectively fortunate rather than nationally formidable. The modern peoples partake of this animus in varying degrees; and the question of any given people's inclusion as a constituent factor in the projected League therefore becomes substantially a question of the degree in which they are imbued with this requisite frame of mind.

In the past, indeed in the recent past—in that recently past time when statesmen still placed their dependence on the Balance of Power—in this past out of which it is hopefully believed that the modern peoples are now emerging, it was an accepted principle underlying all effectual statecraft that no people could hope to be collectively fortunate except at the cost of being nationally formidable. But it is now proposed deliberately to shift the ground of policy from that ancient principle of worldly wisdom to a new principle of what may be called standardised forbearance, whereby it shall cease to be expedient for any nation to be formidable. Under this prospective régime any formidable nation would become a menace to itself and its neighbors alike, inasmuch as it would be a menace to that peace at large within which alone its people can hope to be collectively fortunate. Therefore, incidentally, it becomes the duty of the Pacific League to eliminate all formidable nations.

In varying degrees the modern nations meet these requirements; or it could perhaps rather be said that they are in varying degrees approaching such a frame of mind under the discipline of their war experience; and it may be added that they are due to make a closer approach to this required frame of mind in the further course of the like experience. The chief belligerents on the side of the Entente are already coming to the persuasion that no national aggrandisement and no profits of commercial enterprise are worth the hazard of a return to the *status quo ante.*

It is these chief belligerents, or rather it is such of these chief belligerents as are now in a way to achieve this required spirit of forbearance, that will by force of circumstance be elected to take the initiative, shape its policy, and continue to constitute the core of the Pacific League. There is, at any rate, no prospect that beginning can be made without them. And there is at the same time also no reason to put off this beginning until the close of hostilities. Indeed, the main lines of organisation and administration should best be designed, materialised, and tried out in actual work while the pressure of an urgent present common emergency can still be counted on to keep mutual jealousies and cupidity in abeyance; so that the League would then both serve as a means of conducting the war to a successful issue, and also be ready to enter on the settlement and further conduct of affairs as a going concern.

These chief belligerents that so may hopefully be looked to as the prime movers and the chief support of the projected coalition would be the French and the English-speaking peoples, together with the Chinese and a more or less considerable group of like-minded accessories in Latin America and western Europe. Necessarily included in the League's jurisdiction would also be two further categories: the backward peoples of what are now the colonial possessions of these belligerents and of what have been the colonial possessions of their opponents in the war; and the undemocratic peoples at present comprised in the warlike coalition of the Centrals.

In outline, the forms of organisation, the fashion in which the several constituent peoples are to be articulated into a going concern, and the distribution of responsibilities and obligations among them—in all this it should seem the part of wisdom to draw on the experience of the United States and the British, who have been the chief successful pioneers in the extension of democratic institutions hitherto. Neither has reason to boast of work well done in this respect; the shortcomings of both are sufficiently grave and notorious; but the best, after all, is always better than something else, and between them these two are after all the most signal experiment in democratic pioneering, or rather the nearest approach to a democratic conduct of affairs on a modern scale and over a widely diversified range of peoples and countries. And it should be added that the defects and mistakes which have come to light in the course of these democratic experiments should prove no less instructive for the purposes now in hand.

For the immediate purpose—for an inquiry into the line of policy by which "economic penetration" and investment in foreign parts is best to be controlled—the features which the British and American experiments in democracy have in common are more to the point than their differences; although it may well be that the differences would be no less instructive in another connection. The two are more alike in the working parts of their structure than appears on the surface; the difference being, in good part, that the articulation of the working parts is more sharply defined and more visible in the American case. Loosely, and with a margin of disparities, the working organisation through which co-ordination is effected falls into a three-fold gradation of units in either case, but more obvious in the American case; chiefly a gradation in the scope of such self-direction as they are endowed with. There is in either case a substantial core of constituent communities, in which is finally vested the over-ruling initiative, discretion, and responsibility—the seat of sovereignty, as it would be called in political theory; in the American case this central body is the States of the Union. Then there are the Territories; held under surveillance and concessively vested with a degree of self-government; beyond which come the backward communities of the outlying possessions, who are wards of the Union, held in tutelage and administered under discretionary control. The parallel facts will be visible in the British case to any attentive observer, but they need scarcely be traced out here.

To follow the analogy, in the projected League the substantial core would be constituted, at the outset, by the chief democratic belligerents already spoken of; admission being free to any others possessed of the necessary qualifications. What these requisite qualifications are to be need not detain the argument here, since it does not greatly concern the topic of the memorandum. The second class or group of peoples under the League's jurisdiction—those who would answer to the Territories in the American scheme—would be made up, in the main, of nationalities which are now under German, Austrian, Bulgarian, or Turkish rule; to be held under surveillance, on probation, with so much of self-direction in their administrative affairs as the circumstances would admit, and with a view to their presently coming into standing as qualified members of the democratic federation of peoples. The third and outlying group, the wards of the League, would comprise those characteristically backward peoples that inhabit Colonial Possessions. By grace of fortune, the greater proportion of these pronouncedly backward peoples have now come under the hands of those nations who will presumably exercise the discretion in laying down the lines of the Pacific League's economic policy.

Drawn on these lines, then, the scheme contemplates a very appreciable number and variety of outstanding independent nations; standing outside of the League's jurisdiction by their own choice or because they do not fill the necessary qualifications for admission as democratic commonwealths; and ranging, in point of cultural status, all the way from barbarian Abyssinia to the pseudo-constitutional monarchy of civilised Spain.

Within the confines of the League, it is evident, a sane policy looking to the perpetuation of the peace at large should consistently incline to discard, or at least to disregard, distinctions of nationality, so far as the sentimental preconceptions of its constituent peoples will allow. The most fortunate outcome at this point would be the total obsolescence or obliteration of national demarcations; but the best that can be anticipated, in view of the present state of sentiment, would be a very dubious modicum of approach toward that end.

Abolition of national frontiers would go far to dispose of many questions of economic policy, particularly questions of penetration and trade. Any degree of coalition or federation among these pacific peoples will submerge national distinctions in some degree; and measures are doubtless due to be taken looking to the submergence of national divisions and national integrity wherever their maintenance visibly jeopardises the peace at large. Some appreciable disallowance of national discretion in commercial matters is reasonably to be expected; and an untempered insistence on the removal of whatever is likely to engender jealousy, distrust, and dissension would logically result in the discontinuance of all national establishments, as such. Their place and functions as political or civil units would then be supplied by a neutral scheme of administrative divisions, drawn without regard to present political frontiers and with an eye single to administrative convenience, as determined by the natural—topographical, climatic, or linguistic—parcelment of the countries to be taken care of.

The nationalities so drawn into the scheme of redistricting need not be disturbed in any other respect than that of their civil and political powers. They would cease to have any civil status, but their integrity or solidarity in the cultural and sentimental respect would be left undisturbed and, indeed, legally unnoticed; very much as is now formally the case with various minor nationalities in some parts of the Balkans and the Russian dominions; or, again, the Armenian nation; or the Jews in the English-speaking countries.

Failing that—and there need be no doubt of its failure—any degree of approach to such a measure of neutralisation would be a measure of relief from perplexity in all that concerns international trade relations.

Now, in view of the many-sided uncertainty of the prospective situation, which is still taking shape in ways that had not been foreseen, it is here proposed to argue the questions of "economic penetration" and foreign investments on the broad assumption that the prospective league will be free and competent to deal with all these matters on a footing of neutrality and plenary discretion. From the positions so arrived at it should be practicable to pursue the argument further, as shifting circumstances may dictate, by way of adaptation, reservations, and curtailment of these provisional positions at points where the plan of settlement eventually to be adopted may fall short of full discretionary power.

So also in case the settlement should unexpectedly take the form of a negotiated peace, with treaty agreements covering international trade and investment, the formulations arrived at on the assumption here made could still stand over as a formulation of desiderata to be aimed at by those negotiators with whom the keeping of the peace at large remains the paramount end of endeavor. It will serve as a point of departure for any expedient concession that may have to be made under pressure of stubborn nationalist preconceptions.

As touches the case, then, of such outlying backward peoples as will by force of circumstance come into the status of wards, and so will come under the guardianship of the Pacific League—or in the measure in which any given people comes into this relation—the league will of necessity arrogate to itself a plenary jurisdiction; somewhat after the fashion of that authority over the North American Indians which the United States government has arrogated to itself. In these cases, and they are large, many, and diverse, there is nothing for it but that the League must take over the administration of affairs quite unreservedly; and by the same token it becomes incumbent on the League, in its character as guardian, deliberately and consistently to conserve the natural resources of these countries—mineral, forest, grazing, and agricultural—with a view to the least practicable infraction or exhaustion of the resources that so are taken over in trust.

What will be the practicable minimum of infraction

and usufruct in any given case can of course not be described in a general proposition. The circumstances vary widely. But some degree of administrative surveillance and direction will be unavoidable in nearly every case. Some measure of police surveillance becomes incumbent on the League by virtue of its responsibility as guardian; and in some measure these outlying resources will have to be turned to present account as a source of raw materials indispensable in modern industry—as, e.g., certain cabinet woods, fibers, rubber, and various materials used as drugs, pigments, oils, and varnishes, not otherwise obtainable—and the like holds true for certain fruits and foodstuffs.

On this head there is something due to be said by way of explaining and correcting certain uncritical preconceptions commonly met with; and the same considerations will also apply to "economic penetration" of undeveloped countries more at large, apart from the special case of those outlying virgin resources of the savage world. Popular discussion, in the press and elsewhere, commonly assumes as a matter of course that the speediest and most comprehensive "development" of all hitherto idle resources is altogether desirable and expedient, both for the present inhabitants of these outlying countries and for the nations at the hands of whose citizens the contemplated development is to be effected. On the other hand it is an easy generalisation out of the past history of colonisation that the rate of industrial penetration and conversion to use of any new country may readily be too swift for the continued well-being of the native population; and in taking over the direction of affairs the League will perforce become the guardian of these outlying peoples, and therefore the responsible keeper of their fortunes. At the same time, a Pacific League, whose paramount aim it is in peace and security to hold fast that which is good in democracy, cannot carry on an exploitation of its helpless wards and dependent neighbors, as a side line in its policy of peace and goodwill. Considered simply as a matter of moral profit and loss, dishonesty is not the best policy.

On these grounds of equity and of self-preservation from moral dry-rot, it should fairly be a matter of course that the line to be followed in any effectual industrial penetration of these outlying countries should be a policy of retardation and continence, rather than the reverse. A well-advised and tenacious policy and moderation would appear to be the only salutary course, all the more since—contrary to the prevalent misconceptions—these outlying natural resources are not needed for present use of the civilised nations, apart from a certain special range of raw materials not conveniently to be had elsewere.

As a general proposition, the natural resources already in hand among the modern nations are fully adequate to their current and their calculable future needs; the reservations under this broad rule being that the strategy of competitive investment at present somewhat hampers the use of resources otherwise available, and that a relatively slight supply of indispensable materials will necessarily have to be drawn from these outlying countries beyond the pale. Within the range of those raw materials which are afforded by the temperate latitudes there is no shortage, present or prospective, among the civilised countries, taken in the aggregate and in time of peace. The sole notable exception under this broad statement is the timber supply; which, it happens, is also the particular one among the outlying natural resources that may be largely laid under contribution without danger of exhaustion and without unavoidable risk of cultural disaster to these outlying peoples of the lower civilisation.

There is, of course, an urgent and unremitting pressure for the headlong "Development," that is to say for commercial exploitation, of all these outlying natural resources; but this is a clamor for private gain, not for public use. The promoters and financiers are seeking profitable concessions and investment, and they are actuated uniformly by the businesslike motive of special advantages to themselves, not by considerations of material advantage to any one else or to the community at large; nor is it at all apparent that any net gain commonly accrues to any one else from enterprises of this kind. More frequently than not, the aim is a competitive advantage as against rival business concerns, or the monopolisation of materials with a view to the control of the market.

In those countries where this pursuit of private gain at the cost of the country's resources has been allowed freely to run its enthusiastic career, as, e.g., in America, the consequences have been a wasteful exhaustion of certain natural resources (e.g., the destruction of forests by the lumber interests); together with a hurried appropriation of the tillable land, followed up with a slovenly cultivation and impoverishment of the soil, resulting in low yields and high aggregate cost per unit of goods delivered; so also the speculative holding of natural resources out of present use with a view to a prospective unearned gain (as in American land speculation, rural and urban, and the monopolisations of transportation franchises, water-power, or mineral deposits); and, as will commonly, though it may be less patently, happen in the like case, the gravest mischief has been a pervasive deterioration of industrial enterprise into a collusive chicanery and a speculative traffic in unearned gains.

To such pressure for private gain under the shield of the League's countenance the League can on no account afford to yield; inasmuch as, among other things, all traffic of this kind is a fertile source of commercial jealousies and intrigue, and these habitually give rise to international difficulties and eventual grievances to be redressed. All of which would appear to dictate that these natural resources among the outlying peoples who so come under surveillance should in no case be alienated, that they should at the farthest concession be worked under lease, for a short term only, and under such control and power of revision and revocation as would lower the inducements offered to private enterprise to the practicable minimum. It follows also that permanent improvements and plant incident and necessary to the usufruct of these resources, as, e.g., docks, harbor works, roads, means of storage and transport, should be taken over by the common authority and held in common usufruct under surveillance. And, in general terms, no encouragement should be extended to private enterprise to enter this field, no discrimination is to be countenanced, and no vested interest must be allowed to take effect in these premises.

Larger and more complex and delicate questions of "economic penetration" will arise in connection with those backward peoples who are nominally independent nations and who are outside the jurisdiction of the Pacific League. This class of outstanding nations comprises such countries as, e.g., Abyssinia, Mesopotamia, Persia, and Afghanistan. The traffic between the fed-

erated peoples of the League and these outstanding nations will unavoidably be large, continued, highly diversified, and ever increasing with the passage of time and
the growth of industry. In this intercourse the League
will be dealing with these nations as outside parties; so
that the question resolves itself into a matter of what
regulations can be put into effect within the limits of
tolerance drawn by the consent and goodwill of these
outstanding nations. There are also vested interests
which have already found lodgment in the countries in
question, in the way of investments, concessions, and an
established clientele; and there are further enterprising
persons who are due incontinently to seek similar privileges and opportunities for commercial gain in these
countries so soon as settled conditions return.

It should be recalled that the paramount aim of the
League is to keep the peace on a footing of goodwill at
large; and that the pacific peoples federated under the
terms of the League, therefore, stand to claim no special
or exceptional advantages of trade or investment, for
themselves or their citizens. With this proviso in mind
the logical course to be pursued should not be particularly obscure, in outline; although it may prove perplexing enough to follow out the simple logic of the case in
the face of obstinate preconceptions and a partisan bias
standing over out of the past. Insistence on national
rights and obligations is as incompatible with a safe
economic policy at this point as the primary aim of the
Pacific League is incompatible with that *status quo ante*
against a relapse into which the League is designed to
provide.

The aim here must plainly be to avoid those conflicts
of claims and jurisdiction out of which disputes arise.
To this end, it is plain, all international discriminations

among the associated peoples of the League are to be disallowed. It is with a view to avoiding jealousy and friction of this kind that it has been proposed in an earlier passage to submerge all national distinctions within the League and reapportion the several countries of the League into administrative and electoral districts without regard to previously existing national boundaries. At the same time, the details of usage and civil law vary greatly from one country to another, both among the peoples to be comprised in the Pacific League and among the outstanding nations, and there is little chance of doing away with such differences of use and wont and law within any moderate period of time.

Therefore, the expedient course in dealing with international relations of trade and investments should apparently be to disclaim and disallow all extra-territorial jurisdiction and all extra-territorial enforcement of pecuniary claims, both among the several peoples of the League and as between these peoples and the outstanding nations; in short, all pecuniary claims and obligations should be neutralised, with the effect of throwing their adjudication unreservedly under the local jurisdiction in whose territory they come up.

Commercial traffic and investment would under this rule be accounted a private venture, in pursuit of which the merchant or investor is acting on his own initiative, for his own ends, at his own risk; in which his compatriots share neither profit nor loss, and for the successful issue of which they assume no collective responsibility. What it comes to is that the community will no longer collectively promote or safeguard any private enterprise in pursuit of private gain beyond its own territorial bounds.

That such a plan of neutralisation and mutual disavowal of overlapping jurisdictions should govern trade and investment among the peoples of the League should be plain without argument, and so far it will probably commend itself on slight reflection to most of those concerned. That much would presumably be accepted as a corollary following immediately from the League's primary aim—to keep the peace at large on a footing of goodwill. That the same plan is good and reasonable also for the same kind of relations between the peoples of the League and the outstanding nations may at first sight seem more doubtful. The application of the principle may be more difficult in the latter case, where mutual consent may not readily be had, in the face of national jealousy and national self-interest. But this difficulty appears less formidable on a closer view of the circumstances of the case. The outstanding nations are small and commercially dependent, as compared with the League, and by so much they will be driven to accept any reasonable conditions offered. The League will be in a position to disallow interference from outside in the case of any alien trader, traveler, or investor who has a grievance to present; as well as to disclaim all special rights and immunities of its own citizens in a like case. It may fairly be doubted if public sentiment in any of the pacific countries can be brought to countenance so radical a departure from the established order of national rights and obligations; but it should plainly be the wiser policy to move as far as practicable in this direction, and then to leave an avowed presumption in favor of non-interference in every case of doubt.

To this plan of neutralisation and disclaimer it will be objected that the country's trade and investment interests would suffer irreparably under such a policy, being left at the mercy of these habitually greedy alien nations. It is doubtless true that many an enterprise in the way of investments and concessions in foreign parts would find itself at a disadvantage in its pursuit of gain if it so lost the backing of its home government; but it is equally true that the cost to its home government of keeping such a business concern secure in its pursuit of gain in foreign parts will at an average exceed the advantage which such an enterprise will bring to the rest of the community, who have no share in the gains that may accrue to such an enterprising business concern.

Reduced to elementary terms, the economic effects and bearings of such foreign investments may be described as follows. Investment is made in the foreign country to get a higher rate of profits than at home; which draws a part of the available means of industry out of the country; which advances the rate of profits in the country, or keeps up the rate on home investments, by keeping the productiveness of the country's industry down; which enhances or keeps up prices, and the cost of living; which conduces to activity in industry so long as prices are advancing—in case there is such an advance, which is not always the case. So far the net result is a loss to the home community, though there may be a gain to the interested business concern, except for the (doubtful) gain that may come of enhanced activity—in case such an effect is had. Further, the gains which accrue to the investor from these foreign investments are presumed to be received in cash or its equivalent, by the investor, who is commonly well-to-do; this will then be spent chiefly for consumption, by the recipient or on his account, and largely on superfluities; which acts to advance prices at the same time that it diverts so much of the country's industry to the production of goods suitable for such consumption; which limits the production of goods to meet the ordinary needs of the community by that much; which acts to advance, or to keep up, the cost of necessary consumable goods and thereby to increase or keep up the cost of living. Certain remoter consequences, chiefly having to do with the availability of funds for warlike politics, have no interest in this immediate connection.

Analysis will readily show that the community has nothing substantial to gain in such a case; but it is not overlooked that all modern nations are possessed of a very grave sentimental conviction to the contrary. It is an article of patriotic faith and is accepted as a matter of course and of common-sense. Even the most judicially pacific among them will have great difficulty in persuading themselves to disclaim these presumed national advantages, however illusory they may be in fact. In favor of such a policy of renunciation it will probably be more to the point to urge that the policy can be put into effect at no prohibitive cost, and that something appreciable along this line is urgently needful as a means to the paramount end of keeping the peace at large.

Doubtless, one and another of the outstanding nations may be counted on to watch their chance and take advantage of such forbearance on the part of the League, and to abuse it so far as their short-sighted worldly wisdom will carry them—for they will remain outstanding nations only because and so long as they continue to be dominated by the old-fashioned principles of statecraft according to which a foreign people is always a potential enemy. But it is to be recalled that the Pacific League is designed to comprise the greater part of civilised mankind—at any rate the greater proportion as counted in terms of trade and industry—and that the greater part of the world's outlying resources are also to be held under the surveillance and administered at the discretion of this same coalition of pacific peoples; whereas the outstanding nations, whose mischievous national ambitions bar them out, are a relatively feeble and scattered lot of industrially immature peoples, each pursuing its own archaic illusions and exposed to the vicissitudes of their mutual political intrigue and commercial chicanery. There will, presumptively, be some two or three nations of some appreciable consequence among these outstanding ones—what would be called second-rate Powers, both politically and industrially; but when all allowance has been made, it remains a secure generalisation that the goodwill of the League will be indispensable to the continued prosperity of any one, or of any group, among these outstanding nations. And it follows no less unavoidably from the broad facts that the active goodwill of the peoples of the League will accrue to those among the outstanding nations who conduct their affairs most nearly in the same spirit that moves the peoples of the League.

Still, the limits of human presumption are not easy to define, and it may always come to pass that one and another among the outstanding nations will overpass the limits of tolerance, and so call for remedial attention at the hands of the Pacific League. In such a case, still following the line of neutrality and disallowance, the remedy logically to be sought would appear to be an interruption or curtailment of intercourse with the mischief-making nation. Most conveniently and effectually this would take the form of an export duty on goods destined for the country in question, or in case of urgency, an embargo on traffic with nations who are found to be working at cross purposes with the policy of the League.

Such a Pacific League would, in effect, hold the balance of prosperity and of success between the outstanding nations. From which it follows that the League should be able effectually to govern traffic beyond its confines on much the same lines and by much the same methods as may be found wise and expeditious for the control of affairs among the peoples who are immediately amenable to its jurisdiction. The difficulties to be apprehended are difficulties in the way of its adoption rather than in the way of the successful administration of such a policy, once it has been adopted. What is proposed is little else than an unreserved extension of the principles of free trade, but with the inclusion of foreign investments as well as commercial traffic in the scope of this free-trade policy. The proposed scheme, therefore, has the merits and the defects that attach to any free-trade proposal.

It would be quite bootless to go into an argument here on the merits of a free-trade policy. The objections to such a policy are almost wholly a matter of interest, sentiment, and preconception, and are not amenable to reason. Although the novelty of such a proposal to apply to foreign investments, as contrasted with foreign commerce, may conceivably give it a slightly better chance of reasonable consideration.

What is expedient in the way of a collective policy among the pacific peoples, for the control of economic penetration, foreign commerce, and foreign investments, accordingly appears to be exceedingly simple in principle—so simple as to leave its advocates embarrassed for want of debatable ground. It comes, in principle, to nothing much more than a collusive disallowance of privileges and preference, with safeguarding of the weak and destitute and without respect of persons. How nearly such a single-minded policy could be approximated in any prospective settlement it is presumably not worth while to hazard a guess; but the nearer it comes to being realised, the more promising appears to be the chance of a lasting peace.

Under such a policy private enterprise is not to be supported or countenanced in making use of backward peoples or their resources; foreign investors will take their chances where they find them, without capitalising the support of their home government; justiciable questions will be decided under the law of the place where they arise, without prejudice by the litigants' domicile.

# THE PASSING OF NATIONAL FRONTIERS [1]

It is to be accepted as a major premise, underlying any argument or speculation that bears on current events or on the calculable future, that the peoples of Christendom are now coming to face a revolutionary situation. "It is a condition, not a theory, that confronts us." This will hold true with equal cogency for international relations and for the domestic affairs of any one of the civilised countries. It means not necessarily that a radical change of base in the existing law and order is expedient or desired, but only that circumstances have been falling into such shape that a radical change of base can be avoided, if at all, only at the cost of a hard-handed and sustained reactionary policy. Indeed, it may be an open question whether any concerted scheme of reactionary measures will suffice to maintain or to re-establish the passing status quo. It takes the form of a question as to whether the Old Order can be rehabilitated, not whether it will stand over by its own inertia. And it is, perhaps, still more of an open question what would be the nature and dimensions of those departures from the holding ground of the Old Order which the new conditions of life insist on.

But the situation is of a revolutionary character, in the sense that those underlying principles of human intercourse on which the Old Order rests are no longer consonant with the circumstances which now condition this intercourse. The spiritual ground on which rights

[1] Reprinted from *The Dial*, Vol. LXIV, April 25, 1918.

and duties have been resting has shifted, beyond recall. What has been accepted hitherto as fundamentally right and good is no longer securely right and good in human intercourse as it must necessarily run under the altered circumstances of today and tomorrow. The question, in substance, is not as to whether the scheme is to be revised, but only as to the scope and method of its revision, which may take the direction of a rehabilitation of the passing order, or a drift to new ground and a New Order.

The principles of right and honest living are of the nature of habit, and like other habits of thought these principles change in response to the circumstances which condition habituation. But they change tardily; they are tenacious and refractory; and anything like a deliberate shifting to new ground in such a matter will come to pass only after the old position has become patently untenable, and after the discipline exercised by the new conditions of life has had time to bend the spiritual attitude of the community into a new bias that will be consonant with the new conditions. At such a juncture a critical situation will arise. So today a critical situation has arisen, precipitated and emphasised by the experience of the war, which has served to demonstrate that the received scheme of use and wont, of law and order and equity, is not competent to meet the exigencies of the present.

In the last resort, these changes of circumstance that have so been going forward and have put the received scheme of law and order out of joint are changes of a technological kind, changes that affect the state of the industrial arts and take effect through the processes of industry. One thing and another in the institutional heritage has so been outworn, or outlived; and among these is the received conception of the place and value of nationalities.

The modern industrial system is worldwide, and the modern technological knowledge is no respecter of national frontiers. The best efforts of legislators, police, and business men, bent on confining the knowledge and use of the modern industrial arts within national frontiers, has been able to accomplish nothing more to the point than a partial and transient restriction on minor details. Such success as these endeavors in restraint of technological knowledge have met with has effected nothing better than a slight retardation of the advance and diffusion of such knowledge among the civilised nations. Quite patently, these measures in restraint of industrial knowledge and practice have been detrimental to all the peoples concerned, in that they have lowered the aggregate industrial efficiency of the peoples concerned, without increasing the efficiency, wealth, or well-being of any one of them. Also quite patently, these endeavors in restraint of industry have not successfully prevented the modern industrial system from reaching across the national frontiers in all directions, for materials and for information and experience. Indeed, so far as regards the industrial work of the modern peoples, as distinct from the commercial traffic of their business men, it is plain that the national frontiers are serving no better purpose than a moderately effectual obstruction. In this respect, the national frontiers, and all that system of discrimination and jealousy to which the frontiers give definition and emphasis, are worse than useless; although circumstances which the commercialised statesmen are unable to control have made the frontiers a less effectual bar to intercourse than would suit the designs of national statecraft.

The case stands somewhat different as regards that commercial traffic that makes use of the modern industrial system. Business enterprise is a pursuit of private gain. Not infrequently one business concern will gain at the cost of another. Enterprising business concerns habitually seek their own advantage at the cost of their rivals in the pursuit of gain; and a disadvantage imposed on a rival concern or on a competing line of business enterprise constitutes a competitive advantage. Hindrance of a competitor is an advantage gained. Business enterprise is competitive, even where given business men may work in collusion for the time being with a view to gains that are presently to be divided. And success in business is always finally a matter of private gain, frequently at the cost of some one else. Business enterprise is competitive.

But the like is not the case with industrial efficiency. And the material interest of the community centers on industrial efficiency, on the uninterrupted production of goods at the lowest practicable cost in terms of material and man power. The productive efficiency of any one industrial plant or industrial process is in no degree enhanced by the inefficiency of any other plant or process comprised in the industrial system; nor does any productive advantage come to the one from a disadvantage imposed on another. The industrial process at large is of a co-operative nature, in no degree competitive—and it is on the productive efficiency of the industrial process at large that the community's material interest centers. But while business enterprise gets its gains from industry, the gains which it gets are got in competition with rivals; and so it becomes the aim of competitive business concerns to hinder the productive efficiency of those industrial units that are controlled by their rivals. Hence what has been called "capitalistic sabotage." All this, of course, is the merest commonplace of economic science.

At this point the national frontiers come into the scheme of economic life, with the jealousies and discrimination which the frontiers mark and embody. The frontiers, and that obstruction to traffic and intercourse in which the frontiers take effect, may serve a gainful purpose for the business concerns within the frontiers by imposing disadvantages on those outside, the result being a lowered efficiency of industry on both sides of the frontier. In short, so far as concerns their place and value in modern economic life, the national frontiers are a means of capitalistic sabotage; and indeed that is all they are good for in this connection. All this, again, is also a commonplace of economic science.

In past time, before modern industry had taken on its modern character and taken to the use of a wide range of diversified materials and products drawn from all over the habitable world—in the past the obstruction to industry, and therefore to material well-being, involved in the use of the frontiers as a means of sabotage was of relatively slight consequence. In the state of the industrial arts as it prevailed in that past era, the industrial processes ran on a smaller scale and made relatively little use of materials drawn from abroad. The mischief worked by sabotage at the frontiers was consequently also relatively slight; and it is commonly believed that other, incidental gains of a national character would accrue from so obstructing traffic at the frontiers, in the way of national self-sufficiency and warlike preparation. These presumed gains in point of "preparedness," it has been presumed, would outweigh the relatively slight economic mischief involved in the practice of national sabotage by the obstructive use of the frontiers, under the old system of small-scale and home-bred industry.

Latterly this state of things, which once served in its degree to minimise the economic mischief of the national frontiers, has become obsolete. As things stand now, no civilised country's industrial system will work in isolation. Not only will it not work at a high efficiency if it is effectually confined within the national frontiers, but it will not work at all. The modern state of the industrial arts will not tolerate that degree of isolation on the part of any country, even in case of so large and diversified a country as the United States. The great war has demonstrated all that. Of course, it may be conceived to be conceivable that a modern civilised community should take thought and deliberately forgo the use of this modern state of the industrial arts which demands a draft on all the outlying regions of the earth for resources necessary to its carrying-on; and so should return to the archaic scheme of economic life that prevailed in the days before the Industrial Revolution; and so would be able to carry on its industrial life in a passable state of isolation, such as still floats before the vision of the commercialised statesmen. But all that line of fantastic speculation can have only a speculative interest. In point of practical fact, the nations of Christendom are here together, and they live and move and have their being within this modern state of the industrial arts, which binds them all in an endless web of give and take across all national frontiers and in spite of all the well-devised obstructive measures of the commercialised statesmen.

As an industrial unit, the nation is out of date. This will have to be the point of departure for the incoming New Order. And the New Order will take effect only so far and so soon as men are content to make up their account with this change of base that is enforced by the new complexion of the material circumstances which condition human intercourse. Life and material well-being are bound up with the effectual working of the industrial system; and the industrial system is of an international character—or it should perhaps rather be said that it is of a cosmopolitan character, under an order of things in which the nation has no place or value.

But it is otherwise with the business men and their vested interests. Such business concerns as come into competition with other business concerns domiciled beyond the national frontiers have an interest in the national frontiers as a means of obstructing competition from beyond. For the purpose of private gains, to accrue to certain business concerns within the country, the national frontiers, and the spirit of national jealousy, are valuable as a contrivance for the restraint of trade; or, as the modern phrasing would make it, these things are made use of as a means of sabotage, to limit competition and prevent an unprofitably large output of merchantable goods being put on the market—unprofitable, that is, to the vested interests already referred to, though advantageous to the community at large.

Conversely, vested interests engaged in the pursuit of private gain in foreign parts, in the way of foreign investments, foreign concessions, export trade, and the like, also find the national establishment serviceable in enforcing claims and in procuring a profitably benevolent consideration of their craving for gain on the part of those foreign nations into whose jurisdiction their quest of profits is driving them. At this point, again, the community at large, the common men of the nation, have no material interest in furthering the advantage of the vested interests by use of the national power; quite the contrary in fact, inasmuch as the whole matter resolves itself into a use of the nation's powers and prestige for the pecuniary benefit of certain vested interests which happen to be domiciled within the national frontiers. All this, again, is a commonplace of economic science.

The conclusion is equally simple and obvious. As regards the modern industrial system, the production and distribution of goods for common use, the national establishment and its frontiers and jurisdiction serve substantially no other purpose than obstruction, retardation, and a lessened efficiency. As regards the commercial and financial considerations to be taken care of by the national establishment, they are a matter of special benefits designed to accrue to the vested interests at the cost of the common man. So that the question of retaining or discarding the national establishment and its frontiers, in all that touches the community's economic relations with foreign parts, becomes in effect a detail of that prospective contest between the vested interests and the common man out of which the New Order is to emerge, in case the outcome of the struggle turns in favor of the common man.

# A POLICY OF RECONSTRUCTION [1]

CONSIDERED as a going concern, collectively engaged in the traffic of human living, the American commonwealth is perhaps not ready to go into the hands of a receiver. There is, at the best, a wide-spread apprehension that the affairs of this going concern are in something of a precarious case. The case may not be so grave; but the derangement of conditions caused by the war, as well as the degree in which the public attention now centers on public questions, mark the present as the appointed time to take stock and adopt any necessary change in the domestic policy.

In assuming or accepting the assumption that there is need of some reconstruction, it is supposed that the system of use and wont under which the community now lives and does its work is not altogether suited to current circumstances, it is more or less out of date. This also carries the further assumption that the evil to be remedied is of a systematic character, and that merely palliative measures will no longer serve. This involves the proposition that some realignment of the working parts is necessary even at the cost of deranging any vested rights and interests that may stand in the way. That is what reconstruction means—it is a revision of vested rights, for the common good. What is to be avoided at all costs is the *status quo ante.*

[1] From an address delivered before the Institute of Social Sciences, and reprinted from *The New Republic,* Vol. XIV, April 13, 1918.

An illustrative case may serve to show what is intended by the phrase "vested rights," in the more comprehensive sense. In modern industry as conducted by the methods of big business, it is one of the vested rights of the owner or employer freely to engage workmen on any terms on which they can be got, and to discharge them at discretion. It is another of his vested rights freely to employ as many or as few men as may suit his purpose, which is a quest of profits, and to work his own industrial plant more or less nearly up to its capacity, or not at all, as may suit his own purpose, in his quest of profits. On the other hand, among the vested rights of the workmen, or at least claimed as such, is their right to a job; so also an alleged right to discriminate as to what other men are to be associated with them on the job; also a right to quit work when they choose, i.e., to strike at discretion.

But taken in the large and seen from the point of view of the interest of the community, these vested rights of the two parties in controversy will figure up to something that may be called a right to exercise an unlimited sabotage, in order to gain a private end, regardless of the community's urgent need of having the work go on without interruption and at full capacity. The slowing down or stoppage of the industrial process at any point or on any plea by those who control the equipment or the personnel of industry works mischief to the community by that much, and falls short of that service which the community has a right to expect.

In such a case, it is evident, the vested interests so working at cross purposes are thereby cheating the community of the full benefit of the modern state of the industrial arts; and it is plain that such a case of interests working at cross purposes is a fit subject of revision. It should also be plain that the revision must be made primarily with a view to set up a condition of things that shall bring as much as may be of usefulness and content, and with only a secondary regard to the present vested interests of any one of the persons concerned.

This case of conflict between employer and employees, between the owner of plant and the owner of workmanlike skill and power, may serve to show what is here intended by incompatible or mismated vested interests. It is not here intended to find fault with either party to such a conflict. It is unreservedly assumed that they are all honorable men and all within their rights, as these rights have been allowed to stand hitherto. It is because the existing arrangement, quite legitimately and dispassionately, works out in a running campaign of sabotage, that the whole matter is to come up for a revision and realignment in which vested interests are to be set aside, under a higher necessity than the received specifications of use and wont and law. It is not that the conduct of the persons concerned is to be adjudged immoral, illegitimate, or improper; it is only that it, and the kind and degree of discretion which it involves, have in the course of time become insufferable, and are to be disallowed on the ground of urgent expediency.

The points and passages in the conduct of industrial affairs at which vested interests work at cross purposes among themselves or at cross purposes with the common good, are many and various, and it could serve no purpose to attempt an enumeration of them here. There are few lines of industry or trade where nothing of the sort occurs. The inefficiency of current railway enterprise, e.g., as seen from the point of view of material usefulness, has forced itself on the attention of the Administration under pressure of the war situation; so have the privately owned production and distribution of coal and the handling and distribution of food products. Shipping is coming under the same charge of costly incompetency, and the oil, steel, copper, and timber supply are only less obviously getting into the same general category of public utilities legitimately mishandled for private gain.

But to enumerate instances of such cross purposes between vested interests and the common good would scarcely be fruitful of anything but irritation. It may be more to the purpose to indicate what are the characteristics of the modern industries by virtue of which their businesslike management comes to work at cross purposes with the needs of the community or of a given class in the community; and then to look for something like a systematic remedial treatment, which might hopefully be turned to account—in case some person or persons endowed with insight and convictions were also charged with power to act.

It is believed that this working at cross purposes, commonly and in a way necessarily, though not always, rises to disquieting proportions when and in so far as the industrial process concerned has taken on such a character of routine, automatic articulation, or mechanical correlation, as to admit of its being controlled from a distance by such means of accountancy as are at the disposal of a modern business office. In many, perhaps in most, cases this will imply an industrial plant of some appreciable size, with a correspondingly large force of employees; but much the same outcome may also be had where that is not the case, as, e.g., an enterprise in automatic vending machines, a "news company," so-called, or a baggage-transfer concern of the larger sort.

The mischief which such a situation gives rise to may

be either or both of two distinguishable kinds: (1) disagreement and ill-will between employers and employees; and (2) mischievous waste, expense, and disservice imposed on the concern's customers. Not unusually the large and formidable concerns classed as big business will be found censurable on both counts. Again it is necessary to recall that this is not intended as implying that such management is blameworthy, but only that a businesslike management under such circumstances, and within its prescriptive rights, results in the untoward consequences here spoken of.

If this account of the state of things out of which mischief of this character is wont to rise is substantially correct, the description of the circumstances carries its own suggestion as to what should be a promising line of remedial measures. The mischief appears to arise out of, or in concomitance with, the disjunction of ownership and discretion from the personal direction of the work; and it appears to take on an added degree of mischance as soon as the discretionary control vested in ownership comes to be exercised by an employer who has no personal contact with the employees, processes employed, or with the persons whose needs these processes are presumed to serve—that is to say, so soon as the man or staff in control passes into the class of supernumeraries, in respect of the mechanical work to be done, and retains only a pecuniary interest, and exercises only a pecuniary control.

Under these circumstances, this central or superior control can evidently as well be exercised by some person who has no pecuniary interest in the enterprise; and who is therefore free to manage the industry with a view to its fullest usefulness and to the least practicable generation of ill-will on the side of the employees. Roughly speaking, any industrial process which can, and in so far as it can, be sufficiently well managed from a more or less remote office by methods of accountancy and for financial ends, can also, by the same token, be managed by a disinterested administrative officer without any other than formal recourse to accountancy and without other than a secondary view to pecuniary results.

All of which patently goes to sum up the needs of remedial measures, under two heads: (1) Disallowance of anything like free discretionary control or management on grounds of ownership alone, whether at first hand or delegated, whenever the responsible owner of the concern does not at the same time also personally oversee and physically direct the work in which his property is engaged, and in so far as he is not habitually engaged in the work in fellowship with his employees; (2) To take over and administer as a public utility any going concern that is in control of industrial or commercial work which has reached such a state of routine, mechanical systematisation, or automatic articulation that it is possible for it to be habitually managed from an office by methods of accountancy.

Needless to say that, when set out in this bald fashion, such a proposed line of remedial measures will appear to be shockingly subversive of law and order—iniquitous, impracticable, perhaps socialistic. And it is needless to argue its merits as it stands; particularly not to argue its merits within the equities of the existing law and order. Yet it may be as well to recall that any plan of reconstruction which shall hope to be of any slightest use for its main purpose, must begin by violating one or another of the equities of the existing law and order. A reconstruction means a revision of the present working system, the present system of vested interests, and of the scheme of equities within which that system is now working at cross purposes with the common good. It is a question of how and how far a disallowance of these existing vested interests is to be carried out. And the two propositions set out above are, therefore, intended to mark the direction which such a remedial disallowance of prescriptive rights will obviously take; not the limit to which such a move will necessarily go.

There is no socialistic iconoclasm in it all, either covert or overt; nor need any slightest animus of moral esteem or disesteem be injected into the argument at any point. It is a simple matter of material expediency, in which one of the prime factors to be considered is the growing prospect of an inordinary popular distrust. And the point of it all is that the present system of managing the country's larger industrial concerns by business methods in behalf of vested interests is proving itself bankrupt under the strain of the war situation; so much so that it is already more than doubtful if the community at large will hereafter be content to leave its larger material interests at the mercy of those business motives, business methods, and business men whose management is now shown to work such waste and confusion as cannot be tolerated at a critical time. The system of vested rights and interests is up for revision, reconstruction, realignment, with a view to the material good and the continued tranquillity of the community at large; and there is therefore a call for a workable scope and method of reconstructing the existing scheme of law and order on such lines as will insure popular content. In this bearing, the meaning of "Reconstruction" is that America is to be made safe for the common man—in his own apprehension as well as in substantial fact. Current events in Russia, for instance, attest that it is a grave mistake to let a growing disparity between vested rights and the current conditions of life over-pass the limit of tolerance.

# BOLSHEVISM IS A MENACE—TO WHOM?[1]

WHEN taken at its face value and translated into its nearest English equivalent "bolshevism" means "majority rule." Another equivalent would be "popular government," and still another, "democracy"—although the latter two terms are not so close a translation as the former, particularly not as "democracy" is understood in America.

In American usage "democracy" denotes a particular form of political organisation, without reference to the underlying economic organisation; whereas "bolshevism" has primarily no political signification, being a form of economic organisation, with incidental consequences—mostly negative—in the field of politics.

But in the case of any word that gets tangled up in controversial argument and so becomes a storm-center of ugly sentiments, its etymology is no safe guide to the meaning which the word has in the mind of those who shout it abroad in the heat of applause or of denunciation.

By immediate derivation, as it is now used to designate that revolutionary faction which rules the main remnants of the Russian empire, "Bolsheviki" signifies that particular wing of the Russian Socialists which was in a majority on a test vote at a congress of the Russian Social-Democratic Party in 1903; since which time the name has attached to that particular faction. It happens that the wing of the Social-Democratic Party which so

[1] Reprinted from *The Dial,* Vol. LXVI, February 22, 1919.

came in for this name at that time was the left wing, the out-and-outers of the Socialist profession. And these are they to whom it has fallen today to carry the burden of humanity's dearest hopes or fears, according as one may be inclined to see it. Beyond the Russian frontiers the name has been carried over to designate the out-and-outers elsewhere, wherever they offer to break bounds and set aside the underlying principles of the established order, economic and political.

Bolshevism is a menace. No thoughtful person today is free to doubt that, whether he takes sides for or against—according as his past habituation and his present circumstances may dictate. Indeed it would even be the same for any reasonably intelligent person who might conceivably be standing footloose in the middle, as a disinterested bystander possessed of that amiably ineffectual gift, a perfectly balanced mind. He would still have to admit the fact that Bolshevism is a menace. Only that, in the absence of partisan heat, he would also be faced with the question : A menace to whom?

Bolshevism is revolutionary. It aims to carry democracy and majority rule over into the domain of industry. Therefore it is a menace to the established order and to those persons whose fortunes are bound up with the established order. It is charged with being a menace to private property, to business, to industry, to state and church, to law and morals, to the world's peace, to civilisation, and to mankind at large. And it might prove sufficiently difficult for any person with a balanced mind to clear the Bolshevist movement of any one or all of these charges.

In point of its theoretical aims and its professions, as regards its underlying principles of equity and reconstruction, this movement can presumably make out about as good and wholesome a case as any other revolutionary movement. But in point of practical fact, as regards the effectual working-out of its aims and policies under existing conditions, the evidence which has yet come to hand, it must be admitted, is evidence of a trail of strife, privation, and bloodshed, more or less broad but in any case plain to be seen.

No doubt the available evidence of this working-out of Bolshevism in the Russian lands is to be taken with a much larger allowance than anything that could be called "a grain of salt"; no doubt much of it is biased testimony, and no doubt much of the rest is maliciously false. But when all is said in abatement, there still remains the trail of disorder, strife, privation, and bloodshed, plain to be seen. How much of all this disastrous run of horror and distress is to be set down to the account of Bolshevism, simply in its own right, and how much to the tactics of the old order and its defenders, or how the burden of blame is fairly to be shared between them—all that is not so plain.

Bolshevism is a revolutionary movement, and as such it has necessarily met with forcible opposition, and in the nature of things it is bound to meet opposition, more or less stubborn and with more or less unhappy consequences. Any subversive project such as Bolshevism can be carried through only by overcoming resistance, which means an appeal to force.

The Russian democratic revolution of the spring of 1917 was a political and military revolution which involved a number of economic readjustments. The merits of that move are not in question here. In the present connection it is chiefly significant as having prepared the ground for the later revolution—of November 1917 —out of which the rule of the Soviets and the Bolshevik dictatorship have grown. This latter is an economic revolution in intention and in its main effect, although it involves also certain political undertakings and adjustments. Its political and military undertakings and policies are, at least in theory, wholly provisional and subsidiary to its economic program. Any slight attention to the Declaration of Rights and the provisions of the Constitution, promulgated by the All-Russian Convention of Soviets last July, will make that clear. The political and military measures decided on have been taken with a view singly to carrying out a policy of economic changes. This economic policy is frankly subversive of the existing system of property rights and business enterprise, including, at least provisionally, repudiation of the Russian imperial obligations incurred by the Czar's Government.

These documents of the Soviet Republic, together with later action taken in pursuance of the policies there outlined, give a summary answer to the question: A menace to whom? The documents in the case draw an unambiguous line of division between the vested interests and the common man; and the Bolshevist program foots up to a simple and comprehensive disallowance of all vested rights. That is substantially all that is aimed at; but the sequel of that high resolve, as it is now running its course, goes to say that that much is also more than a sufficient beginning of trouble. In its first intention, and in the pursuit of its own aim, therefore, in so far as this pursuit has not been hindered by interested parties, this Bolshevism is a menace to the vested interests, and to nothing and no one else.

All of which is putting as favorable a construction on the professions and conduct of the Bolsheviki as may be; and it is all to be taken as a description of the main purpose of the movement, not as an account of the past year's turmoil in Bolshevist Russia. But it is as well to keep in mind that the original substance and cause of this Bolshevist trouble is a cleavage and antagonism between the vested interests and the common man, and that the whole quarrel turns finally about the vested rights of property and privilege. The moderate liberals, such as the Cadets, and in its degree the Kerensky administration, are made up of those persons who are ready to disallow the vested rights of privilege, but who will not consent to the disallowance of the vested rights of ownership.

And it is at this point that the European powers come into the case. These democratic or quasi-democratic powers and their democratic or pseudo-democratic statesmen are not so greatly concerned, though regretful, about the disallowance of class privileges and perquisites in Russia. Of course, it is disquieting enough, and the European statesmen of the *status quo ante,* to whom European affairs have been entrusted, will necessarily look with some distaste and suspicion on the discontinuance of class privilege and class rule in the dominions of the late Czar; all that sort of thing is disquieting to the system of vested rights within which these European statesmen live and move. But privilege simply as such is after all in the nature of an imponderable, and it may well be expedient to concede the loss of that much intangible assets with a good grace, lest a worse evil befall. But it is not so with the vested rights of ownership. These are of the essence of that same quasi-democratic *status quo* about the preservation of which these elder statesmen are concerned. "Discontinuance of the rights of ownership" is equivalent to "the day of judgment" for the régime of the elder statesmen and for the

interests which they have at heart. These interests which
the elder statesmen have at heart are primarily the interests of trade, investment, and national integrity, and
beyond that the ordered system of law and custom and
businesslike prosperity which runs on under the shadow
of these interests of trade, investment, and national integrity. And these elder statesmen, being honorable gentlemen, and as such being faithful to their bread, see
plainly that Russian Bolshevism is a menace to all the
best interests of mankind.

So there prevails among the astute keepers of law
and order in other lands an uneasy statesmanlike dread
of "Bolshevist infection," which it is considered will
surely follow on any contact or communication across
the Russian frontiers. There is a singular unanimity of
apprehension on this matter of "Bolshevist infection"
among the votaries of law and order. Precautionary
measures of isolation are therefore devised—something
like quarantine to guard against the infection. It should
be noted that this statesmanlike fear of Bolshevist infection is always a fear that the common man in these
other countries may become infected. The elder statesmen have no serious apprehension that the statesmen
themselves are likely to be infected with Bolshevism,
even by fairly reckless exposure, or that the military
class, or the clergy, or the landlords, or the business men
at large are liable to such infection. Indeed it is assumed
as a matter of course that the vested interests and the
kept classes are immune, and it will be admitted that the
assumption is reasonable. The measures of quarantine
are, accordingly, always designed to safeguard those
classes in the community who have no vested rights to
lose.

It is always as a system of ideas, or "principles," that

Bolshevism spreads by communication; it is a contamination of ideas, of habits of thought. And it owes much of its insidious success to the fact that this new order of ideas which it proposes is extremely simple and is in the main of a negative character. The Bolshevist scheme of ideas comes easy to the common man because it does not require him to learn much that is new, but mainly to unlearn much that is old. It does not propose the adoption of a new range of preconceptions, so that it calls for little in the way of acquiring new habits of thought. In the main it is an emancipation from older preconceptions, older habitual convictions. And the proposed new order of ideas will displace the older preconceptions all the more easily because these older habitual convictions that are due to be displaced no longer have the support of those material circumstances which now condition the life of the common man, and which will therefore make the outcome by bending his habits of thought.

The training given by the mechanical industries and strengthened by the experience of daily life in a mechanically organised community lends no support to prescriptive rights of ownership, class perquisites, and free income. This training bends the mental attitude of the common man at cross purposes with the established system of rights, and makes it easy for him to deny their validity so soon as there is sufficient provocation. And it is scarcely necessary for him to find a substitute for these principles of vested right that so fall away from him.

It is true, these prescriptive rights, about whose maintenance and repair the whole quarrel swings and centers, do have the consistent support of those habits of thought that are engendered by experience in business traffic; and business traffic is a very large and consequential part of life as it runs in these civilised countries. But business traffic is not the tone-giving factor in the life of the common man, nor are business interests his interests in so obvious a fashion as greatly to affect his habitual outlook. Under the new order of things there is, in effect, a widening gulf fixed between the business traffic and those industrial occupations that shape the habits of thought of the common man. The business community, who are engaged in this business traffic and whose habitual attention centers on the rights of ownership and income, are consistent votaries of the old order, as their training and interest would dictate. And these are also immune against any subversive propaganda, however insidious, as has already been remarked above. Indeed, it is out of this division of classes in respect of their habitual outlook and of their material interests that the whole difficulty arises, and it is by force of this division that this subversive propaganda becomes a menace. Both parties are acting on conviction, and there is, therefore, no middle ground for them to meet on. "Thrice is he armed who knows his quarrel just"; and in this case both parties to the quarrel are convinced of the justice of their own cause, at the same time that the material fortunes of both are at stake. Hence an unreserved recourse to force, with all its consequences.

By first intention and by consistent aim Bolshevism is a menace to the vested rights of property and of privilege, and from this the rest follows. The vested interests are within their legal and moral rights, and it is not to be expected that they will yield these rights amicably. All those classes, factions, and interests that stand to lose have made common cause against the out-and-outers, have employed armed force where that has been practicable, and have resorted to such measures of intrigue and sabotage as they can command. All of which is quite reasonable, in a way, since these vested interests are legally and morally in the right according to the best of their knowledge and belief; but the consequence of their righteous opposition, intrigue, and obstruction has been strife, disorder, privation, and bloodshed, with a doubtful and evil prospect ahead.

Among the immediate consequences of this quarrel, according to the reports which have been allowed to come through to the outside, is alleged to be a total disorganisation and collapse of the industrial system throughout the Russian dominions, including the transportation system and the food supply. From which has followed famine, pestilence, and pillage, uncontrolled and uncontrollable. However, there are certain outstanding facts which it will be in place to recall, in part because they are habitually overlooked or not habitually drawn on for correction of the published reports. The Bolshevist administration has now been running for something over a year, which will include one crop season. During this time it has been gaining ground, particularly during the later months of this period; and this gain has been made in spite of a very considerable resistance, active and passive, more or less competently organised and more or less adequately supported from the outside. Meantime the "infection" is spreading in a way that does not signify a lost cause.

All the while the administration has been carrying on military operations on a more or less extended scale; and on the whole, and particularly through the latter part of this period, its military operations appear to have been gaining in magnitude and to have met with increasing success, such as would argue a more or less adequate continued supply of arms and munitions. These military operations have been carried on without substantial supplies from the outside, so that the administration will have had to supply its warlike needs and replace its wear and tear from within the country during this rather costly period. It has been said from time to time, of course, that the Bolshevist administration has drawn heavily on German support for funds and material supplies during this period. It has been said, but it is very doubtful if it has been believed. Quite notoriously the Bolsheviki have lost more than they have gained at the hands of the Germans. And imports of all warlike supplies from any source have been very nearly shut off.

Such information as has been coming through from the inside, in the way of official reports, runs to the effect that the needed supplies of war material, including arms and ammunition, have in the main been provided at home from stocks on hand and by taking over various industrial works and operating them for war purposes under administrative control—which would argue that the industrial collapse and disorganisation cannot have been so complete or so far-reaching as had been feared, or hoped. Indeed these reports are singularly out of touch and out of sympathy with the Associated Press news bearing on the same general topic. It appears, dimly, from the circumstantial evidence that the Bolshevist administration in Russia has met with somewhat the same surprising experience as the Democratic administration in America—that in spite of the haste, confusion, and blundering, incident to taking over the control of industrial works, the same works have after all proved to run at a higher efficiency under administrative management than they previously have habitually done when managed by their owners for private gain. The point is in doubt, it must be admitted, but the circumstantial evidence, backed by the official reports, appears on the whole to go that way.

Something to a similar effect will apparently hold true for the transportation system. The administration has apparently been able to take over more of the means of transport than the Associated Press news would indicate, and to have kept it all in a more nearly reasonable state of repair. As is well known, the conduct of successful military operations today quite imperatively requires a competent transport system; and, in spite of many reverses, it is apparently necessary to admit that the military operations of the Bolshevist administration have on the whole been successful rather than the reverse. The inference is plain, so far as concerns the point immediately in question here. Doubtless the Russian transportation system is in sufficiently bad shape, but it can scarcely be in so complete a state of collapse as had been reported, feared, and hoped by those who go on the information given out by the standard news agencies. If one discounts the selectively standardised news dispatches of these agencies, one is left with an impression that the railway system, for example, is better furnished with rolling-stock and in better repair in European Russia than in Siberia, where the Bolshevist administration is not in control. This may be due in good part to the fact that the working personnel of the railways and their repair shops are Bolsheviki at heart, both in Siberia and in European Russia, and that they have therefore withdrawn from the train service and repair shops of the Siberian roads as fast as these roads have fallen into non-Bolshevist hands, and have migrated into Russia to take up the same work among their own friends.

The transportation system does not appear to have precisely broken down; the continuance of military operations goes to show that much. Also, the crop year of 1918 is known to have been rather exceptionally good in European Russia, on the whole, so that there will be at least a scant sufficiency of foodstuff back in the country and available for those portions of the population who can get at it. Also, it will be noted that, by all accounts, the civilian population of the cities has fallen off to a fraction of its ordinary number, by way of escape to the open country or to foreign parts. Those classes who were fit to get a living elsewhere have apparently escaped. In the absence of reliable information one would, on this showing, be inclined to say that the remaining civilian population of the cities will be made up chiefly, perhaps almost wholly, of such elements of the so-called middle classes as could not get away or had nowhere to go with any prospect of bettering their lot. These will for the most part have been trades people and their specialised employees, persons who are of slight use in any productive industry and stand a small chance of gaining a livelihood by actually necessary work. They belong to the class of smaller "middle-men," who are in great part superfluous in any case, and whose business traffic has been virtually discontinued by the Bolshevist administration. These displaced small business men of the Russian cities are as useless and as helpless under the Bolshevist régime as nine-tenths of the population of the American country towns in the prairie states would be if the retail trade of the prairie states were reorganised in such a way as to do away with all useless duplication. The difference is that the Bolshevist administration of Russia has discontinued much of the superfluous retail trade, whereas the democratic administration of America takes pains to safeguard the reasonable profits of its superfluous retailers. Bolshevism is a menace to the retail trade and to the retailers.

Accordingly it is to be noted that, when details and concrete instances of extreme hardship in the cities are given, they will commonly turn out to be hardships which have fallen on some member or class of what the Socialists call the Bourgeoisie, the middle class, the business community, the kept classes—more commonly than anything of lower social value or nearer to the soil. Those that belong nearer to the soil appear largely to have escaped from the cities and returned to the soil. Now, on a cold and harsh appraisal such as the Germans have made familiar to civilised people under the name of "military necessity," these "bourgeois" are in part to be considered useless and in part mischievous for all purposes of Bolshevism. Under the Bolshevist régime they are "undesirable citizens," who consume without producing and who may be counted on to intrigue against the administration and obstruct its operation whenever a chance offers. From which it follows, on a cold and harsh calculation of "military necessity," that whether the necessary supplies are to be had in the country or not, and whether the transportation system is capable of handling the necessary supplies or not, it might still appear the part of wisdom, or of Bolshevist expediency, to leave this prevailingly bourgeois and disaffected civilian population of the cities without the necessaries of life. The result would be famine, of course, together with the things that go with famine; but the Bolsheviki would be in a position to say that they are applying famine selectively, as a measure of defense against their enemies within the frontiers, very much as the nations of the Entente once were in a position to argue that the exclusion of foodstuffs from Germany during the war was a weapon employed against the enemies of the world's peace.

These considerations are, unhappily, very loose and general. They amount to little better than cautious speculations on the general drift and upshot of things. On the evidence which has yet come to hand and which is in any degree reliable it would be altogether hazardous, just yet, to attempt an analysis of events in detail. But it is at least plain that Bolshevism is a menace to the vested interests, at home and abroad. So long as its vagaries run their course within the Russian dominions it is primarily and immediately a menace to the vested rights of the landowners, the banking establishments, the industrial corporations, and not least to the retail traders in the Russian towns. The last named are perhaps the hardest hit, because they have relatively little to lose and that little is their all. The greater sympathy is, doubtless properly, according to the accepted scheme of social values, given to the suffering members of the privileged classes, the kept classes *par excellence,* but the larger and more acute hardship doubtless falls to the share of the smaller trades-people. These, of course, are all to be classified with the vested interests. But the common man also comes in for his portion. He finally bears the cost of it all, and its cost runs finally in terms of privation and blood.

But it menaces also certain vested interests outside of Russia, particularly the vested rights of investors in Russian industries and natural resources, as well as of concerns which have an interest in the Russian import and export trade. So also the vested rights of investors in Russian securities. Among the latter claimants are now certain governments lately associated with Russia in the conduct of the war, and more particularly the holders of Russian imperial bonds. Of the latter many are French citizens, it is said; and it has been remarked that the French statesmen realise the menace of Bolshevism perhaps even more acutely than the common run of those elder statesmen who are now deliberating on the state of mankind at large and the state of Russian Bolshevism in particular.

But the menace of Bolshevism extends also to the common man in those other countries whose vested interests have claims on Russian income and resources. These vested rights of these claimants in foreign parts are good and valid in law and morals, and therefore by settled usage it is the duty of these foreign governments to enforce these vested rights of their several citizens who have a claim on Russian income and resources; indeed it is the duty of these governments, to which they are in honor bound and to which they are addicted by habit, to enforce these vested claims to Russian income and resources by force of arms if necessary. And it is well known, and also it is right and good by law and custom, that when recourse is had to arms the common man pays the cost. He pays it in lost labor, anxiety, privation, blood, and wounds; and by way of returns he comes in for an increase of just national pride in the fact that the vested interests which find shelter under the same national establishment with himself are duly preserved from loss on their Russian investments. So that, by a "roundabout process of production," Bolshevism is also a menace to the common man.

How it stands with the menace of Bolshevism in the event of its infection reaching any other of the civilized countries—as, for example, America or France—that is a sufficiently perplexing problem to which the substantial citizens and the statesmen to whose keeping the fortunes of the substantial citizens are entrusted, have already begun to give their best attention. They are substantially of one mind, and all are sound on the main fact, that Bolshevism is a menace; and now and again they will specify that it is a menace to property and business. And with that contention there can be no quarrel. How it stands, beyond that and at the end of the argument, with the eventual bearing of Bolshevism on the common man and his fortunes, is less clear and is a less immediate object of solicitude. On scant reflection it should seem that, since the common man has substantially no vested rights to lose, he should come off indifferently well in such an event. But such a hasty view overlooks the great lesson of history that, when anything goes askew in the national economy, or anything is to be set to rights, the common man eventually pays the cost and he pays it eventually in lost labor, anxiety, privation, blood, and wounds. The Bolshevik is the common man who has faced the question: What do I stand to lose? and has come away with the answer: Nothing. And the elder statesmen are busy with arrangements for disappointing that indifferent hope.

# PEACE [1]

INTEMPERATE criticism has diligently sought to find fault with the Covenant which has been devised and underwritten by the deputies of the great powers. The criticism has been animated and voluble, but it has been singularly futile on the whole. At the same time the spokesmen of this Covenant show a singular lack of assurance; they speak in a tone of doubtful hope rather than enthusiastic conviction. And the statesmen who set up this Covenant do so with such an engaging air of modesty and furtive apprehension as should engender a spirit of goodwill and fellowship in the presentation of a doubtfully hopeful enterprise, rather than obstructive tactics and intemperate criticism. They are saying, in effect : We have done the best we could under the circumstances. It is a great pity that we have been able to do no better. Let us hope for the best, and God help us all!

The best must always be good enough, and the Covenant is the best that the political wisdom of the three continents has been able to find in a five months' search for ways and means of avoiding war. But this best will always have the defects of its qualities. And such defects as still attach to the Covenant will best be understood, and may therefore best be condoned and allowed for, when seen in the light of its qualities. Now, as for its qualities, the Covenant is a political document, an instrument of *Realpolitik,* created in the image of nineteenth-century imperialism. It has been set up by political states-

[1] Reprinted from *The Dial,* Vol. LXVI, May 17, 1919.

men, on political grounds, for political ends, and with political apparatus to be used with political effect. It brings to a focus the best and highest traditions of commercialised nationalism, but also it brings nothing else. The outcome is a political covenant which even its friends and advocates view with an acute sense of its inability, perhaps rather a sense of its total vacuity.

Its defect is not that the Covenant falls short, but rather that it is quite beside the point. The point is the avoidance of war, at all costs; the war arose unavoidably out of the political *status quo;* the Covenant re-establishes the *status quo,* with some additional political apparatus supplied from the same shop. True to the political tradition, the Covenant provides for enforcing the peace by recourse to arms and commercial hostilities, but it contemplates no measures for avoiding war by avoiding the *status quo* out of which the great war arose. The *status quo* was a status of commercialised nationalism. The traditions which bind them will not permit anything beyond these political ends, ways, and means of commercialised nationalism to come within the cognisance of the competence of these elder statesmen who have had this work to do. So there is no help for it.

But the Covenant is after all the best that was reasonably to be looked for. It embodies the best and highest traditions of nineteenth-century statesmanship. That it does so, that it is conceived in the spirit of Mid-Victorian liberalism rather than in the spirit of Mid-European imperialism, is to be set down to the account of America and America's President. But that it remains standing as a left-over on that outworn ground, instead of coming up abreast of the twentieth century, is also to be credited to the same power. It is in an eminent sense America's Covenant, made and provided by the paramount advice and consent of America's President. And this paramount advice and consent has gone to the making of the Covenant in the simple faith that commercialised nationalism answereth all things. The unfortunate, and unfortunately decisive, circumstance of the case is, therefore, that the President's outlook and ideals are in this way grounded in the political traditions of Mid-Victorian liberalism, and that his advisers have been animated with political traditions of a still narrower and more antiquated make. Hence the difficulties which arise out of a new industrial situation and a consequent new bias of the popular temper are sought to be adjusted by readjusting the political *status quo ante*.

Now, it should be plain to any one on slight reflection that this Covenant has been forced upon the politicians by the present state of the industrial system. The great war has run its course within the confines of this industrial system, and it has become evident that no nation is competent henceforth single-handed to take care of its own case within this system, in which all the civilised peoples are bound up together. And it should be similarly plain, on similarly slight reflection, that no readjustment of working arrangements among the peoples concerned can hope to touch the core of the difficulties unless its scope is the same as that of the industrial system and unless it is carried out with a single-handed regard to the industrial requirements of the case, and coupled with a thoroughgoing disallowance of those political and nationalist precedents and ambitions that hinder the free working of this industrial system.

The interval since Mid-Victorian time has been a period of unexampled change in the industrial arts and in the working arrangements necessary to industrial production. The productive industry of all the civilised peoples has been drawn together by the continued advance of the industrial arts into a single comprehensive, close-knit system, a network of mechanically balanced give and take, such that no nation and no community can now carry on its own industrial affairs in severalty or at cross purposes with the rest except at the cost of a disproportionate derangement and hardship to itself and to all the rest. All this is simple and obvious to those who are at all familiar with the technical requirements of production. To all such it is well known that for the purposes of productive industry, and therefore for the purposes of popular welfare and content, national divisions are nothing better than haphazard divisions of an indivisible whole, arbitrary and obstructive. And because of this state of things, any regulation or diversion of trade or industry within any one of these national units is of graver consequence to all the others than to itself. Yet the Covenant contemplates no abatement of that obstructive nationalist intrigue that makes the practical substance of the "self-determination of nations."

At the same time, that which chiefly hampers the everyday work of industrial production and chiefly tries the popular temper under this new order of things is the increasingly obstructive and increasingly irresponsible control of production by the vested interests of commerce and finance, seeking each their own profit at the cost of the underlying population. Yet the Covenant contemplates no abatement of these vested interests that are fast approaching the limit of popular tolerance; for the Covenant is a political instrument, made and provided for the rehabilitation of Mid-Victorian political intrigue and for the upkeep of the vested interests of commerce and finance. The cry of the common man has been: What shall we do to be saved from war abroad and dissension at home? And the answer given in the Covenant is the good old answer of the elder statesmen of the Old Order—provision of armed force sufficient to curb any uneasy drift of sentiment among the underlying populace, with the due advice and consent of the dictatorship established by the elder statesmen.

Now, the great war was precipitated by the malign growth of just such a commercialised nationalism within this industrial system, and was fought to a successful issue as a struggle of industrial forces and with the purpose of establishing an enduring peace of industrial prosperity and content; at least so they say. It should accordingly have seemed reasonable to entrust the settlement to those men who know something about the working and requirements of this industrial system on which the welfare of mankind finally turns. To any man whose perspective is not confined within the Mid-Victorian political traditions, it would seem that the first move toward an enduring peace would be abatement of the vested interests and national pretensions wherever they touch the conduct of industry; and the men to do this work should logically be those who know the needs of the industrial system and are not biased by commercial incentives. An enduring settlement should be entrusted to reasonably unbiased production engineers, rather than to the awestruck political lieutenants of the vested interests. These men, technical specialists, over-workmen, skilled foremen of the system, are expert in the ways and means of industry and know something of the material conditions of life that surround the common man, at the same time that they are familiar with the available resources and the uses to which they are to be turned. Of necessity in war and peace, it is for these workmen of the top line to take care of the industrial system and its working, so far as the obstructive tactics of the vested interests and the commercial statesmen will permit; for without their constant supervision and correction this highly technical system of production will not work at all. Logically it should be for these and their like to frame such a settlement as will bind the civilised peoples together on an amicable footing as a going concern, engaged on a joint industrial enterprise. However, it is not worth while to speculate on what they and their like might propose, since neither they nor their counsels have had any part in the Covenant. The Covenant is a covenant of commercialised nationalism, without afterthought.

To return to the facts: The great war was fought out and peace was brought within sight by teamwork of the soldiers and workmen and the political personnel. The cost, the work, and hardship fell on the soldiers and workmen, and it is also chiefly their fortune that is now in the balance. The political personnel have lost nothing, risked nothing, and have nothing at stake on the chance of further war or peace. But in these deliberations on peace the political personnel alone have had a voice. Neither those who have done the necessary fighting at the front nor those who have done the necessary work at home have had any part in it all. The conference has been a conclave made up of the spokesmen of commercialised nationalism, in effect a conclave of the political lieutenants of the vested interests. In short, there have been no Soldiers' and Workmen's Deputies included in this Soviet of the Elder Statesmen which has conferred the dictatorship on the political deputies of the vested interests. By and large, neither the wishes nor the welfare of the soldiers, the workmen, or the industrial system as a going concern have visibly been consulted in the drafting of this Covenant. However, to avoid all appearance of graceless over-statement, it should perhaps be noted in qualification that the American workmen may be alleged to have been represented at this court of elder statesmen, informally, unofficially, and irresponsibly, by the sexton beadle of the A. F. of L., but it will be admitted that this qualification makes no serious inroad on the broader statement above.

Neither the value nor the cost of this Covenant are fairly to be appreciated apart from its background and the purposes and interests which are moving in the background. As it now looms up against this murky background of covert agreements covertly arrived at during the past mónths, the Covenant is beginning to look like a last desperate concert of crepuscular statesmanship for the preservation of the civilised world's kept classes and vested interests in the face of a menacing situation. Therefore, in case the Covenant should yet prove to be so lasting and serve this turn so well as materially to deflect the course of events, what is likely to be of material consequence to the fortunes of mankind is chiefly the outcome of this furtive traffic in other men's good between the deputies of the great powers, which underlies and conditions the stilted formalities of the instrument itself. Little is known, and perhaps less is intended to be known, of this furtive traffic in other men's goods. Hitherto the "High Contracting Parties" have been at pains to give out no "information which might be useful to the enemy."

What and how many covert agreements have been covertly arrived at during these four or five months of diplomatic twilight will not be known for some time yet. A decent cover still hides what may be hidden, which is presumably just as well. And yet, even if one had best not see him face to face, one may still infer something as to the nature of the beast from the shape of his hoof. A little something in that way is coming in sight now in the shameful transaction by which the politicians and vested interests of Japan are given a burglarious free hand in northern China; and it would be both graceless and idle to speculate on what may be the grand total of gruesome enormities which the Oriental statesmen will have undertaken to perpetrate or overlook, for the benefit of the vested interests identified with the European powers, in consideration of that *carte blanche* of indecency. So also is the arrangement between the great powers for the suppression of Soviet Russia, for the profit of the vested interests identified with these Powers and at the cost of the underlying population; the due parceling out of concessions and natural resources in foreign parts, incident to that convention of smuggled warfare, will doubtless have consumed a formidable total of time, ingenuity, and effrontery. But the Covenant being an instrument of commercialised nationalism, all these things have had to be seen to.

# DEMENTIA PRÆCOX [1]

It is evident now, beyond cavil, that no part of Europe is better off for America's having taken part in the great war. So also it is evident that the Americans are all the worse off for it. Europe is balancing along the margin of bankruptcy, famine, and pestilence, while America has gone into moral and industrial eclipse. This state of things, in both cases, is traceable directly to America's having taken part in the war, whatever may have been the ulterior determining circumstances that brought European politics to a boil in 1914.

As regards the state of Europe, the immediate effect of American intervention was to bring the war to an inconclusive settlement; to conclude hostilities before they were finished and thereby reinstate the *status quo ante* out of which the war had arisen; to save the Junkers from conclusive defeat. There is every reason to believe that in the absence of American intervention the hostilities would have been continued until the German nation had been exhausted and the German forces had been broken and pushed back across their frontiers and across their own territory; which would have demoralised and discredited the rule of privilege and property in the Fatherland to such effect that the control of affairs would have passed out of the hands of the kept classes. The outcome should then have been an effectual liquidation of the old order and the installation of something like an industrial democracy resting on other ground

[1] Reprinted from *The Freeman*, Vol. V, June 21, 1922.

than privilege and property, instead of the camouflage of a *pro forma* liquidation in 1918–19 and the resulting pseudo-republic of the Ebert Government. Noske could not have functioned and the Junkers would not have been war-heroes. It was the apprehension of some such eventuality that brought out the Lansdowne letters, which served warning on the kept classes of the Entente and prepared the way for an inconclusive peace—a compact to preserve the elements of dissension, the vested interests and national ambitions out of which the war arose.

There can be no grounded surmise as to what might have been the ulterior fortunes of any conceivable revolutionary establishments that so might have been set up in the German lands on some other basis than vested interests and national ambition; but it may at least be confidently believed that no such foot-loose establishment or group of establishments could have constituted a warlike menace to the rest of Europe, or even a practicable war-bogy. The outcome would presumably have been a serious peaceful menace to absentee ownership and imperial politics, throughout Christendom, but assuredly not a menace of war—Germany would have ceased to be a Power, in the usual minatory sense of the term. And when Germany, with Austria, had fallen out of line as a Power, the rest of the line of Powers would be in a precarious case for want of something formidable to lean against. A practicable Power has to rest its case on a nerve-shattering popular fear of aggression from without.

The American intervention saved the life of the German Empire as a disturber of the peace, by saving the German forces from conclusive defeat, and so saving the rule of the kept classes in Germany. It will be said, of course, by vainglorious Americans and by obsequious politicians of the Entente, that America's entrance into the war decided the case against the Central Powers; which is a sufficiently idle piece of stage-bravery. So also the German war-lords cover their shame with the claim that America turned their assured victory to defeat; but the reason for that claim is the need of it. When the whole adventure is seen in perspective it is evident that the defeat of the Germans was decided at the battle of the Marne in 1914, and the rest of the conflict was a desperate fight for negotiable terms on which the German war-lords hoped to save their face at home; and America's intervention has helped them save the remnants of their face.

If Imperial Germany had dropped out of the running, as a practicable war-Power, at the same time that Imperial Russia had gone into collapse, the French Government would have had no practicable war-scare at hand with which to frighten the French people into a policy of increased armament. On the same grounds coercion and submission would have ceased to characterise the administration of their internal affairs; the existing Government of French profiteers would have lost control; and expenditures would have been covered in part by taxes on income and capital, instead of the present deficit-financiering and constantly increasing debt. France would have returned to a peace-footing. At the same time the prosecution of hostilities through the winter 1918–19 would have carried the exhaustion of French resources and the inflation of French indebtedness to such a point as to ensure a drastic and speedy liquidation of their fiscal and commercial affairs, with a recapitalisation of assets at a reasonable figure, such as to permit French trade and industry to make a new start within a reasonable time.

What has just been said of the French case will hold true for the other Continental peoples in nearly the same degree, with some allowance for local circumstances. The case of the British is not substantially different, except in degree, and except that the outcome of the war has enabled British imperialism to take on an added degree of jobbery and effrontery. The American intervention brought the war to a close before the exhaustion of resources and the inflation of capital and liabilities in Europe had reached the breaking-point, and thereby it has enabled the vested interests to keep their footing on a nominal capitalisation in excess of the earning-capacity of their assets, to maintain prices and restrict output; from which follows unemployment, privation, and industrial disorder. At the same time the inconclusive peace, with the resulting international intrigue, has enabled the politicians of the old line to retain control and continue the old line of warlike diplomacy and coercive administration—a state of things which could scarcely have come to pass except for the formidable intervention of America during the closing months of the war.

It may be said, of course, that the state of things in Europe was not brought on by the American intervention; that even if the contending Powers had been left to their own devices they might not have carried their emulation of the Kilkenny Cats through to the normal Kilkenny finish. Even if the Americans had not come in and upset the fighting-balance, the European statesmen might have seen their way to much the same sort of negotiated peace, with much the same view to renewed hostilities at a future date. Such an outcome would of course have been possible, though it would not seem probable; and in that event the Europeans would presumably have fallen into much the same evil case in which they now find themselves, under the rule of the statesmen of the kept classes. They would have been no worse off, and presumably no better.

But it still remains true that in such event the Americans would have been spared certain untoward experiences that have followed. Most of the war-debt, much of the increased armament, a good share of the profiteering incident to the war and the peace, and all of the income tax would have been avoided. It is true, American statesmen would still have continued to do the "dirty work" for American bankers in Nicaragua; they might still have seen their way to manhandle the Haitians and put the white man's burden on the black population of Liberia for the profit of American banks and politicians; it is even conceivable that they could still have backed the Polish adventures in Russia and have sent troops and supplies to the Murmansk and Siberia to annoy the horrid Bolsheviki; but there is at least a reasonable chance that, in such event, there would have arisen no "American Legion," no Ku-Klux-Klan, no Knights of Columbus, and no Lusk Commission. Presumably there would also have been relatively little of the rant and bounce of Red-Cross patriotism; no espionage act, no wholesale sentences or deportations for constructive sedition, and no prosecution of pacifists and conscientious objectors for excessive sanity. In short, there is a reasonable chance that in such event the Americans might have come through the period of the war in a reasonable state of buncombe and intolerance without breaking down into the systematised illusions of dementia præcox.

It will be said, of course, that the American intervention hastened the return of peace and thereby saved much property and very many lives of men, women, and children that would otherwise have been wasted in hostilities carried on to no effect for another four or five months; all of which is not reasonably to be questioned. But it is also not reasonably to be questioned that the past three or four years of dissension, disorder, privation, and disease that have been brought on by the precipitate conclusion of hostilities, have taken twice as heavy a toll in wasted time and substance and in wasted lives—not counting the debauch of waste and confusion which their unselfish participation in the war has brought upon the Americans.

Assuredly, none of these untoward consequences was aimed at or contemplated by the Administration when it shifted from a footing of quasi-neutrality to formal hostilities in 1917. Still less was anything of the kind contemplated in that run of popular sentiment that came to the support of the Administration in its declaration of war. So far as the case can be covered with any general formula, America entered the war "to make the world safe for democracy." It is only that, instead of what was aimed at, the untoward state of things described above has followed in the chain of consequence. The motives of the Americans in the case are not to be impugned. They were as nearly blameless as might reasonably be expected under the circumstances. It is only that the unintended and unforeseen ulterior outcome of the adventure has now, after the event, shown that America's participation in the war was a highly deplorable mistake. In so far, this unhappy turn of events has gone to vindicate the protests of the pacifists and the conscientious objectors. Their arguments may have been

unsound, and the conscientious objectors have at least
found themselves on the wrong side of the law, and their
motives may have been unworthy as often as not. There
is no call to argue the legalities or the moralities of the
case in this connection. It is only that now, after the
event, it has unhappily become evident that the course of
public policy against which they contended—perhaps
unworthily—was not the wiser course to pursue. Their
morals may have been bad and their manners worse, and
the courts have decided, with great spontaneity, that
their aim was criminal in a high degree, and popular
sentiment has borne out the sentiment of the courts
in this matter, on the whole and for the time being.
Yet the turn of events has, unhappily, gone to show
that, barring the statutory infirmities of their case,
these statutory criminals were in effect contending for
the wiser course. And for so having, in some wrong-
headed way, spoken for a wiser course of action than
that adopted by the constituted authorities, these statutory criminals have been and continue to be subjected
to cruel and unusual punishment. All of which invites
reflection on the vagaries of dementia præcox.

The current situation in America is by way of being
something of a psychiatrical clinic. In order to come to
an understanding of this situation there is doubtless
much else to be taken into account, but the case of America is after all not fairly to be understood without making due allowance for a certain prevalent unbalance and
derangement of mentality, presumably transient but sufficiently grave for the time being. Perhaps the commonest and plainest evidence of this unbalanced mentality
is to be seen in a certain fearsome and feverish credulity
with which a large proportion of the Americans are effected. As contrasted with their state of mind before the

war, they are predisposed to believe in footless outrages
and odious plots and machinations—"treasons, strata-
gems, and spoils." They are readily provoked to a headlong intolerance, and resort to unadvised atrocities as a
defense against imaginary evils. There is a visible lack
of composure and logical coherence, both in what they
will believe and in what they are ready to do about it.

Throughout recent times the advance of exact knowledge in the material sciences has been progressively sup-
planting the received barbarian beliefs in magical and
supernatural agencies. This progressive substitution of
matter-of-fact in the place of superstition has gone forward unremittingly and at a constantly accelerated rate,
being the most characteristic and most constructive factor engaged in modern civilisation. But during the past
six or eight years, since the outbreak of the war, and
even more plainly since its conclusion, the churches,
high and low, have been gaining both in numbers and in
revenues, as well as in pontifical unction. The logical
faculty appears to have suffered a notable degree of
prostration throughout the American community; and
all the while it is the more puerile crudities of superstitious fear that have been making particular and in-
ordinate gains. So, for example, it is since the outbreak
of the war that the Rev. Billy Sunday has effectively
come into his own, and it is since the peace that he has
become such a power of obscurity as to command a
price as an agency of intimidation and misrule. So also
it is during these last few years of the same period of
nervous prostration that the Fundamentalists are effectually making headway in their campaign of obscuration
designed to reinstate the Fear of God in place of common-sense. Driven by a nerve-shattering fear that some
climax of ghostly atrocities is about to be visited on all

persons who are found lacking in bigotry, this grosser sort of devout innocents now impugn certain findings of material science on the ground that these findings are presumed to be distasteful to a certain well-known anthropomorphic divinity, to whom His publicity-agents impute a sadistic temper and an unlimited power of abuse. These evidences of a dilapidated mentality are growing more and more obvious. Meantime even a man of such signal good sense and humanity as Mr. Bryan is joining forces with the Rev. Billy Sunday in the propaganda of intolerance, while the gifts of so engaging a raconteur as Sir Conan Doyle are brought in to cover the flanks of this drive into intellectual twilight.

It may be said, of course, that such-like maggoty conceits are native to the religious fancy and are due to come into the foreground in all times of trouble; but just now the same fearsome credulity is running free and large through secular affairs as well, and its working-out is no more edifying in that department of human conduct. At the date when America formally entered the war, American popular sentiment had already been exposed to a protracted stress of apprehension and perplexity and was ready for alarms and excursions into intolerance. All manner of extravagant rumors met with ready belief, and, indeed, few were able to credit anything that was not extravagant. It was a period dominated by illusions of frightfulness and persecution. It was the peculiar misfortune of the American people that they were called into action only after their mental poise had been shattered by a long run of enervating perplexity and agitation. The measures taken under these circumstances were drawn on such lines of suspicion and intolerance as might be looked for under these circumstances. Differences of opinion were erected into statutory crimes, to which extravagant penalties were attached. Persons charged with these new-found statutory crimes were then convicted on a margin of legal interpretation. In effect, suspected persons were held guilty until proved innocent, with the doubt weighing against them. In one of these episodes of statutory frightfulness, that of the far-famed "Lusk Committee," some ten thousand persons were arrested on ungrounded suspicion, with extensive destruction of papers and property. The foreign-language press was laid under disabilities and the use of the mails was interrupted on general grounds of hysterical consternation. On the same grounds circulation and credence were given to extravagantly impossible fictions of Bolshevik propaganda, and the I.W.W. were by interpretation erected into a menace to the Republic, while the Secret Service kept faithfully on the job of making two suspicions grow where one grew before. Under cover of it all the American profiteers have diligently gone about their business of getting something for nothing at the cost of all concerned, while popular attention has been taken up with the maudlin duties of civil and religious intolerance.

The Republic has come through this era of spiritual dilapidation with an unbalanced budget and an increased armament by use of which to "safeguard American Interests"—that is to say, negotiate profitable concessions for American oil companies—a system of passports, deportations, and restricted immigration, and a Legion of veterans organised for a draft on the public funds and the cultivation of warlike distemper. Unreflecting patriotic flurry has become a civic virtue. Drill in patriotic —that is to say military—ritual has been incorporated in the ordinary routine of the public schools, and it has come to be obligatory to stand uncovered through any

rendition of the "National Anthem"—a musical composition of which one could scarcely say that it might have
been worse. The State constabularies have been augmented; the right of popular assembly freely interfered
with; establishments of mercenary "gunmen," under the
formal name of detective-agencies, have increased their
output; the Ku-Klux-Klan has been reanimated and reorganised for extra-legal intimidation of citizens; and
the American Legion now and again enforces "law and
order" on the unfortunate by extra-legal measures.
Meantime the profiteers do business as usual and the
Federal authorities are busied with a schedule of increased protective duties designed to enhance the profits
of their business.

Those traits in this current situation wherein it is
different from the relatively sober state of things before
the war, have been injected by America's participation
in the war; and it is, in effect, for their failure to join
hands and help in working up this state of things that the
conscientious objectors, draft-evaders, I.W.W.'s, Communists, have been penalised in a manner unexampled
in American history. This is not saying that the pacifists,
conscientious objectors, etc., are not statutory criminals
or that they foresaw such an outcome of the traffic
against which they protested, or that they were moved
by peculiarly high-minded or unselfish considerations in
making their protest; but only that the subsequent course
of events has unhappily brought out the fact that these
distasteful persons took a stand for the sounder side of
a debatable question. Except for the continued prevalence of a distempered mentality that still runs on illusions of persecution, it might reasonably have been expected that this sort of *de facto* vindication of the stand
taken by these statutory criminals would be allowed to

count in extenuation of their *de jure* fault. But the distemper still runs its course. Indeed, it is doubtless the largest, profoundest, and most enduring effect brought upon the Americans by America's intervention in the great war.

Typically and commonly, dementia præcox is a distemper of adolescence or of early manhood, at least such appears to be the presumption held among psychiatrists. Yet its occurrence is not confined within any assignable age-limits. Typically, if not altogether commonly, it takes the shape of a dementia persecutoria, an illusion of persecution and a derangement of the logical faculty such as to predispose the patient to the belief that he and his folks are victims of plots and systematic atrocities. A fearsome credulity is perhaps the most outstanding symptom, and this credulity may work out in a fear of atrocities to be suffered in the next world or in the present; that is to say a fear of God or of evil men. Prolonged or excessive worry appears to be the most usual predisposing cause. Expert opinions differ as to how far the malady is to be reckoned as a curable disease; the standard treatment being rest, security, and nutrition. The physiological ground of such a failure of mentality appears to be exhaustion and consequent deterioration of nerve-tissue, due to shock or prolonged strain; and recuperation is notoriously slow in the case of nerve-tissue.

No age, sex, or condition is immune, but dementia præcox will affect adolescents more frequently than mature persons, and men more frequently than women; at least so it is said. Adolescent males are peculiarly subject to this malady, apparently because they are—under modern circumstances—in a peculiar degree exposed to worry, dissipation, and consequent nervous exhaustion. The cares and unfamiliar responsibilities of manhood fall upon them at that period, and under modern circumstances these cares and responsibilities are notably exacting, complex, and uncertain. Given a situation of widespread apprehension, uncertainty, and agitation, such as the war-experience brought on the Americans, and the consequent derangement of mentality should be of a similarly widespread character—such as has come in evidence.

The peculiar liability of adolescent males carries the open suggestion that a similar degree of liability should also extend to those males of more advanced years in whom a puerile mentality persists, men in whom a boyish temper continues into later life. These boyish traits may be seen in admirably systematised fashion in such organisations as the Boy Scouts. Much the same range of characteristics marks the doings and aspirations, individual and collective, of high-school boys, undergraduate students, and organisations of the type of the Y.M.C.A. In this connection it would perhaps be ungraceful to direct attention to the clergy of all denominations, where self-selection has resulted in a concentration on the lower range of the intellectual spectrum. One is also not unprepared to find a sensible infusion of the same puerile traits among military men. A certain truculent temper is conspicuous among the stigmata. Persons in whom the traits and limitations of the puerile mentality persist in a particularly notable degree are called "morons," but there are also many persons who approximate more or less closely to the moronic grade of mentality without being fully entitled to the technical designation. Such a degree of arrested spiritual and mental development is, in practical effect, no bar against entrance into public office. Indeed, a degree of puerile exuberance coupled with a certain truculent temper and boyish cunning is likely to command something of popular admiration and affection, which is likely to have a certain selective effect in the democratic choice of officials. Men, and perhaps even more particularly the women, will be sympathetically and affectionately disposed toward the standard vagaries of boyhood, and this sentimental inclination is bound to be reflected in the choice of public officials in any democratic community, where such choice is habitually guided by the play of sentiment. America is the most democratic of all nations; at least so they say. A run of persecutory credulity of the nature of dementia præcox should logically run swiftly and with a wide sweep in the case of such a community endowed with such an official machinery, and its effects should be profound and lasting.

# BETWEEN BOLSHEVISM AND WAR [1]

SINCE the return of peace, the civilised nations have come to face a fateful choice between Bolshevism and war. Hitherto no official pronouncement has recognised this state of the case. Neither does the public press comment on this sinister fatality, nor do public speakers call attention to it; which is doubtless quite as it should be in the nature of things—in that nature of things that touches the public press and the public speakers. Of course it is a distasteful state of things, and one would like to overlook it, and it sets up such a dilemma as no aspiring politician can afford to make up his account with. Such a one would have to take sides, and there is small comfort on either horn of the dilemma for any one whose fortunes are to be kept afloat on professions of optimism.

Yet the main fact should be evident to any reasonably well-informed person on slight reflection. It is, in effect, quite the largest and most obvious of the sinister fatalities contained in this twilight peace that has followed the armistice. And among these nations that now stand in the article of decision between Bolshevism and a bootless warfare, America, of course, comes into the case along with the rest of civilised mankind; not so precipitately as some of them, perhaps, but plainly nearer the edge than some others.

That which so confronts the civilised nations is not precisely a question of free choice between two alterna-

[1] Reprinted from *The Freeman*, Vol. III, May 25, 1921.

tive lines of policy. It is rather a question of the drift of circumstances. Just yet it looks like an open choice between alternative lines of conduct, because the ulterior drift of events is not plain, just yet. For the time being the drift visibly sets in the direction of war. But the visible drift is, in the main, the drift of statesmanlike maneuvers, as worked out by the constituted authorities in these various nations; rather then the long-term drift of sentiment among the underlying populations.

The circumstance that these statesmen whose dutiful privilege it is to guide, or to follow, the drift of political maneuvers have made no public acknowledgment of the sinister choice which so faces them, should perhaps be set down to statesmanlike reticence. Statesmanship is necessarily furtive, in the nature of things. It will scarcely do to credit the statesmen with a comprehensive ignorance of the main facts in the situation with which they have to deal. Even the dim religious light of the censored press dispatches allows these main facts to be seen in outline. Whereas the sources of information are all at the disposal of the constituted authorities, and knowledge of the pertinent facts is prudently withheld within the official circle. Indeed, it is plain that the underlying population have ceased to enjoy the confidence of the officials who manage their affairs. So that even in the out-and-out democratic nations the statesmanlike officials find it wise to withhold knowledge of the pertinent facts from their constituencies. There is, accordingly, no reason to believe that the furtive reticence of the statesmanlike officials in this connection denotes any degree of ignorance on their part. And their various proposals and the measures already taken go to say that there are many pertinent facts which the statesmen do not find it expedient to divulge. Therefore it is particularly significant that the visible drift of statesmanlike maneuvers sets consistently in the direction of war as an offset to Bolshevism.

"Bolshevism" is a loose, descriptive term; and it is so used here, without any effort to give it a more precise meaning than it has in popular usage. Popular usage has not yet given the word a well-defined meaning; but as it runs it is definite enough to be understood, in a loose and general way, among those who make use of it. In this popular usage the word has a definite meaning at least to the extent that it always denotes a revolutionary movement of such a kind as to displace the established economic scheme of things. Beyond this there is no reasonable agreement between those who speak for Bolshevism and those who speak against it. It may conceivably signify a peaceable substitution of a new economic order in place of the old, or it may involve a resort to violence; that would depend on circumstances. But in any case Bolshevism is outside the law and in violation of the law, in the sense that it involves a subversion of established law and custom at certain points.

In any case, Bolshevism is not to be reconciled with the established order of things, and the points of conflict are of an economic nature. When reduced to their lowest terms it will be seen that these points of conflict may be drawn together under a single head: The disallowance of Absentee Ownership. On this main head the conflict between Bolshevism and the established order is irreconcilable, and it will be seen on reflection that any of the minor points of conflict follow from this main article of contention. Just yet there is no conclusive ground for assuming that Bolshevism involves any other general principle of action than this one. Bolshevist experience has not yet had the chance to show or to find out if the spirit of it calls for any other principle of action that has anything like the same wide bearing as this one. It appears to be, in effect, a movement to discard this one large institution of Absentee Ownership, which now dominates the economic life of the civilised nations. It is therefore, in effect, a conflict between the absentee owners and the underlying population; in which the constituted authorities come into the case as guardians of the rights of absentee ownership. The constituted authorities are the guardians of the established law and order, which under existing conditions places them in the position of defenders of the legitimate rights of absentee ownership.

So far, therefore, as regards its principles of action, any working definition of Bolshevism need for the present include only this one specification—that it aims to discard absentee ownership, with whatever consequences may follow. But it seems necessary to add that, in point of method, or ways and means, Bolshevism is committed to the Soviet. The Soviet form of organisation appears to be the appointed ways and means of working out this principle of action that inspires the spirit of Bolshevism. It is conceivable that absentee ownership might be superseded by some other form of organisation and control than the Soviet; but any such recourse to some other method of control would scarcely be called Bolshevism. And any disestablishment of absentee ownership by recourse to the Soviet form of administration could scarcely be called anything else than Bolshevism.

In such a movement to dispossess the absentee owners

the Soviet also displaces democracy and representative government, and necessarily so, because democracy and representative government have proved to be incompetent and irrelevant for any other purpose than the security and profitable regulation of absentee ownership. Democratic usage and legal interpretation have taken such a turn in recent times. Hence parliamentary government and democratic legality are due to go in the discard along with their reason for being, so soon as a Bolshevist régime is installed.

In its elements, the Soviet appears to be very closely analogous to the town-meeting as known in New England history. The dictionary meaning of the word is "counsel" and "council." But to let a self-justified town-meeting take over all items of absentee ownership within its jurisdiction would plainly be a revolutionary innovation, a subversion of law and order.

This characterisation of Bolshevism seems colorless and barren, and it will scarcely suit either its friends or its enemies. It has but a slight rhetorical value. Advocates and critics alike have use for terms which will irritate the human sensibilities of their audience. It is necessary for them to raise a sentimental issue; or, as it is also called, a moral issue. And for that use there is need of terms which lend themselves to praise and blame. But since the purpose here is neither praise nor blame, a colorless, descriptive characterisation is all that is wanted. And it is Bolshevism in this objective sense that is here set up as the alternative of war, in the choice of policies that now confronts the governments of the civilised nations. And in so speaking of Bolshevism as the sole alternative of continued warfare and warlike preparation it is by no means intended to claim that

Bolshevism necessarily means peace. The choice between Bolshevism and war need not be a choice between peace and war.

The reason for setting up this simple and objective definition of Bolshevism is partly to avoid unnecessary alarm, partly to avoid confusing Bolshevism with the familiar gestures of the anarchists, or the orthodox Socialists, or the out-and-out Communists. The difference between Bolshevism and an untempered Communism should be plain enough. But it is also not unusual for incautious and intemperate critics to confuse Bolshevism with Socialism and in doing so to disparage both together; and particularly to discredit the Socialists. But neither the Bolshevists nor the Socialists will admit that the two are alike in any substantial way. Indeed, the certified Socialists are among the staunchest enemies of Bolshevism, as is quite intelligible. The Socialists of the stricter observance have consistently spoken for an eventual obsolescence of all ownership, absentee or otherwise, by force of a natural law which governs the sequence of human affairs; and they have now come to an exasperated realisation that Bolshevism is putting that orthodox preconception out of joint and out of date. Socialism is a dead horse; whereas it appears that Bolshevism is not; and the chartered Socialists find themselves seized and possessed of a certain inalienable equity in the remains; all of which does not conduce to a neighborly frame of mind. The Socialists had hoped to preserve the established political organisation intact, and eventually to take it over for their own use; the Bolshevists appear to harbor no such fancy.

This off-hand characterisation of Bolshevism as being no more and no less than a movement to discon-

tinue absentee ownership is likely to be questioned by
partisans, for and against; nor could it readily be made
good with citations of chapter and verse from authentic
sources. The Bolshevist documents which have come
to hand do not commonly speak of absentee ownership
as the particular object of their unfriendly attention;
nor has Bolshevist practice been at all consistent on
this head. Bolshevist practice, and perhaps also Bolshevist profession, has followed a wavering line of compromise and expediency, driven by extreme stress of
necessity. And yet, on the whole, the drift of Bolshevist
policy has after all visibly set that way, with so much
consistency as the stress of shifting conditions would
allow. On the one hand it has become increasingly
evident that ownership of useful property by its immediate users is quite securely an integral part of Bolshevist policy as it is working out, and quite unavoidably so; and on the other hand it is likewise evident
that the enemies of Bolshevism are its enemies because
it denies the rights of absentee ownership, and indeed
for no other cause.

Bolshevism is a menace to absentee ownership. That
is its unpardonable sin. But it is also a sufficiently mortal
offense, inasmuch as it is the sin against the Holy Ghost
of established Law and Order. The disallowance of
absentee ownership would cut away the foundations of
the established order of things economic and political.
For good or ill, it would break up the established order
of law and custom and so bring the current phase of
European civilisation to a close. All of which violates
all that the constituted authorities stand for in all the
civilised nations. It would be a revolt against the constituted authorities on the part of the underlying populations. By virtue of their office the constituted authori-

ties are the appointed guardians of absentee ownership. Any other interests which may still engage the care and attention of the national authorities in any of these civilised nations are quite subsidiary to this main issue; and any such minor interests can still effectually claim official protection or official tolerance only so long as they continue to be subservient to this main interest of the nation's substantial citizens. This follows necessarily from the nature of democratic government as it has taken shape during the recent past in all the democratic nations, and in the same degree as they are democratic within the accepted meaning of the term. A substantial citizen is an absentee owner of much property. In the historical present a democratic government is a government of the underlying population for the substantial citizens, by substantial citizens; whereas a Bolshevist government—if such there were—would, it is alleged, be a government of the underlying population for the insubstantial citizens, by insubstantial citizens—in violation of all current democratic usage. Therefore it has become the first duty of all those statesmen who guide the destinies of these democratic nations to suppress any popular movement of the nature of Bolshevism, far or near, by all means, fair or foul.

Meantime the drift of circumstances following the war and the armistice has brought things to a critical pass in these democratic nations, such that the only practical line of policy still open to the safe and sane statesmen whose duty it is to avert the Bolshevist menace is further warlike enterprise, further continued preparation for war, and the sedulous fomenting of a warlike temper in the underlying population. This is the line of policy on which the civilised nations are now visibly embarked, though without openly avowing it. And this line of policy promises at least a substantial respite from Bolshevist alarms. The prospective cost is high, but the benefits of this policy should be worth the cost; particularly since the benefits inure to the substantial citizens, while the cost falls on the underlying population. Visibly, but with decently voluble disclaimers, the constituted authorities in all the civilised nations have chosen this way out of the dilemma. The peace which has followed the armistice is a peace of increased armaments, increased national jealousies, and unremitting nationalist propaganda.

The practical corrective for all Bolshevist vagaries and illusions is patriotic animosity and a law-abiding submission to authority. Warlike enterprise and warlike preparation induce a patriotic temper in the underlying population, at the same time that they exact a servile obedience to the constituted authorities. These things, therefore, may be counted on to divert the underlying population from spending thought or sentiment on those economic grievances which make for a Bolshevistic frame of mind. And just now there is no other way to accomplish that purpose. Also, patriotism and warlike enterprise have ceased to have any other use.

So long as the underlying populations of these civilised nations are sufficiently taken up with patriotic blare and national jealousy the division of interest and sentiment within these nations, between those who own more than they can use and those who have urgent use for more than they own, will be held in abeyance; a symphony of national hatred and suspicion will be heard in the land, and absentee ownership will be secure. But so soon as conditions of *de facto* peace are allowed to invade the community the underlying population will be due to take stock of their *de facto* dis-inheritance under the established system of law and order; and, for good or ill, there is then presently due to follow such a drift of sentiment as will eventually draw the underlying population together under something like the Red flag, and absentee ownership will no longer be secure—in the absence of unforeseen disturbing causes. That event is doubtless remote, so far as touches America; but America, too, seems to be headed that way. Any community will change its habits of thought only tardily and under pressure, but in case the pressure of new conditions is extreme, uniform, and persistent a wide-reaching dislocation of the traditional habits of thought is to be looked for even in the best regulated community.

The appointed safeguard against this sinister eventuality is "Wars and rumors of wars." In all of this it is, of course, the spiritual benefits of warlike enterprise and military discipline that must be looked to to avert a disastrous spiritual break-down. It is a question of repairing and reinforcing such habits of thought in the community as will continue to favor the security of absentee ownership and the continued maintenance of that system of law and custom that is founded on absentee ownership. In the material respect, of course, warlike enterprise brings no net gain. In the material respect, of course, warlike expenditures are to be counted as net loss—said to amount to something like ninety percent of current Federal expenditures in this country. America is taking war by the forelock—with very decently voluble disclaimers, of course. But the immaterial, spiritual returns from warlike expenditure are quite a different matter and have quite a different value. Warlike enterprise nourishes a harmonious national hatred

of all outsiders, and military discipline induces a virtu-
ously servile temper and an unreasoning obedience to
constituted authority:

> Theirs not to make reply,
> Theirs not to reason why,
> Theirs but to do and die.

All of which makes for what is sometimes called sanity.

The statesmen who guide the destinies of the civilised
nations have reason to be apprehensive of what would
be due to follow in case the attention of their underlying populations should be at all seriously diverted
from the spiritual values of national prestige and
patriotic jealousy, and turn to a consideration of their
own material circumstances as determined by absentee
ownership and control of their industrial system. As
is already becoming evident in more than one of these
nations, in such a case it would be very difficult to persuade the underlying populations that they have anything to lose in discarding the present system of ownership and control. It is not that a better scheme has been
devised and is ready to be put in place of the existing
system, but only that the existing system is proving itself patently unfit to take care of the country's industry
and the material fortunes of its population. What still
stands in the way of a free-swung Bolshevistic temper
and a consequent bull-headed Bolshevist adventure in
these civilised nations is the belated conservatism of the
passing generation, in effect a spiritual holdover out of
an obsolete past, in which absentee ownership had not
yet taken over the nation's industrial system and in
which national jealousy had not yet become patently
imbecile. The established order, economic and political,
rests on material circumstances which ceased to exist

some little time ago; and it can be maintained only by artificially preserving the spiritual counterfoil of that materially obsolete past.

The experience of the past few years has shown plainly enough that the established businesslike system of ownership and control will no longer work. Human nature being what it is, and the state of the industrial arts being such as it has now become, the established order of ownership and control is no longer fit to manage the country's industry in such a way as to yield a decent livelihood for the country's population. This is not saying that a better system is known and ready to be substituted for the obsolete existing system— there is no safe ground for that degree of optimism— but only that the existing system of businesslike control is obsolete.

The present emergency has brought this matter to a test. The war and the armistice have made the world safe for absentee ownership and business as usual; all the civilised nations are in sore need of a full run of productive industry; there is ready and waiting the most efficient industrial equipment, the most abundant natural resources, and the most intelligent and skillful industrial man-power known to history; and for two and a half years the captains of industry and the great statesmen have labored together to turn these unexampled industrial resources to some account under the rules of absentee ownership and business as usual. The best result of their concerted efforts hitherto is an uneasy state of industrial "twilight sleep," hedged about with nightmares of famine, pestilence, and Red riots; and the most sanguine—and doubtful—hope of these civilised nations now is that this incredibly shameful state of things will not grow worse under the continued management of absentee ownership and business enterprise. Meantime the situation has been visibly growing worse during the two and a half years since the armistice, in spite of unusually abundant crops and favorable weather conditions. It is plain that absentee ownership and business as usual are at cross purposes with the country's industrial needs. All of which argues that it is wise for the statesmen to take repressive measures and keep the popular temper irritated about something else.

## EDITORIALS FROM "THE DIAL"

### MAY 3, 1919

IMMANUEL KANT once wrote a sketch, a century and a quarter ago, on Perpetual Peace. He prefaced it with a jest, as tasteless as it was clumsy, to say that the running title under which he wrote—*Zum ewigen Frieden,* that is to say, The House of Peace Everlasting—was borrowed from the signboard of a certain roadside tavern adjoining a certain ancient churchyard. Compounded of bar-room and graveyard, this wise man's jest will to many readers doubtless have seemed as pointless as it is tasteless. But that will be true only of those readers of Kant who have not had the inestimable fortune to live through these days of returning peace and to witness the maudlin deliberations of that conclave of elder statesmen who are now arranging to make the world safe for the vested rights of international dissension. The point of Kant's jest is plain now. Today his readers are in a position to marvel that even that wise old man should have been so wise as all that. It is quite uncanny.

---

### JUNE 14, 1919

*Panem et circenses* was the formula for the politicians of Imperial Rome, on which they relied to keep the underlying population from imagining vain remedies for their own hard case. *Mutatis mutandis,* in the

450

vernacular of the twentieth century, this would be as much as to say, "The Bread Line and the Movies." This is not a literal translation of the Latin motto. It amounts to an equivalence of practice rather than an equivalence of words—*panis,* of course, is Latin for "bread" rather than "the bread line"; and the nearest modern equivalent for *circenses* would perhaps be "the ballfield" rather than "the movies." But then, as the Romans would say, *tempora mutantur.*

*Panis,* of course signifies "bread," a product of the baker's art, rather than the bread line, which is a product of the associated charities. But in effect, as it comes into this Imperial Roman motto, *panem* signified that certain salutary minimum of bread without which the underlying population could not be counted on to tolerate the continued rule of the Imperial politicians and of those vested interests that were entrusted to the care of the politicians. So it appears that the politicians of Imperial Rome allowed the underlying population a ration of actual bread, at some cost to the vested interests. It appears that the astute politicians of Imperial Rome dared go no nearer to the modern democratic institution of the bread line. To those democratic statesmen who now bear up the banners of the vested interests—also called the standards of Law and Order—this prodigal conduct of the Roman politicians will perhaps seem weak and little-minded. But something is to be allowed in extenuation of their pusillanimity. The politicians of Imperial Rome had not the use of Liberty Loans and machine guns; and then the underlying population of that cruder age was perhaps less patient and reasonable, less given to promises and procrastination. *Tempora mutantur.* The democratic statesmen of the twentieth century are more fortunate in both respects. More particularly, the mechanical appliances for preserving law and order have been greatly perfected; and by suitable fiscal methods the underlying population which is to be "kept in hand" can be induced to pay for these mechanical appliances by which they are to be kept in hand. So the statesmen of the twentieth century are enabled to let the bread line serve in place of the bread, and thereby to save the net output of the Republic's industry more nearly intact for the use of the kept classes.

But in the matter of *circenses,* too, there has been change and improvement during these intervening centuries since the Glory that was Rome. Political practice runs on a more economical plan in this businesslike age. The Roman *circenses* appear to have cut somewhat wastefully into the ordinary "earnings" of those vested interests for whose benefit the Roman Imperium was administered; whereas the movies of the twentieth century are a business proposition in their own right, a source of "earnings" and a vested interest. And in ordinary times of peace or war the movies supply what appears to be required in the way of politically salutary dissipation. Yet in times of stress, as is now evident, something more enticing may be required to distract popular attention securely and keep the underlying population from taking stock of the statesmen's promises and performance. At a critical juncture, when large chances of profit and loss for the vested interests are in the balance, it may be well to take thought and add something to the workday routine of the movies, even at some expense. In case of urgent need, to stabilise a doubtfully manageable popular sentiment, the rant and swagger of many subsidised heroes and the pomp and circumstance and moving show incident to a victory loan should have a salutary use of the same kind; expensive, no doubt, but then the cost need not be borne by those vested interests that are to be safeguarded from the corrosive afterthought of the underlying population. And then there are available such heroic spectacles as a "victory fleet," together with parades, arches, and banners—miles of banners and square miles of heroic printed matter; costly, no doubt, but also doubtless salutary. So also, in case of need there is something to be made of such a thing as an overseas flight; particularly if it be abundantly staged and somewhat more than abundantly advertised. It is a potent resource, capable of lifting the common man's afterthought into the upper air, instead of letting it run along the ground of material fact, where it might do mischief; costly, no doubt, but then the cost need not be counted so closely, since it is the common man who pays the cost, the same common man who is forever in danger of getting into mischief by reflecting unduly on what the statesmen have been using him for. And, of course, since it is the common man who is to be relieved of afterthought, it is only reasonable that the common man should pay the cost.

*Panem et circenses:* The Bread Line and the Movies.

---

## JULY 12, 1919

"Open covenants openly arrived at" was the heroic challenge which the President once, in a moment of exaltation, threw in the face of the Elder Statesmen. But it is already a matter of common notoriety how the President's proud words have gone whistling down the winds, while the Elder Statesmen have continued to follow their own devious devices. With jealous care the conclave of Elder Statesmen representing the Great Powers have guarded the secrecy of their deliberations while they have been arranging the world's peace on the good old plan. The Elder Statesmen have been at pains to give out no "information which might be useful to the enemy"; that is to say, to the underlying population of these Great Powers. And among these Great Powers of the secret conclave America is neither last nor least; quite the contrary in fact. Nor is information withheld less carefully from the underlying population of democratic America than from the unfree populace of Europe. "Open covenants openly arrived at" has gone into abeyance. This outcome, of course, marks a defeat of democratic ideals. That it does so may be fortunate or otherwise, but the fact of this defeat should not be overlooked. The fact is to be taken as marking an advance, or at least a conclusive change, in the guiding principles of statesmanship. Democratic methods are no longer safe—if they ever have been. They will no longer serve the uses of statesmanship. The underlying population is no longer a party in interest in national policy or in international negotiations, in such fashion as would warrant consulting their notions of what should be done. Circumstances have taken such a turn that each of these civilised nations is now divided within itself, in such a way that the national administration now represents an oligarchy and speaks for a group of interests rather than for an undivided people at large. This follows unavoidably from the existing economic order, which is built on a division of interests, between the kept classes and the common man. And the events of the past few years have forced this truth upon the conviction of the statesmen, and not least convincingly upon the democratic statesmen of America. They have been brought to realise that their avowed ideals of democratic rule and popular discussion are hopelessly out of date, that the situation which faces them can no longer be handled by democratic methods, that an ever-widening cleavage of interest has arisen within each of the nations between the vested interests and the underlying population, and that it is the part of the statesman unreservedly to range himself on the side of law and order—that is to say, on the side of the vested interests. This conclusion follows because, in the nature of the case, the party of the vested interests is always the party of law and order. Law and order means that legal order which safeguards the established rights of privilege and property. Such being the situation, the underlying population is plainly not to be trusted with a free run of information on public affairs. In effect, the people at large, in these nominally democratic nations, are falling into the position of a subject population; something in the way of a body of alien enemies, to be used, humored, and "kept in hand." There is, for instance, a highly instructive resemblance between the American legislation, late and prospective, designed for the control of American citizens on the one hand, and the notorious Rowlatt Acts by which the gentlemanly British administration is endeavoring to keep their Indian subjects "in hand." Both the Indians and the Americans are to be kept in hand for their own good, no doubt, but more immediately and more obviously for the good of the vested interests of business and office-holding. Therefore, placed in this precarious posture, facing a distrustful underlying population, it has become the first care of these Elder Statesmen in all their deliberations to give out no information which might become useful to the enemy. This strategic secrecy of the peacemaking conclave is presumptive evidence that in the apprehension of these Elder Statesmen the interests which have been guiding their deliberations do not at any substantial point coincide with those interests which the underlying population have at heart. The underlying population want peace and industry; the Elder Statesmen have negotiated an arrangement for safeguarding the vested interests of privilege and property by force of arms. These two lines of interests are out of touch; and they may prove to be incompatible. So the shrewd Elder Statesmen have consumed half a year in carrying out a strategic disposition of their forces under cover of night and cloud, with a view to safeguarding the *status quo;* and so the underlying populations now face a state of *fait accompli,* whereby the resources of these several nations are already committed to an international enterprise in defense of the vested interests, all and several, at the cost of underlying populations. Behind the smoke-screen of the seven censors and the Associated Prevarication bureaus, that much is visible now. But the question remains: Why has that high-hearted crusade which set out to make the world safe for democracy by open covenants openly arrived at come to this inglorious end behind the smoke-screen? The answer appears to be covered by this golden text: Bolshevism is a menace to the vested interests of privilege and property. There need be no question as to the utter good faith of that crusade for democracy and open covenants; no more than there is a question as to its utter defeat. Nor need there be a question as to the paramount responsibility of America's spokesman for this outcome of the peacemaking conclave. No single one of the powers and no coalition of powers has been in a position to make a substantial move at any point in these negotiations without the paramount consent and advice of America's spokesman. Without America's backing the "high contracting parties" are practically bankrupt, all and several; and apart from America's spokesman no two of them could reasonably trust one another out of sight. So that what this conclave of Elder Statesmen has achieved and what it has committed itself to is, in effect, his achievement and his commitment.

America's spokesmen set out with a high and well-advised resolve to make the world safe for democracy; but it was to be a democracy founded in commercialised nationalism, after the pattern of Mid-Victorian times, which being interpreted means a democracy for safeguarding the vested interests of property. Now between the date of the President's high pronouncement on open covenants and safe democracy and the date of the peace-making conclave there intervenes the unlooked-for episode of Soviet Russia, the substantial core of whose policy is the disallowance of these same vested interests of property which make up the substantial core of that Mid-Victorian commercialised democracy that was to be saved. It is easily to be seen that the Bolshevism of Soviet Russia is a menace to that commercialised democracy which Mid-Victorian statesmen are concerned to perpetuate. Indeed, it is easily to be seen that the material interests of the underlying population in the other nations would incline them to fall in with its policy of disallowance, just so soon as these underlying populations come to realise that they have nothing to lose, which is believed to argue no distant date. At least such appears to be the universal conviction among those statesmen who speak for the maintenance of law and order. The situation therefore calls for heroic remedies. The safety of those vested interests of property that now make up the substance of things hoped for could not be jeopardised to make the world safe for a democracy devoid of vested interests. Bolshevism is a menace to these vested interests, and to any Mid-Victorian statesman it is a truism that these interests must and shall be preserved from this menace at any cost—the cost to be paid by the underlying population. This cost at which the menace of Bolshevism is to be averted involves more or less costly and undesirable working arrangements with all the forces of reaction, since none but the forces of reaction can be counted on to take the field openly in the prosecution of such an enterprise. And arrangements of this kind for the support and subsidy of reactionary enterprise, responsible and irresponsible—in effect, for the support of any enterprise sufficiently reactionary to take the field—cannot be openly arrived at by spokesmen of any democratic commonwealth. Hence the secret conclave and the smoke-screen of the seven censors. It is a sufficiently difficult passage, not to say a desperate quandary. However, it appears that under cover of night and cloud arrangements of this kind have been reached which it is hopefully believed will be sufficient; arrangements for the comfort and success of reactionary enterprise in Finland, Livonia, Esthonia, Poland, Czecho-Slovakia, Roumania, and the reactionary factions in Russia, north, south, and east. It is an unfortunate circumstance that all this making of terms with the forces of reaction for the safeguarding of the vested interests will not bear the light. It is unfortunate, but there is no help for it. Needs must when the devil drives, and Bolshevism is largely believed to be of that breed. So it is devoutly to be hoped that these transactions that will not bear the light, these enforced but distasteful concessions of the democratic statesmen to the more shameless powers of reaction, will duly bring in that good fruit of domestic tranquillity which is bargained for at such a price—and all beneath the spreading chestnut tree of commercialised nationalism. *Quod bonum, felix faustumque sit!*

## NOVEMBER 15, 1919

The eleventh November is a day dedicate to the white boutonnière of peace. But the particular Peace to which this day is specially dedicate is the twilight peace of the armistice, which is of a peculiar and distinctive character. It is peace, but it is not marked by any degree of tranquillity or goodwill, nor has it displaced martial law. It is in good part made up of alarms and recrimination, of intrigue and hostilities, and it is hedged about with fire, famine, and pestilence. It is a peace of a very special character, peculiar and distinctive. The twelve months which have elapsed since the armistice will show a larger expenditure for military operations and a larger total of warlike atrocities than any recorded twelve months of war, prior to the Great War of which this Peace is the aftermath. It was a peculiar peace in its inception, in that it was concluded in order to engage in a fight; and it has been a peculiar peace in its further course, in that it shows a steadily rising tide of quarrels, armaments, hostilities, expenditures, bankruptcies, and violations of international law, throughout these twelve months of its prosecution hitherto.

In view of this comfortless state of things it may be worth while to stop and take stock of the circumstances which precipitated this peace of intrigue and atrocities upon the civilised nations; what was bargained for and what has been got. The elder statesmen who negotiated the peace have faithfully observed the punctilios of secret diplomacy, and have given no sign as to what the bargaining was all about; but the past twelve months have brought much circumstantial evidence to the surface. So it is fairly plain now that it was a negotiated peace, in the nature of a compromise with the Central Powers, negotiated hastily to avert a collapse of the German military organisation; such as would unavoidably have followed on a further three months' prosecution of the campaign on the western front. This hasty and, in a sense, premature conclusion of hostilities could scarcely have been other than designed by the high political command which had the bargaining to do. It left the German military establishment standing in a passably serviceable state, and it left also the German Imperial organisation virtually intact under a perfunctory mask of democratic forms. Among the guardians of the established order there appears plainly to have been a growing realisation —first voiced by the Lansdowne letters—that the vested interests of property and class rule in the countries of the Entente must for their own benefit make common cause with the like interests in the countries of the Central Powers if they were successfully to make head against their common enemy—the increasingly uneasy underlying population on both sides. A prostrate and completely discredited German military establishment, such as another three months would have left, and a broken and emptied imperial organisation, such as the same three months would have left—with such an outcome of the war the German states would have gone Red and would have been fit to make trouble for none but themselves. Germany in that case would have been of no use for stabilising things on the basis of the *status quo ante,* and the *status quo ante* has always been the object of the elder statesmen's affections and solicitude. Guardians of the Vested Interests, the elder statesmen sorely needed the bulwark of a practicable German Empire to serve as a bar against the spread of Bolshevism out of Soviet Russia, and they likewise needed the active use of a practicable German military establishment to defeat Bolshevism by fire, sword, and famine, in and out of Soviet Russia. Therefore it would not be expedient to break the Central Powers utterly, by another three months' advance on the western front. The policy with regard to Soviet Russia became the acid test of Entente politics, in war and peace. The line of incentives which under this acid test brought the war to its premature termination, and which has continued to drive the policies of the Allied Powers and direct their maneuvers during the past twelve months, appears to be almost wholly comprised in the proposition that Bolshevism is a menace to absentee ownership. It is another, and hitherto an open question, how near the elder statesmen are likely to realise their sanguine hope of subduing Soviet Russia by use of a subservient German military establishment.

# THE ECONOMIC CONSEQUENCES
## OF THE PEACE [1]

IT is now something like a year since this book was written. And much of its argument is in the nature of forecast which has in great part been overtaken by the precipitate run of events during these past months. Therefore it would scarcely be fair to read the author's argument as a presentation of current fact. It is rather to be taken as a presentation of the diplomatic potentialities of the Treaty and the League, as seen beforehand, and of the further consequences which may be expected to follow in the course of a statesmanlike management of things under the powers conferred by the Treaty and by the Covenant of the League. It is an altogether sober and admirably candid and facile argument, by a man familiar with diplomatic usage and trained in the details of large financial policy; and the wide vogue and earnest consideration which have been given to this volume reflect its very substantial merits. At the same time the same facts go to show how faithfully its point of view and its line of argument fall in with the prevailing attitude of thoughtful men toward the same range of questions. It is the attitude of men accustomed to take political documents at their face value.

Writing at about the date of its formulation and be-

[1] Reprinted from *The Political Science Quarterly,* Vol. XXXV, September, 1920, where it appeared as a review of *The Economic Consequences of the Peace,* by John Maynard Keynes (New York, 1920).

fore its effectual working had been demonstrated, Mr. Keynes accepts the Treaty as a definitive formulation of the terms of peace, as a conclusive settlement rather than a strategic point of departure for further negotiations and a continuation of warlike enterprise—and this in spite of the fact that Mr. Keynes was continuously and intimately in touch with the Peace Conference during all those devious negotiations by which the Elder Statesmen of the Great Powers arrived at the bargains embodied in this instrument. These negotiations were quite secret, of course, as is fitting that negotiations among Elder Statesmen should be. But for all their vulpine secrecy, the temper and purposes of that hidden Conclave of political hucksters were already becoming evident to outsiders a year ago, and it is all the more surprising to find that an observer so shrewd and so advantageously placed as Mr. Keynes has been led to credit them with any degree of *bona fides* or to ascribe any degree of finality to the diplomatic instruments which came out of their bargaining.

The Treaty was designed, in substance, to re-establish the *status quo ante,* with a particular view to the conservation of international jealousies. Instead of its having brought a settlement of the world's peace, the Treaty (together with the League) has already shown itself to be nothing better than a screen of diplomatic verbiage behind which the Elder Statesmen of the Great Powers continue their pursuit of political chicane and imperialistic aggrandisement. All this is patent now, and it needs no peculiar degree of courage to admit it. It is also scarcely too much to say that all this should have been sufficiently evident to Mr. Keynes a year ago. But in failing to take note of this patent state of the case Mr. Keynes only reflects the commonplace attitude of thoughtful citizens. His discussion, accordingly, is a faithful and exceptionally intelligent commentary on the language of the Treaty, rather than the consequences which were designed to follow from it or the uses to which it is lending itself. It would perhaps be an ungraceful overstatement to say that Mr. Keynes has successfully avoided the main facts in the case; but an equally broad statement to the contrary would be farther from the truth.

The events of the past months go to show that the central and most binding provision of the Treaty (and of the League) is an unrecorded clause by which the governments of the Great Powers are banded together for the suppression of Soviet Russia—unrecorded unless record of it is to be found somewhere among the secret archives of the League or of the Great Powers. Apart from this unacknowledged compact there appears to be nothing in the Treaty that has any character of stability or binding force. Of course, this compact for the reduction of Soviet Russia was not written into the text of the Treaty; it may rather be said to have been the parchment upon which the text was written. A formal avowal of such a compact for continued warlike operations would not comport with the usages of secret diplomacy, and then it might also be counted on unduly to irritate the underlying populations of the Great Powers, who are unable to see the urgency of the case in the same perspective as the Elder Statesmen. So this difficult but imperative task of suppressing Bolshevism, which faced the Conclave from the outset, has no part in Mr. Keynes's analysis of the consequences to be expected from the conclave's Treaty. Yet it is sufficiently evident now that the exigencies of the Conclave's campaign against Russian Bolshevism have shaped the working-out of the Treaty hitherto, beyond any other consideration. This appears to be the only interest which the Elder Statesmen of the Great Powers hold in common; in all else they appear to be engrossed with mutual jealousies and cross purposes, quite in the spirit of that imperialistic *status quo* out of which the Great War arose. And the like promises to hold true for the future, until after Soviet Russia or the Powers banded together in this surreptitious war on Russia shall reach the breaking-point. In the nature of things it is a war without quarter; but in the nature of things it is also an enterprise which cannot be avowed.

It is quite needless to find fault with this urgent campaign of the governments of the Great Powers against Soviet Russia or to say anything in approval of it all. But it is necessary to take note of its urgency and the nature of it, as well as of the fact that this major factor in the practical working-out of the Peace has apparently escaped attention in the most competent analysis of the Peace and its consequences that has yet been offered. It has been overlooked, perhaps, because it is a foregone matter of course. Yet this oversight is unfortunate. Among other things, it has led Mr. Keynes into an ungracious characterisation of the President and his share in the negotiations. Mr. Keynes has much that is uncomplimentary to say of the many concessions and comprehensive defeat in which the President and his avowed purposes became involved in the course of those negotiations with the Elder Statesmen of the Great Powers. Due appreciation of the gravity of this anti-Bolshevist issue, and of its ubiquitous and paramount force in the deliberations of the Conclave, should have saved Mr. Keynes from those expressions of scant courtesy which mar his characterisation of the President and of the President's work as peacemaker.

The intrinsic merits of the quarrel between the Bolsheviki and the Elder Statesmen are not a matter for offhand decision; nor need they come in consideration here. But the difficulties of the President's work as peacemaker are not to be appreciated without some regard to the nature of this issue that faced him. So, without prejudice, it seems necessary to call to mind the main facts of the case, as these facts confronted him in the negotiations with the Conclave. It is to be remarked, then, that Bolshevism is a menace to absentee ownership. At the same time the present economic and political order rests on absentee ownership. The imperialist policies of the Great Powers, including America, also look to the maintenance and extension of absentee ownership as the major and abiding purpose of all their political traffic. Absentee ownership, accordingly, is the foundation of law and order, according to that scheme of law and order which has been handed down out of the past in all the civilised nations, and to the perpetuation of which the Elder Statesmen are committed by native bent and by the duties of office. This applies to both the economic and the political order, in all these civilised nations, where the security of property rights has become virtually the sole concern of the constituted authorities.

The Fourteen Points were drawn up without due appreciation of this paramount place which absentee ownership has come to occupy in the modern civilised countries and without due appreciation of the intrinsically precarious equilibrium in which this paramount institution of civilised mankind has been placed by the growth of industry and education. The Bolshevist demonstration had not yet shown the menace, at the time when the Fourteen Points were drawn up. The Fourteen Points were drawn in the humane spirit of Mid-Victorian Liberalism, without due realisation of the fact that democracy has in the meantime outgrown the Mid-Victorian scheme of personal liberty and has grown into a democracy of property rights. Not until the Bolshevist overturn and the rise of Soviet Russia did this new complexion of things become evident to men trained in the good old way of thinking on questions of policy. But at the date of the Peace Conference Soviet Russia had come to be the largest and most perplexing fact within the political and economic horizon. Therefore, so soon as a consideration of details was entered upon it became evident, point by point, that the demands of absentee ownership coincide with the requirements of the existing order, and that these paramount demands of absentee ownership are at the same time incompatible with the humane principles of Mid-Victorian Liberalism. Therefore, regretfully and reluctantly, but imperatively, it became the part of wise statesmanship to save the existing order by saving absentee ownership and letting the Fourteen Points go in the discard. Bolshevism is a menace to absentee ownership; and in the light of events in Soviet Russia it became evident, point by point, that only with the definitive suppression of Bolshevism and all its works, at any cost, could the world be made safe for that Democracy of Property Rights on which the existing political and civil order is founded. So it became the first concern of all the guardians of the existing order to root out Bolshevism at any cost, without regard to international law.

If one is so inclined, one may find fault with the premises of this argument as being out of date and reactionary; and one might find fault with the President for being too straitly guided by considerations of this nature. But the President was committed to the preservation of the existing order of commercialised imperialism, by conviction and by his high office. His apparent defeat in the face of this unforeseen situation, therefore, was not so much a defeat, but rather a strategic realignment designed to compass what was indispensable, even at some cost to his own prestige—the main consideration being the defeat of Bolshevism at any cost—so that a well-considered view of the President's share in the deliberations of the Conclave will credit him with insight, courage, facility, and tenacity of purpose rather than with that pusillanimity, vacillation, and ineptitude which is ascribed to him in Mr. Keynes's too superficial review of the case.

So also his oversight of this paramount need of making the world safe for a democracy of absentee owners has led Mr. Keynes to take an unduly pessimistic view of the provisions covering the German indemnity. A notable leniency, amounting to something like collusive remissness, has characterised the dealings of the Powers with Germany hitherto. As should have seemed altogether probable beforehand, the stipulations touching the German indemnity have proved to be provisional and tentative only—if they should not rather be characterised as a diplomatic bluff, designed to gain time, divert attention, and keep the various claimants in a reasonably patient frame of mind during the period of rehabilitation needed to reinstate the reactionary régime in Germany and erect it into a bulwark against Bolshevism. These stipulations have already suffered substantial modifications at every point that has come to a test hitherto, and there is no present indication and no present reason to believe that any of them will be lived up to in any integral fashion. They are apparently in the nature of a base for negotiations and are due to come up for indefinite further adjustment as expediency may dictate. And the expediencies of the case appear to run on two main considerations: (*a*) the defeat of Bolshevism, in Russia and elsewhere; and (*b*) the continued secure tenure of absentee ownership in Germany. It follows that Germany must not be crippled in such a degree as would leave the imperial establishment materially weakened in its campaign against Bolshevism abroad or radicalism at home. From which it also follows that no indemnity should effectually be levied on Germany such as will at all seriously cut into the free income of the propertied and privileged classes, who alone can be trusted to safeguard the democratic interests of absentee ownership. Such burden as the indemnity may impose must accordingly not exceed an amount which may conveniently be made to fall somewhat immediately on the propertyless working class, who are to be kept in hand. As required by these considerations of safety for the established order, it will be observed that the provisions of the Treaty shrewdly avoid any measures that would involve confiscation of property; whereas, if these provisions had not been drawn with a shrewd eye to the continued security of absentee ownership, there should have been no serious difficulty in collecting an adequate indemnity from the wealth of Germany without materially deranging the country's industry and without hardship to others than the absentee owners. There is no reason, other than the reason of absentee ownership, why the Treaty should not have provided for a comprehensive repudiation of the German war debt, imperial, state, and municipal, with a view to diverting that much of German income to the benefit of those who suffered from German aggression. So also no other reason stood in the way of a comprehensive confiscation of

German wealth, so far as that wealth is covered by securities and is therefore held by absentee owners, and there is no question as to the war guilt of these absentee owners.

But such a measure would subvert the order of society, which is an order of absentee ownership in so far as concerns the Elder Statesmen and the interests whose guardians they are. Therefore it would not do, nor has the notion been entertained, to divert any part of this free income from the German absentee owners to the relief of those who suffered from the war which these absentee owners carried into the countries of the Allies. In effect, in their efforts to safeguard the existing political and economic order—to make the world safe for a democracy of investors—the statesmen of the victorious Powers have taken sides with the war-guilty absentee owners of Germany and against their underlying population. All of which, of course, is quite regular and beyond reproach; nor does it all ruffle the course of Mr. Keynes's exposition of economic consequences, in any degree.

Even such conservative provisions as the Treaty makes for indemnifying the war victims have hitherto been enforced only with a shrewdly managed leniency, marked with an unmistakable partisan bias in favor of the German-Imperial *status quo ante;* as is also true for the provisions touching disarmament and the discontinuance of warlike industries and organisation—which provisions have been administered in a well-conceived spirit of *opéra bouffe.* Indeed, the measures hitherto taken in the execution of this Peace Treaty's provisional terms throw something of an air of fantasy over Mr. Keynes's apprehensions on this head.